ENCYCLOPEDIA OF

LIVING ARTISTS

IN AMERICA

A visual guide to current art in America

Manuscript Editor: Constance Franklin
Associate Editor: Eugene Pera

ENCYCLOPEDIA OF LIVING ARTISTS IN AMERICA

A Visual Guide to Current Art in America

Copyright @ 1987 Directors Guild Publishers

CORRESPONDENCE regarding material should be sent to: Directors Guild Publishers, P.O. Box 369, Renaissance, CA 95962 (415) 381-2729

Library of Congress Cataloging No. 86-072382

 Main entry under title:

Encyclopedia of Living Artists

     1. Artists - United States - Biography. 2. Art, Modern - 20th century - United States.

ISBN 0-940899-00-0

ON THE COVER. . . .

ZAREMBA	KOLDORF	MOSELEY
PERA	LOVE	BREUER
SICRE	SQUIRES	ABRAMOWITZ
YOO	BUCHANAN	HOUSE

*See artists biography
and reproduction
in the Color Section*

Contents

*Color reprints of illustrations provided by Publisher are often
available upon request from the artist's studio or dealer

You stand now at the point where you must necessarily break through to the really high and difficult part of art--the apprehension of what is individual. You must do some degree of violence to yourself to escape theory. The apprehension and representation of the individuality is the very life of art. Do not content yourself with generalities, for almost anyone can imitate you; but in the particular, no one can, and why? Because no others have experienced exactly the same thing.

Goethe

GAYLE L. AL-KAISY

P.O. Box 12573, Portland, OR 97212
Born: 9/5/42
(503) 288-2061
Oregon Free-lance artist.Primary background in retail advertising art.Illustrations are a result of artist's imagination. Art is drawn from theatrics of personal mental imagery and feelings rather than use of specific photos or other posed subject matter.

CULTURAL LEGACY, 15"x20",
Watercolor and ink, NFS

RICHARD J. ALLEN

331 49th St., #2, Oakland,CA 94609
Born: 12/2/45
Represented by Allen Art Services, P.O. Box 3153, Oakland, CA 94609 (415) 658-5958
(415) 654-6600
Painter, Born in Detroit, MI. Studied: California College of Arts and Crafts, Oakland, BFA, MFA 1969. Numerous Local exhibits, Teaching: CCAC,Vista College, Studio One, Oakland. Reviews: SF Chronicle, 9/27/72, Art West, 10/22/74. Prominent Work: San Francisco Bay Mural, in progress to become San Francisco Bay Cyclorama.
SAN FRANCISCO BAY, 15 1/2" x 13 1/2", Acrylic, Price negotiable,

ERIN ALWAY

11738 Citron Street,Honolulu, HI 96826
Born: 11/25/42
Represented by Always Art, 999 Wilder Avenue, #504, Honolulu, HI 96822
Erin Alway focuses her art and passion on portraits and landscapes of the people and places where she has lived and travelled. Her works are in many collections throughout Europe, Canada, USA and Mexico. A professional artist, muralist, designer and instructor, Erin Alway has a freelance business "Always Art" and lives in Honolulu, Hawaii.
MISTY MAUI MOUNTAINS, 24"x 36", Oil, $2,000.00, Owned by Koward Kau of Honolulu

MARGOT ANDREW

1545 Marlay Drive, LA, CA 90069
Born: 1/14/60
Represented by Devorzon Gallery, Pacific Design Center, 8687 Melrose Ave. #188, Los Angeles, CA 90069, (213) 659-0555
(213) 656-7117
BFA Queens University Kingston, Ontario, Canada. MFA, Otis Parsons, Los Angeles, CA Gemini Gel Curator 1986. Devorzon Gallery, L.A., 1986. Otis Parsons Main Gallery 1985. Artsfest, Kingston, Ontraio, 1983

CANADIAN LANDSCAPE SUMMER, CANADIAN LANDSCAPE WINTER, 96"X 96"X 5", Print

GARY ANGELO

65 Bedford St. #2, Waltham, MA 02154
Represented by Bedyk Gallery, 903 Westport Rd., Kansas City, MO 64111
Born in St. Paul and raised in Kansas City, Mo. Began his undergraduate studies in 1979 and graduated in 1983 from the Kansas City Art Institute. In 1984 Angelo entered Boston University. In 1986 Angelo graduated from BU with an MFA in Painting. Angelo was influenced by such people as Stanley Lewis, Lester Goldman and James Weeks.

HEATH ST. NEAR VETERANS HOSPITAL - BOSTON, MA., 26"x28", Oil on canvas, $600.00, owned by Artist

JACQUES AUDERER

575 NE 132 Street, North Miami, FL 33161
Born: 2/1/34
(305) 891-6410
Born in France in 1941, grew up in Paris. At an early age I started to draw. My mother used to call me "Mon petit artiste". I was only eight when I did the picture of King Louis the XIV. Lots of great artists of Montparnasse were interested in my work. My first oil painting was made when I was thirteen. Ever since I am have been painting. I carve wood also.

THE BOY, 14"x16"

2

VICTORIA 'BUNNY' AYERS

Post Office Box 164, Boca Raton, FL 33429
Represented by S.D. Snyder, Agent, 6372
Lacosta Dr. #301, Boca Raton, FL 33433.
At New York School of Industrial Arts she
earned scholarship to Pratt Institute. Worked
as commerical artist in Architectural and
Fashion fields while developing style in Fine
Arts. Painting style runs gamut from Pre-
Columbian, Southwest U.S., Oriental, to
more traditional; as well as unique
personalized horoscope art.

**HOROSCOPE OF DOCTOR R.J.
VENEZIA,** 30"x40", Oil on canvas, NFS,
Owned by Dr. Richard Venezia of Boca
Raton, FL.

HELEN EMREE BANKS

36134 Teaford Poyah, North Fork, CA
93634
Born: 1/20/23
Born in S.F., CA. Ed. at S. F. State Coll. &
S.F. Art Inst. W.W.II, made terraine maps
for Navy, designed toys, lamps, ceramics in
S.F., Chicago, Ill. and Fresno, CA. Awards
incl the Goethe Hon. Purchase award-
Crocker Art Gal. Sacto. CA Inst. Arts &
Crafts and Sculpture to adults in Fresno, CA.
Present studio in Bass Lake Area, Ca.

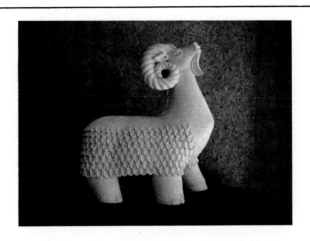

SONG OF THE BIG HORN,
23"x25"x13", Scultpure Clay, NFS, Owned
by Mr. & Mrs. F. Paynter of Fresno, CA

RAYMOND BAREISS

234 Black Horse Pike, Glendora, NJ 08029
Born: 4/9/51
Bareiss has tremendous inner vision and
sensitivity. He is a man who possesses
creative genius and the ability to produce his
visions with his bare hands. He is a self-
taught artist, sculptor, who works in various
mediums. He brings simple objects to life
with his use of shadows and color.

HOT JASMINE TEA, 48"x36", Air
Brush, NFS, Owned by artist

KATE BARNES

4116 Greenwood Ave., Oakland, CA 94602
Born: 1/19/54
Born in Illinois. Education: Kansas City Art Institute 1972-74, Rhode Island School of Design 1974 - 76 BFA. From 1978: One person shows: Nanny Goat Hill Gallery, SF. CA. Juried group shows: Sausalito Arts Fair, Marin Society of Artists, Berkeley Arts Co-op General: oil mural 15'x75', Oakland, CA, various commission works.

DEBORAH, 16"x18", Oil, NFS, Owned by Deborah Johnson

ELIZABETH THERESA BARNHILL

555 Elizabeth Avenue Apt. 13-A, Newark, NJ 07112
Born: 11/5/50
Attended the Newark School of Fine and Industrial Arts. Majored in Fashion Illustration. Worked for Essence Magazine in 1973-75 as a freelance artist. I have also worked for two ad agencies as typesetter. Aside from freelancing I also teach arts and crafts. Other freelance jobs include personal commissions, local newspapers, greeting card companies, etc.

PORTRAIT OF DIANA, 18"x24", Pastel, Owned by Artist

T BARNEY

4370 Pine Flat Road, Healdsburg, CA 95448
Born: 8/8/56
Represented by Landell Galleries, P.O. Box 5807, 9 Deldono Court, Carmel, CA 93921, (408) 625-6555
(707) 431-8378
B.F. A. - Rhode Island School of Design, 1980. Awards - First prize, Central CA Biennial '83, Pacific Grove; Fine Arts Festival Sculpture Award, Denison Univ., OH. '78 Exhibitions - '85: Nine Stone Scultptors, Santa Rosa, Jr. College/Walnut Creek Civic Arts Gallery, CA "Scultura" '84

ATLANTIS 1985, 18"x16"x14", Africastone, $4,000.00

DAN BARTA

160 Otsego Avenue, San Francisco, CA 94112
Born: 1/1/42
Represented by Image Design, 2401 24th Street, San Francisco, CA 94110
Born in Brno, Czechoslovakia. Studied natural history, worked as scientific illustrator in Czech. Acadmey of Sciences. Later as a free lance illustrator & photographer. His work is published in several magazines and 8 books, some in multilingual editions. In creative field received several awards. 1979 came to U.S.. 1980 one man show in Harward. Now lives in San Francisco, CA
MEMORIES

SHELLEY BARTENSTEIN

5831 W. Olympic Blvd., Los Angeles, CA 90036
Born: 6/4/50
Bartenstein works extensively in pen and ink. Her line drawings and cartoons, which have been published to illutrate children's books, greeting cards, and educational texts, reveal an offbeat humor and wry view of man. Bartenstein also does gum bichromate and cyanotype printmaking and conducts workshops on these and other non-silver photographic processes.

INSECTUM REVENGEUM, 12"x16", Ink on paper, NFS, Owned by Artist

---

KARLA M. BATES

3842 Midvale Ave., Oakland, CA 94602
Born: 6/8/54
Artist and Biological illustrator is a native Californian, born and raised in Berkeley . Works in Computer Graphic Tapestry Education, CA 1980 BerkeleyAcademy of Arts. University of SF, BA 1976. Exhibitions : Graphis Arts Gallery Collection in Zurich, Switzerland and Acorn Gallery in San Rafael and Sausalito, CA. Studies and travels in Jamaica, Mexico, Salvador, West Germany, England, France, Italy, Spain & Portugal.

BUTTERFLIES IN SPRING, 8'x24', Computer Graphics, $175.00, Owned by Artist

NELL B. BATES

2364 Vallejo St., San Francisco, CA 94123
Born: 3/23/19
Nell B. Bates began her art education at the SF Art Instutitue studying sculpture, painting and drawing, the latter with Frank Lobdell. She has completed a course in print making at Academy of Art - SF. Juried shows number sixteen since 1971. Prizes include 2nd Prize in oils, and several honorable mentions.

SAN FRANCISCO FLOWER STAND, 16"x20", Oil on Canvas, NFS, Owned by A. Sherman of San Francisco.

HUBERT BAYA

716 7th Avenue, San Francisco, CA 94118
Born: 7/14/53
(415) 752-3411
A promising young painter who had his first successful one-man show in Amsterdam, Rome and San Francisco. In his watercolors, drawings, and ethcings he keenly observes the atmospheres of nature with subtle lines and colors. His recent, more brightly colored monoprints express the vitality of our inner landscapes. He receives commissions for murals and stained glass.
SAN ANDREAS FAULT (Awarded merit, California State Fair, 1986), 22' x 30", Monoprint, $400.00, Owned by the artist

MARY A. BEESON

P.O. Box 3006, Yountville, CA 94599
Born: 1/12/62
Represented by Nelsoin Rockefeller Collection, 707 E. Tahquitz Way, Palm Springs, CA 92262 (6l9) 320-9554
(707) 944-2255
Ms. Beeson is mostly a self taught individualist sculptor. She works in all media, clay wood, stone, bronze. In 1986 she carved marble with Pasquale Martini of Milan, Italy. She is a noted portraitist, interpreting the inner spirit.

THE BROTHERS, 6'x4'x2', Bronze, Copy Available, Owned by United Veteran's Council of Marin County.

6

RUTH BELMEUR

24 Tacoma St., San Francisco, CA 94118
Born: 1/29/28
Sculptor: born Brooklyn. Studied Art Students League, worked as Graphic Artist in NY and SF 1955-1973. Media change to sculpture. Studies: UC Sonoma, College of Marin. Work; art in schoosl, rec'd CAC grant 1978. Sulpture: portraits and figure studies in a variety of clays and fire techniques, also bronze. Production includes limited edition of sculptured tableware and garden sculpture.

ADRIANA, 13"x9"10", Clay-Raku, NFS, Owned by artist

TANYA BENNETT

Rt. 2 Box 132, Hutchins (Dallas), TX 75141
Born: 9/25/61
(214) 225-8320
At an early age I began oil painting. That was a disaster! Years later I discovered acrylics in college and I've been busy creatiing since then. At 19 I received my AAA and began a career in graphic design. I've spent several years experimenting with an acrylic/airbrush combo. The excitement of each new painting is a challenge and it really keeps my life interesting.

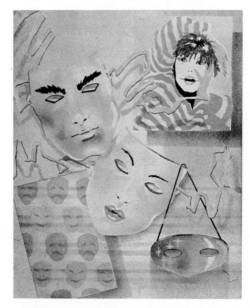

HIDDEN FACES, 11"x14" (framed), Airbrush, $250.00, Owned by artist

GREG BENSON

122 Menores Ave. Apt #6, Coral Gales, FL 33134
Born: 10/24/63
(305) 446-1017
Greg Benson was born in Zionsville, Pennsylvania, a farming community south of Allentown and north of Philadelphia. At age 15, he moved with his family to Perry, Georgia. His studies under James Herbert at the University of Georgia left him with a loose, spontaneous style that ideally leaves room for ambiguity and viewer participation.

FROZEN AFTERNOON, 40"x26", Acrylic, $400.00 Owned by artist

TIBERIU K. BENTE

118-60 Metropolitan Ave. #6B, Kew Gardens, NY 11415
Born:7/21/47
Represented by Stevens Fine Arts, 1437 Center Street, Detroit, MI 48226 (313) 963-0510
(718) 441-5389
MA Academy of Fine Arts, Bucharest. Solo Exhibitions: 1966-1986 New York, Rhode Island, Eket Village, Rockefeller Center, Italy, Rome, Caserta, Regio Calabria, Napli, Bucharest Art Museums. Group Shows, 69 in New York, USA, Italy, Germany

ENERGETIC FOR 9, 29"x26"x23", Cast Bronze, $12,500.00, Owned by Artist

ERNEST R. BERGWALL

1441 N. Jerusalem Rd., East Meadow, NY 11554
Born: 4/29/20
(516) 481-8209
In WW2 traveled all over the pacific in an L.S. T.. My retention of the scenery is clear and valid. Have shown in Calif, Ala, New Jersey, New York. My work also is in many homes in New York area. My background includes the Art Students League and National Academy in New York.

A BAY IN LEYTE P.I., 24"X36", OIL, $500.00

ROD BERRY

5032A Wilder Dr., Soquel, CA 95073
Born: 8/12/50
Presented by Series 20/20, Ltd., 9011 Soquel Dr., Aptos, CA 95073 (408) 688-5803
(408) 476-5834
Rod Berry's landscape paintings are motivated by a need to search out visual solutions that transcend the subject and act as visual metaphors for human qualities. His colors blend harmoniously and shimmer with a quality of light that captures the moods and emotions found in both human and mother nature.
AFTER THE STORM, 48"x60", Oil, $3,000.00

BARRY BICHLER

63 Knollwood Dr., Cherry Hill, NJ 08002
Born: 3/17/61
(609) 779-0782
BFA Pratt Institute. Have had exhibits at the 1985 Paris Air Show & 1984 Farnborough Air Show. Have a painting on display at the Smithsonian Air & Space Museum. Have done work for major aerospace manufacturers and publications. Currently working to produce prints of my art.

ONE DOWN, 30"x40", Oil, $3,000.00, Owned by artist

MARK BIGGS

2688 Folsom Street, San Francisco, CA 94110
Born: 10/8/52
Represented by Third Wave Gallery, 3316 24th Street, San Francisco, CA 94110, (415) 282-4020
(415) 695-8812
Mark Biggs, a native Californian, who has returned to San Francisco after eight years in New York City, has studied under masters of classical western and asian techniques in America and China. He uses Asian design and brushwork with western mediums to create the play of light on moving figures and swirling textures.
SWIMMER, 66"x39", Acylic, $5,000.00

ERWIN BINDER

Born: 1/24/34
Represented by Heritage Gallery, 718 North La Cienega Blvd, LA, CA 90069 (213) 652-7738
First one man show 1976 B Lewin Galleries BH CA 1977-installed large bronze "Sequoia" Southwest Museum LA CA, 1978 installed large bronze "Transcendence of Man", U Jerusalem, Israel; 1979 large bronze "Maize Goddess", Desert Museum, Palm Springs; 1981 Film "Sculptures of Binder: 1982 large bronze "Breeze of the Past" 1985 onyx installed "Fertility Goddess" Butler Inst. of American Art, Youngstown ,Ohio.
CORAZON, 52"x72"x36", Bronze, $50,000.00, Owned by private collector

ROGER BIRD

6710 Hawaii Kai Drive #400, Honolulu, HI 96825
Born : 9/1/41
Four years ago I asked a local artist how could I learn to paint? He replied,"Paint 100 pictures." With a few lessons, I did, then 100 more, etc. I'm an aggressive painter, always experimenting, working in oils and paint everyday. Art has changed my view of life, I find more beauty now. If not, I create it.

TROPICAL MIX, 16"x20", Oil, $400.00, Owned by Artist

HOLLY BLAKE

224 John Street, Santa Cruz, CA 95060
Born: 7/15/52
(408) 429-8044
Born in Newark, OH in 1952. Attended the Columbus College of Art and Design, Columbus, OH, 1971-1979. Exhibited and won awards locally for painting and printmaking. Moved to Sarasota, FL in 1979 and was a member of the Art Uptown Artists' Cooperative. Moved to Santa Cruz in 1985 and is actively seeking gallery representation.

CIRCLES, 24"x36", Mixed media, Owned by Mrs. J.E. Boast, Jr. of Bradenton, FL

VALERIU BOBORELU

45 Kew Gardens Road #3H, New Gardens, NY 11415
Born: 8/3/41
(718) 793-6647
Born in Romania. 1965 MA Nicolae Grigorescu Institutee of Fine Arts, Bucharest. 1966-82 Solo and Romanian State Exhibitions 1983 - Permanent resident in USA 1982 - Young Expression, Paris. 1983 Woodstock School of Art (Awarded). 1983 - Fall Salon Gran Palais, Paris, American Art Annual Exhibition, Ohio. 1984 - Queens Festival. 1985 - Easter Europeans in New York. Paintings in USA and Europe.
COMPOSITION #5, 70"X70", OIL ON CANVAS, $12,000.00, Owned by Artist

10

SKIP BOLEN

JAF Box 895, GPO New York City, NY
10116
Born: 4/1/56
Represented by Mario Villa Gallery, 3908
Magazine St., New Orleans, LA 70115 (504)
895-8731 & Eagles Nest Gallery, 1202 San
Antonio St., Austin, TX 78701 (512) 453-
2012
BFA from Univ. of Southwestern Louisiana.
He has been exhibiting his art since 1979 and
included nationally in many shows and
private collections.
**HER BLACK LATEX GLOVED
HAND NEVER ONCE TOUCHED
THE ELECTRIC I GAVE HER**,
23"x29", Gouache and permanent inks,

CRYSTAL BORIS

70-20 l08 Street, Apt 15C, Forest Hills, NY
11375
Born: 12/25/31
Represented by Lerner Gallery, 241 East 76
St., NY,NY 10021
Born in Poland. Studied Plocer's School of
Fine Arts, Israel 63-64. Work Museum Tel-
Aviv, Roerich Museum, NY Museum of
Modern Art and numerous other museums.
Exhibits in Europe, Asia, Africa and USA.
Awards: Gold Medal, Accademia Italia 1980-
82, Member Artist Equity Ass Art League,
NY
**OUR PLACE
WE** 24"x36"x30", Oil, $12,000.00, Owned
by Roerich Museum

PAMELA BORNE

11 Warner Court, San Rafael, CA 94901
Born: 12/12/39
(415) 485-1606
Originally from Sydney, Aust. Pamela has
been painting all her life with no formal fine
art training. One Woman shows in Sydney
and Marin and in art galleries in San
Francisco. Pamela also designs quilts and
banners. "The hills of Marin are my
inspiration".

SAUSALITO HOUSEBOAT, 18"x24",
Acrylic, $175.00, Owned by artist.

LEONARDA BOUGHTON

32 Columbine Road, Milton, MA 02186
Born: 06/26/62
Born in Bayside, WI, Leonarda started drawing very young. It hasalways been a natural extension of herself, not something that has been formally trained. She has been working as a freelancer for the past several years. The work that she most enjoys is wine label design, portrait work and children's books illustration.

UNTITLED, Pastel, Owned by artist

BARBARA BRIODIN

3429 Larissa Dr., LA CA 90026
Born: 10/20/48
Artisttpoet since age 2. Exhibited in Los Angeles and St. James Palace, London, England. Published poetry volume, 1984, Heart & Wings. Her painting, poetry and eggshell doll sculptures (created since 1968) are inspired by nature, the emotions and by the colours and pageantry of her work on stage from ages 4-19 as dancer/actor/singer.

CONFLICT, 25 1/4" x 24 3/8", Watercolour, $500

STAN BRODSKY

7 Glenna-Little Trail, Huntington, NY 11743
Born: 3/23/25
(516) 549-3763
Born in Bklyn, MFA Iowa '50. Solo shows: Roko, Lerner-Heller Galleries, NY, Heckscher, Mus. L.I. Group Shows:: Butler Inst. Of Del., U. Biennial; Pensacola Mus., Fla. Philamus. Collections: Heckscher, parrish Mus. L.I. Newsday; Pt. Auth., NY; Film: "Infusion" folio, "Influence of Landscape" List Who's Who, NY Rev. of Art '87. Fellowships: McDowell, VA. Center creative art, Prof. CW Post, L.I.U.

ENCLSOURE III, 40"x30", Oil, $1,600.00, Owned by artist

JACK BRUSCA

109 W26TH St 5A, NYC, NY 10001
BORN: 11/18/39
Born NYC, studied at the School of Visual
Arts. 15 One Man Shows. Collections:
Chase Manhattan Whitney Museum, NY
Aldrich Museum, Chrysler Museum,
Corcoran Museum, Queens Museum, NY
William Benton Museum, Univ. of Sydney
JFK Univ. CA Atlantic Univ. FLA. Roberto
Marinho Brazile Seymor Knox NY Inmont
Corp Owen Corning, Fiberglass Corp,
Minnesota Mining Co. ,Prudential Ins. Co.

SECRET LIFE OF A POLITICIAN,
42"x60", Acrylic, NFS, Owened by Marcio
Roiter of Rio, Brazil

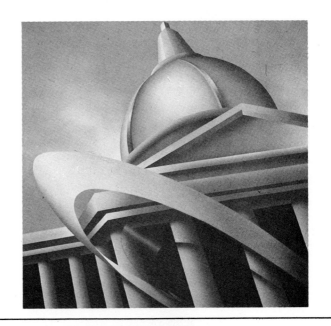

A.E. BUNKER

2137 Beach St., San Francisco, CA 94123
Born: 5/11/54
Represented by H.R. Mahany, Jr., 201
California St., 3rd Floor, San Francisco, CA
94111
Currently pursuing a BFA, minor in
computer graphics and a commercial arts
degree at the Academy of Art College, SF,
CA. Foundations award 1984. Academy
spring show 1983, 84,85,86. Sutter Gallery
exhibit 1985. Crocker Kingsley 61st annual
1986. Sacramento Union showcase, review
1986. Somar Gallery merit cash award
1986. Scotland traveling exhibition 1986.
**RUNNING FULL SPEED, JUST TO
STAY EVEN,** 100"x62", Acrylic/Tempra,

e.g. BURNS

800 El Camino Apt. 5, Vacaville, CA 95688
Born: 2/24/44
Represented by Oberon Gallery, 1130 Main
St., Napa CA 94559 (707) 255-7882
(707) 446-1057
Exhibitions: Oberon Gallery in Napa, CA,
Triangle Gallery Washington DC, National
Apeture Winston, Salem, NC. First prize for
national photo competition 1985. Formerly
on Marin Arts Guild Board of Directors.
Presently with Vacaville Arts Council. I've
been photographing for 10 years. I enjoy
landscapes and people as well as blending
images together artistically.
DAYS END, 8"x12", Photograph,
$100.00, Owned by artist

BRAIN CALLAGHAN

17 Harrison Commons, Shirley, NY 11967
Born: 1/16/53
The subject matter of my work is "visual commentary". This is the visual editorialization of the events and conditions that shape the world in which we live. These works are created in various media including watercolor, pen and ink, colored pencil and oils. I welcome all inquires. I am a Bachelor of Fine Arts (Media Arts) graduate of the School of Visual Arts.

FOR THE CHILDREN....A LEGACY IN PERPETUITY....14"x18", Oil

JOHN PHILIP CAPELLO

1115 Quentin Road, Brooklyn, NY 11229
Born: 10/23/39
Represented by Onyx Gallery, 411 Atlantic Avenue, Brooklyn, NY 11217 (718) 834-1700
(718) 336-3212
Self taught. Paintings, murals, stones sculpturee. Affiliations: National Society of Mural Painters, President of All Communities Arts, Audubon Artists Assoc., City Arts Workshop, Awards: 3 Mollie Parnis Awards for Public Murals, 3 BACA awards for mural designs, 6 ACA awards for easel paintings and sculpture.
PATH TO YOUR DREAMS, 10'x 22', Acrylic mural (outdoor)

LEONILDE CARABBA

2316 Elm Rd., P.O. Box 676, Bolinas, CA 94924
Born: 11/28/38
Born in Milano, Italy. She was born, as artist, in the Milano of the sixties where her masters and friends were: Fontana, Crippa, Fautrier and others. She exhibited in Milan, Rome, Berlin, Frankfurt, Bruxelles, Hamburg and more. In 1983 she moved to California. The cultural shock gave an extra boost to her creativity. Her style is New Age Renaissance.
SELF-PORTRAIT OF THE YOUNG MAN THAT I LOVE, 40"x40", Acrylic, NFS, Owned by Marine Mourier of Occidental, CA

CATHY CAREY

4908 Regent Road, Richmond, VA 23230
Born: 9/27/60
Education: Corcoran school fo Art-Painting
and printmaking. VA Commonwealth Univ.
- BFA Painting and printmaking. SHOWS:
Boardwalk and Neptune Festival Art Shows,
VA Beach, VA. In my paintings, I use layers
of patterns to simultaneously reveal and
camoflauge an object. I use strong color and
perspective distortions to show abstract
qualities within realistic areas.

CHAMPAYNE GLASSES, 18"x24",
Acrylic, $300.00, Owned by artist

BERTHA CATHERINE CARTWRIGHT

105 Keer Ave., Newark, NJ 07112
Born: 6/8/62
Graduated from Rutgers University in 1984
with a bachelor of Arts degree in visual arts.
In sophmore year, I was told by an assembly
of 6 professors I did not have enough ability
to remain in the BFA program. At Mason
Gross School of the Arts, I was a late
bloomer, and as a result created a new
portfolio in the summer of 1982 which this
drawing came from.

MICHAEL PARE, 10 3/8"x 14 1/16",
Pencil, NFS

LEON CARVER

5550 S. Corchester, Chicago, IL 60637
Born: 11/14/60
1982 BFA Graduate and 1986 MFA graduate
from the school of the Art Institute of
Chicago. Presently pursuing galleries to
exhibit my airbrush screen print technique
developed while in school. Actively
working freelance in design and illustration,
with plans to open an inhouse print and
illustration studio.

MISSION OF A MIND, 15"x20",
Screenprint, $600.00

PHILLIP PAANG CHAN

5225 Edgeworth Rd., San Diego, CA 92109
Born: 7/11/46
Born in Canton, China. Study: Univ. of
Calif. @ Berkeley. Exhibited: SFMuseum of
Art, SF Art Inst., Des Moines Art Center,
Ackland Mus., Huntsville Mus Art, Artmisia
Gallery, Univ. of Houston, Parsons Gallery;
Teaching: Univ of North Carolina, Univ of
Vermont, Oberlin College, Skidmore,
College, Univ Texas; Awards: National
Endowment Arts, MacDowel

UNTITLED, 22"x28", Oilsticks, Owned
by artist

JOHN CHIP

P.O. Box 2, Chadds Ford, PA 19317
Born: 2/11/50
Represented by Ellin/Baker Gallery, 102
Chestnut St., Philadelphia, PA 19106 (215)
923-6257
(215) 793-1150
Living and painting along the Brandywine
River in Chadds Ford, PA brings a realistic
painting tradition to bear on John's work.
Doctoral studies in creativity, travels among
primitive cultures. Classical art training in
Europe and America give the foundation to
this artist's compelling style.
A SECOND LOOK, 40"x34", Oil,
$3,000.00 Owned by Ellin/Baker Gallery of
Philadelphia.

JACK CHIPMAN

P.O. Box 1429, Redondo Beach, CA 90278
Born: 10/31/43
(213) 376-2964
Birth Place: Los Angeles. BFA - Chouinard
Art Institute. Exhibited: Oakland, Long
Beach, U. Santa Clara Museums, Solos
Shows: Long Beach Museum, U. Santa
Clara, Brand Library, Glendale, Sawyer and
Grapestake Galleries, San Francisco.
Museum collections: Oakland, Long Beach,
U. Santa Clara. Seeking gallery affiliation.

XAXIS 14, 72"x48 1/2", Mixed, $500.00
Owned by artist

CHARLES CHRISTOPHER

887 Bush St., #609, San Francisco, CA
94108
Born:2/7/29
(415) 771-8964
Born Charles Christopher Hovine, Chicago
Ill. Studied in NY Art Career School 53-54,
Ozenfant 55-56, Archipenko 57-58, His
absorption with painting as a catalyst for the
meditative mind stylistic forerunners are Ad
Reinhart and Mark Rothko exhibited in the
NY 10th St. Cooperative Galleries, The Brata
Goup, the Loft, Etc. 59-65.

DIAMOND SUTRA 60-61, 5"X5";, Oil,
NFS, Whereabouts unknown

LINDA M. CLEMENT

28 Warren Avenue #1, Somerville, MA
02143
Born: 4/6/51
Graduated Rhode Island School of Design in
1973 - BFA in Communication Design. 12
years experience working as a
designer/illustrator and art director. Have
done most of my three-dimensional work on
a commissioned basis. Continuing to build a
series of automobile replicas-but seek
illustrative applications and challenges, using
this medium.

1937 JAGUAR SS 100, 8"x8"x8", Soft
Sculpture, NFS, Owned by Mr. Drew
Epstein of Swampscott, MA

JOSEPH COCO

247 Van Houten Ave., New Jersey, NJ
07055
Born: 3/8/51
Represented by Luminarios Art, 438 West
37th St., New York, NY 10018
"Combining drawn or painted images with
my original music I use pretaped video loops
as an installation counterpart. The solar
eclipse series will tour the next 14 years
culminating at a permanent location. With
354 works in 176 collections Mr. Coco has
had 23 solo shows since 1974 with an MFA
from Rutgers Univ.
**GHOULS OF THE EART, Solar
Eclipse and a Nuclear Holocuast**
(series), 18"x 24", Chalks/Paper, NFS

PHILIP COLGAN

279 Frederick St., Hanover, PA 17331
Born: 1/7/56
Attened the former York, PA Academy of Arts before embarking on an extensive art study through Europe. The recipeint of numerous awards and honors and the veteran of exhibits through the eastern US, the artist now owns and maintains a successful gallery-studio in his hometown. Here he sells original works and accepts some commission projects.

WILLIE SMITH-BLUES PAINIST, 22" x 34", Oil, Owned by Philip Ridder of Houston, TX

OLAV COLN

1065 Las Ovejas Ave., San Rafael, CA 94903
Born: 4/12/18
Studied painting with Tom Buchanan and on his own. Primarily abstract semi-abstract oils. Member of Marin Arts Guild and MSA. Exhibited in local shows such as San Francisco Art Festivals, Los Gatos Fiesta des Artes, MSA and TLAA Annual Shows and at Shorebirds Gallery. Has privately owned works in San Francisco, Oakland, Seattle, Los Gatos and Marin County.

TAHOE, 30"x40", Oil, NFS, Owned by artist

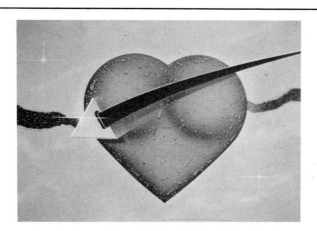

A.D. COOK

P. O. Box 1181, Clackamas, OR 97015
Born: 3/9/61
I am a self-taught artist with 10 years of airbrush experience, specializing in commercial illustration and design with a strong background in commercial and residential murals and wall graphics. Other areas of expertise include the design and execution of sets, props, and backdrops for photographers. I also enjoy teaching airbrush skills at local high schools.

UNTITLED, 14"x17", Ink, Owned by artist

SCOTT CORAN

160 University Avenue West, Saint Paul, MN 55103
Born: 9/10/52
Through research, I construct artworks specializing in the aesthetic experimentation of high voltage fluorescent light. Placed in highly visable locations, these sculptures involve the viewer through curiosity.

24MMX12M, 2'x4'x6', Flourescent Light, NFS

TERRY CRANE

15037 Dobson Avenue, Dolton, IL 60419
Born: 12/20/61
(312) 849-3874
Born in Cedar Falls, Iowa. Studied Fine Art at Northern Illinois University and Thornton Community College. Although watercolor is my primary media, I also produce oils and acrylics, many of which are sold to private collectors and businesses. My goal as an artist is to provoke serious thought by using elements of humor.

H. DUMPTY, 25"x21", Watercolor, NFS, Owned by Carol Lambert of Atlanta, GA.

SARA E. CULMONE

7701 Westlawn Avenue, Los Angeles, CA 90045
Born: 8/7/47
I believe that humor can keep us going when all the reasons in the world would fail us. I have been testing the limits of computer graphics at UCLA. I am illustrating a book and am looking for other frontiers to challenge. I was a founding member of The Maple Creek Papermaking Studio. I graduated from San Diego State University in Art/Printmaking and Enameling.

SPECIAL PASSAGE FOR PARENTAL COMMENT, 18"x22", Viscosity Print, $1,000.00, Owned by artist

DAVID CULP

348 Douglas St., Los Angeles, CA 90026
Born: 1/8/42
(213) 413-8210
EDUCATION: BA Degree Whittier College, 1963; Majored in Psychology. I am a self taught artist. Group Exhibition: Ariel Gallery, NY, 1986. Limited Edition of Three works by Graftek International, 1986. I have sold my work at the Beverly Hills "Affaire in the Gardens" Festivals and the Long Beach Art Museum Artist's Market.

LA MAISON ROSE, 20"x26", Acrylic, $300.00, Owned by artist

ZELMA DALE

2200 Sacramento #505, San Francisco, CA 94115
Born: 5/18/11
Represented by SF Women Artists, 451 Hayes, San Francisco, CA, 94102 (415) 552-7392
(415) 346-2675
BFA in Painting from U. of Okla. Art Students League, NYC, Rome, Italy, Tasos, New Mex. Resided 20 yr Caracas, Venezuela. Paint oils, acrylics, water colors, serigraphs. Exhib. Museo Bellas Artes, Vaauw Gallery, Centro Ven. America Galleria, Botto.

ALONG HI-WAY 5, 12"x18", Watercolor, $300.00, Owned by artist

HELEN DAPHNIS-AVLON

463 West St., NYC, NY 10014
Born: 6/18/32
Represented by Gallery I-Westbeth, 155 Bank St., NYC, NY 10014
Provincetown Permanent collection Museum and Art Assoc. Gallery, One Westbeth NYC. Bertha Schaeffer Gallery, NYC, Brata, Phoenix Galleries, Forum, James. Chrysler Museum, Provincetown, Mass. Gallery East, NYC Center Gallery, Environmental show videos available. UFS Show, Colorado Spring Fine Art Center, Hudson Guild Silvermine Guild, Chelsea and Avant Garde Art Festivals.

CLOUD CELESTIALS, 4'x4', Oil and acrylic, Owned by artist

DAVID CANNON DASHIELL

400 Duboce Avenue, #411, San Francisco,
CA 94117
Born: 7/4/52
EDUCATION: California Institute of The
ARrts, BFA 1974, MFA 1976.
EXHIBITIONS: "Art for Life," CNA
Gallery, San Francisco, 1986; "Metaparty",
AAA Gallery, San Francisco, 1982;
"Artwords and Bookworks", Los Angeles
Institute of Contemporary Art, Los Angeles,
1977; "Southland Video Anthology", Long
Beach Museum of Art, Long Beach, 1975.

PLAGUE JOURNAL, 1985, 56"x108",
Pastel, NFS, Owned by Daniel Buckler of
Boulder Creek, CA

MARIA S.C. DAVI

2660 Rim Rd., Tara Hills, San Pablo, CA
94806
Born: 9/3/47
(415) 222-4092
Born in El Paso, Texas. Education: Interior
designing. Languages: Several. Experience:
Art instructor since 1970, private and public,
all ages, in several recreational centers.
Private studio. Freelance: newspapers,
brochures. Media: oil, acrylic, porcelain,
ceramic, watercolor, ink. Art Work: original,
reproduction and portraits.

THE GUST (Porcelain hand-painted dish),
8"x8", $49.00, Owned by Mrs. Arnoni

DAN DAVIDSON

6910 Greenbrook Circle, Citrus Heights, CA
95621
Born: 1/10/65
(916) 722-5489
Dan Davidson enjoys painting in a neo-
surrealistic style. He works primarily with
oils, but also uses watercolors, pencils, ink
and multi-medias. He began oil painting in
1980 after receiving a book on Rene
Magrette. Dan is working to improve his
techniques and to develop a more individual
style. Dan's goal is to contribute to a modern
version of surrealism.
**ECLIPSE OF MEMORY;
VARIATIONS ON A THEME OF
SADNESS**, 36"x 24", Oil

YBETH DAWNING

23800 Morrell Cutoff, Los Gatos, CA 95030
Born: 11/2/37
Ybeth was born in Los Angeles. Though principally self taught she received training at Otis-Parsons Art School. and Marin and Cabrillo Colleges. A visionary artist, her work is owned by numerous private collectors. She has done commissions of people and animals. Her works include pen/ink, acyrlics, sculpture/clay, and wearable art.

LIGHT VISION, 3'x4', Acrylic, $500.00
Owned by artist

BETTY DECTER

5412 W. Washington Blvd., Los Angeles, CA 90016
Born: 4/2/27
Painter, sculptor, writer. Her work includes room installations, mural sized paintings and bronze sculptures from the "Wandering Through Life and Dancing Toward Death" series and "The Red Shift" series. Member of the Dean's Council, Otis/Parsons. Board of Directors, Woman's Bldg. in private and corporate collections in France, Holland, USA. Published author.
FRAMENTS FROM "A TON OF KIMONOS" SERIES, 43"x7", Acrylic & mixed media, NFS, In Collection of Ivey's, Florida

ANNABEL DE LA TORRE-BUENO

15111 Otgego St., Sherman Oaks, CA 91403
Born: 1/18/14
(818) 784-5040
Annabel de la Torre-Bueno has been a painter all her life. She sees deep into her subject capturing inner strength and beauty. She works only from life sittings unless subject is deceased. She received a BFA degree from Colorado U and was winner of the Frank Alvah Parsons Scholarship for study in Paris. Solo shows in London, Sussex, Colorado, Los Angeles.

RICHARD DE LA TORRE-BUENO PORTRAIT, 34"x 48", Oil/Canvas, NFS, Owned by artist

GEORGE DENNINGER

3250 Braemar Dr., Santa Barbara, CA 93109
(805) 682-3299
Born NY. Degrees: Engineering and Product design. One-of-a-kind metal, mixed media. Work includes sculpture, architecture, product prototypes, furniture, piano cabinetry. Pianos shown at Smithsonian and Metropolitan Museum of Art. Focus on promoting uplifting ideas through form. Latest works emphasize light. Available for commissions.

FOREST SHADOW BOX 12"x19"x8", Wood, glass, $1,500.00, Owned by the artist

PHIL DIERS

1362 Hayes St., San Francisco, CA 94117
Born: 2/23/57
(415) 567-7032
Phil Diers has created visual art most of his life and has worked extensively in sculpture, photography, filmmaking and architectural miniatures. A film production major; he is currently working in portrait and figure sculpture and designing architectural details: "In whatever art I do, I want to create an enveloping moving experience for the viewer".

APOLLO I,47"x 24"x 12". Sculpture, $1,200.00, Owned by artist, Limited Edition #1 of 25.

JACK DODD

1504 Cabrillo, San Francisco, CA 94118
Born: 4/15/55
(415) 752-6938
A Native of the San Francisco Bay area, Jack Dodd studied art at the University of California, Santa Cruz, where he developed his interest in painting dramatic California landscapes. Most recently his watercolor work was represented in the Bay Area Regionalists Exhibit, Bay Area Seen II.

THE WAVE, 17"x25", Watercolor, $425.00, Owned by artist

RICHARD DOERER

183 Livingston St., New Haven, Ct. 06511
Born: 10/16/58
Represented by Phase One Gallery, 857 West Armitage, Chicago, IL 60614 (312) 887-7435
(203) 776-0203
Born Ann Arbor, MI. BFA Western Mich Univ 1981. MFA Yale Univ 1984. Select Exhib: Art l6' 85 Basel Switz.(Schweyer Galdo Galleries) '85 Art in Heaven, New Haven, CT '86 College of William and Mary, Group/ Figure Invit., Williamsburg, VA **THE RECAPTURE OF NUMBER #17**, 84"X 60", Oil on Canvas, NFS, Owned by Dr. Stephen Friedlander of Knoxville, TN

ARDIE DUNNING

8621 Coolwoods Way, Sacramento, CA 95828
Born: 3/7/34
(916) 689-6436
Born and raised in Colorado. Moved to CA. Raised 4 children. Moved to Nevada City, 1980, where I engaged in art classes. Was a member of Pioneer Art Club, Displayed oils at fairs and local art shows. Besides canvas, I paint on shovels, saws, glass and Christmas ornaments. My "Winter Scene" won 1st place at Stu Milluer Christmas Extravaganza, at Cal Expo in Sacramento **SWANS IN SERENITY**, 18"x24", Oil, NFS, Owned by Connie and Presley Herndon of Kansas

LAWRENCE EGE

7425 N. Sheridan Rd., Chicago, IL 60626
Born: 12/31/55
(312) 338-6375
I was born in Chicago, Spent most my youth in Indiana and moved to New Jersey at 18 attending Gloucester Co. College and Glassboro State College. There I received a BFA from the Art Institute of Chicago in 1981 and have been working professionally since 1984. I work in oils and watercolor primarily.

STILL LIFE WITH CANTELOUPE AND CHERRIES, 11 1/4"x 17 1/4", Watercolor, $700.00, Owned by artist

CHARLES EGRI

125 West 16 St., New York, NY 10011
Born: 7/13/09
(212) 929-7522
Nat'l Academy of Design NYC: Art Students League, NYC: Pratt Graphic Center, NYC: SOlo Show Nat'l Art Center, NYC: Group-Gallery Modern Art NM: Sixth Sense Gallery-Group: ACA Gallery, NYC Group: Collection-Johnson Whaling, Museum PrinctonDupont Office, Wilmington, Del: Thomas Funding, Atlanta, GA

THE MAGIC CITY, 30"x22", Mixed Media, $1,200.00, Owned by artist

SHEILA ELIAS

2323 E. Olympic Blvd, Los Angeles, CA 90021
Represented by Alex Rosenberg Gallery, 20 West 57th St., NY 10019 (212) 757-2700
(213) 689-9198
Selected Solo Exhibitions: '86 NYU Loeb Center, Danville Museum of Fine Arts, '84-'86 Stella Polaris Gallery, LA. '83 San Jose Museum. Group Exhibitions: '86 Louvre, "Liberty": Institute Des Decorifs, Paris, France; NY Public Library, NYC; New Z Gallery, Tokyo, Japan. '85 "Objects for New Rituals", Pictogram gallery, East Village, NY
MARY AND MISS LIBERTY, 36"x47", Handmade paper, NFS, Owned by Mr. & Mrs. Resnic of New York

MERIAM JEAN EMANI

1691 Dickinson Drive, Wheaton, IL 60187
Born: 8/10/62
Studying fine arts in HS lead me to a BA in Illustration. I studied my first 2 years at the California College of Arts and Crafts, Oakland. I then transferred to Columbia College, Chicago, finishing off 3 more years. I wish to work in a studio and participate in gallery showings. To view more works, write me at the given address.

UNDERWATER WORLD, 16"x11", Colorpencils, NFS

JOHN EVANS

9011 Soquel Drive, Aptos, CA 95003
Born: 12/18/43
Represented by Series 20/20, 9011 Soquel
Drive, Aptos, CA 95003
Using original poetry as the main expression
with other forms, handmade cotton paper and
carvings, are combined to create an unique
artpiece. Set in a museum mounting, the
papercasting and corresponding etching float
in a dimensional sequence. This piece is a
signed and numbered limited edition.

TRAVEL YOUR ROAD, 18"x24"x3",
Paper

DEBORAH EVERETT

566 Henry Street, Brooklyn, NY 11231
Born: 3/20/51
(718) 643-9642
Born Galveston, TX. BA 1969-73. Worked
full-time 1973-75. 1975 entered art school,
Univ. of TX, studied with Gary Winogrand,
Janis Provisor, Susan Whynne; 1978
awarded Ford Foundation Grant, BFA.
MFA Rutgers Univ. 1979-82. Group shows:
Small Walls Gal, 1983, City Arts
Organization, 1984. Works reproduced:
New York Art Review 1987.

DRIFT, 48"x 36", Oil, $2,000.00

NICK FALCONE

27853 West Oakland, Bay Village, OH
44140
Born: 10/25/42
I have been painting professionally for the
past ten years. My following is a group of
individuals who purchase my work because it
not only challenges one's imagination, but at
the same time makes a personal statement,
whether that statement is political, religious
or humane, it must generate a reaction by it's
viewers.

BROTHERS IN ARMS, 21"x16", Oil,
NFS, Owned by Artist

VICTOR Q. FAN

370 Noe Sreet, San Francisco, CA 94114
BORN: 2/2/53
(415) 621-2415
I was born in China, immigrated to US in
1980. I got my MFA in painting when I
graduated from Academy of Arts College in
1983. In 20 years I concentrated to depict the
different people, variety and lifestyle,
especially about subculture. My works are
exhibited in several countries and were
awarded prizes. I like music, sport and
travel.

CAT, 40"x30", Oil $4,000.00, Owned by
artist

LEONARD FARACE

11 Hazel Avenue, West Orange, NJ 07052
Born: 12/16/50
(201) 731-6965
As a painter, I explore the visual possibilities
which exist between realism and abstraction
and how these possibilities can be applied to
evoke a positive intuitive response. My
paintings reveal a multi-dimensional world
which is easily accessible to the viewer. My
work has been exhibited in museums and
galleries throughout New Jersey.

P O L A R I T Y , 3'x3', Oil/Canvas,
$2,000.00, Owned by artist

DIANE FEDORIW

2316 W. Rice St., Chicago, IL 60622
Born: 2/2/57
(312) 486-6865
Born in Chicago, Diana is an emerging media
artist who works with photo, film and video.
Her serial photo postcards arrive in
installments in Japan, Germany, Britain and
the US. Her work has also appeared in the
literary journals, OYEZ and Red Shoes
Review. She is currently working on a video
tape that deconstructs the classic movie
Western.

**NO. 2, FROM SELF-PORTRAIT IN
SILVER MYLAR SERIES,** 11"x14",
Ektacolor, $350.00

K. ROXI FELFE

212 Burton Hill Rd., Fort Worth, TX 76114
Born: 12/27/62
(817) 738-7572
Now in her early twenties, Roxi is virtually a self taught artist who places extreme emphasis on fine detail and photographic realism. She favors the dramatic appeal pencil on black paper. Her favorite subject matter is people, animals, and guitars because she only feels compelled to draw "that which has life, breath, and a living soul."

WHERE THERE'S SMOKE...,
12"x16", Pencil NFS, Owned by Eric Trent

CHARLES A. FILIUS

3060 Bel Pre Road Apt. 1B, Silver Spring, MD 20906
Born: 1/24/61
(301) 871-3926
I'm a native West Virginian educated at Fairmont State College and Art Institute of Pittsburgh. Employed as a graphic artist near Washington, DC, I'm building a strong freelance following. My work's been exhibited and has won various honors and awards. Areas of experience: Cartooning, Illustration, Portraits, graphics, Logos and Film/Television production.

JEAN HARLOW, 12"x17", Acrylic, NFS

TOM FITZWATER

P.O. Box 847, Greenfield, CA 93927
Born: 5/2/43
(408) 674-5335
Tom Fitzwater received MA in art at CSULB (1972). Past exhibits in CA galleries/Museums. Responsible for statue of John Steinbeck (Salinas, CA). Paintings of the old west, a series of "Historic Photo-transforms of figurative artlandscapes, portraits, and wild-life scenes. Just completed model of proposed monumental gas-relief triptic sculpture: John Muir in Yosemite Park.
NIGHT RIDERS STOP, 72"x40", Oil/Canvas, NFS, Signed numbered Ed. prints on canvas available.

28

CHRISTINA J. FLEISCHBEIN

P.O. Box 2124, Ft. Lauderdale, FL 33303
Born: 1/5/57
(305) 462-2997
Christina received her BFA from Virginia Commonwealth University in 1979, with a double major in painting and printmaking and a minor in theology. Her work has been exhibited in area shows and galleries. She has received awards from the Torpedo Factory, Alexandria, VA. and several of her pieces have been purchased by the World Bank and the State Department.

UNTITLED, 6"x8", Collage, $220.00

A. STEVE FLEMING

1080 San Miguel Rd. SP158, Concord, CA 94518
Born: 4/5/42
(415) 827-4916
1986 - One man exhibit at Kaiser Aluminum Headquarters in Oakland CA. A series of 12 cartoons depicting the takeover attempt by J.A. Frates group of KACC. Wildlife and cartoon art relating to the California delta. Commissions of artwork relating to the oil industry. Caricatures. Oils, watercolor, pen and ink and pencil.

SUNSET AT THE RIG, 20"x 30", Airbrush/Pen and Ink, $310.00, Owned by the artist

ANTHONY CHARLES FLETCHER

2719 Speakman Place, Wilmington, DE 19802
Born: 12/22/56
Represented by Ariel Gallery Soho, 76 Greene St., NYC, NY 10012 (212) 226-8176
(302) 764-7443
His incredible techniques (oils, too) combined with spiritual intensity & lush colors make Fletchers works unique and always exciting. Executed in dramatic compelling arrangements that capture the interest of the viewer, his works convey a hidden message for humanity.

VULBERABILITY, 29 1/2" x 36", Pencil, $1,500.00, Owned by Artist

MARK J. FREDENBURG

112 North Pershing Road, Waukegan, IL 60085
Born: 7/22/55
Represented by Laura Stankovitch, 2217 North Bonnie Brook Lane, Waukegan, IL 60085
In common with professional artisans of our century, Mark Fredenburg's work is being noted. He attributes his browing recognition to his properly concentrated thoughts and his classical disciplines gained while an apprentice to Mustafa Naguig.
To every soul bring beauty near. Emerson
PRAYER, 32"x10"x15", Limestone, NFS

VALERIE FREEMAN

150 West 55th St. #7F, New York, NY 10019
Born: 2/12/60
BFA Pratt Institute NY Multi mixed media artist. Installations, performance-video against nuclear Society. Grants from Ford Foundation, Experimental TV center. Exchibit at Red Spot Outdoor Slide Theater NY & Miami, Wallagerie Germany, Suffolk County video Festival NY cable TV. Art performance at NY Tech. Has received many reviews in NY Times High Performance Mag.
NUCLEAR AVENGER FROM 'DIOXIN DANCE', Video Still, 18"x24", Cibrachrome, $500.00 Owned by artist

MICHELLE FRIDKIN

P.O. Box 55278, Tucson, AZ 85703
Born: 6/19/46
Represented by Ann Original Gallery, 4811 E. Grant ,Suite 153, Tucson, AZ 85712
(602) 299-4521
(602) 299-3097
Michelle, like many great american artists, has honed her craft through years of illustration work. She received her art degree from the University of MA in 1968. Her illustration credits include McGraw Hill; Random House; Macmillan and Prentice-Hall.

TRANSITIONS, 20"x 26", Mixed, $2500.00, Owned by artist

JAKE GAEDTKE

3550 So. Kendall 2-203, Denver, CO 80285
Born: 3/l6/54
Jake is a self-taught artist who has been
drawing since he could hold a pencil in his
hand. He has studied under professional
artists in Kansas City and Colorado. The
Rocky Mountains provide him with the
inspiration to further his skills as an artist.
Jake chooses oil and pastels as his favorite
medium. Jakes work is found in collections
throughout the country.

THE BEAVER HAT, 18"x24", Charcoal,
NFS, Owned by Dr. and Mrs.. David Katzen
of Estes Park

ED GEDROSE

18822 SE Mildred, Milwaukie, OR 97267
Born: 9/16/49
(503) 657-0608
Ed began his career in Portland, Oregon
working as a portrait artist. After exploring a
wide range of techniques and subject matter,
he later turned hisattention to illustration and
the world of fantasy art. Today, Ed's goal is
to illustrate books and book covers and
eventually illustrate his own book of fantasy
art.

THE DANCING FAIRY, 12"x18,
Colored Pencil, In private collection

ROGER GERBERDING

843 West Belle Plaine #1-S, Chicago, IL
60613
Represented by Studio View Gallery, 1627
North Damen Avenue, Chicago, IL 60647
(312) 384-4441
(312) 929-1206
Attended the Chicago Academy of Fine Art.
Has exhibited widely in the midwest,
including appearances at the Atrium Gallery,
The Evanston Art Center, Artemisia, The
Norris Cultural Center, and the Koehnline
Gallery . His graphic work has appeared in
Tomorrow, Fantasy Tales, Etchings land
Odysseys, the Rockford Review
THE WAY WE SAY GOODBY,
36"x36", Oil/Acrylic, $1,000.00, Owned by

SUSAN LEE GERINGER

60 North Stamford Rd., Stamford, CT 06903
Born: 9/18/58
(203) 329-7228
Su holds a BS in Social Sciences, a BFA in painting from Purchase College. Exhibits in NYC, NY, NJ and CT. Represented in International Art Expo '86. Her colorful, gestural abstracts are inspired by nature and its interactions by dance and movement and by psychic phenomenon.

SECOND SIGHT, 36" x 60", Mixed media, $1800, Owned by artist

JIM GILBERT

P.O. Box 1543/530 Archibald Ct., Colton, CA 92324
Born: 12/28/48
(714) 825-7648
James Gilbert has always been fascinated with the female form, and for the past 20 yrs has strived to perfect his exotically beautiful women. His latest series is a combination of classic cars and beautiful women (Reflection is the first to be published). James Gilbert is a multi-talented artist and designer whose style and imagination set him apart from the rest.

REFLECTION, 22"x30", Acrylic, Prints available

LAURETTE GNAEGY

160-13 84th Avenue, Jamaica, NY 11432
Born: 11/27/58
Laurette Gnaegy is a 1981 Ford Foundation Scholar. She has studied at the Byamshaw School of Art in London, The Miami Art Center, the Art Students League and earned her BFA at Pratt Institute in NY where she lives. She has exhibited in numerous group shows, received commissions and is represented in many private collections is a member of NYAE.

BIRD, 48"x36", Acrylic, NFS, Owned by Christopher Kovary

SHEILA GOLDEN

P.O. Box 183, Penngrove, CA 94951
Born: 1/5/43
Represented by Vorpal Gallery, 393 Grove St., San Francisco, CA
Born and raised in NY. Studied painting under abstract expressionsist Morris Davidson. First exhibit 1964 Satori Gallery, NYC. Worked as graphic designer in SF and NY. BA degree, Fine Art 1980. Solo Show Vorpal Gallery, SF. 1985 selected for Contemporary Women Artists Calendar. Presently living in Sonoma County, CA

HOLIDAY, INTERFACE SERIES, 16"x 20", Watercolor, $325.00, Owned by artist

SONIA HAIG GOLDSBOROUGH

1651-215 S. Juniper, Escondido, CA 92025
Born: 5/1/26
Born SF. Training SF Academy of Art College under Richard Stevens SR., Howard Brodie. SF Museum of Modern Art Alexander School of Painting. Other instructors: Martin Snipper, former SF Art commissioner, Brook Temple. Exhibited 2 paintings by jury selection for "American Painters in Paris", French-American bicentennial celebration Paris, France.

BREAKTHRU, 32"x 32", Oil, Owned by artist

DOROTHY GOLDSTEIN

36 West Culver, Phoenix, AZ 85003
Born: 5/7/45
Represented by Sunbird Gallery, Ann Kristin Hansson, 243 Main St., Palo Alto, CA 94022 (415) 1941-1561
(602) 253-6796
Brooklyn born, self trained artist. Specializes in intricate and imaginative prismacolor and pen and ink drawings of urban scenes and designs. Goldstein's works are fantasy, fun, futuristic and full of things to look at.

SILVER CITY, 18"x24", Prisma colors and Ink, $1,500.00, Owned by artist

JANE A. GOSS

P. O. Box 107, Kensington, MD 20895
Born: 10/21/49
A graduate of the MD Institute College of Art, Ms. Goss resides in the Washington, DC area where she has been in shows including the 22nd Area show at the Corcoran Gallery. Her first solo show was at the National Arts Club in New York. She has also been in International shows and has received awards for painting, drawing and photography.

AMARILLUS, 39"x27", Mixed Drawing, $600.00, Owned by artist

MAX E. GOTTFRIED

82-60 116 St. #CC3, Kew Gardens, NY
Born: 3/31/53
Represented by Field Gallery, 43 East 10 St., NY, NY 10003 (212) 473-2168
(718) 441-9868
Max Gottfried graduated Pratt Institute in '75 (BFA). Formally trained as a illustrator he later developed his current artistic philosophies. Film-noir, fashion, comics and eclectic music help from Gottried's "Retro Nouveau" style of painting. Gottfried has been involved in all phases of media ranging from film to a broadway musical to self publishing venues.
THE CONTINENTAL, 40"x50", Gouache, NFS

JEAN GREGG

RR 2 Box 425, Kapaam, HI 96746
Born: 4/28/24
Represented by Pine Street Gallery, 114 Pine St., Troy AL 36081
BS in Art Ed, Miami U. Resident of Hawaii since 1946. Active in several art groups. Received awards for drawings, photographs and watercolors in local and mainland judged and juried shows. Prefer drawing and watercolors. Have studied with Island NM and east coast artists. Favorite subjects: florals and old buildings.

OLD PINE, 4 1/2"x6 1/2", Pencil, $95.00, Owned by artist

GRIFFE RONALD GRIFFITHS

Box 608, Woodacre, CA 94973
Born: 10/9/36
Born Liverpool, Eng. Education: Trade school, Southport College of Art and Design 57-58. Designed and built stage sets. Far east study of Oriental Art 60-61. Studio NYC 64. Faculty Sarah Lawrence College, Theatre '65. Reside CA. I work in sheet bronze using the pierce repousse chasing techniques. My latest work is a series of masks and wall plaques.

MASQUE IBAN, 8"x10", Sheetbronze, NFS

GREGORY GRONOWSKI

805 N4th Ave. #303, Phoenix, AZ 85003
Born: 4/14/53
Represented by John Douglas Cline, 424 Nth Central Ave., Phx, AZ 85004 (5602) 258-5859
(602) 252-9301
Born: Panama City, Florida
Education: 1972-74 Columbus College of Art and Design: 2 year scholarship: 1974-77 studied with Fred Graff, Medina, OH: 1977-79 Studied landscape and abstract painting with Fred Leach AWS Avon, OH: 1981-82 Began printmaking: 1982-86 Paint-sculpture-printing

MAN'S TOYS, 72"X72", Oil/Canvas, $1,500.00, Owned by Artist

KATHY A. HALAMKA

180 Harbor Drive Suite 202, Sausalito, CA 94965
Born: 11/24/62
(415) 332-1050
My life has always been art. I have worked professionally in the field from a very early age. To compliment my career, I hold a BA in Fine Art from Stanford. My work looks at the richness of life and at universal human perceptions: mood, emotion, sensation. I work in the realist style and focus on images in nature using watercolor for its vibrancy.

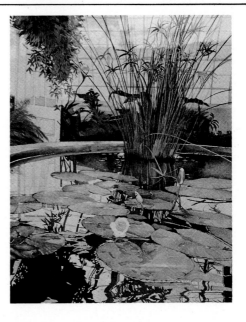

ARBORETEUM 36 POND AND RUSHES, 30"x22", Watercolor, NFS

STEPHEN MICHAEL HAMILTON

150 Sherwood Drive #116, Salinas, CA 93901
Born: 1/8/61
Represented by Sallie B. Mitchell, 2486 Fulton St., San Francisco, CA 94118 (415) 751-8077
(408) 757-7053
The Artist was born in New York City. He attended the High School of Art and Design, where he studied graphic art and illustration. He joined the service and moved to California; where he is now an aspiring artist.

TIGER FAMILY, 11"x14", Acrylic, NFS, Owned by Ms. Antonia Wark of Monterey, CA

MARY A. HAMMOND

16 Trillium Lane, San Carlos, CA 94070
Born: 3/3/34
A professional potter since 1973, I have grown from a production potter in my home studio to doing non-functional, one of a kind pieces. Influenced most by studying with Richard Neutsch at UC Santa Cruz and Paul Soldner at Scripps College, Claremont, CA. Now working out of a studio in Berkeley.

CERAMIC MASK #7, 14"X7"X3", CLAY

THOMAS HANFORD

2966 Diamond St., Suite 140, San Francisco, CA 94131
Born 1/3/52
Have shown at P.S. 122 and 22 Wooster, NYC and at SFSU. Drawings used by Indie record labels for album jackets and published by OP magazine and other periodicals. Paintings reviewed by M. Brenson, New York Times, 8/19/83. In the collection of The Museum of Art of The Americas, Leon, Nicaragua. Themes include peace and social justice and American Folklore.
SALVADORAN MOTHER AND CHILD (STOP THE BOMBING), 36"x54", Oil Stick, $1,000.00, Owned by artist

IRENE HANSEN

532 N. Beachwood Dr., LA, CA (0004
Born: 4/20/45
Represented by Bella of Solvang, 1580 Copenhagen Dr., Solvang, CA 93463 (805) 688-0569
(213) 463-6769
I was born in Copenhagen, Denmark, where I graduated in Fine Art. I also studied at Sorbonne in Paris, and in Switzerland. I came to USA in 1967. I have had many shows here in LA. I participated in the Pacific Design Center Art Festival, L.A. Zoo Art Show and at Southcoast Botanical Garden.
SWAN IN IRISES, 21"x27", Watercolor, $450.00, Owned by Bella of Solvan

MARY L. HARBERT

739 l/2 Pershing, San Bernardino, CA 92410
Born: 8/10/55
Student at Cal State Univ. "The Cross", Oil 48"x48" exhibited at the National Art Gallery, NY 1972. Now in a private collection in Iowa. I love nature, thus recreate in oils, charcoal, markers, and watercolor. Unfortunately, at this time the majority of my works and I can only be seen at home (usually in my 'undies') - Serious about my art....but humor never hurts.

GREEN SCAPE, 16"x20", Oil, NFS

MARK ANDREW HARDIN

50 Balboa Avenue, San Rafael, CA 94901
Born: 3/18/61
I was born in a town which is known as the garlic capital of the world. My family soon moved to San Rafael, a small industrial city, where I was raised and educated. In 1983 I went to study art at San Diego State University and I soon graduated in 1986. In Fine Art I strive to express my perceptions of the time and environment in which I live.

SATAN'S COLLAR, 1"x6"x1.5", Copper, silver, NFS, Owned by artist

ANN HARDY

20483 Brook Drive, Sonora, CA 95370
Born: 8/25/18
Represented by Glory Hole Gallery, 28 So. Washington St., Sonora, CA 95370 (209) 533-1466
(209) 532-5434
Painting spans lifetimes, primarily in oils. Interest in primitive approach upon urging by family to "put something live" into compositions. Themes inspired from childhood experiences; also subject matter gathered in Calif's mother Lode -- present residence, Sonora. Past 15 years include awards and a gradual increase in numbers of patrons and collectors.
SONORA PARADE, 30" x 40", Oil

JILL S. HARDY

16620 Beekman Place, NW, Washington, DC 20009
Born: 4/28/50
(202) 667-4245
Univ. of Cinn, School of Design, Art and Architecture 1968-70, Fashion Design Major, Parsons School of Design, NY 1970-73. Assoc. Certificate, Fashion illustration. The New School for Social Research, NY, BFA degree 1973. The Hecht Co. Staff illustrator 1973-75. Bonwit Teller, Lord & Taylor, Ralph Lauren Womenswear, NY 1975-81. Freelance illustrator 1981- present

UNTITLED ILLUSTRATION

DEIRDRE DALLAS HARRIS

366 Crown St., Brooklyn, NY 11225
Forn: 4/11/51
BA Fine ARt - Brooklyn, Coll 1974
Dipl Coml Art - Art Inst. of Atlanta, 1984. Mem"Where We At" Black Women Artist 1976-78. Instru Brooklyn Museum 1976-77. Mural Artist, NYC, Arts Prog. 1980. PU and Mech Artist-Minkus Stamps and Publ Co. 1984-85 Exhib. New Muse Comm Museum, Dorsey's Gallery, Medger and Evers Coll, Brooklyn Col, Art & Cultural Ctr of Restoration Plaza, Fulton Art Fair.

UNIFICATION OF KINGS, 20"x24", Oil , NFS (Print available), Owned by artist

STEVE HARRIS

7632 Arbory Ct., Laurel, MD 20707
Born: 11/15/46
Represented by Foundry St. Studios, P.O.
Box 504, Savage, MD 20763 (301) 776-0825
(301) 776-9357
BA U of MD '68, GWU '85 Collections include GWU, UofMD, Corporate and private, awards include '85 MCAA Merchants award, '84 David Lloyd Kreeger award lst prize painting Dimock Gallery '83 P.G. Co. Artists Today travelling exhibit '81 Merchants award Jubilee '81 Membership Baltimore Watercolor Society, Artist Equity.
ORANGE KONTERRA, 28"x36", Acrylic, $1,000.00, Owned by artist

CAROLYN HARTMAN

14498 Triadelphia Mill Road, Dayton, MD 21036
Born: 5/26/43
Fine Art BA from U of MD where she also worked as graphic designer. She explores watercolor, focusing on nature. She considers her self an American Impressionist painting a broad range of subjects. Fascinated recently by carousel horses, she also offers a LIFE SIZE fiberglass jumper in soft pastel colors available in a limited edition.

CAROUSEL HORSE WITH ROSES, 30"x38", Watercolor, $450.00

LYNN HASSAN

253 Railroad, Woodacre, CA 94973
Born: 1/8/46
(415) 488-0474
1962-63 Art Center
1963 Calif. Institute of Art
1965 Otis Art Institute
1966 CA Inst. of Art
1983-84 Studied with GageTaylor and Judy North
1985 Group Exhibit
1986 Group Exhibit
1987 One Person Show

OWL WOMAN, 15 1/2"x 19 1/4", Watercolor, $625.00, Owned by artist

HIKARU HAYAKAWA

2605 Pamoa Rd, Honolulu, HI 96822
Born: ll/ll/62
1962 Born in Japan
1986 Graduated from Kyoto Seika College of Art
1985 JACA Japanese Illustration Exhibition, Japan-LA
1986 JACA Japanese Illustration Exhibition, Japan-Australia
1986 One Man Exhibition Gallary Suzuki, Kyoto Japan
In addition, many group shows
At present, studying at the University of Hawaii
MAN'S MAN'S WORLD, 23"x15"x8", Polyester, Owned by artist

ANITA EGAN HEALY

320 Montero Avenue, Balboa Peninsula, CA
Born: 2/6/38
Represented by Renee Carr, 621 36th St., Newport Island, Newport Beach, CA 92663
Anita Egan Healy is a native New Yorker. Her watercolors, mixed media and assemblages all have a contemporary tone of abstraction. Classical music is the catalyst that triggers and shapes all of her visual statements. The music dictates her brush strokes. The spontaneity of her work is due to her emotional involvment with the music and the media.
OUT OF BOUNDS SERIES NO. 1, 2'x4', Acrylic, NFS, Owned by Andrea Yates of Venice, CA

GREG HEIN

13065A Shadyside Lane, Germantown, MD 20874
Born: 3/7/60
Greg's earliest artwork was painted in primary colors directly onto the walls of his home. This use of primary colors carried over into his work of the late l970's and early l980's. Since earning his degree from the Univ. of MD he has devoted himself to painting. Today, he lives with his wife, Bari, in Maryland, and paints in his loft studio.

XOX, 80"x60", Acrylic, NFS, Owned by artist

DORIS HENDERSON, S.W. A.

4 Hilltop Lane, Vacaville, CA 95688
BORN: 3/23/31
(707) 446-7545
Realist painter of landscapes and still lifes in watercolor and oil. Born in Houston, Texas. Credentials include BFA from University of Houston. Experience as commercial artist, and is signature member of Society of Western Artists (SWA). I paint daily on location or in my Vacaville studio. Am an art instructor. Paintings have been published in print form.

OCTOBER EVENING, 24"x36", Oil, NFS, Owned by the Artist

JOSEPH HNIZDIL

217 East 85th St, Box 236, NY, NY 10028
Born: 7/13/52
1986 Now Gallery, NY
Storefront Gallery NY
Moosart Gallery, Miami, FL
1985 Now Gallery
Eastman-Wahmendorf NY
1984 Soho Center for Visual Artists, NY
Art Forum Studio Kausch
Kassel West Germany
V H S Kunstation
Kleinsassen W. Germany

THE PRISONER, 26"x21"x18", Plaster Oil, $1,500.00, Owned by artist

JACK HOAG

65 Sleepy Hollow Lane, Orinda, CA 94563
Born: 7/2/29
MFA CCAC (Sculpt) '54, EdD UC Berk (Child Creativity) '58; Taught CA Univ. San Jose '58-60; Art Supv. UC Berk.'68; Many Natl. commissions, exhibitions and awards. Presently exploring new ways of rendering forms to imply inner dimensions and energy events. Current prints and sculpture are characterized by a strong sense of form and pattern based upon nature.

STORM SPIRIT, 46"x53"x7", Silicon Rubber, $20,000.00

NG HON

203 Van Duzer Street, Staten Island, NY 10301
Born: 9/13/34
Represented by Parker Bratton Gallery, 322 East 11th St., New York City, NY 10009
Ng Hon was born in Shanghai, China and came to US in 1967, attending the school of Museum of Fine Art, Boston MA., as well as Visper George School of Commerical Art. Learned watercolor from George Carpenter. Member of Copley Society of Boston, MA and North Shore Art Assoc. of Glochester MA. Now residing at Staten Island, NY.

TIME SQUARE NEW YORK, 15"x22", Watercolor, $500.00, Owned by the Artist

HEIDI HOOPER

43 Montfern Avenue, Brighton, MA 02135
Born: 10/23/58
BFA in Sculpture and jewelry from Virginia Commonwealth University. Presently showing in Boston Galleries including Goldsmith Copley Place. Works are primarily in silver with precious stones. Each piece is designed with "My hand firmly on the torch and my tongue firmly in my cheek." Works include pins, pendants, and boxes - each one individually designed.

UNCLE BOB AND FRIENDS, 1"x 1 1/8"x 1/2", Silver, NFS

MICHAEL HOPKINS

302 N. Pine Ave., #3W, ArlingtonHeights, IL 60004
Born: 10/9/58
(312) 253-9228
Born in Illinois, attended the following schools: W.R. Harper College, American Academy of Art, Art Institute of Chicago, (BFA). Mono-prints at Van Straten Gallery Chicago, IL. Currently teaching at W.R. Harper College

SERIES 84W-FIGURE NO. 1, 14"x17", Oil Stick, $350.00, Owned by the Artist

HOWARD HOPKIRK

6608 Chabot Rd., Oakland, CA 94618
Born: 2/10/52
BFA 1974 Californai College of Arts and Crafts
BA 1985 Western Design Institute

DISCO BURGERS, 41"x94", Acrylic, $1,000.00

CHANDRALA LINDA SUE HUBBARD

1087 Stanford Avenue #D, Oakland, CA 94608
Born: 6/11/53
(415) 654-1774
Mediums: Dance/drawing/sculpture. BFA ceramics, Louisiana. MFA Sculpture, Montana. Raised in the south and east. Main interest include contemporary primitive, folk, and native American art. Greatly influenced by the richness and spirit of traditional cultures.
'VILLAGE' NEWSPAER, WILLOW AND SPIRIT, Size of Room 40'x60'18', Tower is 15' Tall,; Fence: 40' long. Mixed media, Photo documentary, $200.00

SHARON HUTCHCROFT

2201 NW 122nd #404, Oklahoma City, OK 73120
Born: 3/1/61
I am a student of the Fine Arts. I graduated with a Bachelor of Fine Arts degree from the University of Northern Iowa. My emphasis was on drawing, illustration, and graphic design. I currently reside in Oklahoma City, where I am involved with the design industry,

OLYMPIC STAMP 1984   (9" x13", Prismacolor

JAMES C. IANZITI

2069 Wilkins Ave., Napa CA 94559
Born: 12/28/21
A member of the Society of Western Artists who earned his signature award in 1982, Jim teaches watercolors, judges art shows, demonstrates for art groups and conducts critiques. A native of the Napa Valley, Mr. Ianziti is a retired Naval Architect who has been a fine arts painter since 1971. Current works can be seen at the address listed.

NATURE WALK, 14"x19", Watercolor, NFS, Owned by artist

TONY C. IATRIDIS

705 Fourth Ave., Brooklyn, NY 11232
Born: 11/18/61
(718) 788-0309
Mr. Iatridis works as a freelance illustrator, fine artist and designer. His work has appeared in several national publications and gallery showings. He is a graduate with honors of Pratt Institute in New York City, and served as apprentice to the noted Russian Avant-Garde painter, Anton Refrieger.

REAGAN AND CHERNENKO, 10"x15", Collage $800.00

GEORGE IVANCIU

30-40 82St APID, Jackson Hts, NY 11370
Born: 5/20/51
(718) 898-3783
Born in Bucharest RSRI received my diploma in Fine Arts from Nicolae Grigorescu Institute of Art in Bucharest, Romania. I left Romania in 1978. In Sept 1985 I became an American Citizen. One man show, 1980, Gallery Borghi in Ft Lauderdale, FL.; Art Expo, Dallas, TX 1984; Maurice Hayot Gallery in NY, May 1985.

SPRING TIME, 26"x 38", Oil Linen, 27.000, Owned by artist

JOHN IWANSKI

7418 W. Myrtle, Chicago, IL 60631
Forn: 10/14/60
Represented by Merrill Chase, 89 Oak Brook
Center, Oak Brook, IL 60521
Former all-star secondbasemand for the
Chicago Cubs. Won rookie of the year
honors in 1980 by hitting .327 with 35 home
runs and 114 RBI's. Gold glove winner 5
consecutive years - 1981-85. NL's MVP in
1984. Led the major leagues in fewest errors
(3) in 1985. When a knee injury ended his
baseball career in 1985, he took up painting.

SUMMER OF '79, 30"x24", Acrylic,
$500.00, Owned by the artist

ANNETTE MARIE IZAC

2615 South 8th Street, Arlington, VA 22204
Born: 2/11/43
Over 7 years commercial art training.
Graduated Maga Cum Laude from Northern
VA community college with 2 art degrees.
Has previously taught art to high school
students and currently is employed as a
technical illustrator while also doing part
time freelance work as well as a personal fine
arts project. Award winning work in all
media.

MATCHO JOCK, 32"X40", Mixed
Media, NFS, Owned by artist

ROBERT EMMETT JACKA

1295 E 34th, San Bernardino, CA 92404
Born: 3/30/61
Represented by San Bernardino Art, 1640 E.
Highland, San Bernardino, CA 92404
Fine Art Institute 1981 Inland Exhibition 17,
19, 20 1982 1984 1985 Redlands Multi
Mini Media 1983 2nd pl 1985 Brea
Traditional Art 1983 Zanor Gallery NY
1984 Ink and Clay 1983 84 84 International
Art Competition Brand Library Los Angeles
Tradition & Alternatives NY 1984 Purchase
Award BA CAL State Fullerton. Commerical
Artist for TGS Technologies, Norton AFB
MAN IN HIS ENVIRONMENT,
20"x26", Monoprint $500.00, Owned by
artist

TIM JACKSON

5861 North Winthrop Ave., Chicago, IL 60660
Born: 1/16/58
Cartoonist and illustrator, born in Dayton OH. First published at the age of 16. Presently living in Chicago where he runs a free lance art service to provide illustrations for individuals and organizations. Published titles: Friends are for Singing, Just like a Happy Family, That's All they're Good For, Friends Are for Being Different.

ENCOUNTER WITH LOUIE, 10"x15", Ink and Markers, NFS, Onwed by artist

MARSHALL JACOBOWITZ

306 East 5th Street #34, New York, NY 10003
Born: 5/7/56
(212) 533-0968
I received a BFA from the Cooper Union Art School, NY. in 1978. In my recent work I have been attempting to breathe new life into abstraction by combining complex linear structures with worldly symbols and a sense of narrative. In this way I hope to have the best of two worlds in the pursuit of, hopefully, an ever expanding vision.

HOPE OF LIGHT IN THE HEART OF DARKNESS. 50"x60", Oil on linen, $2,000.00, Owned by artist

XUE BING JIANG

405 N. Wabash, Chicago, IL 60611
Born: 10/1/41
Represented by Tolford Galleries
(312) 467-1237
Born in Shanghai, China. Dir. of Shanghai Decorative Pkg Assoc. Director of China Arts & Crafts. VP of Shanghai Arts & Crafts Assoc. Member of Shanghai Assoc of Aesthetics. Sr. Dir. & Designer of China Tourism souvenirs joint development Corp. Decorated Pres. Nixon's suite in China. Decorated Mao Tse Dong's mausoleum in Beijing. Designed Beijings first subway station.
C R A N E ' S, 32"X 22", Watercolor, $5,000.00, Owned by artist

JOAN JOHNSON-SCHEURING

9225 Willoughby Road, Pittsburgh, PA
15237
Born: 3/16/38
Born in Toledo, Ohio. BA Degree Fine Art,
Marygrove College, 1960, Detroit, MI.
Additional study with Vincent Nesbert.
Taught art in Des Plaines, IL., public
schools and painting class at Carnegie
Institute, Pittsburgh, PA. Her subjects
include portraits and landscapes done in
pastel and oil. Shows work in Pittsburgh
Regional Exhibits.

THE BLUE HOUSE, 19"x23", Pastel,
NFS, Owned by artist

JACQUELINE JONES

10 Fair Drive, San Rafael, CA 94901
Native Californian resides in Marin County,
CA. Education: San Jose State University;
University of CA, Dominican College, CA;
Instituto Allende, San Miguel, Mex.
Selected Exhibitions: Ca Women Artists;
Crown Zellerbach, San Francisco; Wild Blue
Gallery, LA; Barlett Gallery, Pleasanton, CA;
Biblioteca de San Miguel De Allende, Mex.

CHICHEN ITZA DAWN, 23"x32",
Mixed Media, NFS, Owned by Mr. & Mrs.
Lynn Upshaw of Marin, CA

JANE JORDAN

1405 Akin Drive, Evansville, IN 47714
Born: 11/10/23
Represented by Catherine Sulak, 1120
Galvez Drive, Pacifica, CA 94044
Jane Jordan feels there is value in revealing
the often remarkable beauty of the common
simple things surrounding us. Her
representational technique reveals a personal
viewpoint with a subtle message. She paints
in oil and transparent watercolors. She
recently had two series published; the
majority of her work is in private collections
nationwide.

CABBAGES AND KINGS, 30"x 22",
Oil, Owned by Florida art collector

MURIEL SHEERR KAPLAN

339 Garden Road, Palm Beach, FL 33480
Born: 8/15/14
Represented by Portraits Inc, 985 Park Ave., New York, NY 10028 (212) 879-5560
(305) 842-3139
Education: Cornell U., Sarah Lawrence College - graduate work, Art Students League Exhibits: Brooklyn Museum, Newark Museum, Sculptors Guild National Academy of Art. Collections: JFK School, Jerusalem Israel, Columbia U, U of Texas, Headquarters Empire State Building Co, **PORTRAIT OF JOHN F. KENNEDY,** 19"x10"15", Bronze, $15,000.00, Owned by JFK School, Israel, U. of Texas (Johnson Library)

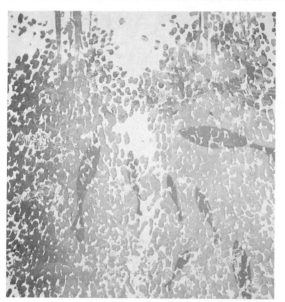

LIENKE KATZ

54 Lochinvar Rd., San Rafael, CA 94901
Born: 8/16/44
Born in Holland, Studied languages at Leiden University. Attended on year at CCAC in Oakland and one year at the Royal Academy of the Hague in Holland. Later studied printing classes at the Palos Verdes Art Center in Los Angeles. Works out of her home in Marin County.

REFLECTIONS IN THE WATER, 15"x17", Monprint, $125.00, Owned by artist

MELINDA O. KAY

1504 Kenny Road, Columbus, OH 43212
Born: 6/9/57
Melinda Kay's work blends ritual qualities with artifice in the formation of her wooden wall constructions. She has shown widely in individual and group shows around the nation. She received her BAE and MFA from The Ohio State University. She has taught art overseas and most recently as an Instructor at the Ohio State University at Marion.

SEVER, 42"x9"x14", Wood, NFS, Owned by Helen May Wortman

MICHAEL KENT

4122 Edmunds Street NW #4, Washington, DC 20007
Born 1/8/58
Michael Kent was born outside of Paris. His father, an amateur artist, encouraged him to paint as a child. Early influences include comic strips as well as the "Greats". At Bowdoin College, he studied drawing, painting and photography, as well as English. Since, he has continued to produce many other paintings, reminiscent of Cezanne and Hopper.

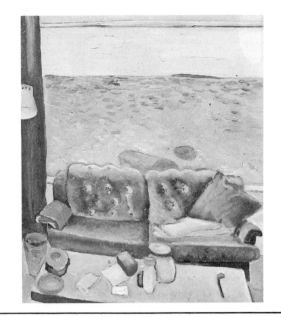

LIVING ROOM AND OCEAN, 20"x23", Oil, NFS, Owned by artist

JEFF KIMERER

P.O. Box 1169, Haleiwa, HI 96712
Born: 7/10/49
A native of California and graduate of Chico State University in Art in 1976. While painting he had a variety of jobs, from a ranch hand to an IRS agent before moving to Hawaii in 1983. On a hike up a mountain trail he paused to paint this North Shore beach scene.

PUPUKEA, 16"x20", Watercolor, $375.00, Owned by artist

KATRINA KIRKPATRICK

816 SW Eleventh Ave., Ft. Lauderdale, FL 33315
Born 2/5/47
(305)\524-2927
Katrina could best be described as a modern day Renaissance woman. She is an accomplished musician (classical guitar and bass), with a sultry singing voice. As an artist, she excels in graphics and commerical design; has received numerous awards and accolades, and her paintings reflect a Santa Fe consciousness, with pale colors and a relaxed, peaceful grace.

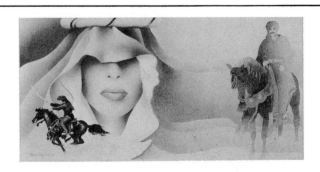

THE SHEIK, 15"x30", Dyes and Acrylic Airbrush, NFS, Owned by artist

**COLOR
SECTION**

M.D. ABRAMOWITZ

401 East 80 St. Gracie News, New York, NY 10021
Born: 3/7/48
(212) 570-6629
1985 - Wrote and illustrated with 40 watercolors - The Rarebit Fantasy, a children's book of historical overtures. 1986 - Created an erotic zodiac - 60"x48" - Oils within Graham's Mathematical Solution. 1986 - Has shown at the Michael Katz Gallery, Houston St. and Jacqueline's, East 61st, New York, NY. Summer 1984 - Guest lectures of Art, Chateau D'O, Mortree, France.
PICNIC, 48"x60", Oil, $7,500. Page 57 #1

SIA BAYAT

1760 Pacific Ave. #4, San Francisco, CA 94l09
Born: 8/2/50
Graduated from London, England. Graphic design, publication specialist. Recently moved to San Francisco from Washington DC where I worked as a designer and taught at the open University. I have started "Sia Ink" graphic design studio where projects ranging from Corporate identities to brochures and annual reports are designed and completed for production.

BUTTERFLY, 16" x 24", Airbrush, $450.00   Page 57 #2

NANCY BAYTOS

905 Ford St., Burbank, CA 91505
Born: 2/24/48
Kent State University 1966-1970
The Film School 1975-1976
Currently working on a series of acrylic paintings and assemblages concerning environmental and political issues.

DOWNWIND, 48"x60", Painting,
NFS   Page 57 #3

IBBY V. BENTE

118-60 Metropolitan Ave. 6B, New York
Kew Garden, NY 11415
Born: 5/10/47
Academy of Fine Arts Bucharest. Solo exhibitions:1986-1979 New York, Italy, Roma, Caserta, Napoli, Romania, Bucharest. Group exhibits: NY , ,Rockefeller Center , Park Gallery, RI Brown University, Delaware University ,Romania ,BUC Art museums and galleries. Documentation Paris, Italy, Budapest, Israel. Private collections in Belgium, Italy, France and Canada.
INFINITE & NATURE, 80"x53", Oil on canvas, $6000.00   Page 57 #4

LEN BERZOFSKY

11620 Texas Ave., Los Angeles, CA 90025
Born: 6/21/34
Represented by Bojennie, 11620 Texas Ave., Los Angeles, CA 90025 (213) 478-1965
Born in N.Y. F.F.A. degree from Pratt Institute, N.Y. Art Director and artist for movies, T.V., Books, and posters. International museum exhibit touring the world. Presently exhibited through L.A. Art Museum Rental Gallery.

STATUE OF LIBERTY, 36"x72"x1 1/2", Mixed Media, $3,000.00   Page 57 #5

JEN BICKSLER

2503 Smouldering Wood Drive, Arlington, TX 76016
Born: 7/21/61
Born near Washington D.C. and raised in Mobile, my family and friends always encouraged me artistically. My aunt Jen Ayres, a fine-artist from Virginia, taught me to create by utilizing all of my senses. I thank her for this lifelong gift.

ALMOST PARADISE, 15' x 18", Water Color, NFS, Owned by artist Page 57 #6

HENRY BREUER

190 Miller Ave., Mill Valley, CA 94941
Born: 1/10/36
Leaving the concrete canyons of New York as a young man, I travelled west to the open hills and seashore of California. Here, I think, is more natural beauty than anyplace I've lived. After 20 years as an art director, I've honed my illustrative and painterly skills, and now devote more and more of my time painting the natural beauty of California.

THE BATHERS, 16"x20", Watercolor, $700, Owned by the artist   Page 58 #7

CATHERINE BUCHANAN

6 Moss Avenue, Oakland, CA
Born: 2/7/57
Born in Canada. Moved to California in 1974. Studied photography at SF State University. Currently living and working in Oakland, CA. Latest work includes a series of photographs that catalog ordinary collections of objects as well as photographs of animals by using the contact sheet as a format.

ANGIE, 16"x20", Photography, $300.00, Owned by artist   Page 58 #8

MAUDE CHURCH

5412 Bryant Avenue, Oakland, CA 94618
Born: 6/15/49
(415) 547-5630
Graduate study: 1973 Byam Shaw College, London. Undergraduate: 1967-72. Teaching: 12 yrs. CSPP, Berkeley, CA Her acrylic paintings and drawings are in over 50 collections in the U.S. and Europe. She has exhibited in the Oakland Museum and the Anhalt Gallery, Los Angeles, among others. Her themes have direct reference to the human condition. Photos available.
SURVEYOR, 48"x48"x3", Acrylic, NFS, Owned by V. Aitro Collection of Oakland, CA   Page 58 #9

54

THOMASINA JOSHEPINE DE MAIO

2 De Soto St., San Francisco, CA 94127
Born: 1/22/51
(415) 239-4164
Museo Italian Aug-Oct 1986, Museum Modern Art Rental Gallery 11/85, SF Arts commission Gallery 12/84, New Langdon Arts Gallery 12/84, South of Market Cultural Center 1984, 37th Annual Arts Fest (award) 1983, Art Against War 1983, Southern Exposure Gallery SF 1983, Education BA 1983 SFAI, MFA 1985 SFAI

LAST TANGO, 6'x 10', Oil, NFS Owned by artist   Page 48   #10

MS. PRICE DERATZIAN

P.O. Box 1942, Mill Valley, CA 94942
Born: 9/6/63
BFA Cornell University, 1986; Studied in the Soviet Union and Europe. Have exhibited paintings and prints in the US, Europe and Japan. Presently photographing the America's cup races for various national and regional publications in Australia.

THE THINKER, 48"x62", Acrylic, $2,000.00, Owned by artist   Page 58   #11

PETER MICHAEL DU FORE

15189 Holleyside Dr., Dumfries, VA 22026
Born: 7/15/47
Represented by Joseph Jacoby, 2309 Ross Rd, Silverspring, MD 20910
(703) 680-0220
A former New Yorker who extended his life and love of music in the world of jazz at an early age. He attended the HS of art and design, the School of Visual Arts with a BFA. Three of his works are presently hanging in the Poland National Radio Hall.

SOMBRERO SAM BLUES FOR THE INVICIBLE TORRO, 24"x30", Oil, $1,100.00, Owned by Artist   Page 58   #12

THOMAS W. FROST

224 E. Graham, Lake Elsinore, CA 92330
Born: 4/22/49
(714) 674-8343
Thomas W. Frost, born in Los Angeles, currently living in Lake Elsinore, CA. Shades of Purple II is one from a set of 3. Tom has created over 300 art manifestations in all sizes. Creating a personal collage out of your own photo albums is a specialty of his, and has kept him alive in the art world. He is a family man with a wife and 2 children.

SHADES OF PURPLE II, l0 1/4"x17 1/4", Collage, NFS, Owned by artist Page 59   #13

ROBIN C. GAYNES

226 Eastr 13th Street, Apt. #14, New York City, NY 10003
Born: 12/7/50
Represented by Ceres Gallery, 91 Franklin St., NY, NY 10013 (212) 226-4725
(212) 677-9178
BFA Univ of Texas, Austin: MFA City College of : Sunset on Vinyl Solo Exhibition NY: Vinyl Meditations, Solo Exhibition NY: Ceres Gallery Solo Exhibition : 1985 New American Talent Laguna Gloria Patterson Sims Juror: 10th Annual drawing show Ivan Karp Juror:
OCEAN   PAINTING; 48"x66", Oil, $10,000.00 Owned by Artist   Page 59   #14

CHRIS HEDRICK

4622 Cedar, Bellaire, TX 77401
Born: 2/5/55
Houston area artist, Chris Hedrick works mainly with acrylics and an airbrush on canvas. Receiving a BFA in commercial art, Hedrick currently works as a graphic artist for a large corporation by day and paints at night. His art work is in a number of private collections and has been shown in both regional and national exhibitions.

PERFECT   PEAK, 24"x40", Acrylic, $1,400.00   Page 59   #15

MARGARETE HEISING

1298 Windermere Way, Concord, CA
Born: 12/28/40
(415) 671-7309
Born in Denmark, she received art education as an illustrator. She worked as art teacher and illustrator of classical books. Painted in oil since age of 12. She has exhibited oil paintings and linocuts in Copenhagen since 1970 and in the SF Bay Area, Oregon, and Nevada since 1981. Published a book "Next Step Same Year" with 52 full page linocuts.

EARTH   MOTHER, 40"x36", Oil, $4,500.00, Owned by the artist Page 59   #16

JOEL MICHAEL HOUSE

37 Edwards St., Sausalito, CA 94965
Born: 7/14/47
(415) 332-6530
Painter born in Los Angeles. Moved to Larkspur, CA in 1969. BA Cal State Sonoma 1971. MFA San Francisco Art Institute 1975. Early work rooted in abstract expressionism. In 1981 direction changed to impressionistic portraiture. Now works on a personal commission basis only.

NANCY IN TUB, 36"x48", Oil, NFS, Owned by artist   Page 59   #17

SHIH-CHIEH HUNG

APSC, 3860 Vale Ave., Oakland, CA 94619
Born: 2/2/28
Represented by Hung's Art Studio, 3645 MacArthur Blvd, Oakland, CA 94619 (415) 482-2365
Famed artist born in China, he and his family immigrated to Oakland, CA 9n 1980. His very best subject matter are human lifeforms and portraits. He has painted noted portraits of President and Mrs. Reagan and of Attorney General Edwin Meese. Facts about Mr. Hung appear in the "Directory of American Portrait Artists" (pages 111 & 112).
SUNBATHING, 38"x48", Oil on canvas, $25,000.00, Owned by artist Page 59   #18

GORDON A. HUTHER

1673 E Street, Napa, CA 94559
Born: 7/18/59
(707) 255-5954
Huther's main focus has been in glass and it's various forms for many years. The works are now taking on an architectural mood. His large flat glass commissions reiterate the structural environment of their location, his more intimate sculptures utilize neon and plate glass. He was born in Rochester, NY and resides in the Napa Valley, CA

BREAKING THE ICE, 32"x6"x10", $1,600.00   Page 60   #19

ART JASIK

3536 West 72nd Street, Chicago, IL 60629
Born: 9/21/43
Graduate of American Academy of Art-Chicago. Member of Chicago Artist coalition and registered with the Illinois Arts Council. Has had work published by Catholic Forester Magazine and General Learning Corp. Specializes in portraits and illustrations. Works in watercolor, pastels, acrylic and ink.

#4 PORTRAIT, 19"x25", Pastel, $300.00
                                    Page 60 #20

LAWRENCE D. KOLDORF

21 Garden Oval, Springfield, NJ 07081
Born: 9/8/55
Art is aesthetic communication and a language may not be spontaneously understood . One may have to attend school to do so! Modernish, post-modernism, these have appeared more comprehensible to particular experiences. I hope to communicate to those who have experienced, understood and loved the NYC suburbs, and punk, and their aesthetics.

BLUE CHARLEIM, 54"x40", Acrylics, $1,000.00, Owned by the artist Page 60 #21

NEUMAN LOVE

P.O. Box 73, San Anselmo, CA 94960
Born: 3/4/41
(415) 485-5603
Newman Love is known for his dynamic, kinetic sculpture and dramatic, non-figurative water' colors. The watercolors are holographic; each smaller segment of every painting is whole and complete with its own integrity and detail He is self and friend taught in the arts, innovating new styles and techniques. His degree in philosophy is from UC Berkeley.

ALIVE!, 22"x30", Watercolor, NFS, Owned by artist   Page 60 #22

JAVIER MANRIQUE

2629 Central Avenue, El Monte, CA 91733
Born: 2/4/58
Represented by Artspace-Ceci, 35 East Montecito Ave., Sierra Madre, CA 91024
(818) 355-4778
(818) 350-8044
Born in Mexico where for the last five years has lived partly and part time in California. Javier has exhibited in Mexico City and other cities in the country as well as in California. Though most of his work is graphic, painting makes up part of his repetoire. He has worked as a photographer, illustrator, projectionist and stage technician.
JON, 16"x26", Photography, NFS, Owned by Rocio Lopez (Marion)   Page 60 #23

STEVE MARSHALL

PO Box 884653, San Francisco, CA 94188
Born: 9/27/49
Born in St. Paul, MN. Began painting at age 6, majored in art at school, developed a style for portrait painting while attending SFSU extention in 1972. Awarded for the first showing of a portrait titled "Bobby" in 79, when working for Gentey engineers, as a draftsman. Became art director in 83 for SF Boys Club; as of 86 the ASI Gallery exhibits "Bobby" in SF.

NANCY GREY, 24"x 36", Oil/canvas, $2,500., Owned by artist   Page 60 #24

#1 #4

#2 #5

#3 #6

57

#7 #10

#8 #11

#9 #12

58

#13 #16

#14 #17

#15 #18

#19 #22

#20 #23

#21#24

60

#25 #28

#26 #29

#27 #30

#31 #34

#32 #35

#33 #36

#37 #40

#38 #41

#39 #42

#43 #46

#44 #47

#45 #48

STEVE MILLER

505 Court Street 3D, Bklyn Hts , NY 11231
Born: 10/31/60
Represented by Civilian Warfare, 614 East 9th Street, New York, NY 10009 (212) 475-7498
(718) 643-2162
1982 BA, Drew Univ, Madison, NJ. 1982 Parsons School of Design, MFA Program. Select exhibitions: 1982 Drew Univ, Korn Gallery, Madison, NJ 1984 Drew Univ, Korn Gallery, "Selected Prints" 1985 Downtown Beirut, New York, NY, Inauguration Exhibition 1985 Downtown Beirut, NY, NY 1-man show 1985
TWISTED, 36"x 48", Charcoal/Ink, Owned by artist   Page 61   #25

HELEN M. MONTGOMERY

780 Las Colindas Road, San Rafael, CA 94903
Born in Canada. Moved to San Rafael 1956. Studied at Coll. of Marin and with Eliz. Boyd of Larkspur. 1971-1980 Associated with Terra Linda Art Gallery winning many merit awards. 1980 to present associated with Marin Soc. of Artists winning a cash award at their 53rd annual members only show. 1981 won best in show and cash award at Santa Rosa Statewide Exhibit.

ELIZABETH NO. 2, 24"x36", Oil, NFS, Owned by artist   Page 61   #26

MICHAEL MOORE

1565 Vendola Dr., San Rafael, CA 94903
Born: 1/13/50
I am a subject painter and enjoy creating the illusion of space, mass, depth, and humanity on a flat surface. I want the viewer to participate and relate to the image on some level even if it is negative. Any reaction is better than none.

CHRISTOPHER, 34"x42", Oil, $6,000.00, Owned by artist   Page 61   #27

TIMOTHY WRIGHT MOSELEY

901 Cedar Hill Ave., Suite 227, Dallas, TX 75208
Born: 4/22/57
(214) 942-8874
Born in Orange, CA. Residing in Texas. Self taught from 12 years of age. Received scholarship from Texas Fine Art Association May, 1975. Received BFA degree (Honors) Studio Art, The University of Texas at Austin. Attended 1978-80. Also attended NISU 1975-78. Exhibited in various Texas galleries and colleges 1980-86. Currently working as painter/designer.

TWILIGHT JOURNEY, 36"x48", Oil, NFS, Owned by artist   Page 61   #28

PERA

P.O. Box 369, Renaissance, CA 95962
Born: 3/16/26
Represented by Constance Franklin, (415) 527-4373
It is hard to believe that when I die I'll be discarded like an overripe melon. My body yes, but not my soul! But what is my soul? Is it something behind my eyes when I look at the mirror? Is it the accumulation of my life experiences? I know that it is not my toenails or my beard. It is something like light, like energy, like myself that appears often in my paintings....
FRAU MONREAL, EAT IL TUO PAMPLEMOUSSE, QUERIDA..., 32"x44", Acrylics, $3,000.00 Page 61   #29

SALLY S. ROCKEFELLER

1620 West Cullom, Chicago, Il 60613
Born: 5/10/46
(312) 472-6426
Media: acrylic, graphite, pen and ink, watercolor, collage. Subjects: cityscapes, animals, women, plants, flowers, buildings: especially intersted in texture, pattern, design. BS in Fine Arts (studio major): Northeastern Univ. Boston, MA. Former member of the Boston visual artists union and sigma epsilon rho honor society. Relocated to Chicago, Dec 1984.

CITYSCAPE - RED SKY I, 39"x57", Acrylic, $850.00   Page 61   #30

RICHARD RALPH ROEHL (RRR)

P.O. BOX 1111, Venice, CA 990294
Represented by Thinking Eye Gallery, 1318
S. Figueroa Street, Los Angeles, CA 90015
(213) 748-3411
(213) 857-0222
I prefer to sell only to well established collectors who are knowledgeable and appreciative of contemporary art objects....after all, being happy is the best revenge   A sense of humor with every piece....

NINE TWO FIVE, SERIES F, 24 1/2" x 23", Oil and glass, NFS   Page 62   #31

SY SAJID

311 N. Desplaines St., Suite 607, Chicago, IL 60606
Born: 1/5/50
(312) 993-0494
Born in India. Father renowned artist taught and influenced. In 1970 finished college and traveled and studied throughout Europe and US. In 72 established studio in Chicago. In 76 became US Citizen. Illustrators workshop with top US illustrators. Studied at Art Institute of Chicago. Established fine and com. art firm. Executed murals for media nationwide.

SHE IS LOOKEN AT YOU, 40"x 54", Mixed media, NFS   Page 62   #32

MARTHA SALAS

5405 Gate Lake Rd., Fort Lauderdale, FL 33319
Born: 5/29/59
(305) 721-3891
Born in Caracas, Venezuela. BA Fine Arts Instituto de Diseno, Caracas. AS advertising design Art Institute Ft Lauderdale 1983-present Art Director. Exhibits: Ceramics, Broward Comm College 1986. Graphics, paintings, exhibtis Art Institute Ft. Laud. Etchings, TAGA, Caracas 1980. Honors: Award of Excellence, Poster Competition, Aspen. Fundacion Ayacucho scholarship 1980-1983.
YELLOW FIRST, YELLOW LAST, 12"x18"x8", Clay, $150.00   Page 62   #33

66

J.L. SICRE

1966 San Francisco Ave., Long Beach, CA 90806
Born: 4/15/56
Represented by Dubois Inc., 321 Cedar Ave., Long Beach, CA 90802
His grandfather and cousin were leaders of Cubas avant-garde. By the time he graduated University, Sicre had developed a stylistic identity which would evolve into one of great range. 1981 was his first solo show. By age 26 he had been in four New York shows (3 in Soho) and two museums.

THE THREE GRACES, 11"x14", Watercolor   Page 62   #34

ELLY SIMMONS

Box 463, Lagunitas, CA 94938
Born: 6/11/55
Represented by J. Noblett Gallery, 139 E. Napa, Sonoma, CA 95476 (707) 996-2416
(415) 488-4177
Shows incl: "New Art in the West", Vorpal Gallery, SF. CA, "Neo-rustic Artists" Liason Show, Theater Arts Gallery, LA "Artquest 85, University Art Museum, Long Beach, CA. Solo Exhibit, J. Noblett Gallery, Sonoma, CA. Represented by: Beverly Gordon Fine Arts, Dallas, Tx, San Francisco Museum of Modern Art Rental Gallery, SF.

THE HERALD, 23 1/2"x 29 1/2", Oil on paper, $1000.00   Page 62   #35

NORMA-JEAN SQUIRES

2764 Woodwardia Drive, Los Angeles, CA 90077
Born: 2/14/45
(213) 474-6364
Edu: Cooper Union, NYC, BFA CSUN, MA Exhibits: 6 1-woman shows plus Group shows: Martha Jackson, NY; Albright-Knox, Buffalo, La Jolla Mus.; Newport Harbor Mus.; LACMA Rental Glry; David Stuart Glry; Baxter Art Galry; etc. Collections: City Investing, NY Security Pacific Bank, LA; Warner Bros; Galeria Vandres, Madrid.

AS THE WORLD CHURNS, 63"x45", Acrylic, pastel & Letraset on board, $2200.00, Owned by artist   Page 62   #36

RICK SUSOEFF

1670 Market St. #46, San Francisco, CA 94102
Born: 5/21/51
Attended Santa Rosa Jr. College 1969-72. Studied drawing, painting, and silkscreen printing. Air brushed garments 75-77. Resumed painting in 84. Resumed airbrush work in 86.

FASHION ROBOTS, 30":x 40", Acrylic, $500.00, Owned by artist   Page 63   #37

R.V. SWIDERGAL

316 NE 50th, Seattle, WA 98105
Born: 2/13/49
Currently working as a free lance glass artist. Education: Southern Illinois University - Carbondale BS, 1981

PRECOCITY, 11 1/2"x 11 1/2"x 5 1/2", Blown Glass, NFS   Page 63   #38

ELIZABETH A. SYKES

113 Ripley Street, San Francisco, CA 94110
Born: 9/29/61
Elizabeth Sykes is a surrealistic illustrator that employs mysticism to art in order to give inanimate objects the illusion of life. Born in New York, Sykes is currently continuing her education in art. Among her many honors and awards, she has received the 37th Anniversary pen Women's Award for art and will have a children's book published shortly.

LADIES OF LAND AND SKY, 12 1/2" x 16 1/2"   Page 63   #39

JANICE FAGLIANO TEW

P.O. Box 193, Cromberg, CA 96103
Born: 12/10/52
Reprsented by Tew Eggs Studio, Suite 8 Blairsden Station, Blairsden, CA 96103
(916) 836-2143
Since graduating from Humboldt St. Univ in 1975, Jan Tew has pursued a career as an artist. Jan's interest in eggshell painting began in 1976, when she was introduced to Ukrainian pysanky. Since then, she has carefully developed her own technique and style based on this ancient art.
ORIGINALLY DESIGNED HAND PAINTED EGGS, Analine dye, $30.00-$150.00, Owned by artist   Page 63   #40

NIXON THORSTAD

4362 2nd St., Pleasonton, CA 94566
Born: 1/29/53
Earned BA degree in Art from Cal State University, Hayward in 1983. Have entered in Alameda County Fair, 1983-86; also entered in LAA/PAL Spring shows 1983-86. Awarded merit award 1985. Exhibited bronze sculpture in a two man show at Evergreen Gallery, Mill Valley, CA 1985. Rendered illustrations for advertising and magazine stories and articles.
THANKS DAD, 7"x16", Prismacolor, NFS, Owned by Kaiser Hospice Unit, Walnut Creek   Page 63   #41

MILLICENT TOMKINS

31 Shell Rd., Mill Valley, CA 94941
Born: 8/23/29
Born SF, 6 yrs at SF Art Instit., MA, UC Berkeley, '51: Wash. DC, Peabody Conservatory of Music, shows at Artists Mart, 2nd Prize Soc. of Wash. Artists. '69 to Mill Valley, CA. Rep. in numerous Priv. Collections including Dr. Herbert Boyer, Chiron, CSF, Brooklyn Museum, Portland Museum. Musical series reproduced. Mediums: Oil, watercolor, ink, etching.

MUSICAL STILL LIFE WITH CHAISE A LYRE, 17"x23", Watercolor and ink, NFS   Page 63   #42

SEA TRISDALE

744B Antelope Rd, Citrus Heights, CA 95621
Born: 12/17/46
(916) 722-1504
Sea has pursued her art for over twenty eyars and has exhibited in numerous juried and solo shows, winning several awards. Her paintings are comprised of an exquisite blend of fabrics which may include; silks, satins, tapestries, velvets, laces, or leather, and various mixed media such as pastels, pencil, or acrylic paints. Sea invites portrait commissions.

TAHITIAN TRILOGY Page 64 #43

RENE WESTBROOK

331 Western Avenue, Cambridge, MA 02139
Born: 5/2/50
I am a multidisciplinary holistic artist interested in visualintelligence and creative thinking. Fine art, media, writing, theater and poetry make up the basic forms of art I explore. Awards include: 1980 Danforth Foundation Finalist in Sculpture, 1986 grant from Polaroid for photography, 1986 Coleman award for excellence in fine art.

R A C H E L, 18"x24", Craypas, NFS, Owned by artist Page 64 #44

MICHAEL JAMES WHITE

41 Bishop St. New Haven, CT 06511
Born: 4/24/64
Michael White is a science fiction fantasy illustrator, from S.C. From criminal composits to computer graphics, White reflects a variety of skills. A 1985 graduate of the Ringling School of Art, he now pursues his career from his New Havent, CT studio. This talented artist seeks a steady career in book cover/poster/graphic novel, markets.

VALLEY OF THE SERPENTS, 20"x24", NFS Page 64 #45

JOANNA G. WHITNEY

309 West 109th St., #4C, New York, NY 10025
Born: 10/18/62
(212) 662-8193
I was born in Berkeley, CA. I grew up in the Bay Area and moved to New York City at 18 to attend the School of Visual Arts. I graduated in June of 1985 with a BFA in illustration and am presently working as a free lance illustrator, while keeping other avenues open.

SUBWAY I, 45 1/2" x 62", Oil/Canvas, $1,000.00 Page 64 #46

KYUNGAE YOO

22 Tamarack Rd., Somerset, NJ 08873
Born: 3/10/64
I was born in Inchun, Korea. I came to America in 1978. In 1982 enrolled in Mason Gross School of the Arts at Rutgers University majoring in Graphic Design and minoring in Printmaking, specifically silkscreen. Graduated in 1986 with BFA degree. Currently working as a graphic designer.

S K Y C R A P E R S, 15 3/4"x 22 1/2", Serigraph, $400.00 Page 64 #47

JAN ZAREMBA

2000 N. Ivar Ave., Hollywood, CA 90068
Born: 1/30/41
Studies with German Expressionist Schwaderer 60's; in Europe, India, Himalayas 70's. Monk 72-75. Declared a master of Sumi-e by his teacher Hisashi Ohta, Living National Treasure of Japan. His work is an important East-West bridge. Listed in Who's Who in CA 86. Repr. in collections in Germany, USA, England, France, Japan, Isreal, Mexico, Finland. Teaches at Japanese Cultural Center LA
RED CITY, 24"x30", Oil on canvas, $5000,00, Owned by artist Page 64 #48

ELLEN LEE KLEIN

139-12 84th Drive, Briarwood, NY 11435
Solo shows include Green Mountain Gallery, Maples Gallery, Fairleigh Dickinson Univ. Pratt Institute, Ward-Nasse Gallery, Phoenix Gallery.
Group Shows include Hudson River Museum, Sothebys, Arthur Charles Gallery, Wash. DC, Zoma Gallery, Gallery Carron, Avery Fisher Hall, Lincoln Ctr, Hobart & William Smith Colleges, Aaron Davis Hall, CCNY.

BRIDGING THE GAP, 60"x48", Oil, Price on request, Owned by artist

MICHELE KORTBAWI

1008 Tysley Place, Raritan, NJ 08869
Born: 1/20/61
(201) 685-0204
Michele is a self-taught artist, following a life long love of birds and wildlife. She has won numerous ribbons and awards. Michele has recently become competitive on a national basis. She was a finalist in So. Carolinas 1986 Duck Stamp contest, a finalist in WAN remarque contest and placed second and third in Lehigh Valley's Conservancy Print contest.

SNOW LEOPARD, 5"x 7", Acrylic, NFS, Owned by Dr. M. Ornstein of New Jersey

KRASH

110 East 15th St., 3rd Floor, Los Angeles, CA 90015
Born: 9/7/60
(213) 746-9917
Born Kathleen Stenson, I began making art objects at an early age while growing up in Northern Michigan. I was interested in music also, and studied piano, guitar, and drums before I started college. In college I focused on painting and drawing , deviating to experiment in music and performance. Currently, I'm juggling them all.

THE SHAPE THAT CREATED THE WORLD, 7'x8'8', Oils, $30,000.00, Owned by the artist

AL KRYSZAK

107 David Rd., Cheektowaga, NY 14225
Born: 6/19/61
(716) 894-8687
Al Kryszak's work has recently involved woodburning effects. The boundary between surface and medium becomes vague, as characters or objects are influenced by the wood's contours. This element of transition is also present in Kryszak's music and playwrighting.

SPORTS GUY WITH HORSE, 17"x52", Burnt Wood, $2,000.00, Owned by artist

MANFRED KUPPER

POBox 643, Folsom, CA 95630
Born: 4/21/50
Manfred Kupper was educated at Kolner Werkschulen in Koln, Germany and at Sir George Williams university in Montreal, Canada. Mr. Kupper is presently a freelance illustrator living in Fair Oaks, CA.

N, 12"x 20", ,Owned by Barbara Segschnieder of Roseville

SEVERINO LABAYEN

224 51 Street, West New York, NJ 07093
Born: 9/9/56
Birthplace, Caolod City, Philipines. Graduated from University of Santo Tomas, Manila, Philippines with a bachelors in Fine ARts - advertising major, 1977. Also a graduate of New York University of 1986, with a masters degree in art and art education, studio art program. REal name is Maria Socorro S. Labayen.

NOT ONLY THE HUNGRY...., 44" X 66", Oil, acrylic, $800.00, Owned by artist

DANA CHESTER LASCONIA

430 Keoniana St., #1301, Honolulu, HI
96815
Born: 9/24/59
Born and raised in Alameda, CA. Attended
UCLA; studied under such artists as Tom
Wudl, Lee Mulligan and William Brice.
Received BFA in 1982 with an emphasis on
painting. Major concerns in her work:
People related to environment; light, color
and temperature.

THE BOYS, 48"x73", Oil, $2,500.00,
Owned by the artist

VICKI LAVORINI

2730 - 39th Ave., San Francisco, CA 94116
Born: 5/24/29
Mixed media works on gold and silver leaf.
Representational acrylic and watercolor
paintings. Member and past president of
Society of Western Artists, Presidnet Natl.
League Amer. Pen Women of Norcal.
Schools: Calif. School of Fine Arts; Jean
Turner School of Design; Cal College Arts
and Crafts. Exhibits in Northern California
and Nationally.

TULIPS, 22"x26", Mixed Media, $250.00,
Owned by artist

WING LAW

108 Burlwood Dr., San Francisco, CA
94127
Born: 5/11/52
American Citizen born in Hong Kong. MFA
(Design), MA (Design), Univ. of Iowa,; BA
(Chemistry), BA (Biology) Luther College.
Work in design (2D & 3D), ceramics,
furnishings, sculpture, typography,
photosilkscreen. Exhibition record 1986:
Luther College; Iowa State Fair; Museum of
Art, Univ. of Iowa; Central States Exhibition;
20th Annual Small sculptpure and drawing.

LAMP, 3 1/2" x 3 1/2"(Base), 15" tall,
Ceramic, Owned by artist

LAZAN

P.O. Box 612, Malibu, CA 90265
Born: 10/9/63
Who's Who of California. Published Dad's Car care Book 1984. Work can be seen in various museums around the country including the Virginia Museum, The Anderson Gallery, UC Irving, The Museum of Anthropology Calif. State Chico and many others. Celebrity clientelle and following. Includes various international actors and athletes; Malayasian, Mexican, and US diplomats.

UNTITLED

CHRISTIANE LAZARD

2509 Scott St., San Francisco, CA 94115
Born: 2/16/35
Represented by Fine Arts in Metal, 825 North 10th St., San Jose, CA 95112
Sculptor born in New York. Studied and worked in Paris, France from 1948 to 1982. Have shown in group shows in France and Belgium and have had two one woman shows, one in Paris and one in San Francisco at the Palace of the Legion of Honor. My works are also in private collections throughout France and the US. I now live and work in San Francisco.
TOWARDS INFINITY II, 39"x48"x40", Brass, $3,500.00, Owned by artist

KEITH A. LEAMAN

3530 Damien #245, La Verne, CA 91750
Born: 9/19/45
Keith, a native Indianan, studied art and anthropology at California State University and in Nayarit, Mexico. He has exhibited award winning oils and aqueous-feather works in California, Wisconsin, Minnesota, and at the Institute of American Indian Art Museum in New Mexico. The work shown is slated for exhibit at the Smithsonian Institute, Washington, DC

QUAIL GETS UP, 15"x22", Aqueous, NFS Owned by IAIA Museum , Santa Fe, New Mexico

CATHERINE LE CLEIRE

1899 California St., Apt 6, San Francisco, CA 94109
Born: 11/22/52
(415) 885-5202
I am a California printmaker who has been working in the medium of monoprint because of its spontaneous, experimental and unpredictable nature. I have also been teaching in all areas of printmaking on the college level for several years. While showing and producing my own work in both California and national shows.

THE CATCH, 40"x60", Monotype, $750.00, Owned by the artist

ANNE DIXON LEDING

3233 Red Oak Lane, Beford, TX 76021
Born: 1/29/47
(817) 540-2296
Anne Dixon Leding is a freelance artist in Dallas/Ft. Worth. She was born in Forth Smith, Arkansas. At age eight she won her first art contest. In high school she became a serious art student. After studying as a commercial art major in college, she began teaching art, music, and freelancing. Anne is married and has two children.

AMERICAN HEROS, 17"x19 1/2", Watercolor, NFS, Owned by artist

ABBY J. LEVINE

20 Tompkins Place, Brooklyn, NY 11231
Born: 1/3/55
Represented by Jim Diaz Gallery, 223 E. 10th St., New York, NY 10003 (212) 420-9174
(718) 596-4230
Abby Levine was born in Newark, NJ. She holds a BFA from the Tyler School of Art in Philadelphia. Her work has been exhibited in Philadelphia, the Boston, area, the Mid-west and New York City. Her first NY solo show will run from 11/28 to 12/23 at the Jim Diaz Gallery. Ms. Levine is also a freelance illustrator specializing in album cover art.
WHEEL OF FORTUNE, 40"x50", $1,500.00, Owned by artist

BARBARA LITKE

510 Main Street, Roosevelt Island, NY 10044
Born: 3/26/28
Master of Fine Arts: Grants/artist in residence: YADDO, the Millay Colony for the Arts, The Virginia Center for the Creative Arts - Poet and illustrator of poems

FALLING LEAVES, 20"x 24", Ink and pencil, $350.00, Owned by artist

VIRGINIA MARY LOGSDON

P.O. Box 1121, Oceanside, CA 92054
Born: 2/13/49
Born in Quincy, Illinois, Ms. Logsdon is a naturally talented artist who graduated from Illinois Central College. A recipient of several awards, she has done work as an illustrator and portrait artist. She has recently exhibited at Cranell Gallery in Fallbrook, CA. She is interested in being represented by other galleries or an agent in the future.

VIETNAMEZE MOTHER AND CHILD, 18"x24", NFS, Owned by artist

ANDREJ LOHNERT

3707 1-2 E. 4th St., Long Beach, CA 90814
Born: 1/19/50
(213) 438-8232
Born in Holic, Czechoslovakia. In 1973 graduated at Comenius University, majoring in art history. Between 1968-1982 exhibited with unofficial artists in Czechoslovakia. In 1982 defected to west. Since 1983 lives in the USA. Works as a freelance artist, portraitist and painting conservator.

SONG OF SOUTHWEST, 24"x36", Oil on Canvas, $900.00, Owned by artist

SANTOS LOPEZ

235 East 84th St., New York City, NY
10028
Born: 1/4/57
I am a commercial artist living in Manhattan
who enjoys roller skating. With dedication I
have developed my interests into skills. I
was an art director for Nadi Magazine, and I
have done illustration for Ski Magazine.
After a leg injury in the Navy, I took up
skating as therapy. Since then I have become
well known and respected on the New York
skating scene.
**A ROLLER SKATER MAKES HIS
OWN DECISIONS, A BEGINNER
OBEYS PUBLIC OPINION,** 11"x18
1/2", $15,000.00, Owned by artist

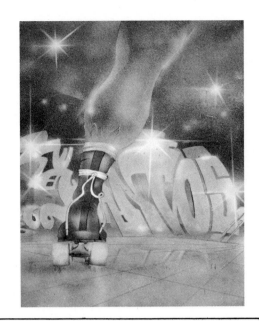

Y HALOP LORD

8683 Rawhide Lane, #27, Wilton, CA 95693
Born: 8/5/42
Represented by Penhallow Gallery, Oak Leaf
Plaza, 5707 Marconi, Carmichael, CA 95608
(916) 483-4158
Reside and have studio at Rawhide nudist
resort. Have shown numerous locations
throughout Bay Area and Sacramento.
Studied under Millard Sheets; Loma Linda
UN, UCD, & CCAC. I am represented in a
number of private collections. Artist believes
God created mankind, in his own image. We
are born nude. Only through grace of God is
artist able to work.
EMERGING WOMAN, 48"x36",
Acrylic, $750.00, Owned by artist

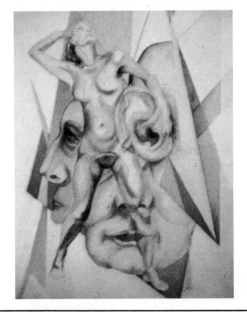

ARLINE COLL LOWE

311 Pompton Ave., Pompton Lakes, NJ
07442
Born: 12/18/36
Artist is art Director for Duro-Test, a NJ
industrial lighting firm. Exhibitions include
shows at State museum, Trenton, Bergen
Community Museum, Paramus, NJ, Pratt
Institute, Bklyn, NY, William Paterson
College, Wayne, NJ. Studied at Ringling
School of Art, Sarasota, FL, Penn. Acad.
Fine Art, Phila, PA. Received MFA from
Pratt Institute, Bklyn, NY, NY in 1984.

OLYMPIAN LEDA, 36"x40", Oil on
canvas, $1,500.00, Owned by artist

BARBARA LUCKE

654 Santa Alicia Drive, Rohnert Park, CA 94928
Born: 7/23/64
I was raised on the Chesapeake Bay of Maryland and left in 1982 to study weaving and textile design at Rochester Institue of Techhnology in Rochester, NY. It was here that I began to utilize painting to relieve the tedium of weaving. Watercolors seem to be the perfect medium for me. They gave me a freedom and spontaneity that fiber art could not.

UNTITLED, 34"X52", Watercolor, $800

WENDY LYONS

92 Fleet Street, Jersey City, NJ 07306
Born: 11/25/58
Wendy Lyons developed her abstract style of representing the human form since graduating from college 16 years ago. These works use simple shapes, rhythm, and color to highlight emotion and action. A resident of New Jersey, Ms. Lyons has exhibited in the metropolitan New York area for several years.

PIECES, 16"x21", Watercolor, Owned by artist

BARBARA MACDONALD

P.O. Box 701, Woodacre, CA 94973
Born: 1/16/25
Chicago Acad Fine arts 1950. Calif. State Univ Long Beach BA 1968; MA 1972 (environmental sculpture). Member San Francisco Women Artists, lives in Bay Area. Work held in private collections. Paintings shown nationwide until 1965. Varied media since: Bronze, wood, stone; now mixed-media of found objects in contained environment assemblage (boxes).

DOWN TO THE SEA IN SHIPS, 12"x12"x4", Mixed, Owned by artist

LILI MAGLIONE

30 Harbor Road, Sands Point, NY 11050
Born: 1/30/29
Represented by Gallery 84, 30 West 57th St., NY, NY 10010 (212) 581-6000
(516) 883-4048
NY born and raised, Lili Maglione received her degree from Traphagen. She also studied at the Art Students League and NYU. Her paintings have been shown, collected and commissioned throughout the US, Canada, and Japan and have won numerous awards and honors. Recently she represented the US at the United Nations Art Festival and Benefit Ball in New York.
SEAPENS, 42"x70", Acrylic, $4,000.00, Owned by artist

MARIE D. MALONEY

41 Vallejo Way, San Rafael, CA 94903
Marie studied at the MuseumSchool of Art, Columbus, GA. before moving to Marin. She continued her studies at the College of Marin and has shown her work in SF and Marin County. Marie has had many one-woman shows in Marin since 1970. She belongs to Society of Western Artists, Marin Arts Guild and Golden Gate Branch of American Pen Women.

HILL OF VIOLETS, 11"x9", Mixed-media, NFS, Owned by artist

ANN E. MANCINI

 34 Front St., Marblehead, MA 01945
Born: 3/3/53
Artist and Poet, Ann Elizabeth Manicini creates her landscapes not only in expressions of love for the visual form, but also from an awareness of inner feeling and reflection. She classifies her landscapes as narrative images searching the soul. Intertwined with the visual expresion is Anns poetry reflecting her deep faith. Ann is also an accomplished photographer.

SOME THINGS STILL REMAIN STABLE, 27"x39 1/2", Pastel, $12,00.00, Owned by the artist

PAUL MARKS

45-06 102 Street, New York City, NY 11368
Born: 10/31/50
(718) 803-2341
Education: Master of Fine Art - 1981 Queens College. Exhibitions (Group): Franklin Furnace 1/84-3/84. International Center of Photography 12/83. Queens Museum 12/82-1/83, 1/81, 2/81. Future events: Focal Point Gallery (solo) '87-88; Los Angeles Photography Center '87-'88. Publications: Mudfish Ed: J. Gallen and V. Urban; Viewpoint Ed: R. Terner with Exhibition.

GLADIATOR NUMBER 172, 14"x28", Oil/Linen, $1,919.19, Owned by artist

ELIZABETH MARTIN

31 Hope Rd., Hingham, MA 02043
Born: 8/26/60
At 26 years old, I reside in Hingham, MA, the place of my birth. I went to New England School of Art and Design , Vesper George School of Arts and I finally graduated from Bridgewater State College with a bachelor of art degree. In my art I concentrate on portraiture and design. I am now a production designer at a local company.

PORTRAIT OF JOHN, 14"x17", Pastel, NFS, Owned by Catherine Martin of Hingham, MA

CAROL MARTIN-DAVIS

Box 435, Bolinas, CA 94924
Born: 2/24/43
Native and long time resident of Northern CA. Education: BA, UC Berkeley; Ft. Mason Art Center. Professional artist since 1978. Specializing in fabric or "soft" sculptures, fabric pictures, wearable art. Member Gallery Route One, an Artists Association, Pt. Reyes Station, CA.

FABRIC OUTLET, 87"x23"x28", Fabric, $350.00, Owned by artist

LINDA ADAIR MARTINEZ

Box 455, Nevada City, CA 95959
Born: 7/17/47
Linda Adair Martinez was born and raised in the San Joaquin Valley of California. She has been painting professionally for the last ten years. Ms. Martinez has had numerous exhibitions in Northern California. Three of her watercolours are in the permanent collection of Bank of America in San Francisco. The natural flora of the sierra foothills are her inspiration.

AU NATUREL, 18"x24", Watercolour, NFS, Owned by the artist

SKEETER MASON

583 Deer Ridge Dr., Bayfield, CO 81122
Born: 4/28/54
Represented by C. Lynne White
Mason began oil painting at the age of 9 and began his career in 1976. He has, through out his life, had a strong love for the wilderness. With the grace of a mountain man, Skeeter wishes to share the spirit of the wild through his paintings and his lifestyle. His theme is what he lives and knows about mans relationship to the creation in its natural state.

THE BLIGHT, 30"x 40", Alkyd oil, $3000

MIKE MASTERS

600 Three Island Blvd, St 1222, Hallandale, FL 33009
Mike has had several major shows including two at Edinburgh Festival. Works have been used for bookcovers, in hotels, colleges and even a famous pub. He has designed every cover fo the leading Scottish magazine, Business Insider. Currently working on interior design for new Hotel and first limited edition prints.

THE RUNNING MAN (KEEP IT UP MISTER JONES), 40"x28", NFS

GLORIA M. MATTIS

346 Keystone Court, San Rafael, CA 94903
Born: 9/13/48
Represented by The Gallery, 329 Primrose Road, Burlingame, CA 94010 (415) 347-9392
(415) 492-1694
SF Bay Area Artist. Born Japan. Educated Univ. of Calif., Berkeley, BA 1969, SF State Univ. Teaching credential-secondary 1972. Numerous awards juried shows throughout California. Member Artists for Social Responsibility. Currently working on exhibition entitled "Our Children: An Endangered Species?" which is scheduled to open in Oregon 1987.
FISH, 56"x40", Prismacolor, $1,300.00

ERIN MAUTERER

4840 Coco Palm Drive, Fremont, CA 94538
Born: 8/3/58
Graphic Designer, San Francisco, CA
BS Graphic Design, San Jose State University, CA
AA Fine Arts, Prince Georges College, Maryland
Commissioned illustrator/Designer
Northern CA; Washington, DC

TR-HANDS-FORMATION II, 9"x12", Watercolor/Gouache, Prints @ $80.00, Owned by artist

ROBERT MAYO

9 Stanford Ave., Colonia, NJ 07067
Born: 3/7/54
(201) 382-4730
Middlesex County College 72-74; School of Visual Art 75; New School of Social Research; Graphic artist - profession. Shows: Lynn Kottler Gallery, NY; Guild of Creative Art; Somerset Art Assoc; Garden State Arts Festival, Momouth; St. John's Church, Newark, NJ; Somerset County College School of Visual Arts

UNTITLED, 18", 15", 21", Mixed media assemblage, Owned by artist

ELEANOR B. MCCARGAR

12235 Indian River Dr. EQ 19, Apple Valley,
CA 92308
Born: 8/30/13
Over 600 commissioned portraits in 9 states
and 4 foreign countries. Prefers painting
from life. Interviewed on Cable TV in Maine
and CA. Featured in several news articles.
Distinguished alumnus in The Arts Award
from U of Maine. M Grumbacher Inc. Ward
for outstanding contribution to the arts.
Specialized in corporate and childrens
portraits. Financing available.

RT. REV. FREDERICK WOLF,
40"x42", Oil, NFS, Owned by Episcopal
Cathedral of Diocese of Maine

DYAN M. MCCLIMON

3447 Colfax Avenue South, Minneapolis,
MN 55408
Born: 9/26/49
Represented by Peter M. David Gallery, 400
1st Ave., North Suite 236, Minneapolis, MN
University of Iowa, Iowa City, MFA 1979,
MA 1977 St. Ambrose Davenport, Iowa BA
1971 Exhibits: Peter M. David Gallery, Cray
Research, Gannett Corp, Washington, DC,
Macalester College St. Paul, Art Expo,
Chicago. Collections: Pillsbury, Amocco
Oil, 3M Corp, First Bank Systems Mpls & St
Paul & La Crosse, Wis, Dallas Bank, &
Trust, Paine Webber
PICTURES FROM MY TRIP, 39"x40",
Watercolor mix silk on paper, $1,350.00

KATE MCDANIEL

Rt. 1 Box 817, Crawford, OK 73638
Born: 8/24/27
Represented by Pear Tree Gallery, 708 Main
St., Woodward, OK 73801 (405) 256- 4513
(405) 983-2374
Kate McDaniel and her husband live on a
ranch in a remote area of Roger Mills Co. in
Okla. She has had lessons from a master and
has painted in oil for 15 years. She has had
many one person shows. Kate loves to paint
alone in the surrounding red hills, plus still
life and abstract visions from her soul.
**LIFE IS BEAUTIFUL EXCEPT FOR
THE LITTLE AGGRAVATIONS,**
24"x30", Oil on Canvas, $4,000.00, Owned
by artist

JOHN MC MAHON

25200 Malibu Rd., Malibu, CA 90265
Born: 5/12/44
Born in Honolulu, HI. Studied film at CSU Northridge with a BA/1976. Spent 8 yrs in graphic arts with various publications and turned to photojournalism and sculpture for another 5 yrs. Published in Random House in photography and won various photography awards before taking up painting in 1976. Today concentrates with abstracts using acrylics.

MUDSLIDE, 18" x 22", Acrylic, $350.00, Owned by artist

PATRICIA MCMURTRY

P.O. Box 441, El Verano, CA 95433
Born: 11/5/47
(707) 996-1448
Born in St. Helena, CA, raised in Sonoma, CA. Seriously pursued painting for 20 years. Completely self taught. Developed a unique style in response to European symbolistand surrealists. Paintings typify the Northern California outsiders School of Eccentric Folk Art.

FISH, NFS, Owned by Otto Teller of Sonoma, CA

MAYRIE MEANS

737 Carnival Ave., Port St. Lucie, FL 33452
Born: 11/3/41
Mayrie Means gained background in commercial graphic arts at Florida Atlantic Univ. and the correspondence Famous Artists School; in fine art through self study. Her paintings contain elements of both. She has exhibited in numerous juried compeititons in FL (recently the Allied Artists 77th Annual Show, NYC) and her works are in many private ocllections.

SOLAR RAIN, 16 1/4"x24 1/2", Oil on wood, $600.00, Owned by the artist

LINDA MEDLEY

98 Desmond Road, Salinas, CA 93907
Born: 5/17/64
(408) 663-2406
I'm a freelance illustrator specializing in old-fashioned, highly detailed illustration in the tradition of Arthur Rackham and Edmund Dulac. I emphasize historical research, costume design and character development brought together with good solid drawing skills. I graduated from the Academy of Art College in San Francisco with a certificate in illustration.

THE WIZARD, 8 1/2"x11", Watercolor, NFS, Owned by artist

LOUIE MEI-LING

14 Fifth Avenue, East Northport, NY 11731
Born: 9/14/51
Ms. Louis is a fiberartist. Works include fashion, costumes, softsculpture and products. Fashions seen in McCalls, Ladies Home Journal, Woman's World. Designs available through Vogue Patterns. Costumes for Big Apple Circus, Great Adventure, Robert Wilson. Her product line "Beasts-of-Burden" are mans-best-friend as luggage, accessories and wearables.

THE ONE THAT GOT AWAY FROM BEASTS OF BURDEN COLLECTION, Silk, NFS, Owned by artist, Silk painting by Georgina Morgese, Photo by Maje Waldo.

SIMIN MEKADEH

178 Avenida Miraflores, Tiburon, CA 94920
Born: 11/19/41
(415) 435-1366
Member of Marin Society of Artists, Free Painters, Sculptures London. Prize winner F. Young Gallery 1985-86. Exhib: Chelsea Westminister Inst, Chelsea Art Soc. Ann Exh London 1981-1982. Paintings sold to priv. coll, London, CA. Studied Tehran in London, SF Art Inst. Married with 3 children. Born Iran to Abbas Massoudi, author, publisher, Ettelaat newspaper.

GREGORY, 44 1/2", 32", Acrylic, $1200.00, Owned by artist

RENEE MELLENA

583 Kamoku St., #1107, Honolulu, HI 96826
Born: 7/6/53
(808) 942-2523
I create art to share a brief sensation with other people: a sort of mini conversation. My art is my language, my release, my dreams. It is a necessity in my life, without it I would have to go to parties.

ALONG THE STRAIGHT AND NARROW, 4 1/2"x9"x9", Ceramic, NFS, Owned by artist

GRACE MERJANIAN

18701 Deodar Street, Fountain Valley, CA 92708
Born: 9/9/24
Represented by Mariners Fine Arts, 34505 Street of Golden Lantern, Dana Point, CA 92629 (714) 496-2330
(714) 968-5983
Grace has been painting for thirteen years. Even though she did not start until she was forty-nine, she has won over six awards including "Best of Show" and "First Place" for her oil and watercolor paintings. Her works are in the US, Canada, France, Lebanon and Germany.
STORMY PACIFIC, 21"x29", Watercolor, $1,800.00

NANCY ROSE ANNE MIDDENDORF

4934 Brock St., Apt. 102, Indianapolis, IN 46254
Born: 11/30/60
1984 Honors graduate of Ivy Tech, Columbus, IN: received Associate of Applied Science degree. Currently working for audio/visual company. Have illustrated for Binty Baladi, a middle eastern dance magazine. Also I illustrated children's books. Work primarily in prismas and pencil, but also work well with pen as well as oils and 3-D pieces.

TWIN NEPHEWS, 8"x10", Prismas, NFS, Owned by Suzanne & Joe Arruda of Topeka, KS

MR. JAN MIDTUN

2126 17th St., NE, Rochester, MN 55904
Born: 5/2/41
(507) 281-2805
Born Bergen, Norway, emigrated to USA in 1973. Studied at Bergen Art & Design School for 3 years. MA degree in Art. Works in all media from oil to airbrush. Have attended many car show and exhibition set up. Have client like General Mills, Control Data, Gates Rubber, Webb Publishing, Norwegian Caribbean Cruise LIne etc.

CLENET CLASSIC CAR, 30"x40", Oil on canvas, $1,800.00, Owned by artist

CATHEY MOORE MILLER

312 W 105 #5FE, New York, NY 10025
Born: 6/23/63
Attended Southern Methodist University and Art Center College of Design
Currently living and working in New York City.

UNTITLED, 19"x24", Oil, NFS, Owned by Dina Wallace of Dallas, TX

ALI MIRANDA

555 NE 34th St. Apt. 1105, Miami, FL 33137
Born: 1/29/54
(305) 576-0520
Born in Cuba; raised in Miami. Studied art, photography, and film at the School of Visual Arts in NY and the Academy of Arts College in SF, holding a degree in Fine Arts from the latter. Presently working as a commerical photographer in the Miami area, Ali's career has taken him to Europe, Mexico, Central and So. American and the Caribbean.

UNTITLED, Photography, Owned by artist

JOSEPH MITCHELL

1479 North West 73rd St., Miami, FL 33147
Born: 8/18/56
Joseph studied art at Miami-Northwestern Sr. High, Atlanta Art College, Miami-Dade Community College, University of Miami, and The Art Instruction Schools. I've experienced working as a fashion artist and a graphic artist. My work has been shown throughout the state of Florida. My work was also shown in Paris and France art galleries where I was highly honored.

UNTITLED, 30"x39", Pencil, $3,000.00, Owned by artist

ALEX T. MIZUNO

140 Harold Ave., San Francisco, CA 94112
Born: 9/27/55
(415) 239-4886
Graduated from Nihon University, College of Arts in Japan. Worked for a Japan's legendary avant-garde stage compnay, Tenjo-Sajiki, as a production artist. In the States, as a freelance illustrator and graphic artist, designed a dozen posters for plays, film festivals and concerts and several album covers.

FAREWELL, TERAYAMA, 19"x 14", Supracolor II, Owned by the artist

WELLS MOORE

4St. Marks Place, New York City, NY 10003
Born: 3/8/51
Art Director by trade, painter by heart. Currently seeking professional help in freelance market. Portraits, forgeries and margaritas by appointment.

RAYA, 18"x24", Acrylic, NFS, Owned by Raya Keis, of New York City

RAY MORELLI

650 East 231 Street, Bronx, NY 10466
Born: 9/24/39
Born in Bklyn NY studied comm and fine art
under the direct. of H. Maurer & N. Myers at
the Amer. Art School. In 1969, I was a 1st
place winner in a design contest sponsored
by 3M and ABC for a TV spec called Africa
the Continent. Art Dir at Natl design Ctr and
research Inst of Amer. I'm now freelancing
spec in rendering & illustrations in various
mediums.

THE ROAD TO DARTHMERE, 24"x
36", Oil, NFS

VINCENT MORIN JR.

2543 Highwood Dr., Dallas, TX 75228
Born: 1/15/52
(214) 328-7345
Vincent Morin's work is usually labeled
surrealism. He simply calls it a universal and
psychological omnibus on canvas. In his
interpretations, he offers orchestrations of
Gossamer imagery. His art touches all the
senses and emotions while giving the mind a
chance to create the story or meaning within
it's content. In every life, there is a story to
be told.

CAPTIVE CYCLE, 1978, 72"x48",
Acrylic on Canvas, $2,500.00, Owned by
artist

ZENAIDA TALBOT MOTT

16 Garden Road, San Anselmo, CA 94960
Born: 2/26/38
(415) 457-5292
BA UC Berkeley, Davis. Lived and painted
extensively Africa, Asia, Europe; studied
painting in Nigeria, Japan, Cambridge, MA,
Marin, CA. Elizabeth McDaniel, Maria
Sanchez. Member Marin Society of Artists,
MAC; Guest Artist CSPF. Magazine cover
paintings; Exhibited San Francisco, Marin
Galleries. Media: Oil, acrylic, pen and ink.

THE WEST GARRISON, 30"x40",
Acrylic, NFS, Owned by State Park
Foundation of California

KATHLEEN L. MUELLER

RR 4 Box 97, Mankato, MN 56001
Born: 12/10/65
Represented by Upstairs Gallery, 918 South Front Street, Mankato, MN 56001 (507) 625-7044
(507) 245-3181
Born in Mankato, MN. Graduated from St. Clair High School in 1984. Was accepted by various art schools, but chose to attend Minneapolis College of Art and Design. I will begin school in January of 1987. I am currently working for a major printing corporation in Mankato, MN, as a commerical artist.
YOUNG GIRL, 8"x10", Pencil, $500.00, Owned by artist

BRIAN E. MURPHY

300 West 12th St., Spt 2G, NY, NY 10014
Born: 7/30/59
(212) 243-2720
A graduate of Rhode Island School of Design with a BFA in illustration 1982. Studies included heavy emphasis of painting and drawing. Work selected for illustration/painting exhibit at Woodsgerry Gallery. Presently freelancing as an illustrator in NYC. Work exhibited in NY at the Salmagundi Clubs 8th Annual juried non-member show.

THREE AND TWO, 24"x 30", Oil, $1100

PATRICIA ANN MURRAY

1270 Monterey Blvd, San Francisco, CA 94127
Born: 12/16/39
(415) 626-1175
Pat Murray was educated at the University of Michigan with a master degree obtained from Washington University in Saint Louis. Locally, she attended the San Francisco Academy of Art. She works in the San Francisco Bay Area, but her work reflects her time spent in the Orient and the island of the Caribbean.

NEW BEGINNING, 20":x24", Oil, NFS, Owned by Hugh Fraser

MYRRH (GERTRUDE REAGAN)

967 Moreno Ave., Palo Alto, CA 94303
Born: 9/18/36
(415) 856-9593
In 1981, Myrrh founded the Art Group, Ylem: Artists using science and technology. She has used science images in her work since 1969. She works on paper, using resist techniques she once used on cloth, to create aerial landscapes. Studied: Stanford, fiberworks. Artist-in residence, Villa Montavlo, 1983. Collection: The Ribbon, Smithsonian Institution, 1985.

ISTHMUS, 25"x40", Shibori Painting, $500.00, Owned by artist

MARIA LYNN NESBITT

300 Sea Avenue 17B, Pt. Pleasant Beach, NJ 08742
Born: 9/2/61
Represented by Ocean Artists, Inc., Pt. Pelasant Bewach, NJ 08742 (201) 892-1999
(201) 892-4597
Maria is a 1983 graduate of Seton Hall University. In addition to being a marketing rep for Spencer Gifts, Inc., she is also the proprietor of Nessie Graphics, Pt. Pleasant Bch, NJ. She is presently working with interior decorators designing paintings for their clients. Maria specializes in custom graphic designing, large canvas, and murals.

GRAPHIC GLIDE, 28"x36", Acrylics, $250.00, Owned by artist

ROBERT NEWMAN

2 Xerman Place, Weehawken, NJ 07087
Born: 8/17/52
Represented by Semaphore Gallery, 137 Green St., NY, NY (212) 228-7990
(201) 348-6721
Born in NYC, raised in NJ. Graduated Rutgers U. Received MFA degree from Rutgers in 1977. Currently working as an art therapist. Participated in a group show at the Semaphore Gallery in the summer of 1986.

UNTITLED, 22" x 26", Oil, $2,500.00, Owned by artist

MARIA NICHOLAOU

891 Menlo Drive, P.O. Box 3300, Big Bear Lake, CA 92315
Born: 8/13/63
Born on Long Island, New York, I attended high school in Athens, Greece and the School of Visual Arts in Manhattan, New York. Since then, I have been in the graphic arts field, and freelancing artwork. I would like to thank both my families, who made this particular painting possible.

RELIGIONS' TOLL, 18"x22", Watercolors, NFS

JEFFREY I. NICHOLS

5345 Brophy Dr., Fremont, CA 94536
Born: 11/20/45
Represented by Syt Galerie, 39040 Fremont Hub, Fremont, CA 94536 (415) 1795-1335 (415) 791-0666
Jeff Nichols has spent most of his life in California where he now teaches and paints in his Fremont home studio. His work displays a special and unique style and use of color. Jeff has always been expecially fond of painting florals but he also teaches and paints landscapes and seascapes.

BIRTH OF A ROSE, 16"x20", Oil on canvas, NFS, Owned by Roland R. Finch of Thomasville, GA

DOROTHY ELIZABETH NOSENZO

172 Corwin St., San Francisco, CA 94114
Born: 12/28/49
Represented by Stephen Wirtz Gallery, 345 Sutter St., San Francisco, cA 94108
Born and raised Italian-American in San Francisco. Studied art from childhood. Educated in mid-west; bronze work at Univ of Kansas and Oxbow Foundry. Artist and consultant to architectural projects, esthetic communities and private commisions throught the US. Extensive travel throughout Europe and the Middle East.

EQUISTRIAN-PIECE.KINETIC.,
51"x 96"x96", Bronze-Steel, $15,000.00, Exhibited by Modesto Lanzone, Opera Plaza, San Francisco, CA

GEOFFREY IHEANYI NWOGU

425 Lyon St., #5, San Francisco, CA 94117
Born: 6/17/49
Represented by Wajumbe Cultural Inst., 762
Fulton, SF.CA 94102 (415) 563-3519
(415) 931-5096
A third generation award winning Nigerian
artist. Has been showing for 18 yrs and
represented in museums, public galleries and
homes in Africa, Europe and USA.
UNEXCO appointed observer International
Congress of Artists, Finland, 1983.
Represented in the collection of Pope John
Paul II, Vatican.
RITUAL PROCESSION, 48"X24",
Wood, NFS, Owned by IMO State
Government Gallery of Nigeria

STEVEN OERDING

6248 Westwood Dr., Rocklin, CA 95677
Born: 4/22/59
(916) 786-3701
Born in Portland, Oregon, I have been a
practicing artist since age 6, having little
formal training at college. Mostly self taught
through books, others artwork and the
practice of trial and error. This art was done
in watercolors applied with airbrush then
acrylics applied by hand on cresent board.
The inspiration came from Clint Eastwood in
"Dirty Harry".

MAKE MY DAY, 18"x20", Watercolor,
NFS, Owned by artist

TIMOTHY P. OJILE

1421 S. Beretania St., Honolulu, HI 96814
Born: 6/29/48
(808) 955-1251
Graduated University of Minnesota 1970 in
Eastern Art History and English Literature.
Lived New York 1973-1981. Moved Hawaii
1981. Work in various mixed media.
Numerous awards. Art in collections of
Honolulu Academy of Arts, Hawaii State
Foundation, Contemporary Art Center of
Hawaii and Collections in Hawaii and US
mainland. 3 shows Japan summer 1986.

UNTITLED, 30"x22", Mixed, NFS,
Owned by Honolulu Academy of Arts

ANN M. OLMSTEAD

1450 Hidden Bridge Road, Folsom, CA 95630
Born: ll/l/43
Reprsented by Friday House Gallery, 2936 Mosquito Road, Placerville, CA 95667 (916) 621-1661
(916) 933-2223
Featured Artist Garden Silks Gallery, Friday House Gallery Best of Show - Friday House Gallery, May '86 Group show City Callery July 86 Group Show Rara Avis Gallery, Aug 85. Instr Arch. Drftg. Display designer major Dept Store. Interior Designer. Needlepoint designer .
BEYOND OUTER LIMITATIONS, 32"x30", Watercolor with ink, $600.00

JOSE LUIS ORTIZ

312 E. 93rd St., New York NY 10128
Born: 7/.19/45
Jose Luis Ortiz was born in Mexico in 1945. In Mexico he studied at the National School of Fine Arts, the School fo Design and The Molino De Santo Domingo. After moving to New York, he studied at Art Students League and Printmaking workshop. Mr. Ortiz has exhibited his paintings, prints, and casting paper in Mexico, New York, Washington, DC, Canada and Latin America.

MY KING AND MY QUEEN, 50"x38", Oil/canvas, $3,000.00, Owned by the artist

ALAN OSBORNE

825 North Tenth Street, San Jose, CA 95112
Born: 11/13/49
Represented by Charles Campbell, 647 Chestnut St., San Franicsco, CA 94133(415) 441-8680
(408) 292-7628
Alan Osborne was born and raised in the San Francisco Bay Area. He is co-founder and president of Fine Arts in Metal, Art Foundry in San Jose. For the past seventeen years, Alan has been a prolific sculptor as well as a dedicated foundry man.

SAMURAI ARMOR XLIX, 22 1/2"x18"x9", Sculpture, $3,500.00 Owned by artist

92

IRIS OSTERMAN

240 East 25th Street, New York, NY 10010
Born: 10/4/50
Represented by Bowery Gallery, 121
Wooster St., NY. 10012
BFA Boston Univ; MFA American Univ;
Shown in numerous 1 person and group
exhibitions on the East coast; Fellowship
recipient - Millay Colony for the Arts,
Ossabow Island Foundation, Virginia Center
for the Creative Arts, Dorland Mtn Colony,
Cummington Community for the Arts.
Works primarily in oils, as well as several
graphic mediums

UNTITLED, 48" x 72", Oil, $1,200.00,
Owned by artist

ED OSTERMAYER

12121 Northwest Freeway #119, Houston,
TX 77092
Born: 3/25/55
(713) 896-1017
Born in Baytown, Texas; presently lives in
Houston. Graduated from the University of
Houston and studied under Mark English.
Worked two years at the Houston Chronicle
as editorial illustrator. For six years, has
freelanced commercial art, fine art-abstract
and realistic, architectural rendering, posters,
and airbrush. Painting reprinted courtesy of
The Houston Chronicle
**CASTRO'S SUPPORT OF SPORTS
AND THE OLYMPICS,** 10"X17",
ACRYLIC, NFS, Owned by artist

SUSAN PARENTE

PO Box 258, Salisbury Mills, NY 12577
Born: 5/25/51
Won full scholarship to small New England
college. Worked as artist on Jackson Sq,
New Orleans. Taught and showed in local
galleries. BFA school of visual arts NYC.
Society of Illustrators 1981. American
illustration annual 1986. Harris memorial
award Hudson Valley 86. Currently working
NYC area as illustrator, while pursing
interests in fine art.

UNTITLED, 6 1/2" x 7", Mixed, NFS,
Owned by artist

NORMAN PARISH

1207 Jamie Lane, Homewood, IL 60430
Born: 8/26/37
Represented by Isobel Neal, Ltd., 200 W. Superior Suite 200, Chicago, IL 60610 (312) 944-1570
1960 Graduate School of the Art Inst. of Chicago. Exhibits include - Galerija Art Gallery, Museum of Science & Industry, First Pacific Bank, Monroe Gallery, Purdue University and Garland Building. Wards - Intergraph Computer Art Competition, Union League Annual Art Show and pruurchase prize Chicago City Bank

CHICAGO 1981, 48"x48", Oil, $2,000.00, Owned by artist

PETER C. PARLAGRECO

15 South Saxon Ave. Apt. A, Bay Shore, NY 11706
Born: 6/8/61
(516) 666-0575
In 1981, with an AA Cum Laude, I entered a studio position at HG Industries, a Long Island toy co. In less than 6 months I became studio manager, and later Asst. Art Director. After 3 years, I left to pursue personal artistic goals. Recently, I have been concentrating on advancing my freelance work into the illustrative field; working in assorted media

MADAME BUTTERFLY, 15 1/2"x 22 3/4", Ink and watercolor, $300.00, Owned by artist

DAVID W. PELSUE

16729 Cedarwood Circle, Cerritos, CA 90701
Born: 6/5/58
(213) 404-7947
Self taught, born and raised in Southern California. Ten years experience in commercial art and industrial design. Last five years at Nissan Motor Corp. As a graphic designer. Also freelance: preproduction design, graphics, and miniatures for film and TV. Product design, murals and posters. Hobbies: Porsches, Shelbys, sculpting, scuba and WWII reenacting.

UNTITLED, 16l/2"x26", Watercolor, NFS Owned by Nissan Motor Corp.

MARGOT PEPIN

1178 Reggio Pl, Pomona, CA 91766
Born: 3/7/63
(714) 623-2716
Margot was born In Quebec City. She studied art at College Jean-De-Brebeuf in Montreal from 1980 to 1982, then pursued her education in California graduating with a BA in art from Cal Poly Pomona University in 1985. Mainly a painter, she is also a printer and ceramist, and is currently studying computer art and animation at Otis Parsons in Los Angeles.

A CRUCIFIXION, 5'x4', Acrylic, NFS

BOB PETERS

3924 Warren Avenue, Bellwood IL 60104
Born: 7/9/63
(312) 544-1360
Bob Peters is a 1985 graduate of Northern Illinois University. He is currently the Art Director for Pro Football Weekly and freelances as a graphic artist and illustrator. He has had several of his illustrations published this year

BLEACHER   DAZE, 14"x17", Prismacolor, NFS

LOUISE M. PETOSA

426 West Broadway, New York, NY 10012
Born: 3/5/56
Photographer born and raised on Staten Island (NYC). Trained at Parsons School of Design, NYC and Paris. BFA 1978. Architectural photographs published in NYC Winter Antiques Show Catalogue. Works in color and black and white. Graphic design work selected for graphis and NY Art Directors Club annuals. Member AIGA. Travels to experience and record foreign cultures.

XIAN, CHINA, 11"x14", Photography, $500.00, Owned by artist

RICHARD PHELPS

8842 11th Ave., SW, Seattle, WA 98106
Born: 5/22/54
Represented by Terrie Mitchell, P.O. Box 47297, Seattle, WA 98126
Richard was born in Hawaii, and lives in Seattle. He is devoted to his life's love, painting. Walking into his home is like walking back in time, the rooms teeming with antiques and photographs from the turn of the century. He would argue the whereabouts of the last Indian battle, and paint his own depiction. His ancestors have been craftsmen for 600 years.

MY BROTHER'S BATHTUB, 48"x41 1/2", Acrylics, $1,200.00, Owned by artist

P.H. PHILLIPS

56 Lucky Drive, Greenbrae, CA 94904
After many years of traveling and studying on the east and west coas of the US, the artist now resides in Marin County and creates images in different media from the exposure to this exquisite area of wild life and flowers.

PAPER IMAGE, 18"x24", Mixed media, NFS, Owned by artist

MICHAEL PIERSANTI

1043 Plainfield Ave., Plainfield, NJ 07060
Born: 11/5/60
(201) 757-0208
I am presently working as an art director for an ad agency in NJ. I have been doing airbrush illustration for 6 years. I specialize in full color renderings and illustration as well as black and white retouching.

TDK, 14"x20", Gouache, NFS, Owned by artist

AUGUST A. PIERUCCI

68 Cypress Drive, Fairfax, CA 94930
Born: 7/11/23
Born in San Francisco, he joined the Calf.
Nat'l Guard in 1938 lying about his age.
Discharged from army in 1945 as 1st Sgt Inf.
Paratrooper. Retired with 30 years service
from SFFD . After retirement fulfilled
lifetime ambition to paint and enjoy the arts.
Having no formal art education. He enrolled
in class taught by Odette Littee of San Rafael,
CA

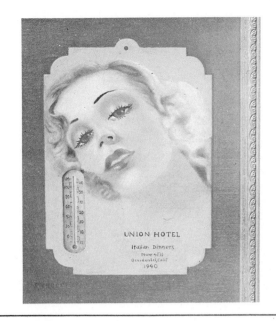

OCCIDENTAL LADY, 9"x12", Oil, NFS

GINGER GAY PLUMB

P.O. Box 46396, Los Angeles, CA 90046
Born: 12/4/50
Represented by Plumb Productions, P.O.
Box 46396, Los Angeles, CA 90046
Ginger has been painting since the age of 8
years old. She has an AA in graphic art
advertising. She is presently a photo-
journalist free lance for magazine and
newspaper. She owns her own company
Plumb Productions and plans on publishing
her own magaine in the near future. Her
paintings are of mixed media. She paints
from fantasy to realistic colorful.

UNTITLED, 18"x24"x24", Mixed media,
NFS, Owned by artist

R. H. POLLETTE

725 Minna, San Francisco, CA 94103
Born: 9/16/48
Represented by Max West Assoc, 725
Minna, San Francisco, CA 94103 (415) 621-
3627
(415) 621-3627
R.H. Pollette aka Internationaly under the
name, Max West, currently lives and works
in San Francisco. Pollette considers himself
a world citizen and is an avid traveler and
recognized reveler.

**OUTSIDE SIKA (aka) THE
SADISTIC GEISHAS,** 36"x60",
Mixed/Oil, Owned by Jilla Omari of Tokyo

MARILYN JEAN POPE

226 McKendry Drive, Menlo Park, CA 94025
Born: 11/27/49
I have been painting for the last sixteen years. My artwork has been purchased by architects, decorators, corporations and private collectors through the US and four countries. The character of my work is luminosity movement and color, all arranged to produce the feeling of space and hope. Currently teaching fine arts to children in Menlo Park, CA

ENERGY, 3'x3', Oil, $1,500.00, Owned by Claude and Nadine Dawson of San Francisco, CA

GERALDINE A. PROVOST

3665 24th Street, San Francisco, CA 94110
Born: 10/23/64
(415) 648-3157
Born in Holyoke MA and moved to Califonria. Studied art at Chicoper High school and Holyoke Community College both in MA. Studied drawing and design 1/2 year in college. Showed work at exhibit during school years. Currently working on projects at home in SF. Most works done in mixed media.

VICTORIAN HOUSE IN NEW ENGLAND, 17 1/2" x 11 1/2", India Ink, NFS, Owned by David Lawrence Dodge of SF

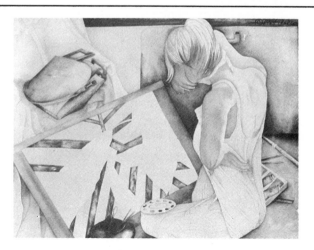

KAREN J. PULEO

382 Jefferson Court, Vernon Hills, IL 60061
Born: 11/17/54
Represented by David M. Stern, 651 First Bank DRive, Palatine, IL 60067 (312) 358-9202
(312) 367-7137
I have been painting for 8 years, with the last five being devoted sole to watercolor. I received a BFA from Barat College, Lake Forest, IL and am presently enrolled at the Art Institute of Chicago as the recipient of theSmith Award. I hope to successfully blend editorial illustration and fine art into my paintings.

SELF PORTRAIT WITH BOTANIC II, 22"x30", Watercolor, NFS

RICHARD THOMAS RABE

3103 Rogers, Covington, KY 41015
Born: 8/10/52
Graduate of Northern Campbell Tech and
Northern Kentucy State. Attended Pratt
Institute of Art and Design.

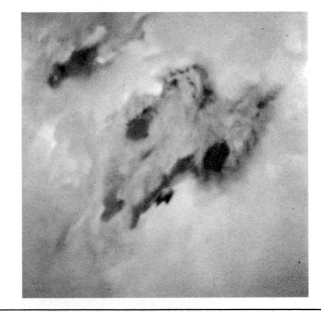

BEYOND THE REEF, 18"x21", Tempra,
$800.00

GARY RAGAGLIA

26 Archdale St., Roslindale, MA 02131
Born: 6/13/58
Photography is, I think, the visual beginning
and end - truth after all is much stranger than
fiction.

BUILDINGSPEAK,   Kodachrome,
Owned by the artist

RICHARD C. RANCITELLI

22 Roosevelt Ave., West Caldwell, NJ
07006
Born: 1/18/54
(201) 575-8928
Born in Newark. Attended Parsons School
of Design, Rutgers Univ. Exhibited, among
others, Salmagundi Club, Nabisco Corp.
Headquarters. Drawn for Worldview,
Working Women, Sin Embargo, And Casa
del Tiempo Magazines. Lived in Mexico,
1982. Artists most admired: Sheeler, De
Muth, Lozowick, Los Trest Grandes de
Mexico. Long live the precisionsts and their
descendants.

PLANT   NO.   6, 7"x4", Pencil, Ink,
$125.00

RANDEE RANKIN

256 NW 7th St., Boca Raton, FL 33432
Born: 11/2/49
Represented by Fran Murphy, 401 Clematis St., (Stephen Lloyd), West Palm Beach, FL 33401 (305) 659-6200
Born and raised at Purdue University, Randee has been painting since a child. She graduated from Prudue in visual and package design which is the main basis for her visual illusion, 360 degree room graphics which she has won awards for, however, her paintings are just as important because, "The main thing to me is communication and to make people feel great!"
DIETRICH IN AIRBRUSH, 59"x49 1/2", Airbrush, $1,800.00, Owned by artist

RAGNHILD REINGARDT

21 Andem Place, Brookline, MA 02146
Born: 4/8/36
Born and educated in Sweden. Advanced visual studies at Harvard University and Massachusetts Institute of Technology, Cambridge, MA Selected exhibitions and events: Red Banner, ArtPark, Lewiston, NY; Liljevalchs Knosthall, Stockholm, Sweden; Dreamscreen, Sigma, Bordeaux, France; Form reflections, City Hall, Boston, MA; the Avant Garde Festival World Trade Center, NY, NY

RED BANNER, ARTPARK, VISUAL ART 1983, 65'x122', Sewn Nylon, $10,000, Owned by the artist

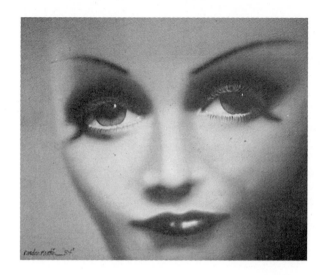

LINDA REVEL

2862 Folsom St., San Francisco, CA 94110
Born: 4/28/53
Intaglio printmaker with background in filmmaking; have worked and exhibited with Fort Mason Printers and graphic arts workshop. Shown in Crocker Kingsley, No. Regional Print Show and Alexandria, LA Museum. Focus of work is on social irony and human injustice. Studied at school of Visual Arts, NYC and informally in London and Amsterdam; BFA degree.

CULTURE SHOCK, 24" x 19", Intaglio, $250, Owned by artist

ROBIN REBECCA REYES

267 Miller Avenue, Mill Valley, CA 94941
Born: 11/24/57
I began drawing human and animal forms at age 3. I use oils, watercolors, pastels and pen and ink in creating portraits and landscapes. My work has appeared in libraries throughout the US as part of the Traveling Art Show, and in a variety of N. Calif. galleries. My next series of paintings focus on beach lines of the West and East Coasts.

MAIN STREET, SAINT HELENA, 29"x27", Watercolor, NFS, Owned by artist

JENNY KIRST REZ

329 Belmont St., Glendale, CA 91206
Born: 9/21/58
AA Degree in Art from Cabrillo College; Aptos, CA
BA Degree in illustration from Art Center College of Design, Pasadena, CA
Now working as a freelance illustrator in Los Angeles

FACE, 4 1/2"x6", Gouache & Ink, NFS, Owned by artist

DALE RHYMER

6817 Santa Susana Pass Road, Santa Susana, CA 93063
Born: 3/3/58
Education: CSUN, MA in Art 1 - 1983
CUSN BA in Art, 6 -1980
Exhibitons:
Bachofner Gallery: Consignment 1-8, 86
LA Municipal Art Gallery, "Artists Select Artists", 1984
CUSN Gallery, "Marvin Garden: a Tribute", 1984
Conejo Valley Art Museum, "Third Annual Juried Show", 83

)offal #24, 8"x96", Mixed, NFS, Owned by artist

ROATS (DOROTHY R. MYERS)

210 E 63rd St. 2E, #34, New York, NY 10021
Born: 3/24/21
Represented by Morin-Miller Gallery, 119 W. 57th St., #805, New York, NY 10019
(212) 757-7822
(212) 838-0932
Internationally accredited to jury exhibits. Studied Corcoran Gallery; Art Students League. Member Salmagundi and Affiliated Clubs in London, Paris, Amsterdam, Montreal, Toronto, and US; Art Students League; NY Artists Equity; (others). Official US Coast Guard Artist.
PATERNITY, 8"x10", Oil on Canvas, $300.00, Owned by the artist

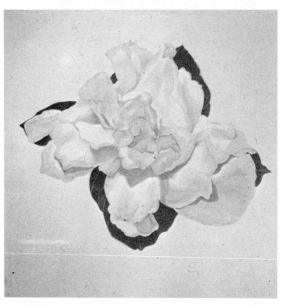

MARK ROBINSON

19-30 202 Street, Bayside, NY 11360
Born: 3/17/47
A regard for nature and delicate sensibility is critical to success of the work. A mastered direction for technique revers subject with skill and tact. A diverse versaility is apparent in the body of work dealing with major and minor subjects and mediums; including oil, tempera, watercolor and drawing.

GARDENIA, 30"x30", Oil, $1000.00, Owned by artist

BOB ROCK

5239 Buchanan Trail-East, Waynesboro, PA 17268
Born: 2/16/61
(717) 762-9044
New as a professional freelancer, I specialize in two areas. One is cartooning, whether it be a single-panel or comic strip, or as magazine illustration. The other area is Fine Art illustration, where my work is pen and ink drawings or impressionistic pastel paintings. I have a flair for portraits and caricature and try to convey a sense of humor in my work.
GOOD HEAVENS PAUL, LOOK! IT'S WELTY'S BRIDGE!, 17"x23", Inkpen, Wash, $100.00, Owned by artist

KITTY SCHEUER RODRIQUEZ

40 Sterling Ave., Yonkers, NY 10704
Born: 3/29/32
Born in Vienna, Aust., Kitty studied art in NYC. She specialized in portraiture, working primarily in oils and pastels. She is a member of various art associations. Her work has been shown in several galleries, as well as local and national juried competitions. She has won numerous awards. Many of her works are in private collections both here and abroad.

IN THE GARDEN, 24"x30", Oil, $1,500.00, Owned by artist

LLYOD N. ROGNAN

3620 Linneman St., Glenview, IL 60025
Born: 6/14/23
(312) 729-0898
Lloyd studied in France 5 yrs., and USA. Encyclopedia artist. Historical illustrator. Cartoonist Brown & Bigelow calendar art & limited edition plates. Picard art editor, United Card Co. Art accepted in Vesterheim Museum, Decorah, Iowa. Currently working on portfolios of western art and landscapes, animals and historical turn of the century farm life. See Who's Who of Midwest - World.

REWARDS OF A FARMBOY, 12"x16 1/2", Mixed media, Owned by Artist

RAFAEL ROPEK

187 Duane St., New York City, NY 10013
Born: 1/12/48
Represented by Neo Persona, 51 Hudson St., NYC, NY 10013 (212) 406-9835
Born NYC. Educated Art Students League. Artist in Residence Royaal School of Ballet Covent Garden, England 1968-69. Ruropean studies 1968-1973. Exhibitions: Tucson Museum 1974, 75, 76, Scottsdale Center 76, 77, Grapestakes Gallery, San Francisco, 78, Even Mannes Gallery, Atlanta, GA 79-84, Alan Stone Gallery NYC 81 82, Neo Persona Gallery, NYC 85 86.
THE CURRENCY OF MODERN ART WAS FORGED IN THE PAST, 72"x96", Acrylic, $5,000.00

NORMAN RUBINGTON

13 Bleecker St., New York, NY 10012
Born: 5/20/21
Born New Haven, Conn. Studied at Yale School of Fine Arts, '39-43. Served in China, 44-46. Lived and worked in Paris, 46-69. Exhibited in salons, group shows etc. in Europe and US Prix de Rome, Tiffany Scholarship, Guggenheim Fellowship. Works in private collections, Hirschorn Purchase, Grace Cathedral, San Francisco. One man shows Paris, Rome, NY, Boston. At present in NY.

STILL LIFE, 30"x40", Oil, Owned by artist

R. KAY RUDISELL, OPAA

Route 6 Box 53-B, Hamilton, AL 35570
Born: 11/16/61
(205) 921-2907
Self-taught pastellist with special interest in impressionistic painting and portraits. Art memberships include a titled membership in the Oil Pastel Association of New York, with charter memberships in the Pastel Society of the West Coast in California, the Degas Pastel Society, of New Orleans, and the National Museum of Women in the Arts, in Washington DC.

ORIENTAL FISH, 21"x17 1/2", Soft pastel, Owned by Mr. DAvid Markham of Tuscaloosa

BETH L. SAGE

310 Ravine Forest Drive, Lake Bluff, IL 60044
Born: 2/9/63
Born in Aberdeen MD, originally from Gaithersburg, MD. Moved to Kansas City, MO where I went to Kansas City Art Institute for training in painting and illustration. My painting concentration to date has been in perceptual nature working in oils. I also like to work in collage and constructions. I now reside in Lake Bluff, IL.

GIRAY HUN, 44 1/2"x 32 1/2", Oil, NFS, Owned by Nihal Emsun of Lake Bluff, IL

MELINDA M. SAMINSKI

45 Cowart Ave., Manasquan, NJ 08736
(201) 223-5937
Freelance New York illustrator currently working on 2 murals and various editorial work. Experienced in broad spectrum of commercial art.   Designed Tiffany style mirrors and etched glass. Extensive window painting and sign work, with expereince in photography.   Published illustrations in several publications.

MICK JAGGER, 18"x 24", Acrylic

ROBERT JOHN SANDERS

930 East 260 St., Euclid, OH 44132
Born: 11/16/61
Represented by CCXA, 23632 Mercantile Rd, Beachwood, OH 44122 (216) 831-8011
(216) 289-6559
After spending most of my life in a small town of Auburn, New York, I continued my education in Pittsburg, PA.   Therefore completing my student identity and pursing a "Professional" job structure which brought me to Cleveland, Ohio to practice my trade amongst my fellow artists.

CRY THE BLUES, 4 1/4"x 5 3/4", Ink, NFS, Owned by artist

BEN SATUREN

2040 East 17th Street, Oakland, cA 94606
Born: 12/10/48
Represented by Colleen Francis, 2040 E. 17th St., Oakland, CA 94606
Underseascape was inspired by snorkeling in the Red Sea. When I record on canvas precise and believable images of undersealife, I combine my photographic and drafting skills with first hand scuba diving observations. Essentially self taught, my paintings and seriagraphs have been exhibited in Los Angeles, San Francisco, Berkeley, Beijing and Shanghai, China.

UNDERSEASCAPE, 37"x72", Oil, NFS, Owned by Steven L. Jarvis, of Torrence, CA

ANTHONY MICHAEL SCARANO
PO Box 541, Santa Cruz, CA 95061
Born: 9/2/51
Represented by Robert L. Kidd Gallery, 107 Townsend St., Birmingham, MI 48011
My mentor Robert Kidd taught me to appreciate the visual arts. I see the medium of photography as the most creative and truthful forms of expression/the camera never lies. It is only reality in an altered form. The best for me is when one of my images affects someone-negatively or positively- while the worst is for someone not to react at all.

FIREWORK FANTASY, Diptych, 40" x 34", Photography, NFS, Owned by Robert Louis Kidd

RON SCARSELLI

311 Isabel Street, Los Angeles, CA 90065
Born: 6/7/55
I consider the work that I do as being "primitive impressionism" with emphasis on form and feeling as opposed to technique. Technique will develop as more images are produced.

THE PATH OF LEAST RESISTANCE, 24"x36", Oil/Canvas, NFS, Owned by Arturo Heredia

AMANDA SCHAFFER

330 E. Bellevue #3, Pasadena, CA 91101
Born: 89/25/59
(818) 449-6738
Born and raised in Michigan, I enjoyed drawing during childhood. After graduating from college with a liberal arts degree, I entered Art Center College of Design in Pasadena. There I discovered painting and found I best expressed myself by using color in a gestural style. I hope to continue finding new ways of applying and combining techniques of paint.

SATURDAY MORNING, 22"x28", Oil, NFS

106

LELA R. SCHAUS

195 Mountain Spring Road, Farmington, CT
06032
Born: 7/21/61
My interests lie in both arts of the past and of
the present. My painting is strongly
influenced by the masters, and I can
appreciate the history as well. I graduated
with a BA in Art History in 1983 from
Denison University, and spent a year in
Florence, Italy painting in 1985. Painting is
something I enjoy and practice on the side,
which might turn to full time.

COMTEMPLATION, 26 1/2" x 19", Oil
on Paper, NFS

CATHERINE SCHMID-MAYBACH

284 32nd Avenue, San Francisco, CA 94121
Born: 8/5/58
I was born in San Francisco. I received a
BFA from California College of Arts and
Crafts in 1980, and a MA from San
francisco State Univ. in 1986. I have lived in
Germany and New York and traveled in
Europe and America. My work is mainly
figurative. I use a variety of clays and
glazing techniques and am combining glass
and metal elements with clay.

UNBEARABLE LIGHTNESS,
6"x6"x23", Clay-glass, $450.00

DEBRA J. SCHNEIDER

17302 SE Todd Place, Gladstone, OR 97027
Born: 11/29/56
Believes capturing the mood or personality of
the subject is one of the most important
aspects of art. Always studying and
practicing at various schools or on own to
improve still. Loves the challenge and
experience of all freelance art jobs. Favorite
medium is oil painting.

GRANDMOTHER'S DEATH, 36"x48",
Oil, NFS, Owned by artist

FRED W. SCHULTZ

8239 Melrose Lane, El Cajon, CA 92021
Born: 10/22/03
Born in Crescent, Iowa on a farm. Attended school in Council Bluffs, Iowa, St. Johns, Winfield, KS and Concordia, St. Louis. First painted in oils in early 1930's. Raised family in Tulsa, OK. No more painting until retirement and moved to Calif. Took only few classes in San Diego. Learned from book and TV artists. Paints only for friends and relatives and personal satisfaction.

PURPLE MOUNTAIN FOSTER BOOK 1954 by Wm F. Powell Inst., 16"x 20", Oil, NFS, Owned by Laura Curtis of Norman, OK

SCHWARTZ & SWANSON

RD10 Churchill Rd., Carmel, NY 10517
Born: 7/29/59 & 7/9/57
(914) 225-1057
Kurt Swanson and Lisa Schwartz have been working together in glass for the past four years. All of their work is collaboratively designed and produced. The incorporate both of their interests, skills and senses of humor, in order to produce sculpture, lighting and vessels that are innovatively designed and express both beauty and wit.

TRAVELERS TROPHY, 21"x6"x7", Blownglass, NFS

SEIHO

c/o Sullivan, Box 111, Foxton, CO 80441
Born: 9/15/40
Represented by Creative Endeavours, 16 Bent Street, Taos, NM 87571
Seiho is the "brush-name" given to M. Justin Sullivan by Harada Kampo, in the classic Japanese tradition. Seiho works entirely with traditional oriental materials to produce works which blend eastern calligraphy and western abstract-expressionism, in both color and black and white. He lives in seclusion in the Colorado Rockies, some forty miles SW of Denver.

KLINE'S GHOST #1, 1986, 30"X42", Sumi Inks, $325.00, Owned by the artist

JUDITH QUITTNER SEIZYS

708 West Grace, Chicago, IL 60613
Born: 8/27/56
aka Jaquin. Encouraged to seek a career other than fine arts, she studied textile design, but soon found graphics at the School of Design, NCSU. She first began painting when corporate design proved dissatisfying in Philadelphia, and is now pursuing freelance graphics and painting in Chicago.

GOLD IN THE GLEN, 30"x30", Acrylics, Owned by Andy Kalman of Century Graphics

MICHAEL F. SHEA

P.O. Box 7299, New York, NY 10116
Born: 1/15/52
Mike has studied at the College of Dupage, the American Academy of Art of Chicago and the Art Students League of New York. He is also a member of the Salmagundi Club of NY. He works in oils, acrylics and ink on canvas. His work in ink can be seen at Taylor's Gallery, Santa Fe, NM. He has also illustrated for Contemporary Books, Inc.

GIRAFFE, 16"x20", Acrylic, NFS, Owned by Kevin and Lynn Dempsey of Chicago, IL

ROSE E. SHOOP

2 East Main St., Waynesboro, PA 17268
Born: 8/6/62
Coming from an artistic family, I was mostly self taught before studying art in college. After obtaining an art degree, I began a small art business from my home, specializing in portraiture. Pencil and watercolor are my main mediums, although I also work in oil. My other interests include animal illustration and murals.

FLAG WAVER, 18"x24", Pencil, NFS, Owned by the artist

YVETTE M. SIKORSKY

P.O. Box 146, Lake Mohegan, NY 10547
Born: 9/9/31
(914) 737-5167
Born in Paris, France. Graduated there. Held designing position. Wallpapers, murals, textiles and fine art in USA. Exhibited for years in France. Received honorable mention in 1965, Bronze medal in 1973 from City of Paris for watercolour. I was at the Salon Des Nations 1985, Exhibiting 14 paintings, among those The Four Horses I have made some video and exhibits in this country.

THE FOUR HORSES, 30"X36", Watercolor, $25,000.00, Owned by the artist

ERICK J. SIMONS

1422 B Del Rio Circle, Concord, CA 94518
Born: 1/23/59
Represented by Daystar Inc.
Born in Lansing MI to Mr. & Mrs. MU Simons, youngest of 4 children. Began photographing simple landscapes at age 10. Graduated high school 1977 in Houghton Lake, MI. Studied fine art at Northern MI Univ. Graduated 1982 BFA. Moved to surburban San Francisco in 1983. Began photographing Californias Sierras in large format. Influence; Ansel Adams, M. Zehnder.

UNTITLED, Photography

ALAN D. SINGER

70 Prospect Park West, Brooklyn, NY
Born: 6/19/50
Represented by Mona Berman Gallery, 168 York St., New Haven, CT 06510 (203) 562-4720
(718) 768-6664
Painter, illustrator, teacher; and writer on art. BFA from Cooper Union, MFA from Cornell University. Recent solo shows at 55 Mercer Street Gallery, NYC and Long Island University. Receipient of awards from Artquest '86, also Skowhega School and Yale University.
AT NIGHT THE DESERT COMES ALIVE, 100"x148", Oil on Linen, $5000.00

110

KATHERYN ANNE SINS

299 Dekalb Avenue #2, Brooklyn, NY
Born: 6/12/53
Represented by Allan Stone Gallery, 48 East
86th Street at Madison Ave., NY.NY 10028
Born in West Leyden, NY. BFA - Syracuse
University 1973. Mst in Art Ed from RIT in
1974. MFA in 1981 from Pratt Institute.
Taught art in college, high schools and
elementary schools for 12 years. Currently
freelance artist in New York City. Current
artwork uses mixed media to survive in New
York - both reflective and humorous.
**RELIQUARY TO ILLUSIVE MS.
LIBERTY - JOURNEY OF THE
BROKEN DOLL,** 9"x12"x8", Mixed
media, $1500.00, Owned by artist

DAVID SKORA

ARI Box 483, New Buffalo, MI 49117
Born: 3/9/58
Graduated with a bachelors degree from
Western Michigan University. My paintings
have been included in various group and one
person exhibitions. I am the recipient of
several awards. For the past 5 years I have
lived and worked in the mid-west.

**ISN'T IT ABOUT TIME YOUR SON
FOUND A JOB,** 60"x48", Acrylic,
$1,500.00, Owned by the artist

DARYL BRENT SMITH

5101 NE 55th #102, Seattle, WA 98105
Born: 10/2/54
Represented by Gallerie Elisabeth, 2119
First Ave., Seattle, WA 98121
Born in Seattle, Daryl earned his bachelor's
degree in art studio and art history/criticism at
the University of California, graduating with
honors in 1982. Since then he has actively
pursued commissions for public sculpture
installations, and has produced several life-
size bronze portraits. His work reflects his
interest in the realities of daily life.

AT GRAM'S, 52"x48"x48", Bronze,
$18,000.00, Owned by Windermere Vista
Apts of Seattle

111

HENRY W. SMITH

P.O. Box 1599, Twain Harte, CA 95383
Born: 5/1/17
Represented by Glory Hole Gallery, 42 So. Washington St., Sondra, CA 95370
Almost a half century ago an art critic praised Henry Smith's ability to paint with subtlety and delicacy the scenes of his native Canada. Today this ability to capture the mood and character of a locality is evident as he depicts scenes of California's Mother Lode, the Sierra's of the ghost towns of the Eastern plateau. He is represented in public and private collections in the US and Canada.

VICTORIA HARBOR, 22"x 30", Watercolor, $1,200.00

LAURETTA JEAN SMITH

RR 2, Box 355-A, Muncie, IN 47302
Born: 3/8/61
Born: Muncie, Indiana. Education: Ball State University: Muncie, IN. Professional art curriculum; fine art/sculptural major. Degree granted: Bachelor of Science, 1985. Shows & Exhibits: BSU 50th Annual student show (juried), Syracuse University., Drawing Exchange. BSU: Solo exhibit Edmund Petty Gallery, Developed new technique for casting plastics.

FRAGMENTARY MATRIX VESSEL III, 15"X 7"X 4", Bronze, $300.00, Owned by artist

NEAL SMITHWILLOW

1657 Squire Dr., Atlanta, GA 30060
Born: 3/25/41
BFA Ringling School of Art, Sarasota, FL 1966
MFA Instituto Allende San Miguel De Allende Guanajuato Mexico 1972

SLEEPER, Oil/Canvas

YUNG KWANG SO

2316 Ashglen Way, San Jose, CA 95133
Born: 1/12/43/
(408) 258-6670
BA in Fine Art from Hong-IK University
1970. First prize in Republic of Korea
Students Art Exhibition 1961. Came to US in
1973. Now US Citizen. Work in oil and
watercolors in art gallery in San Francisco.
Now work in own art studio in San Jose,
CA where subjects are the views, flowers,
animals, figures, etc. Also instructor for
students.

PEACEFULL NOON, 28" x 22", Owned
by artist

BEVERLY SOBIESKI

1922 W. Chicago Ave. 3 East, Chicago, IL
60622
Born: 11/12/49
B. Sobieski is currently the artistic director
for a major party planning company in
Chicago, where she paints renderings,
designs backdrops, and makes oversize
props. Within her 8 year career in this
business she has worked with hundreds of
hotels, TV stations, and has designed parties
for 2 Presidents. Bev has a degree in set
design from Goodman Theatre.

50'S OUTDOOR DRIVE IN DINER,
10'x20', Laytex, $800.00, Owned by Juke
Box Saturday Nite of Chicago

JAN STAFFORD

3535 SW Canby, Portland, OR 97219
Born: 12/7/49
Art education: NYC - studied painting and
illustration; West Virginia - studied graphics
and textiles; Tokyo, Japan studied ink
drawing   Group showings: Art Students
League, NYC, NY - Sunrise Art Gallery,
Charlston, WV and private institute in
Tokyo. Presently working on a showing of
drawings for a gallery in Portland, Oregon

PERSIMMON, 10"x12", Sumi-e, NFS,
Owned by artist

ERNEST A. STIFEL

3245 Countryside Drive, San Mateo, CA
Born: 8/30/59
Represented by Joseph C. Dopson, 359
Northam Ave., San Carlos, CA 94070
Mr. Stifel was born in Denver, Co, and received his degree in art, with an emphasis in painting and printmaking from San Francisco State University. His work has been accepted in numerous local juried art shows and has received several awards. Mr. Stifel prefers doing portraits and figure studies, working in oils or pencil and also acrylics.

PENCIL STUDY FROM 'SPORTS ILLUSTRATED', 10 1/2"x 15", Prismacolor, NFS, Owned by artist

LEONARD ST. JOHN

1528 Walnut St., Berkeley, CA 94709
Born: 5/22/43
Began painting/sculpture 1963 Chicago, IL. Moved to Berkeley in 1967. Colleges: UCB 1967, UCSB 1971, Cal State Univ, 1977-78, UCB 1979-81. Mural at UCSB 36x110 Ft. Musee Cheret, Nice, 1975. Exhibit: Oakland Museum 1970, College of Marin, Black Invitiation 1970. Collections: Esther Bear, NAACP, Prof's E&S Gilbert, UC Davis, APK Van Sergae, Honolulu, HI

BLUE MOON, 32" x 40", Acrylic, $1500.00

LIZ STOCK

Born: 8/12/61
I was born in a remote mountain village in Haiti. When both of my parents died from eating dead peoples brains I was left alone to be raised by a pack of wild sheep and so for many years they taught me their sheep-like ways. Soon after that I jumped a Dutch freighter eating nothing but leaves and roots. Then I drew 50 beautiful pictures. This is one of them.

REINCARNATION, 1'x2', Pen and ink, NFS, Owned by Suzanne Fassl

TREE STOKES

704 N. Stockton St., Stockton, CA 95203
Born: 6/28/51
(209) 466-0137
'81 MFA, ASU, Tempe, AZ. Solo shows: '84 Louisiana World's Fair, Great Hall, New Orleans. Group shows: '85 "Emerald City Classic", Nepenthe Mundi Soc., Wichita, KS. Awards: Best of classic, best of watercolor 2nd, 3rd place. '85 "Ariel Gallery First International Competition", Ariel Gallery, Soho, NY. Private collections: M. Foley, Former Asst Dir Leo Castelli Galleries, NY
VENUS REVISIONED 3, 30"x 22", Watercolor, Owned by R. Kristian Morton of Stockton, CA

TAMARA STRICKHOUSER

421 West Side Drive, #301, Gaithersburg, MD 20878
Born: 5/3/62
(301) 869-2216
Tamara is an accomplished freelance illustrator and graphic designer living in the Washington, DC area. Proficient in a variety of mediums, her diversity has allowed her to work on books, brochures, calendars, annual reports and greeting cards. She has worked for retail and corporate agencies and holds a BFA in illustration from Moore College of Art, Phila.

THE SIX SWANS, 12 1/2"x 15 1/2", Watercolor, $600.00, Owned by artist

THOMAS E. STUBBS

580 East Lemon Ave., Glendora, CA 91740
Born: 10/6/56
Represented by Stein Fine Arts Ltd., 620 North Michigan Ave., Suite 340, Chicago, IL 60611
Thomas E. Stubbs, MA has exhibited in shows in New York and the West Coast. He is carried by two major galleries in Chicago. He is in numerous collections all around the country. In 1983 and 1984 he did two TV presentations for Cox Cable and Metrovision. He is currently an Art instructor at Mt. San Antonio College and the Hollywood Art Center.
FEMINIST REGIME, 15 3/4 "x 20", Watercolor, $1,500.00, Owned by artist

MATHEW SUMICH

2485 Tuscan Rd., Palm Springs, CA 92262
Born: 9/19/31
Designer, sculptor, painter, graphic artist, draftsman, landscape and exhibit designer. Education: Chouinard Art Institute and Isomata. Artwork published in Arch. Digest. Solo Exhibits in private and community colleges. Intl art competition award. Commissioned work private, public and commercial. Designed Palm Springs Desert Museum sculpture gardens.

UNTITLED, 12"x6"x16", Aluminum, NFS, Owned by artist

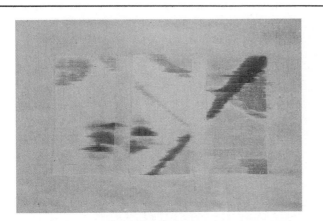

MARIE SUMMERS

46 Castle Street, San Francisco, CA 94133
Born: 3/15/56
Represented by Sarah Volpe Designs, 63 W. 38th St., New York, NY 10018
Marie Summers is a textile artist currently designing fabrics that are represented in New York. She studied art at the University of Calif. Berkeley and the Rochester Institute of Technology, NY. She worked on historical textiles at the Metropolitan Museum, NY and the Textile Museum, Washington DC and studied and worked in Paris, France.

UNTITLED, Silk Damask, unpainted warp, 12"x 18", Textiles, NFS, Owned by artist

SUZANI

10316 Main Street, Fairfax, VA 22030
Born: 5/11/60
Represented by Fairfax Art Supplies, 10316 Main Street, Fairfax, VA 22030 (703) 691-0530
(703) 691-0530
Specializing in realistic pencil renderings, stylized pen and ink, airbrush illustrations and custom typgography. Sophisticated, futuristic, erotic. Gallery Exhibits. Complete portfolio available for review. Prints for sale.

DANCERS, 16"x22", Graphite, NFS, Owned by Christina Little of Fairfax, VA

116

TAMARA SWEGER

1727 Woodland Ave., #18, Palo Alto, CA 94303
Born: 9/2/51
(415) 322-9371
Tamara Sweger was exposed to the world of art from the beginning by her mother, an artist and teacher, and her father who is a photographer. Her accomplishments include painting in oil and acrylic, soft sculpture, papier mache figurines, and full color pen and ink drawings as theme, illustrations for children's books, calendars or note cards.

MAY FLOWER GARDEN, 9"x12", Marking pen, NFS, Owned by artist

TABRA

P.O. Box J, Forest Knolls, CA 94933
Born: 12/31/43
(415) 488-9161

Tabra@ is a jewelry manufacturing company located in Northern California, named after the owner/designer, Tabra Tunoa. The jewlery consists of unusual earrings with a shophisticated gypsy flair made of sterling silver, 14 kt gold-fill, niobium, copper and brass with cascades of glass beads, stars, moons, semiprecious stones, etc. Emphasis is on the unique.

EARWING EARWRAP, Jewelry, $130.00, Onwed by artist

TA TA CHOOK

2615 Granite Creek Road, Santa Cruz, CA 95066
Born: 6/12/48
Born in New York City; graduate Parsons School of Design; BA Goddard College; MA San Jose State Univ. 1983 Grand Prize Central CA. Biennial; 1st Prize Professional 1982 New York Glassmasters Guild; Award "Selections" 1981 Ca. Polytechnical Stan. Univ; member Society of North American Goldsmiths; Glass Art Society; International Sculpture Center; American Craft Council.

DE ANGULO FELLOW, 61"x43"x23", Mixed media, Owned by artist

ROZ TANZMAN

Represented by Grace Mittleman, 80 Quail Close, Irvington, NY 10533
Born: 8/18/40
My art is inspired by the endless energy and mystique of both the city and the natural world. Although much planning precedes each painting, I seek to capture my spontaneous reaction to these subjects. Color, rhythm, and composition are the tools with which I express the vitality that these subjects generate in me.

LOOKING UPTOWN, 66"x 44", Oil, $1,000.00, Owned by artist

JAMES SCOTT TAYLOR

6691 Dorene Place, San Jose, CA 95120
Born: 11/19/57
(08) 375-3528
James Scott Taylor is a noted animal artist, who paints horses, dogs, and cats, as well as exotic wildlife, from lions to llamas. His portraits are included in the private art collections of top Hollywood stars. Taylor is known for capturing the true-to-life personality of each pet he portrays, using a unique, realistic style of watercolor painting.

THE WHITE HORSE, 23" x 27", watercolor, NFS, Owned by private collector

JEANNE WESTRICK TAYLOR

1201 Seafarer Circle #304, Jupiter, FL 33477
Born: 2/26/57
A native of Michigan, I have lived in South Fla and New Orleans for the past 15 years. I have traveled various southern regions including Molokai, Hawaii, a most remote island. From this experience I put forth an entire exhibition of 122 large watercolor paintings along with 7 small ink screens

MOLOKA'I LANDSCAPE, 39"x32", Watercolor, $1,500.00

O. V. TAYLOR

1031 Suntan Lane, Palm Springs, CA 92264
Born: 4/4/32
Represented by Florence Art Gallery, 2500
Cedar Springs, Dallas, TX 75201
EducationBFA Pittsburg St. Univ, Pittsburg,
Kansas. Chounard Art Institute, LA, Calif.
Art Center College of Design, LA, CA.
Exhibitions: One Man Shows - 4 at Gallery
Vanderwoude, Palm Springs, CA, Classic
Potomic MD, Artists I Gallery, Hollywood
Riviera, CA, Gallery 21, Marina del Rey,
CA. Numerous group shows. Publications:
Palm Springs Life, Artists USA, Tennis
Talk, Congoleum.
#320 TWO FIGURES, 72"x48", Mixed
media, $3,l00.00, Owned by artist

SHARON TEABO

P.O. Box 1077, Petersburg, WV 26847
Born: 11/20/52
Represented by Pine Tree Gallery, 11 Pine
Street, Troy, AL 36081
Teabo's work has appeared in various
publications and has been shown in many
group and solo exhibitions across the United
States and part of Europe. She has illustrated
a children's book and currently is adjunct
faculty for Shepherd College in West
Virginia.

ALMOST HEAVEN, 13 1/2"x 15 1/2",
Watercolor, $300.00, Owned by the artist

MAGGIE TERRY-VIALE

2219 Gramercy Ave., Torrance, CA 90501
Born: 7/26/49
Represented by LAART, 112 Mercer St.,
New York, NY 10012
Grants: Pollack-Krasner, 1986; selected
Exhibits: 1986,New Works, LAARt, New
York, NY: Contemporary Women Artists,
Warm Art Gallery, Minneapolis; West Coast
works on paper, Humboldt State University,
Purchase award; all Cal Biennial, Riverside
Art Museum, CA; 1985: State of Art, Orange
Co. Center of Contemporary Art; MFA
Exhibit, For Mason, SF.
RED HOUSE WITH TWO DOORS,
22"x28", Acrylic, $600.00, Owned by the
artist

CRAIG STIRLING THOMPSON

600 E. Ocean #508, Long Beach, CA 90802
Born: 2/10/61
Represented by Jan McGrath, 5549 Romaine, Hollywood, CA 90038 (213) 460-4950
Graduate of the Art Institute of Fort Lauderdale, attended the Colorado Institute of Art. Held title of West Coast Advertising Coordinator for the Guardian Angels. Acrylic on canvas exhibits through Los Angeles.

UNTITLED, 24"x24", Acrylic, $210.12

JOAN THORNTON

12211 Sir Francis Drake, Inverness Park, CA Born: 1/3/32/
Represented by Gallery Route 1, P.O. Box 937, Point Reyes Station, CA 94956 (415) 663-1347
(415) 663-1752
Joan Thornton was born in Massachusetts. She received her MFA in painting from the San Francisco Art Institute. Emphasizing both the irrational and the beautiful in nature, her bold landscapes are lively and personal.

RAVEN ON FENCE, 60"x48", Oil/Canvas, NFS, Owned by Ingrid and Larry Golden of Claremont

TAMARA TISMINETSKY

37-41 81st Street, New York A. Hgts, NY 11372
Born: 1/24/53
MA - 1976 "N. Grigorescu" Academy of Fine Arts - Buch. Worked there and in New York since 80 as fashion designer, illustrator and art instructor. The art works have been exhibited in Buchare St. - at "Atelier 35" - 78, "Hanulcu Tei" Galleries - 79, Paris - "Le Salon International de L'artisanat d'art" - '84

Group Shows. Certificate of Honor - Design International (San Francisco) 1985.

BLACK AND WHITE, 201/2"x 16 1/2", Watercolor, $300.00, Owned by artist

WING TONG

19 Home Place (West) #5, Oakland, CA
93610
Born: 9/30/63
Born in Hong Kong. I am the youngest of
four. My family migrated to the US in 1969
and arrived in Sacto, CA where I spent my
youthful years. After graduating from
McClatcy High, I went onto college at UCB.
4 years later, I got my BA in architecture.
My first work, Metropolis, was completed in
1983. My specialties are photo-realism and
impressionism.

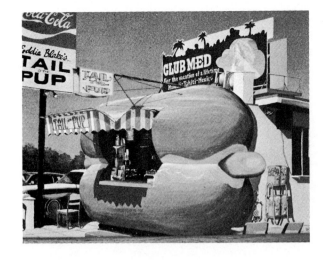

TAIL OF THE PUP, 18"x 24", Acrylic,
NFS, Owned by artist

CARMEN TOSTADO

P.O. Box 7943, Long Beach, CA 90807
Born: 1/10/49
1977-BFA Calif State University LB. 1981-
MFA UCLA 1983 Architectonic Install LB
1985 "Screens by Artists" Kuhlen Schmidt-
Simon Gallery LA CA 1984. "Olympic
Exhibition" Caponigro Gallery, 1983. Shakti
Gallery "3 Artists" LB, CA 1982.
"Stoffwechsel KI8 Kassel, West Germany
1981 . Installation Wight Art Gallery
UCLA, 1980 Zerox Book, 1980 UCEM
Gallery UCSB and 667861 West Germany

TUNNEL WALL 1986, X 1/2"x6"x16",
Mixed media, NFS, Owned by artist

CHERYL TROTTER

461 Gibson Avenue, Pacific Grove, CA
93950
Born: 2/25/58
Represented by Robin Colgan, 5351 Godbey
Drive, La Canada-Filtridge, CA 91011
Cheryl Trotter received a certificate of
achievement in photography from Monterey
Peninsula College in 1981. Her non-silver
photographic prints are produced by the 19th
Century cyanotype process, on which she
then watercolors.

**STILL WATERS, WATER COLORED
CYANOTYPE,** 14"x11", Mixed media,
$200.00, Owned by artist

BARBARA G. TUMMOLO

12 Greenridge Way, Spring Valley, NY 10977
Born: 1/5/56
Attended school of Visual Arts, Parson School of Design in NYC, University of Miami and then San Francisco Art Institute. Barbara has been painting for 15 years professionally and has had a few local one-woman exhibits. Presently taking commissions for portraits with a special love and talent for painting animals photorealist. Seeks a gallery for representation.

TARA AT MY FEET, 30"x36", Oil, $800.00, Owned by artist

SUSAN TOURNAI

446 School Road, Novato, CA 94947
Born: 11/3/57
I am a native Californian. I attended the California College of Arts and Crafts in Oakland, CA. My work is an attempt to bring into view useen aspects of life, to give others a means through which they may look inside.

TO BE A FAIR WITNESS, 32"x40", Mixed media, $350.00, Owned by artist

RICHARD B. VALDES

2202 Northside Drive, Montebello, CA 90640
Born: 5/20/49
Represented by Goez Art Gallery, E-13 Olvera Street, Los Angeles, CA 90012 (213) 617-7642
(213) 728-3412
Born in East Los Angeles, and known locally for 18 years, I have sold many oil paintings to private collectors. I have never had a one man show in a gallery. In 1971 I received a BFDA at Chouinard Art School.

PUEBLO, SCENE, 12"x16", Oil, NFS, Owned by Tom and Helen Snyder of Glendale, CA

122

VITORIA

18722 CR 14, Bristol, IN 46507
Born: 1/25/37
Exhibits: Midwest Museum of Art in 1982-84, Council Del Artists 1973, Matrix GAllery 1982, Greenhill Gallery, Phil. 1972, Delaware Art Museum 1972
Education BFDA Mass College of Art 1959, MFA Cranbrook Academy of Art MI 1961, Pro Exp Univ. Del Asst Prof Art 1969-73, Millersville Col of Art, PA Asst. Prof Art 1968-69, Ind. Univ. Instructor 1964-68.

COUTURE, 36"x51 1/2", Mixed paper, Owned by artist

GERALD A. WAGNER

535 Delaware Avenue, Glassport, PA 15045
Born: 3/7/55
Craftsman's Gallery, NY
Incorporated Gallery, NY
Elements Gaqllery, Conn.
Ten Arrrow, Mass.
The Clay Place, PA
Sylvia Ullman Gallery, OH
Martha Schneider Gallery, ILL
Clay & Fiber Gallery, NM
Ree Schonlau Gallery, Neb
Elizabeth Fortner Gallery, CA
Free Hand, CA
Susan Cummins Gallery, CA
TURQUOISE VESSEL, 5"x15"x14", Ceramic, NFS

DAVID WALKER

P.O. BOx 388, Boonville, CA 95415
Born: 1/13/59
(707) 895-2144
Born in Long Beach, California. Lives and maintains
studio in Boonville, CA. He is a self taught artist. Holds a SOC full-time vocational teaching credential for having over nine thousand hours independent work in the fields of art and design. Current work on display in the St. Eligius Figurative Sculpture Gallery, 1748 Union St., SF

FACE POT POP, 12"x9"x9", Terra Cotta, $485.00

RAPHAEL LYLE WARKEL

Box 772, Carmel, IN 46032
Born: 6/27/42
Represented by Traci's Recollection, Box 772, Carmel, IN 46032 (317) 846-3719
Realist oil painter and illustrator born in Phila. Although primarily self-taught, he has had some formal training at the Art League in Indianapolis. He paints sensuous women in the nude in mysterious or erotic situations with psychological and surrealistic undertones. An added symobolic content is used to solidify the structure of his painting.

BLOND WITH CLOWNS, 30": x 24", Oil, NFS, In private collection

LIZ WASP

170 Willow Ave., Fairfax, CA 94930
Born: 11/2/54
Holds a BFA degree from the California College of Arts and Crafts. Professional in the ceramic ware industry. Along with maintaining a personal studio for development of personal artistic exploration. Presently a freelance artist producing murals, sculpture, decorative and functional ware.

AMIGA, 24"x32", Ceramic, $650.00, Owned by artist

MARION WEBER

Bolinas, CA 94924
(415) 868-2113
Associated with Artisans in Mill Valley. Focus is art for healing. Does her own work by presenting images and works with clients to bring forth imagery. Does sandtray with cancer patients at Commonweal in Bolinas "through play the participants activates the powers of unconscious imagery which awake and constitute the healing process:. First one lady exhibit "Art as a Healing Foce" at Artisans, April 1985.

IRIS, 4'x 4', Owned by William and Elizabeth Collins of Berkeley

HARRY WEISBURD

Box 10036, Oakland, CA 94610
Born: 2/18/38
Represented by Farnsworth Gallery, 2426
Fillmore Street, San Francisco, CA 94115
(415) 824-1554
Born NYC. MFA, California College of Arts
and Crafts, Oakland, CA. Numerous one
man shows: Boston, NY, SF. Work in
numerous private, public collections,
including Bank of America and Holiday Inns.
Mr. Weisburd has been a professor of Art,
Univ. of Connecticut, and Westfield State
College, MA. He has also won numerous
awards and prizes on both coasts.
YELLOW SAND, 32"x40", Acrylic,
$2,300.00, Owned by artist

DANIEL M. WENK

8207 S. Newland, Burbank, IL 60459
Born: 6/6/64
(312) 430-4814
Daniel M. Wenk is a graduate of Northern
Illinois University with a BFA in Illustration.
Although skilled in many forms of media,
Mr. Wenk prefers working mostly in water
colors. He is currently freelancing out of his
home near Chicago, Ill.

PORTRAIT OF ARTIST, 11"x14",
Watercolor, NFS, Onwed by Y.M. Avery

MICHELE WESEN

235 West 75th St. , New York, NY 10023
Born: 6/1/54
At 32, Michele Wesen is an established
illustrator of mens', womens'., and childrens
wear for magazines, brochure, catalogs and
retail advertising. Educated at St. Martins
School of Art in London and Parsons School
of Design in NY, she worked hard learning
to draw well and avoid cliche. Michele
works in NYC and recovers on weekends in
Ulster County.

125

BRAD WEST

3009 E. Brill, Phoenix, AZ 85008
Born: 11/5/59
(602) 244-0236
Brad West began drawing at an early age.
BFA from Arizona State University. West
persues illustration and fine art with both
drawing and painting. An ongoing interest is
films and he would like to get involved in
production of storyboards.

UNTITLED PROMOTIONAL PIECE,
22"x30", Mixed media, NFS, Owned by
artist

JAMES A. WHITNEY

56 Spring VAlley Rd., Oradell, NJ 07649
Born: 1/25/52
Born in Teaheck, NJ, graduated from
Bergenfield HS in 1971 majoring in design
and fine arts. Employed as a packaging
engineer for the past 6 yrs. Interests in
sculpture, engraving, oil painting, sketching,
pastels, chalk and photography. Several first
place awards in local art shows. Present art
exhibit at the Patton Museum, Fort Knox,
KY . Married with 2 children.

WINE DRINKERS, 18"x24", NFS,
Owned by Lt. Comm. Michael Giorgino of
Newport, RI

NOEL ANNE WILKINS

881 Lorraine #207, Wheaton, IL 60187
Born: 2/8/63
Graduated from the School of The Art
Institute of Chicago. I work primarily in
pastels and oilsticks, creating images
concerning the psychological conditions of
urban life. I am currently living in the
Chicagoland area.

MEN WITHOUT CLASS, 15"x20",
Oilsticks, NFS

126

BUD WILLE

9230 SW 178 St., Miami, FL 33157
Born: 3/30/33
(305) 255-2362
Growing up on the horicon marsh and the woods of Wisconsin prompted my love for wildlife and the outdoors. Sketching birds at an early age soon turned to painting, carving and photographing all types of wildlife. Freezing an exciting scene on canvas so it can be remembered forever is the greatest reward in painting.

WINTER WIDGEON, 22"x28", Acrylics, $250.00, Owned by artist

VALERY A. WOLFE

48A Shirley Lane, Jamestown, NY 14701
Born: 4/26/31
(716) 664-6765
The artist has worked in all fine arts media and has done various types of art, eg . painting, school logo, history books, art on printed pamphlets, programs, booklets, oil painted photos, interior decorating. Gives private art instruction. She has judged exhibits and has been honored many times for her own work in exhibits and showings.

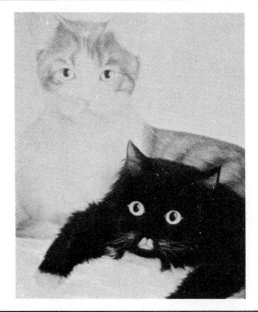

CAT PORTRAIT-TIGER AND BOOTSY, 24"x30", Oil, NFS, Owned by Gayle Howell of Florida

KAREN FRIMKESS WOLFF

431 Venice Blvd., Los Angeles, CA 90015
Born: 12/30/40
(213) 748-1822
Born in Los Angeles, CA. Studied at UCLA. Began work with sound as a graphic medium in 1974. Makes drawings with paper and on cavnas with dry pigment and pencil. Uses sound media (words on tape, electronic tones or bells) in drawing environments. Subjects usually derive from feelings or responses to events. Major works involve change, motion and passing time.

RESURRECTION, 60"x90"x60", Electronics, wood, celotex and paint, NFS

STEPHEN K. H. WONG

1212 Masonic Avenue, Berkeley, CA 94706
Born: 3/13/41
Represented by Art Co-op, 1652 Shattuck Avenue, Berkeley, CA 94709
Born Ipoh, Malaysia
Education Kirkby College, England, 1961. CCAC Oakland 1973. BFA with distinction 1983. One man show Chinese Cultural Center, San Francisco, 1984 Award in drawing, Berkeley Art Center, 1985. Juror's merit award Pacific States print and drawing show, Hawaii 1985. Bay Arts San Mateo County, CA.

SELF-PORTRAIT, 44"x48", Oil, NFS, Owned by artist

RALPH M. WYSER

14552 Martha St., Van Nuys, CA 91411
Born: 9/13/26
Wyser has been a representational oil painter of the western USA since 1963. Born and educated in Zurich, Switzerland and now lives in Van Nuys, CA, since 1967. He has studied at Long Beach City College and was a pupil of Arden Von Dewitz. He has traveled and worked in Europe, Australia and Alaska. He is an active member of the San Fernando Valley Art Club.

MINING SHACKS RANDSBURG MINING DISTRICT CALIFORNIA, 16"x20", Oil, $150.00, Owned by artist

NOTES TO ARTISTS

Having been an artists agent for some time and then participating with the publication of this book, I feel that the following information will be of assistance to those artists who might be new in promoting themselves.

I have found it usually best to procure an agent. One that you can trust, and also get along with, as you will be spending much time conversing about different aspects of your art and the business world. Most artists need to keep their energy in the direction of the creative mode. If you have an agent that works for you, you will have more time to devote to your creativity. The freedom of this arrangement can be immense for an artist.

The agent is not there to change your morals or standards of painting, but to promote your present works, and those that come in the future. If the agent doesn't have a clear understanding of your mode of painting, they probably aren't the correct agent.

If you wish to continue without an agent, there are some notes that you might try to follow:

When sending information to publishers, send only what they request. i.e. a short biography; this most likely means 1 page or at the most 2 pages. Volumes of literature are to cumbersome, unless it is specifically requested. If you are unsure what to send, it is better to call and ask, or be as concise as you can in what you send.

When sending slides to ANYONE (gallery, publisher, friend), send them in the clear plastic sheets that you can buy at photo stores. (Glass slides should not be sent through the mail). Any other means of protection is not really necessary. In this way they are very easy to pull out and view. When a publisher gets a slide wrapped in 10 layers of paper and scotch taped shut, it is very frustrating to open . Make it as easy as possible for the viewer to easily see the slide. Also mark clearly the top front, as well as noting on the slide the title and your last name.

Best of luck in your career.........

Constance Franklin

If you are interested in becoming part of the next publication please send a brief statement (no more than one page) and 2 color slides of what you feel is your most representative work. When considering the slide you send please make sure:

1. It is full frame, or screened off with appropriate tape
2. It is in focus
3. It does not include anything but the piece of art (no friends, pets, or self)
4. Mark clearly on the slide the top front viewing point.
5. Also note the title, and your last name on the slide.

When taking slides use a solid white background for paintings, drawings and sculpture. Use a solid dark background for white marble or chrome sculptures. Large scale murals should have a detail singled out for better reading and/or use a 2 slides. Don't use any scotch tape or glue.

Enclose a self addressed stamped envelope and mail to Directors Guild Publishers, P.O. Box 369, Renaissance, CA 95962. Please write "ATTN: 1988 " on envelope for easier separation.

Should your piece not be selected, it will be returned in the self addressed stamped envelope (make sure the return envelope has the same amount of postage as it took to send the original).

We will begin choosing slides in March for the 1988 edition.

SHARKS

First edition, second revise
Published by Reader's Digest (Australia) Pty Ltd
26-32 Waterloo Street, Surry Hills, NSW 2010

Reprinted 1994, 1995

Edited and designed by Capricorn Press Pty Ltd (Inc. in NSW)
3/9 Oaks Avenue, Dee Why, NSW 2099

National Library of Australia
cataloguing-in-publication data
Sharks, silent hunters of the deep
    Includes index.
    ISBN 0 86438 047X.
    1. Sharks. I. Reader's Digest (Australia) Pty Ltd
597'.31

SHARKS
Silent hunters of the deep

Reader's Digest

Sydney London New York Montreal Cape Town

Contributors

Alice Alston

Ian Close, BA(Hons)

Perry W. Gilbert, PhD
is Director Emeritus of the Mote Marine Laboratory, Sarasota, Florida, and Professor Emeritus of Neurobiology and Behavior at Cornell University, Ithaca, New York. He has studied the biology and behaviour of sharks in many parts of the world for the past 45 years, and is currently working with the sensory and reproductive systems of sharks.

Peter Goadby
is a world famous Australian big game fisherman with a special interest in sharks. He is a regular contributor to many international publications and has one of Australia's best private collections of rare books on fish and fishing.

Robert Pullan

Olaf Ruhen

Julian G. Pepperell, BSc (Hons), PhD
has worked in the field of marine recreational fisheries for over 10 years. He is a senior biologist with the Fisheries Research Institute, NSW Department of Agriculture, and specialises in the study of large pelagic predatory fishes. He is responsible for the Australian Gamefish Tagging Programme.

Ron and Valerie Taylor
are perhaps the best known husband and wife diving team. Their work with sharks, particularly the large, dangerous species, has given them more practical experience in this field than anyone else in the world.

Susan Turner, PhD, AMA, FGS, FLS
is an Honory Research Fellow of the Queensland Museum. She has studied the ancient jawless fishes — the thelodonts — for 20 years, and the similarity of their scales to those of modern sharks led to her study of cartilaginous fishes. Since 1980 she has been researching fossil sharks from Australia and China.

C. Scott Johnson, PhD
was trained as a physicist, and has spent the past 23 years studying hearing and echolocation in dolphins, shark behaviour, the electrical senses of sharks and various countermeasures to the dangerous species.

Noel R. Kemp, DDA, DipEd, MSc, MAIG
has been Curator of Geology at the Tasmanian Museum since 1973. Among his particular interests are the teeth of sharks from the last 70 million years, the taxonomy of these fossils, and their relationships to modern species.

Nick Otway, BSc(Hons)
is conducting marine biological research for his doctorate at the University of Sydney. His research interests lie in the field of experimental marine ecology, and he has participated in several shark tagging studies while working with the CSIRO.

Design
Lawrence Hanley

Art
Alistair Barnard

Head of a grey nurse shark.

Contents

Gills slits and pectoral
fin of a grey nurse shark.

Head of a grey nurse shark
Eugomphodus taurus.

World of the shark

Men and sharks

Denticles glisten on the skin of a grey nurse shark.

Facts about sharks and shark attack

INTRODUCTION

Few creatures on earth are as much feared, and as little understood, as sharks. Lions eat people; they are given special reserves and the title 'King of the Beasts'. Sharks eat people; their name has become a byword for ferocity, and people demand their extermination.

For centuries sharks have been merely objects of terror. A real understanding of their lives and habits only came with the invention and development of free-diving equipment after World War II. We were among the first to film sharks underwater in the 1950s, and have taken an active part ever since in bringing the extraordinary wonders of the ocean world to a wider audience through film, television and still photography.

We hope that this magnificent book will help readers to see sharks as we do – to appreciate the important role that they play in the complex web of underwater life. Certainly large sharks can be terrifying creatures. They are formidable and efficient predators and demand respect. Certainly people are occasionally injured, or even killed by them, and few deaths can be as terrible. We ourselves have been frightened on occasions during the 30 years we have worked closely with large, so called 'maneating', sharks. We have been jostled and bumped by them as they snatched food from the water around us, yet we have only ever received minor, accidental injuries. The truth is that most sharks ignore people – they are neither friends nor enemies.

Many eminent, internationally renowned scientists, researchers, writers and photographers have contributed to this important book. All are experts in their own fields, and over the years we have had the pleasure of working with many of them in their attempts to unravel the mysteries of shark biology and behaviour. Their contributions have brought together all the important facts about sharks, in what is certainly the most informative, entertaining and beautifully illustrated book ever published on this subject.

Many people will be drawn to this book by the terrifying stories it contains. We hope that they will come away with a greater appreciation of a sadly misunderstood group of complex and fascinating creatures.

Ron &
Valerie Taylor

A sinister shape, lurking in the shadows – two divers confront the ultimate underwater nightmare. Despite its menacing appearance, this grey nurse shark is quite harmless.

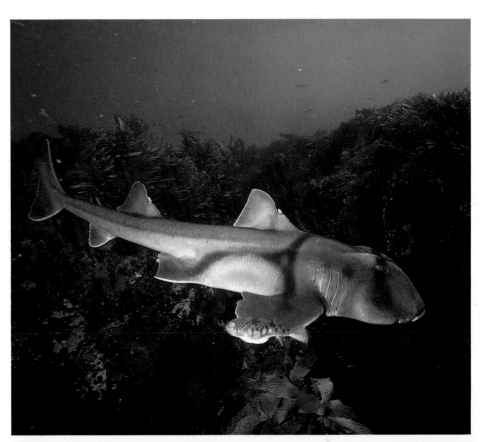

Sharks are an extraordinarily diverse group of creatures – only a minority conform to the popular, sleek, 'maneater' image. Illustrated here are a wobbegong (above), a Port Jackson shark (right) and a hammerhead (below), all from Australian waters.

Tab. VII

Mandibula Canis marini
des meer hunds gebis.

Canis Carcharix
dentium series
Meer hund gebis

2

1

Galeus
Centrina dictus

Sawhund

4

Vulpecula Marina

Fuchs Hund Meer fuchs

3

Alius Galeus seu Centrina
Sauhund ander aert

5

6

Simia Marina

Meer Aff

Simia Marina Danica

7

8

Zygana

Meerschlegel

Meerwag

Zygæna seu

Libella altera

9

Part One

1

World of the Shark

Sharks are difficult
to study. Many details
of their lives remain a
mystery to this day. The
extraordinary behaviour of this
ancient group of animals and
their strange abilities are
only now beginning to be
understood by scientists.

Illustrations of sharks
from Conrad Gesner's
Fisch-Buch, first
published in 1670.

Realm Of The Shark

For most people the watery world inhabited by sharks is almost as alien as the surface of another planet. Even the most experienced of divers are usually restricted to nearshore waters. The great ocean depths – little known and little explored – still harbour many mysteries.

The earth, viewed from far above the Pacific Ocean, deserves the name given to it by astronauts: the blue planet. This one ocean alone covers 181.3 million sq. km (70 million sq. miles), and is 17 700 km (11 000 miles) across at its widest.

The motions of the atmosphere, traced out by clouds, and the size of the oceans dominate the view of earth from space. So vast are the oceans, in fact, that they take up almost 71 per cent of the entire surface of the globe. The combined area of the oceans and seas is 361 million sq. km (139 million sq. miles).

The oceans of the earth have an average depth of 3730 m (12 230 ft), and reach their deepest point in the Marianas Trench in the north-western Pacific Ocean at 11 038 m (36 204 ft) below sea level. The ocean basins hold at least 1185 million cu. km (285 cu. miles) of water. Scientists believe that this vast quantity of water arose from the earth's interior as it cooled.

The water in the oceans and seas is a solution of many elements and chemical compounds which give it its distinctive salty taste. After some early fluctuations, the chemical composition of seawater stabilised, and it has remained more or less the same since early Palaeozoic times, about 600 million years ago.

Approximately 2730 million tonnes of dissolved solids are poured into the oceans each year by rivers. This material is almost enough to account for the saltiness of seawater, but analysis shows that there are more of some elements in the oceans than there are in river water, so there must be another source of dissolved minerals.

This additional source was not found until about the middle of this century when the mechanisms responsible for continental drift were investigated. Meandering through the ocean basins are the mid-ocean ridges where fresh rock flows up from deep in the earth, causing the sea floor to spread. Accompanying this rock are virgin waters rich in salts and trace-elements that are less abundant in water that runs off the land.

The total quantity of dissolved solids in seawater – its salinity – is about 35 parts per thousand, and oceanic water generally ranges from 34 to 37 parts per thousand. Variations from place to place are due to factors such as rainfall, evaporation, biological activity and radioactive decay.

Fresh supplies of salts are now being added to the oceans at roughly the same rate they are being removed by various physical, chemical and biological processes.

Measures of salinity do not include the dissolved gases in ocean water, many of which are important to marine life. All of the gases found in the atmosphere are also present in seawater, and the major ones in air – nitrogen, oxygen, argon and carbon dioxide – are also the most abundant gases in the oceans. The gases come from a variety of sources. Nitrogen, for example, enters the ocean dissolved in rainwater, whereas oxygen is produced by marine plants during photosynthesis, and also enters through the aerating action of waves. Factors such as temperature, salinity, depth, the state of the sea surface and biological activity all affect the distribution and abundance of gases.

The temperature of the oceans varies enormously according to season, latitude and depth. The warmest waters are at the surface near the equator where they average about 28°C (82.4°F). The coldest waters are found in the depths of the Arctic and Southern Oceans where the average is -2°C

IN THE DEPTHS OF THE OCEAN

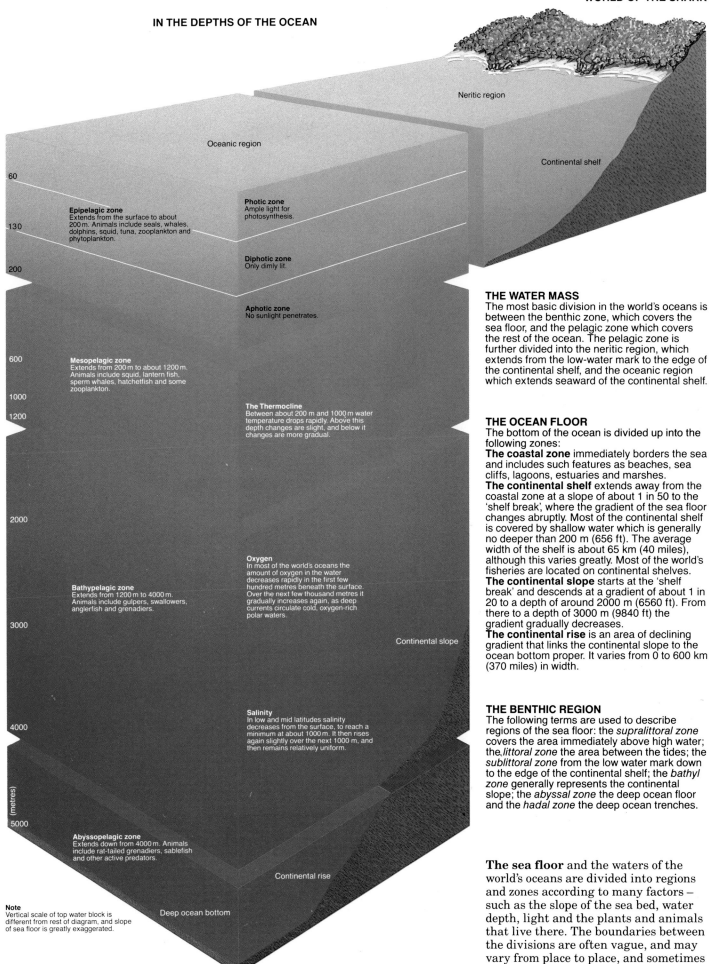

Oceanic region

Neritic region

Continental shelf

60

Epipelagic zone
Extends from the surface to about 200 m. Animals include seals, whales, dolphins, squid, tuna, zooplankton and phytoplankton.

Photic zone
Ample light for photosynthesis.

130

200

Diphotic zone
Only dimly lit.

Aphotic zone
No sunlight penetrates.

600

Mesopelagic zone
Extends from 200 m to about 1200 m. Animals include squid, lantern fish, sperm whales, hatchetfish and some zooplankton.

1000

1200

The Thermocline
Between about 200 m and 1000 m water temperature drops rapidly. Above this depth changes are slight, and below it changes are more gradual.

2000

Oxygen
In most of the world's oceans the amount of oxygen in the water decreases rapidly in the first few hundred metres beneath the surface. Over the next few thousand metres it gradually increases again, as deep currents circulate cold, oxygen-rich polar waters.

Bathypelagic zone
Extends from 1200 m to 4000 m. Animals include gulpers, swallowers, anglerfish and grenadiers.

3000

Continental slope

Salinity
In low and mid latitudes salinity decreases from the surface, to reach a minimum at about 1000 m. It then rises again slightly over the next 1000 m, and then remains relatively uniform.

4000

(metres)

5000

Abyssopelagic zone
Extends down from 4000 m. Animals include rat-tailed grenadiers, sablefish and other active predators.

Continental rise

Note
Vertical scale of top water block is different from rest of diagram, and slope of sea floor is greatly exaggerated.

Deep ocean bottom

THE WATER MASS
The most basic division in the world's oceans is between the benthic zone, which covers the sea floor, and the pelagic zone which covers the rest of the ocean. The pelagic zone is further divided into the neritic region, which extends from the low-water mark to the edge of the continental shelf, and the oceanic region which extends seaward of the continental shelf.

THE OCEAN FLOOR
The bottom of the ocean is divided up into the following zones:
The coastal zone immediately borders the sea and includes such features as beaches, sea cliffs, lagoons, estuaries and marshes.
The continental shelf extends away from the coastal zone at a slope of about 1 in 50 to the 'shelf break', where the gradient of the sea floor changes abruptly. Most of the continental shelf is covered by shallow water which is generally no deeper than 200 m (656 ft). The average width of the shelf is about 65 km (40 miles), although this varies greatly. Most of the world's fisheries are located on continental shelves.
The continental slope starts at the 'shelf break' and descends at a gradient of about 1 in 20 to a depth of around 2000 m (6560 ft). From there to a depth of 3000 m (9840 ft) the gradient gradually decreases.
The continental rise is an area of declining gradient that links the continental slope to the ocean bottom proper. It varies from 0 to 600 km (370 miles) in width.

THE BENTHIC REGION
The following terms are used to describe regions of the sea floor: the *supralittoral zone* covers the area immediately above high water; the *littoral zone* the area between the tides; the *sublittoral zone* from the low water mark down to the edge of the continental shelf; the *bathyl zone* generally represents the continental slope; the *abyssal zone* the deep ocean floor and the *hadal zone* the deep ocean trenches.

The sea floor and the waters of the world's oceans are divided into regions and zones according to many factors — such as the slope of the sea bed, water depth, light and the plants and animals that live there. The boundaries between the divisions are often vague, and may vary from place to place, and sometimes even from one time of year to another.

Invertebrates are one of two major divisions of the animal kingdom. The name means 'without a backbone', but apart from this distinction most have little else in common. The group ranges from plankton to jellyfish and from worms to prawns.

Vertebrates – animals with backbones – include all the most highly evolved creatures on earth. The most numerous vertebrates in the oceans are the bony fishes, but the group also includes whales, dolphins, seals, turtles and of course sharks and rays.

(28.4°F). Radiation from the sun is the most important source of heat for the oceans, but radioactive decay and heat from the earth's interior also contribute. Currents in the oceans and atmosphere distribute the heat around the globe.

Temperature and salinity are critical to life in the oceans because they can affect the rate at which chemical reactions take place, including those involving the enzymes essential to all living cells. As a consequence, many animals can only live in water where temperature and salinity fluctuate slightly. Others, however, can tolerate conditions which vary a good deal.

Many of the salts in the oceans, especially the calcium salts, are used to build animal skeletons. The shells of molluscs, the spines and tests (cases) of sea urchins and the teeth and bones of fish are all made up mostly of calcium carbonate absorbed from water. Nitrates and phosphates, also present in seawater, are essential to plant growth and are easily extracted and used. The concentrations of these chemical compounds can directly affect the number of phytoplankton – tiny floating plants – in the water.

A final vital component of seawater, and an important source of food for many ocean dwellers, are the millions of tiny particles of organic matter that come from dead and decaying plants and animals. A constant rain of these particles sinks gradually to the ocean floor, often to be returned to the surface by currents.

The energy that drives the ocean's circulation comes almost exclusively from the sun. Surface currents transport enormous volumes of warm water to the polar regions, while deep currents move water from one hemisphere to the other. On a smaller scale, storms and strong winds may cause local upwellings of cold water.

Ocean currents also play an

Zooplankton

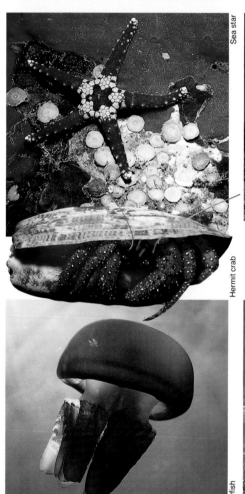

Sea star

Hermit crab

Jellyfish

Galapagos shark

Loggerhead turtle

Coral cod

Fur seal

important role in distributing gases throughout the ocean. Descending currents at the poles, for example, take oxygen-rich surface water to the ocean depths where it is used by the animals living on or near the sea bed.

Light is extremely important to life in the oceans because it is needed by plants for photosynthesis – the process by which sugar is created from carbon dioxide and water, using light for energy.

Sunlight can only penetrate to a maximum depth of 600 m (1970 ft) in clear seawater, although the actual amount of light at any depth can vary from place to place for many reasons, including reflection from the water surface, refraction, and the murkiness of the water. This means that marine plants can only live in the upper part of the oceans where there is sufficient light for photosynthesis. The distribution of plants in turn governs the areas where plant-eating animals can live. Light also affects the behaviour of animals in the ocean – many rise to the surface to feed at night.

The oceans can be divided into two basic regions, the benthic and the pelagic – the former covering the ocean floor and the latter the rest of the water mass. Organisms that live in the pelagic zone are known either as nekton – the active, free-swimming animals – or plankton – small plants and animals that float or drift passively near the water surface. There are two types of plankton – the phytoplankton, made up of millions of microscopic plants, and the zooplankton, tiny animals which include the eggs and larvae of many of the ocean's larger inhabitants.

Phytoplankton are the primary producers of the ocean. They convert energy from the sun into living plant tissue, and thus form the basis of most food chains. As much as 80 to 90 per cent of all the photosynthetic activity that takes place on earth is carried out in the upper 100 m (328 ft) of the oceans.

Zooplankton are usually much larger than phytoplankton, although many are less than 10 mm (0.4 in) long. Most of them can swim, although they are usually only able to travel up and down through the water. Zooplankton generally feed on phytoplankton, and they are therefore the second step in the food chain, coverting plant into animal tissue. Zoo-plankton are, in turn, preyed on by larger animals such as fish, squid and some sharks.

Most free-swimming animals in the oceans are vertebrates – they have backbones – such as sharks,

OCEAN FOOD CHAINS

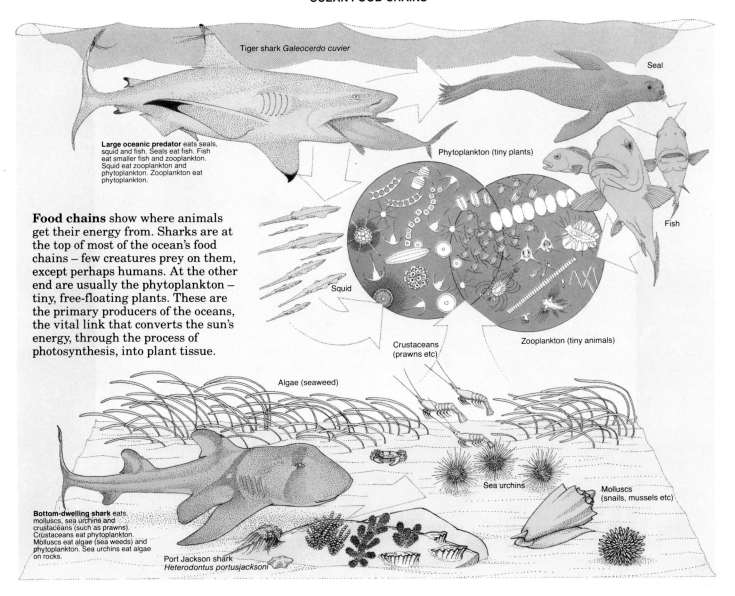

Tiger shark *Galeocerdo cuvier*

Seal

Large oceanic predator eats seals, squid and fish. Seals eat fish. Fish eat smaller fish and zooplankton. Squid eat zooplankton and phytoplankton. Zooplankton eat phytoplankton.

Phytoplankton (tiny plants)

Fish

Food chains show where animals get their energy from. Sharks are at the top of most of the ocean's food chains – few creatures prey on them, except perhaps humans. At the other end are usually the phytoplankton – tiny, free-floating plants. These are the primary producers of the oceans, the vital link that converts the sun's energy, through the process of photosynthesis, into plant tissue.

Squid

Crustaceans (prawns etc)

Zooplankton (tiny animals)

Algae (seaweed)

Sea urchins

Molluscs (snails, mussels etc)

Bottom-dwelling shark eats molluscs, sea urchins and crustaceans (such as prawns). Crustaceans eat phytoplankton. Molluscs eat algae (sea weeds) and phytoplankton. Sea urchins eat algae on rocks.

Port Jackson shark *Heterodontus portusjacksoni*

Bony fishes have evolved along quite a different path to that taken by the sharks, and they are the most successful of the ocean's vertebrates. There are at least 20 000 (known) species alive today, and they may be found in salt and fresh water, in almost every part of the globe.

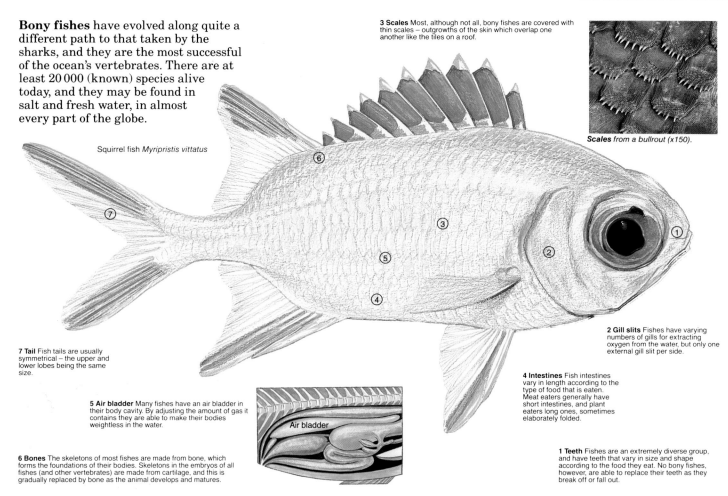

3 Scales Most, although not all, bony fishes are covered with thin scales – outgrowths of the skin which overlap one another like the tiles on a roof.

Scales from a bullrout (x150).

Squirrel fish *Myripristis vittatus*

Air bladder

7 Tail Fish tails are usually symmetrical – the upper and lower lobes being the same size.

5 Air bladder Many fishes have an air bladder in their body cavity. By adjusting the amount of gas it contains they are able to make their bodies weightless in the water.

6 Bones The skeletons of most fishes are made from bone, which forms the foundations of their bodies. Skeletons in the embryos of all fishes (and other vertebrates) are made from cartilage, and this is gradually replaced by bone as the animal develops and matures.

2 Gill slits Fishes have varying numbers of gills for extracting oxygen from the water, but only one external gill slit per side.

4 Intestines Fish intestines vary in length according to the type of food that is eaten. Meat eaters generally have short intestines, and plant eaters long ones, sometimes elaborately folded.

1 Teeth Fishes are an extremely diverse group, and have teeth that vary in size and shape according to the food they eat. No bony fishes, however, are able to replace their teeth as they break off or fall out.

tuna, herring and whales. These animals are generally carnivorous, preying on zooplankton or other vertebrates. In contrast to these free-swimming animals, there are those that live on the sea floor which are either permanently attached to rocks, or are relatively slow moving. They include crabs, lobsters, abalone, oysters, starfish, sea urchins, corals and sponges. The plants that live on the sea floor, such as green, brown and red algae (seaweeds), are restricted to areas that are reached by enough sunlight for photosynthesis.

Many of the animals that live in the oceans share a phase of their life cycles, when their eggs or larvae, or both, become part of the zooplankton. They are then food for other zooplankton and many free-swimming species, and are also completely at the mercy of ocean

currents which can transport them over great distances.

The free-swimming animals of the oceans are dominated by the fishes, sharks and rays. The structure of a fish body is designed for ease of movement, and this is especially true of the sharks. This ability to move easily, without having to rely on water currents to carry them about, has enabled fishes to exploit most parts of the world's oceans, and this is reflected in an extraordinary variety of sizes and shapes.

There are many species of bony fishes, sharks and rays, and an understanding of the relationships between them is based on detailed studies of their anatomy, development, and on the sometimes scanty fossil record. What is known of the earliest fishes has been gleaned from fragments of bone taken from

rocks of the early Ordovician age, which are approximately 480 million years old. Some researchers think that the origins of fishes may go back further in time because the two major groups – the Agnatha or jawless fishes, and the Gnathostomata or jawed fishes – were so well established at the beginning of the Silurian period, about 435 million years ago.

The most primitive of living marine vertebrates are the cyclostomes – the lampreys and hagfishes – which are greatly modified descendants of the Agnatha. They have a skeleton made of cartilage – a tough, elastic tissue – instead of bone, and do not have jaws. These slimy, eel-like animals are adapted primarily for scavenging and for life as parasites.

Modern jawed fishes fall into two groups – the cartilaginous

ETWEEN SHARKS AND FISHES

Sharks are, in many ways, more highly evolved than many of the bony fishes, although they have been less successful in terms of numbers and distribution. There are 344 (known) species and they are found almost exclusively in salt water, although some occasionally venture into rivers and lakes.

Blacktip reef shark
Carcharhinus melanopterus

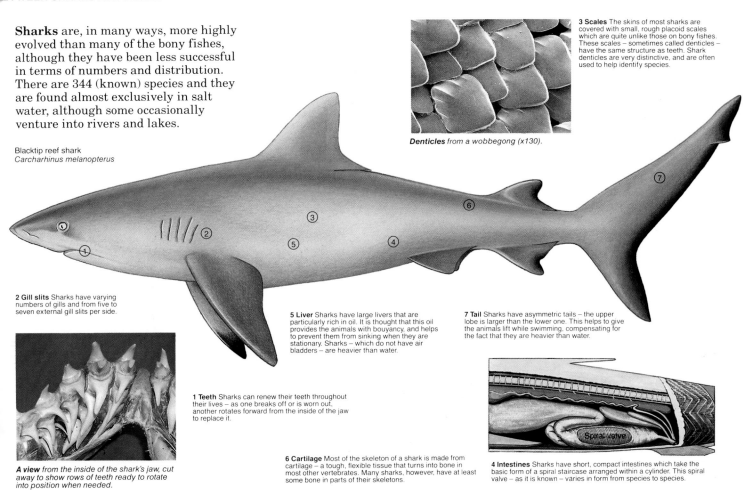

3 Scales The skins of most sharks are covered with small, rough placoid scales which are quite unlike those on bony fishes. These scales – sometimes called denticles – have the same structure as teeth. Shark denticles are very distinctive, and are often used to help identify species.

Denticles from a wobbegong (x130).

2 Gill slits Sharks have varying numbers of gills and from five to seven external gill slits per side.

5 Liver Sharks have large livers that are particularly rich in oil. It is thought that this oil provides the animals with buoyancy, and helps to prevent them from sinking when they are stationary. Sharks – which do not have air bladders – are heavier than water.

7 Tail Sharks have asymmetric tails – the upper lobe is larger than the lower one. This helps to give the animals lift while swimming, compensating for the fact that they are heavier than water.

A view from the inside of the shark's jaw, cut away to show rows of teeth ready to rotate into position when needed.

1 Teeth Sharks can renew their teeth throughout their lives – as one breaks off or is worn out, another rotates forward from the inside of the jaw to replace it.

6 Cartilage Most of the skeleton of a shark is made from cartilage – a tough, flexible tissue that turns into bone in most other vertebrates. Many sharks, however, have at least some bone in parts of their skeletons.

4 Intestines Sharks have short, compact intestines which take the basic form of a spiral staircase arranged within a cylinder. This spiral valve – as it is known – varies in form from species to species.

AN ANCIENT PAST

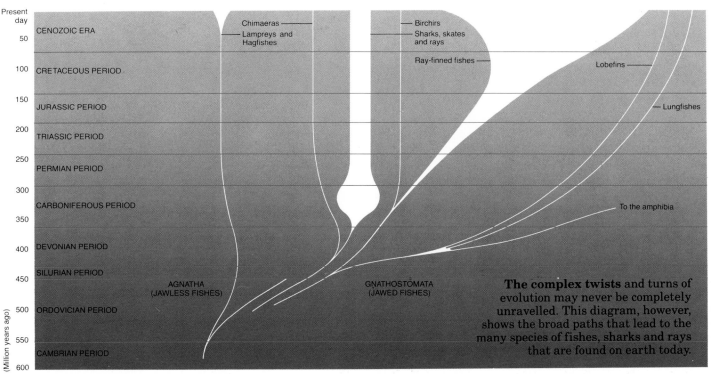

Present day

(Million years ago)	
50	CENOZOIC ERA
100	CRETACEOUS PERIOD
150	JURASSIC PERIOD
200	TRIASSIC PERIOD
250	PERMIAN PERIOD
300	CARBONIFEROUS PERIOD
350	
400	DEVONIAN PERIOD
450	SILURIAN PERIOD
500	ORDOVICIAN PERIOD
550	CAMBRIAN PERIOD
600	

Chimaeras
Lampreys and Hagfishes
Birchirs
Sharks, skates and rays
Ray-finned fishes
Lobefins
Lungfishes
To the amphibia

AGNATHA
(JAWLESS FISHES)

GNATHOSTOMATA
(JAWED FISHES)

The complex twists and turns of evolution may never be completely unravelled. This diagram, however, shows the broad paths that lead to the many species of fishes, sharks and rays that are found on earth today.

fishes (Chondrichthyes) such as sharks, rays and rat-fishes (chimaeras), and the bony fishes (Osteichthyes). There are more than 20 000 species of bony fishes which are divided into four main groups – the lungfishes, the lobefins, the ray-finned fishes (which make up the majority) and the birchirs and reedfishes. Bony fishes are found in both the oceans and in fresh water, a habitat which has never been successfully colonised by the sharks and rays. Most fishes are carni-

vorous, but a few feed on algae, such as seaweeds.

The cartilaginous fishes are divided into two sub-classes – the Elasmobranchii or sharks, skates and rays, and the Holocephali or rat-fishes (chimaeras), rabbit-fishes and elephant-fish. Fishes in this last sub-class live close to the ocean floor and have retained many primitive features. They have no stomach; their teeth are in large plates firmly attached to their jaws; they have small apertures for their

mouths; and their upper jaws are fused to their skulls. They feed on molluscs, other invertebrates and sometimes small fishes.

The sharks, skates and rays are not quite the masters of the oceans that the bony fishes are, but they are well adapted to their environment and survive in large numbers. Almost all are carnivores or scavengers, although the species that live close to the sea floor feed mostly on invertebrates. Three distinctive features identify all

Living sharks are divided into eight orders – groups that are used by scientists to collect together animals that have certain common characteristics. One member from each order is illustrated here. It is not, however, possible to illustrate one shark that is 'typical' of each order, because their external appearance can vary greatly. The carpet sharks (*Orectolobiformes*), for example, include the whale shark – the world's largest fish – and the wobbegongs, patterned sharks that live on the sea floor.

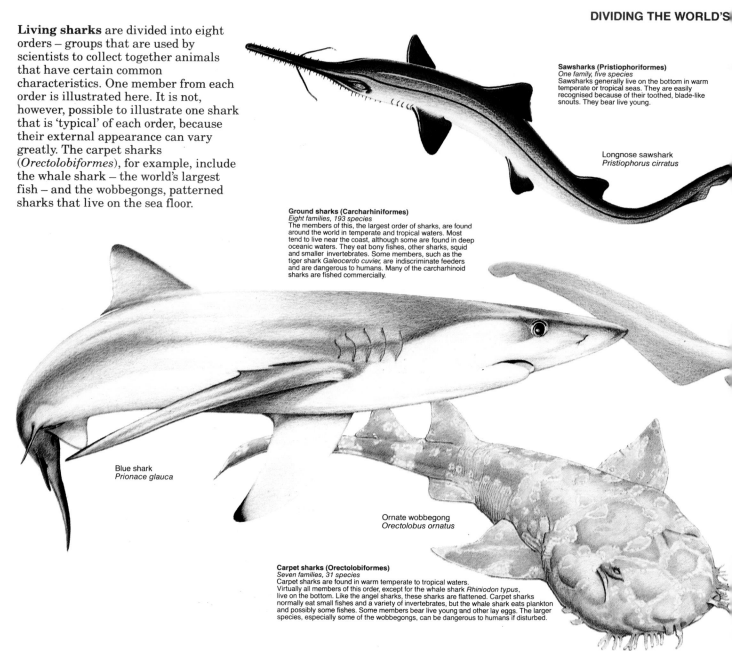

Sawsharks (Pristiophoriformes)
One family, five species
Sawsharks generally live on the bottom in warm temperate or tropical seas. They are easily recognised because of their toothed, blade-like snouts. They bear live young.

Longnose sawshark
Pristiophorus cirratus

Ground sharks (Carcharhiniformes)
Eight families, 193 species
The members of this, the largest order of sharks, are found around the world in temperate and tropical waters. Most tend to live near the coast, although some are found in deep oceanic waters. They eat bony fishes, other sharks, squid and smaller invertebrates. Some members, such as the tiger shark *Galeocerdo cuvier*, are indiscriminate feeders and are dangerous to humans. Many of the carcharhinoid sharks are fished commercially.

Blue shark
Prionace glauca

Ornate wobbegong
Orectolobus ornatus

Carpet sharks (Orectolobiformes)
Seven families, 31 species
Carpet sharks are found in warm temperate to tropical waters. Virtually all members of this order, except for the whale shark *Rhiniodon typus*, live on the bottom. Like the angel sharks, these sharks are flattened. Carpet sharks normally eat small fishes and a variety of invertebrates, but the whale shark eats plankton and possibly some fishes. Some members bear live young and other lay eggs. The larger species, especially some of the wobbegongs, can be dangerous to humans if disturbed.

sharks, skates and rays – their skeletons are made of cartilage and not bone; their skin is covered with denticles and not scales; and they have from five to seven gill slits per side, and not one per side like all bony fishes.

Sharks are superbly adapted to their environment. Most possess a keen sense of smell, a large brain, good eyesight and a highly specialised mouth and teeth. Their bodies are usually heavier than water and they do not have an air-filled swim bladder for buoyancy like most bony fishes. All sharks have an asymmetric tail fin, with the upper lobe being larger than the lower one, although this is less noticeable in fast-swimming species. This feature, together with flattened pectoral fins, and an oil-filled liver compensates for the lack of a swim bladder.

There are 344 known species of sharks (to date) living in all parts of the oceans, from shallow to deep water, and from the tropics to the polar regions. A few even venture into fresh water and have been found in rivers and lakes. Contrary to popular belief, most sharks are harmless to humans.

Sharks are classified into eight orders (see illustration below). Unfortunately very little is known about the general biology and behaviour of most of the world's sharks. Research is concentrated almost exclusively on the few species considered to have commercial potential.

SHARKS INTO EIGHT ORDERS

Dogfish sharks (Squaliformes)
Three families, 73 species
These bottom-dwelling, deep-water sharks are distributed worldwide. All bear live young and eat bony fishes, crustaceans, squid and other sharks. Several species are fished commercially. None are considered harmful to humans, although their fin spines can inflict painful injuries.

Leafscale gulper shark
Centrophorus squamosus

Bullhead sharks (Heterodontiformes)
One family, eight species
These sharks generally live on rocky reefs where there are plenty of cracks and crevices. So far they have only been found in the eastern and western Pacific Ocean and in the western Indian Ocean. Bullhead sharks generally eat invertebrates such as sea urchins, molluscs and crustaceans. They are of little interest to fishermen.

Angel sharks (Squatiniformes)
One family, 13 species
These are flattened, bottom-dwelling sharks that look very like rays. They are normally found on the continental shelves and upper slopes of cold temperate to tropical seas. They have very sharp, awl-like teeth that are used to impale small fish and crustaceans. Some species of angel sharks are fished commercially.

Sand devil
Squatina dumeril

Port Jackson shark
Heterodontus portusjacksoni

Goblin shark
Mitsukurina owstoni

Frilled shark
Chlamydoselachus anguineus

Mackerel sharks (Laminiformes)
Seven families, 16 species
A small, highly diverse order, the members of which are usually found in tropical to cold temperate and even Arctic waters. Some are oceanic while others are found near the coast. Most grow quite large and eat bony fishes, other sharks, squid and marine mammals. The basking sharks and megamouth, however, are plankton eaters. This order includes some partially warm-blooded sharks, such as the mako and great white, both of which are known to attack humans.

Frilled or cow sharks (Hexanchiformes)
Two families, five species
These are primarily deep-water, bottom-dwelling sharks with a worldwide distribution. They are easily recognised because of their six or seven gill slits (all other sharks have five pairs, except for the sawshark Pliotrema, which has six). They bear live young and generally eat bony fishes, crustaceans and other sharks.

THE MYSTERIOUS LIVES AND HABITS OF SHARKS

Sharks are hard to study. Many species, including the ones most dangerous to humans, cover great distances in their daily routines. In order to see them at all it is usually necessary to put bait in the water, and then only feeding behaviour is observed. Our present knowledge of sharks is about equivalent to our understanding of other animals at the beginning of the twentieth century.

In spite of the difficulties involved, a great deal has been learned about sharks and their cousins, the rays, skates, and chimaeras (fishes with large heads and long, tapering tails), in the past several years. The general view of sharks is changing. Once thought of as stupid – a swimming nose attached to an eating machine, a fish that should have disappeared with the dinosaurs – they are now viewed as highly evolved and efficient predators with brains, in proportion to body size, larger than many birds and mammals. Sharks can learn faster than bony fishes, at a rate comparable to white rats and pigeons. At various laboratories young nurse sharks *Ginglymostoma cirratum* have been trained to come when signalled, to touch paddles and other objects and, on command, to retrieve a ring that is thrown into their holding tank.

There are great differences in size and shape among the 344 species of sharks known to exist. The largest fish in the world is the whale shark *Rhiniodon typus* which reaches 12 m (40 ft) long, and the smallest shark is the dwarf shark *Squaliolus laticaudus* which matures at a length of 150 mm (6 in). Sharks inhabit all the oceans of the world from the Arctic to the Antarctic. They frequent, if not inhabit, many rivers that flow into the oceans, and at least one lake, Lake Nicaragua. Actually only one species, the bull shark *Carcharhinus leucas*, is known to frequent fresh water routinely. At one time it was thought that there were three species of fresh water sharks: the Zambezi River shark, the Ganges River shark, and the Lake Nicaragua shark, because they were found frequently in the lake and the two rivers. It has now been determined that they are all the same species, the bull shark. The bull shark is one of the most dangerous to humans, having been responsible for many attacks in all parts of the world.

The migratory patterns of several shark species have been studied, and temperature is a major environmental factor affecting their movements. Some sharks are known to be warm blooded: the three species of thresher sharks *Alopias vulpinus*, *A. superciliosus* and *A. pelagicus*, the great white shark, two species of mako sharks *Isurus oxyrinchus* and *I. paucus*, the salmon shark *Lamna ditropis*, and the porbeagle shark *L. nasus*. But most sharks are cold blooded. The benthic species, living at the bottom in deep water, are in an environment that is probably never more than a few degrees above 0°C (32°F). Northern hemisphere pelagic species, seen near the surface in deep water, tend to migrate north as the water temperature rises in the spring and summer, and south as the temperature drops in autumn and winter. The reverse is true in the southern hemisphere. These movements are also affected by warm and cold currents. The great blue shark *Prionace glauca* likes

Sharks that live in the ocean can be divided into two main groups: the shallow water species that spend most of their lives on the continental shelves, and the deep water species that live in some part of the deep oceans. The deep water sharks are further divided into: the benthic sharks that live at the bottom in deep water, the pelagic sharks that live in the upper few hundred metres, and the mid-water sharks between the extremes.

Only two specimens of the remarkable megamouth shark *Megachasma pelagios* have ever been captured. Both were males, 4.5 m (14.8 ft) long. One was caught near the Hawaiian Islands and the other off the coast of California. Megamouth, like the whale and basking sharks, is a filter feeder, and yet anatomically it is related more closely to the great white shark *Carcharodon carcharias*.

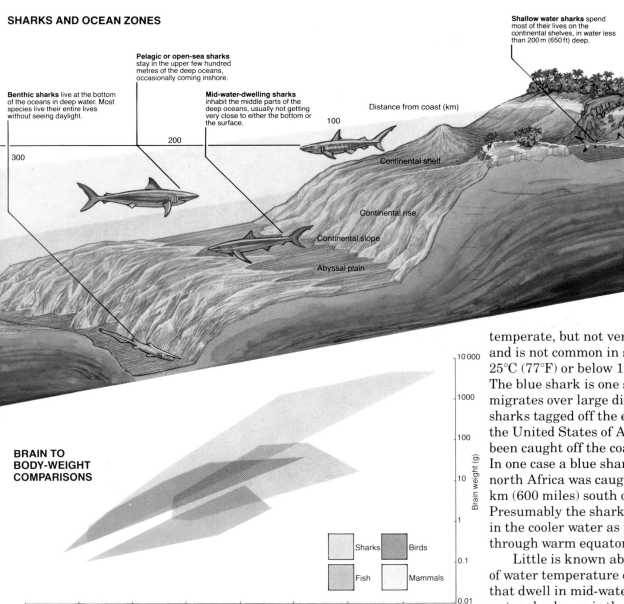

SHARKS AND OCEAN ZONES

Shallow water sharks spend most of their lives on the continental shelves, in water less than 200 m (650 ft) deep.

Pelagic or open-sea sharks stay in the upper few hundred metres of the deep oceans, occasionally coming inshore.

Benthic sharks live at the bottom of the oceans in deep water. Most species live their entire lives without seeing daylight.

Mid-water-dwelling sharks inhabit the middle parts of the deep oceans, usually not getting very close to either the bottom or the surface.

Distance from coast (km)

100

200

300

Continental shelf

Continental rise

Continental slope

Abyssal plain

BRAIN TO BODY-WEIGHT COMPARISONS

Sharks	Birds
Fish	Mammals

Body weight (kg): 0.001, 0.01, 0.1, 1, 10, 100, 1000, 10 000, 100 000

Brain weight (g): 0.01, 0.1, 1, 10, 100, 1000, 10 000

Claims that sharks are stupid are not borne out by comparisons of brain to body-weight ratios among a range of animals. Some sharks have larger brains, in proportion to body weight, than most bony fishes, many birds and some mammals.

Proof of the ability of sharks to learn has come from experiments such as those conducted in the United States of America with these nurse sharks, which were conditioned to press a target in order to receive food.

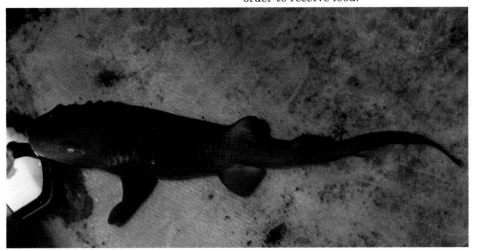

temperate, but not very cold, water and is not common in seas above 25°C (77°F) or below 15°C (59°F). The blue shark is one species that migrates over large distances. Blue sharks tagged off the east coast of the United States of America have been caught off the coast of Africa. In one case a blue shark tagged off north Africa was caught again 965 km (600 miles) south of the equator. Presumably the shark swam deeper in the cooler water as it moved through warm equatorial seas.

Little is known about the effects of water temperature on the sharks that dwell in mid-water. Shallow water sharks, as is the case with pelagic sharks, move in response to temperature changes. In the tropics where temperature changes are not great, the sharks may stay in a relatively limited area for most of their lives. Some shallow water sharks, such as nurse sharks, do not appear to migrate with changing temperatures – they simply become less active as the water gets cooler. Food supply as well as temperature affects movements.

Because all sharks receive their oxygen supply from the water via their gills they tend to avoid very warm water – above 32°C (90°F) - which has a lower oxygen content than cooler water. High water purity is also important, particularly for the long term health of captive sharks. Sharks, as is the case with bony fishes, do not survive well in polluted water.

Sharks, specially large sharks,

ANATOMY OF A SHARK

The bodies of sharks vary enormously – there is no 'typical' shark. However, the following descriptions of this shortfin mako Isurus oxyrinchus *also apply to most other species.*

1 Eye *Most shark eyes have immovable lids, but a few species (not the mako) have an eyelid – the nictitating membrane – that can completely cover the eye to protect it.*

2 Nostril *Shark nostrils are very sensitive and in tests have responded to extremely low concentrations of some chemicals.*

3 Ampullae of Lorenzini *Sensors within these small pores on the heads of sharks detect minute electric fields, and are used to find prey buried under sand.*

4 Gill slits *Sharks have from five to seven gill slits per side.*

5 Spiracle *These apertures – one per side – behind the eyes of most sharks are vestigal gill slits which play a role in aerating blood.*

6 Teeth *Shark teeth vary greatly in shape according to the way in which the animal feeds. The thin, sharp teeth of makos are adapted for seizing the fish that they eat.*

7 Skull *The shark's skull is a compact block of cartilage containing the brain as well as the auditory and nasal capsules.*

8 Gill arches *These support the gills.*

9 Auditory capsule *A shark's ears are hidden within its skull and are connected to the exterior of the animal by narrow canals.*

10 Skeleton *The skeleton of a shark is made up almost entirely of cartilage – a tough flexible tissue.*

11 Dorsal fin
12 Second dorsal fin
13 Pectoral fin
14 Pelvic fin
15 Anal fin
16 Caudal fin *Most sharks have assymetric tails – the upper lobe being larger than the lower. This is less noticable in fast swimming sharks such as the mako.*
17 Caudal keel *The bodies of many fast swimming sharks are slightly flattened at the back which may help them to move quickly. However, this feature is also present in some slow moving species, such as the plankton-eating whale shark.*
18 Muscle structure

19 Dark muscle *A few fast swimming sharks (including the mako) have a body temperature that is higher than the surrounding water. The reason for this is that warm muscle is more efficient than cold. The dark, warm muscle is used by the animal for swimming continuously at cruising speed. Heat generated in the muscle is used to warm cold blood coming from the gills.*
20 Lateral cutaneous artery *This artery is the major source of blood only in warm-bodied sharks such as the mako and porbeagle.*
21 Fin structure *It is the horny rods used to support the fin internally that are dried and extracted for use in soup.*

22 Liver *Shark livers have two lobes which almost completely enclose the digestive tract. In a large tiger shark the oil-rich liver can weigh up to 80 kg (176 lb).*
23 Spiral valve *The intestine in a shark is short and compact. Internally it is like a spiral staircase arranged within a cylinder.*
24 Stomach *Shark stomachs are U-shaped.*
25 Pancreas
26 Heart
27 Skin *Shark skin is rough because it is covered with tiny denticles. These small, hard scales have the same internal structure as the animal's teeth, and are unique to sharks and rays. Denticles vary in shape from species to species.*

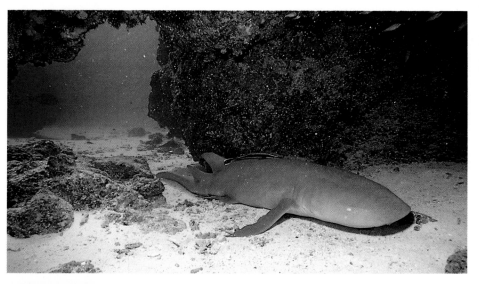

Nurse sharks *Ginglymostoma cirratum* are one of several species that are known to rest on the sea floor. At one time it was thought that sharks had to keep moving in order to extract enough oxygen from the water.

are surprisingly fragile. While it is sometimes very difficult to kill a shark quickly, it is easy to injure one during capture and transport. Injured sharks frequently die in a few days or weeks. Many injuries result from the fact that sharks have no bony skeleton to support their vital organs. On the other hand, disease is almost unknown in sharks. Most sharks have parasites, both internal and external, but none is life-threatening. The greatest threat to their lives comes from humans and other sharks.

Sharks live fairly long lives. The spiny dogfish *Squalus acanthias* is estimated to live more than 30 years. This small and harmless shark grows very slowly, only reaching a maximum length of 1 to 1.5 m (39 to 59 in). Females are sexually mature at about 12 years, and males at 9 years.

It is not known what factors determine the maximum size of sharks, but, as in humans and other mammals, growth hormones may perform this function. In the case of one of the larger species, the tiger shark *Galeocerdo cuvier* which grows to over 5 m (16.4 ft), it has been suggested that their maximum size may be limited by the size of their livers. These contain large quantities of oil which provide the shark with buoyancy (see box story far right).

Another shark, the sandtiger *Eugomphodus taurus*, which often swims very slowly, virtually hanging still in the water, may have developed an alternative way of acquiring buoyancy. Sandtigers sometimes come to the surface and appear to gulp air into their stomachs, and this may help to prevent them from sinking to the bottom when they are not moving.

At one time it was thought that many species of sharks never slept or stopped swimming for very long because they had weak gill muscles, and had to keep moving to get

oxygen from the water. The only ones that appeared to sleep were the nurse sharks, bullhead sharks, cat-sharks, carpet sharks and a few others. As time progresses, and more observations are made of both captive and wild sharks, the number of species that are known to stop swimming and lie on the bottom for extended periods is increasing. Bull sharks and grey reef sharks *Carcharhinus amblyrhynchos* have both been observed to do this. So far none of the pelagic sharks have been seen resting on the sea floor.

Sharks swim by moving their tails from side to side in an undulatory motion, like many other fish. All sharks have asymmetric tails, the upper lobe of the tail being larger than the lower lobe. Many bottom dwelling sharks have no lower lobe at all. A larger upper tail lobe is needed to provide downward thrust to balance the lift

Most sharks are hosts to a variety of parasites – both internal and external — like these sea lice living in the mouth of a great white shark. Despite the fact that some sharks carry enormous numbers of parasites, especially internal parasites such as tapeworms, they seem to be little affected by them. Sharks tolerate remoras, or sharksuckers, because they feed on external parasites.

generated by pectoral fins at the front of the shark so that they can swim level. The great white shark, and all the warm blooded sharks, have the most nearly symmetrical tails, except for the thresher shark. Thresher sharks are asymmetric in the extreme. They do have a small lower lobe, but the upper lobe makes up about 40 per cent of their overall length. The long tail is used to strike the water surface and stun bait fish so that they are easier to catch and eat.

Sharks generally cruise around at a relatively slow one to two metres per second (0.7 mph), but some are capable of short bursts of relatively high speeds. One mako shark has been estimated to have exceeded 32 km/h (20 mph) for a few seconds. Sharks tire quickly under the stress of fast swimming. The most powerful swimmers are the warm blooded sharks. This is because warm muscles are stronger

Shark tails differ in size and shape according to the species. In every case, however, the upper lobe is larger than the lower lobe so that the shark can create downward thrust to counteract the lift generated by the pectoral fins.

Upper lobe

Lower lobe

Tiger sharks are slower swimmers than porbeagles and whites, and also have markedly asymmetrical tails.

Nurse sharks spend much of their time lying on the sea floor. Their tails have almost no lower lobe, and consequently they swim in an eel-like manner.

Porbeagle sharks are fast swimmers and have more-nearly symmetrical tails than other species. They are capable of rapid acceleration.

Thresher sharks have the most extraordinary tails, with the upper lobe making up 40 per cent of the length of the shark's body.

Great white sharks also have almost symmetrical tails, which seem to be a major source of thrust when swimming.

Cookiecutter sharks have large tails, probably so they can accelerate rapidly to catch their prey – whales, dolphins and large fish.

than cold ones. A 3°C (6°F) increase in temperature doubles muscle strength, and muscle temperatures of up to 8°C (16°F) above the surrounding water have been measured. These warm blooded species also have smoother skins than other sharks, thus reducing water drag and increasing swimming efficiency. The skins of most sharks are designed for protection, not drag reduction. Sharks are not adapted for sustained swimming at high speeds, it uses too much energy. Rather they are designed for long periods of slow cruising. The drag on a brown shark *Carcharhinus plumbeus* has been measured at eight to ten times that of a similar sized Pacific whiteside dolphin *Lagenorhynchus obliquidens*.

Compared to other fish, sharks are not particularly powerful. A 1.5-m (4.9-ft) bull shark was measured to develop a maximum

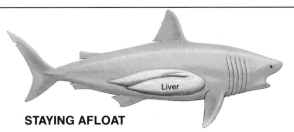

Basking sharks need a large liver to provide them with enough buoyancy to remain just beneath the water surface for long periods of time.

STAYING AFLOAT

The size of a shark's liver may be the key to its overall length. Unlike many other fishes, sharks do not have air-filled swim bladders to give them buoyancy. They are therefore heavier than water by a few per cent, and must produce lift in order to swim off the bottom of the sea.

Like aeroplanes in air, sharks 'fly' underwater using their pectoral fins like wings. If the fuselage of an aircraft is doubled in size, then the wing area must be more than doubled if the 'plane is to fly. This is because a doubling in size cubes the volume of the fuselage, but only squares the area of the wings.

In tiger sharks the fin area of a two-metre-long (6.6-ft) specimen is just half that of a 4-m (13.1-ft) shark. In order to compensate for the loss of lift caused by having a bulkier body and relatively smaller fins, the 4-m (13.1-ft) shark increases its liver size by considerably more than twice that of the

2-m (6.6-ft) shark. The liver contains oil, and it is this that gives the larger shark the increased buoyancy that it needs.

Sharks obviously cannot keep giving over a larger and larger proportion of their body cavity to house the liver, otherwise there would be no room for other organs. This theory therefore predicts that there should be a maximum size for any species of shark. Calculations so far have only been made for tiger sharks, and these suggest that the maximum length for that species should be around 5 to 6 m (16 to 20 ft), a figure which agrees with records of large specimens captured so far.

The livers of large sharks can reach a great weight – sometimes up to 91 kg (200 lbs). In the days when sharks were fished for the oil in their livers it was reckoned that a well-fed, 4-m (13-ft) tiger shark might contain a liver that would yield as much as 81.8 litres (18 gallons) of rich oil.

The swirling bodies of a group of grey reef sharks *Carcharhinus amblyrhychos* in a feeding frenzy present an awesome spectacle. In these circumstances sharks will attack anything around them, even one another.

Sharks have teeth adapted to deal with their food. The Port Jackson shark, for example, has small, pointed teeth at the front for seizing prey, and large molars at the back for crushing the shells of the molluscs it eats.

swimming power of about 0.2 kW (0.25 horsepower), while a 1.2-m (3.9-ft) barracuda *Sphyraena barracuda* produced a maximum of more than 0.6 kW (0.75 horsepower). Barracuda are adapted for remaining almost still and then accelerating quickly to high speed to catch prey.

The mating of all sharks is much like that of many mammals: the male introduces sperm directly into the female's reproductive tract. Males have two organs, called claspers, for doing this, but probably only one is used at a time. The claspers are extensions of the male's pelvic fins. Pre-mating behaviour and actual copulation have been observed in only a few species. In some instances mating appears to be a rather violent activity. Adult females have been seen with lacerations on their pectoral fins and on their backs and sides between the dorsal fin and tail, where the males bite them before mating. In some species the males have smaller teeth than females, and female blue sharks have skins that are twice as thick as males in the critical areas. The best guess as to how males identify receptive females is through their extremely acute sense of smell.

Shark young are brought into

the world in three different ways, with some variations. As with most mammals, many sharks bear live young which are nurtured in one of the female's two oviducts through umbilical cords. No care is given to the young after they are born. Some sharks lay eggs, and as with the live bearers, once the eggs are laid they receive no future care. The whale shark lays pillow-shaped eggs almost 500 mm (20 in) long. One of the most interesting egg layers is the Port Jackson shark *Heterodontus portusjacksoni* from Australia. The eggs of this species are shaped like large truncated wood screws 150 mm (5.9 in) long, with spiral flanges on the outside. Some scientists think that the female carries the eggs around in her mouth after they are laid, and deposits them in reef crevices where, because of the shape, they become securely lodged.

In the third method of bearing young, the females produce eggs and carry them internally until the young hatch. There is no attachment to the mother. The young are nourished by their large egg yolks. An unusual case is that of the sandtiger shark which produces hundreds of pea-sized eggs throughout a long gestation period of several months. One of the first

eggs in each oviduct develops into a baby shark before the others, and each baby sustains itself until birth by cannibalizing its undeveloped brothers and sisters as they are produced by the mother. Sandtigers only produce one large baby shark – 40 per cent of the length of the mother – from each of the two oviducts. While probing the uterus of a pregnant sandtiger a scientist was bitten by an unborn pup. While not the smallest, this was definitely the youngest shark to have attacked a human! The incident has been classified as a provoked attack.

The gestation period in sharks varies from about nine months to as long as twenty-two months for the spiny dogfish. The number of young produced varies from species to species, but ranges from one to close to a hundred in the tiger shark.

In spite of the fact that inanimate objects are frequently found in shark's stomachs, they are all entirely carnivorous. Food ranges from the smallest plankton to the largest whales. Sharks prefer live fresh food but do sometimes eat decaying flesh. There are, however, no vultures in the shark family that specialize in eating only dead flesh. A favourite food is apparently shark pups. When sharks are first caught and brought into captivity it is

These teeth all come from large, fast-swimming, flesh-eating sharks, and they all have the same basic characteristics – they are pointed and extremely sharp. Teeth from the upper and lower jaws of the same shark are often different shapes because of the way in which such sharks feed. Prey is first impaled on the teeth of the lower jaw, which are generally pointed, and those in the upper jaw are used to 'saw' away a section of flesh. The serrated edges on the teeth of some species help with this process.

Although sharks' teeth are sharp, they are also brittle, and are constantly breaking off. Fortunately for the sharks, new ones are being created all the time, and these rotate quickly into position from the inside of the jaw as they are needed.

often difficult to get them to take food. This can sometimes be remedied by giving them live baby sharks or fresh shark liver. It is thought that bull sharks have their pups in fresh water to protect their young from being eaten by other sharks. Some bottom-dwelling sharks, such as the Port Jackson shark, feed extensively on crustaceans and shellfish. These sharks have molars at the backs of their mouths for crushing shells, and sharp teeth at the front for seizing small prey.

Among the sharks that are dangerous to humans, the shape of the teeth ranges from long, narrow and pointed, as in the mako shark, to broad and somewhat less pointed in the case of the tiger shark. In every case, however, the teeth have edges that are razor-sharp – quite sharp enough to easily shave the hairs from an arm. In many of the dangerous species the teeth in the upper jaw are broader and more triangular than those in the lower jaw. In all shark jaws there are several sets of teeth – five or more – present at the same time. Behind the set of teeth visible and being used by the shark are the other sets, folded back into the jaw tissue. When a sharks loses a tooth, a replacement rotates out of the jaw

THE TEETH OF A PREDATOR

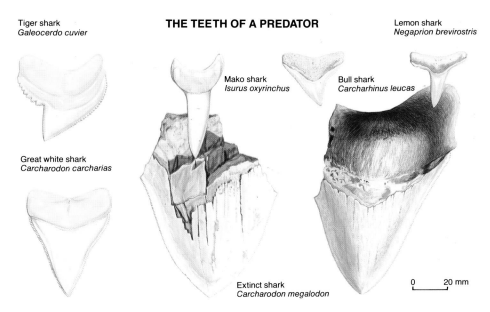

Tiger shark
Galeocerdo cuvier

Mako shark
Isurus oxyrinchus

Lemon shark
Negaprion brevirostris

Bull shark
Carcharhinus leucas

Great white shark
Carcharodon carcharias

Extinct shark
Carcharodon megalodon

0   20 mm

The razor sharp teeth of the little (500-mm; 20-in) cookiecutter shark (left) can cause considerable damage, even to the rubber casing on submarine components (above).

SOLVING THE COOKIECUTTER RIDDLE

When submarines surface after dives there is the ever-present danger of collision with one of the growing number of surface ships plying the oceans of the world. To help avoid this problem United States Navy submarines have a listening device that can be raised far enough above the boat to hear surface ships. This listening device is covered with a 13-mm (0.5-in) rubber coating. About 10 years ago it was found that these rubber coatings were being damaged. Crescent shaped slashes were somehow being cut out of them.

At first it was thought that the damage was due to some kind of animal bite, but since none of the biologists that were asked could identify the animal responsible, they were assumed to be due to mechanical failure. Exhaustive tests could not reproduce the slashes. Finally, quite by accident, a scientist who studied both whales and sharks was shown some of the slashes. 'Of course,' he said, 'these are caused by the cookiecutter shark which feeds by biting chunks out of whales and large fish. The cookiecutter must mistake submarines for whales!'

Once the source of the damage was identified it was a simple matter to cover the rubber coating with a layer of fibreglass too hard for the little shark to bite through.

Some 30 submarines had been damaged in this way. Fortunately, none of the sharks had ever bitten all the way through the rubber coating. If this had happened, the oil in the listening device would have leaked out, making it useless, and a collision might have resulted. A 500-mm (20-in) long shark could have caused the loss of a submarine.

Despite their small size, cookiecutters are fierce fighters and many fishermen have reported extensive damage to nets in which the sharks have been caught. The injuries to the cookiecutter's living victims are distinctive and take the form of a 50-mm (2-in) wide hole where flesh and skin have been gouged out. Until quite recently the resulting scars on whales and dolphins were thought to be caused by a bacterial infection, or some sort of parasite.

tissue to take its place. In small, growing sharks, each tooth is replaced once every one to two weeks. In adults this rate probably slows to replacement every month or two. Even so, every shark must produce hundreds of sets of teeth in its lifetime.

Not all sharks lose teeth one or two at a time. Some species lose a whole set at once. An example of this is the cookiecutter or cigar shark *Isistius brasiliensis*. This little shark, which grows to 500 mm (20 in) in length, lives in the mid-water volume in deep tropical oceans. It eats by biting chunks the size and shape of half a tennis ball out of whales, tuna, squid and other larger animals. Its upper jaw contains several rows of needle sharp teeth which protrude 1 mm (0.04 in) from the jaw. In the lower jaw are 25 to 30, 3 mm (0.12 in) long teeth that are strongly attached to one another, forming a band. The jaws are surrounded by muscular

lips which form a suction attachment when it attacks its prey (see box p.27). Once attached to the smooth surface of its victim, the needle-like teeth in the upper jaw prevent the shark from slipping off, and it then scoops out a hemispherical chunk of flesh. On occasions the shark swallows its teeth at the same time as its meal. Complete sets of teeth have been found in the stomachs of many captured specimens.

The cookiecutter shark is also one of the several species of sharks that have luminescent organs on the outsides of their bodies. These may be used to attract prey in the deep, dark waters they inhabit. Megamouth sharks *Megachasma pelagios* have luminous organs inside their mouths which may be used to attract the small fish and squid they filter from the water.

Because sharks have such sharp teeth they do not need extremely strong jaw muscles. Even so,

measurements have shown that some species can generate impressive forces when they bite. Up to 587 newtons (132 pounds-force) have been measured between the jaws of a 2-m (6.6-ft) dusky shark *Carcharhinus obscurus*. Because this force is concentrated at the fine cutting edge of the shark's teeth, it is amplified to 3 tonnes per sq. cm (21 tons per sq. in), which is enough to severely damage oceanographic instruments and other important equipment, not to mention fragile human bodies.

Sharks that live high enough in the ocean to be exposed to sunlight feed mostly at night and are especially active on dark, moonless nights. Their eyes are adapted to see well in low light levels. All sharks also have electrical receptors which detect the weak electric field that surrounds all animals, including humans. Sharks have the highest sensitivity to electric fields of any known marine animal, and

Copulation has been observed in very few sharks, particularly in the wild. The best observations are probably those made of nurse sharks which will mate in captivity, but it is not clear if their mating behaviour is 'typical'.

Male sharks have two claspers with which to introduce sperm into the female cloaca, in the same way as a penis is used in mammals. Opinion is divided on whether one or both of the claspers are used during mating, as both possibilities have been reported by researchers. Claspers vary in shape according to the species (those below are of a great white shark), and are equipped with hooks and spurs, presumably to keep them in place.

Pre-mating behaviour in many sharks

is highly complex, perhaps because a high degree of cooperation is required during copulation. Males will often bite females on their fins and bodies, possibly to stimulate a sexual response, and the wounds created are often severe (below). In nurse sharks insertion of a (single) clasper and copulation takes only about a minute or so.

The corkscrew-shaped eggcase of a Port Jackson shark *Heterodontus portusjacksoni*. Some researchers believe that the female carries the egg cases in her mouth to underwater rocks, and then inserts them into a crevice. Their shape makes them difficult to dislodge. The eggcases of other shark species come in many shapes and sizes.

this gives them a great advantage over their prey. They can find crabs and fish buried in the sand, and detect fish and other creatures in complete darkness, when many animals are not active (see p.35).

It is generally thought that if dolphins are sighted, the area must be free of sharks, because sharks and dolphins are thought to be mortal enemies. Such is not the case. Sharks and dolphins have been seen swimming together on many occasions. There are many reported instances of dolphins attacking and killing sharks. Dolphin remains have been found in sharks and many live, healthy dolphins have been captured bearing large scars which were probably caused by shark bites. The conditions under which these violent encounters occur are not known. Experiments have been conducted in which captured sharks and bottlenose dolphins *Tursiops truncatus* have been placed together in the same enclosure. Under these conditions the behaviour of both species indicated awareness of each other's presence, but there was no aggressiveness shown by either. The sharks tended to swim around the perimeter of the enclosure, while the dolphins kept to the centre. Both groups of animals competed for food without incident.

At the Mote Marine Laboratory at Sarasota, Florida, a bottlenose dolphin was trained to chase and attack sharks. These experiments showed that bottlenose dolphins can tell one shark species from another, for the dolphin would only attack the species with which it had been trained. It ignored any others.

Sharks have few natural enemies, apart from other sharks. The only predator large enough to tackle a shark is a killer whale, although no encounters have been reported. A shark was, however, once taken from the stomach of a sperm whale.

Blackie (above) chasing young blacktip sharks through the shallow waters of Canton Island's lagoon. The dog and his owner, Tonga John (left), solved a pressing scientific puzzle.

THE SHARK-CATCHING DOG OF CANTON ISLAND

The study of sharks in the wild can present researchers with many unexpected problems, not the least of which is that of cornering a suitable specimen.

Canton Island is a small atoll in the Phoenix group, located about 965 km (600 miles) north of Samoa, 1290 km (800 miles) west of the Gilbert Islands and about 3220 km (2000 miles) south-west of Hawaii. This group of islands has now been handed over to the Gilbert Islanders, and is part of the tiny nation of Kiribati.

Canton Island was brought to the attention of scientists from Hawaii and California several years ago by the United States Air Force. The Air Force had based a tracking station on the island for monitoring missile and space flight tests. For reasons unknown to this day, an 8-m (26.5-ft) female whale shark had swum into Canton's shallow lagoon, and Air Force officials feared that the great fish was trapped and would die if not rescued. The shark stayed for over a year, despite all efforts to set her free. Residents of the island named her Mimi, and on days off they would swim with her and feed her shrimps and fish. However, she apparently became bored with all the attention and one day swam away and was never seen again.

During trips to the island scientists noticed that Canton's reefs were a treasure-trove of marine life, and several new species of fish were discovered. There was also an abundant supply of juvenile, 450 to 600 mm (1.5 to 2 ft) long, blacktip sharks *Carcharhinus melanopterus* — a species that is commonly found around many Pacific ocean reefs and islands.

These small sharks swam in very shallow water near the shore where their larger cousins could not make a meal of them. It appeared to be a simple task to net the

sharks and transport them live to various aquariums and oceanariums for display and study.

As it turned out, the sharks had other ideas, and after three exhausting days spent chasing sharks around in the equatorial heat only six had been caught. By now the catching crew had dwindled to one scientist – all the rest found more pressing work to do. In desperation the remaining scientist enlisted a local civilian Air Force employee from Tonga, aptly named Tonga John.

The island had been deserted between the end of World War II and recent Air Force occupation, except for several dogs which had been left behind when the last inhabitants had departed. A descendant of these dogs, named Blackie, had adopted Tonga John.

The scientist, Tonga John and Blackie went off to collect sharks. When they arrived at the appropriate spot the scientist explained to Tonga John the procedure used to catch sharks. John was not very enthusiastic about the method, but agreed to give it a try. They picked up the collecting nets and turned to find a squirming shark at their feet, with a wet dog, one foot holding the shark down, wagging his tail furiously. The scientist asked where the shark came from. 'Oh', John replied, 'Blackie, he catchum, dats his favourite ting, catchin sharks.' For the next hour Tonga John sat in the shade sipping beer while Blackie, assisted by the scientist, caught the last eight sharks needed. Everyone was happy: the scientist got his sharks plus a great story for cocktail hour, Tonga John got a day off and a few free beers, and Blackie, well, Blackie got to do two of his favourite things – catch sharks and eat all the ice cubes that he wanted.

A unique sequence of photographs (reading down from the top) show the actual birth of a lemon shark pup *Negaprion brevirostris*. This event, which had never been seen in a shark in the wild before, took place in Bimini Lagoon in the Bahamas. The mother – which was about 2.6 m (8.5 ft) long – had been captured for study and was anchored to the scientist's boat by a hook in her mouth and a rope around her tail. As each pup was born it would lie briefly on the ocean floor before swimming away, straining against the umbilical cord until it broke, leaving a small depression in the baby shark's belly. The remoras swimming around the mother would dart in rapidly after each pup was born to devour the afterbirth. Altogether 10 pups were born, each about 610 mm (2 ft) long, although the last was born dead. Once free of their mother these baby sharks must survive on their own.

THE SHARK'S REMARKABLE SENSES

Sharks have a range of sensory systems on their heads and bodies with which to explore the environment, pursue prey, and avoid predators. In addition to touch, taste and a keen sense of smell, sharks possess excellent vision at close range and unique vibration and electromagnetic senses. Armed with such equipment, it is not surprising that they have survived so successfully for more than 200 million years.

The shark has frequently been referred to as a 'swimming nose' and there is considerable support for this claim. The nostrils, located on the underside of the snout just ahead of the mouth, open into spacious sacs lined with many folds of tissue which contain the cells responsible for detecting smells. When a shark takes water into its mouth to constantly aerate its gills, suction causes some water to flow in and out of each nasal sac. In addition, the forward motion of the shark brings water through the funnel-shaped nostrils into the sacs. A fleshy flap extending across the opening of each sac separates water flowing in from water flowing out. The odour-detecting system of a shark is therefore constantly bathed by a current of water whether the shark is swimming or resting. In one of the oddest of all sharks, the hammerhead, the nostrils, as well

as the eyes, are located far apart at the ends of the 'hammer'. This fact, coupled with the shark's habit of swinging its head from side to side through a considerable arc as it swims, enables it to sample the smells in a much wider path through the water than would otherwise be possible.

Ralph E. Sheldon, working at the Marine Biological Laboratory in Woods Hole, Massachusetts, was the first to demonstrate scientifically that the sense of smell is important in guiding sharks to a meal. He found that smooth dogfish had no difficulty distinguishing a cloth-covered packet that contained crushed crabmeat from identical packets containing stones. When Sheldon plugged the sharks' nostrils with cotton wool so that a current of water could not enter the nasal sacs, they no longer homed in on the food packets, although they swam

quite close to them. To eliminate the possibility that the cotton wool plugs merely made the sharks uncomfortable and discouraged them from eating, Sheldon plugged the nostril on one side only of several dogfish. After a brief period of adjustment all but one of the animals readily located the packet containing food.

Several years ago, at the Lerner Marine Laboratory, scientists tested the sense of smell of lemon sharks *Negaprion brevirostris* by implanting electrodes in various parts of their brains (see box below). They concluded that the sharks were capable of detecting dilutions of one part of tuna juice to 25 million (10^6) parts of seawater. Albert Tester conducted laboratory tank experiments at Eniwetok in the 1960s and found that 'the response of blacktip and gray sharks to a standard extract increased under conditions of progressive starvation.' He found that starved blacktips were so sensitive to smells that they responded to concentrations of grouper flesh in dilutions of only one part in 10 billion (10^9) parts of seawater.

Sharks have excellent vision

REASSESSING THE MENTAL ABILITIES OF SHARKS

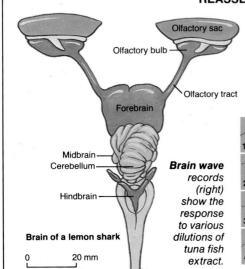

Brain of a lemon shark

Labels: Olfactory sac, Olfactory bulb, Olfactory tract, Forebrain, Midbrain, Cerebellum, Hindbrain

0   20 mm

***Brain wave** records (right) show the response to various dilutions of tuna fish extract.*

Sharks are often described as having 'primitive' brains – a claim that has not been borne out by recent studies. Brain size and complexity vary greatly from species to species, but some sharks obviously have considerable mental ability, and are capable of simple feats of learning. A comparison of brain to body-weight ratio (see p 21) shows that sharks compare well with many other vertebrates. The species with the largest brains in comparison to their body weights are the dusky shark and the scalloped hammerheads. In general, the active, fast-moving sharks have larger and more complex brains than the slower, bottom-dwelling species.

1 Sea water — Brain wave
2 Tuna extract
3 Tuna extract
4 Tuna extract

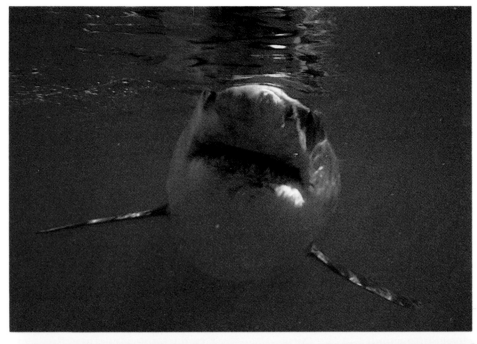

A great white shark 'sniffs' the surface of the water as it homes in on the source of a smell. Sharks trace odours by following the scent and always turning upstream when it is detected (see p.83).

The nostrils of the grey nurse shark *Eugomphodus taurus* are divided externally by a flap of skin. Water flows in through the openings on the outside of the nostrils, and out through the openings on the inner side of the flap. Once inside the shark's head the water passes through a funnel-shaped passage and into the nasal sacs, which are lined with sensitive cells.

Sharks' eyes vary greatly in size and shape according to the species concerned. Not all have nictitating membranes as shown in the diagram (left). There has been some disagreement among researchers on whether the lens can be moved in and out to focus the eye on near and far objects.

In dim light the platelets of the *tapetum lucidum* reflect light back into the retina and improve the eye's sensitivity.

In bright light pigment cells obscure the platelets and prevent any light from being reflected back to the retina.

Labels in diagram: Cornea, Ligament, Lens, Light entering eye, Iris, Muscle, Immovable eyelid, Nictitating eyelid, Fibrous sclera, Choroid, Tapetum lucidum, Retina, Vitreous humour, Optic nerve

Labels in upper right diagram: Retina, Light reflected from platelets, Light striking retina, Retinal nerve ganglia, Migratory pigment cells, Platelets

Labels in lower right diagram: Light striking retina, Pigment covers platelets

and experimental studies have now dispelled the widely-held notion that they have poor eyesight. As early as 1960, experiments were conducted in which large lemon sharks had discs placed over their eyes to blind them temporarily. The blinded sharks were then released into pens at the Lerner Marine Laboratory on Bimini in the Bahamas to compete for food with other sharks that had normal vision. The adult lemon sharks with unimpaired vision had no trouble homing in on and consuming a 113-kg (250-lb) chunk of blue marlin, while those temporarily blinded were unable to locate such an attractive feast. Other studies at this laboratory confirmed that sharks were attracted to bright objects while non-reflective, dull colours were generally avoided.

A shark's eye is a somewhat flattened version of the same eye that all vertebrates have, with an iris, lens, and retina, and three fluid-filled chambers contained within a tough envelope of cartilage, the sclera. In the shark, the aperture of the iris (pupil), varies in shape and, again, contrary to popular belief, may open and

close quite rapidly. In the nurse shark *Ginglymostoma cirratum,* for example, the pupil can dilate to its maximum size 24 to 30 seconds after entering the dark, and can constrict to its minimum size 5 to 13 seconds after emerging into the light again. In the brown shark *Carcharhinus plumbeus* maximum dilation and constriction take place in 40 and 25 seconds respectively. In every case the shark's pupil constricted in bright light more rapidly than it dilated in dim light or darkness.

The retina of the shark's eye contains many light-sensitive rod and cone cells, with there being many more rods than cones. The cone cells determine the extent of the animal's visual acuity and colour vision, and the large number of rod cells improve a shark's visual sensitivity, and therefore its ability to tell the difference between an object, especially a moving one, and its background in very dim light. In recent years experiments have shown that sharks have much greater visual ability than researchers first thought.

The sensitivity of the shark's eye in dim light is greatly improved

by a remarkable structure, the *tapetum lucidum,* a mirror-like reflecting layer that lies under the retina. The *tapetum* is made up of tiny platelets, silvered with guanine crystals, that can reflect incoming light back through the retina to restimulate the light-sensitive rods and cones. The *tapetum* therefore enables sharks that feed at night – as most species that live in the open seas do – to make the most of the small amount of light that is available.

The *tapetum,* however, has an even more remarkable ability. For those sharks that also feed during the day, bright light must be prevented from reaching the delicate cells of the retina. This is achieved not only by reducing the size of the opening in the pupil, but also by a curtain of pigment that temporarily screens each of the tiny platelets of the *tapetum.* Each platelet is covered by cells that contain pigment, and black granules temporarily fill the cells in bright light, thus preventing light from being reflected back into the retina. Conversely, as the shark's eye becomes accustomed to the dark, these black granules

The bulbous ampullae of Lorenzini are shown in this cross-section connected to canals that lead to the skin surface, and to nerves. The diagram of the shark's head shows the locations of skin pores leading to both the ampullae of Lorenzini and the lateralis system.

Skin pores show up clearly in this view of the head of a grey nurse shark. They lead to the ampullae of Lorenzini – sensory organs which enable sharks to detect very weak electric fields, and therefore any prey that may be buried under sand on the sea floor.

withdraw to the base of the cells to expose the reflective surface of the platelets again.

The lens of a shark's eye is nearly spherical and rigid, unlike the ellipse-shaped, elastic lens that mammals have. Some sharks can focus on an object by moving the lens towards or away from the retina, much as a camera can be focused. The movement of the lens is controlled by a muscle – the protractor lentis.

It has now been conclusively demonstrated that sharks can locate their prey in the open sea by detecting the minute electric fields they generate. One of the first to suspect that sharks may be sensitive to tiny electric currents was Sven Dijgraaf, working at the University of Utrecht more than 45 years ago. He noticed that the blindfolded, small-spotted catsharks *Scyliorhinus canicula* he was using in behavioural experiments would turn rapidly away from a rusty steel wire located a few centimetres from their heads. However, when a glass rod was held at the same distance it did not produce the same response. Dijgraaf assumed that his sharks were responding to electric currents

A researcher uses an electrode at the end of a pole to test the electrical sense of this shark. The extraordinary sensitivity of this sense has only been fully appreciated in recent years.

generated at the surface of the rusty wire. But what receptors did the sharks employ for doing this? A clue was provided in the early 1960s by R.W. Murray who demonstrated that the ampullae of Lorenzini on the snouts of sharks responded to

weak electric fields. When Dijgraaf and one of his bright graduate students, A.J. Kalmijn, severed the nerves to these ampullae the sharks were no longer able to detect electric currents.

It remained for Kalmijn to show that a shark may employ these unique electroreceptors to locate prey. In a classic series of experiments he demonstrated that a small-spotted catshark can locate a live flounder buried beneath the sand in a laboratory aquarium. It did this by detecting minute electric pulses generated by the resting flounder. The shark was even able to find the flounder when it was placed in an agar chamber that permitted seawater and electric pulses to pass through. When the agar chamber was covered with a plastic film, electric pulses from the flounder were blocked, and the shark could not locate it. Finally, when a pair of electrodes were buried in the sand to simulate the flounder, Kalmijn's sharks attacked the electrodes.

During the summer of 1976, Kalmijn and K.J. Rose continued their work in the open sea off Cape Cod, Massachusetts. They succeeded in getting the nocturnal,

The lateralis system alerts sharks to low-frequency vibrations, such as distant disturbances in the water made by struggling fish, or the erratic movements of a human swimmer. This sensitivity to vibration is shared by most fishes and some aquatic amphibians. There are still many unanswered questions about the role that this system plays in the everyday lives of sharks, in spite of the fact that it has recently been the subject of considerable research.

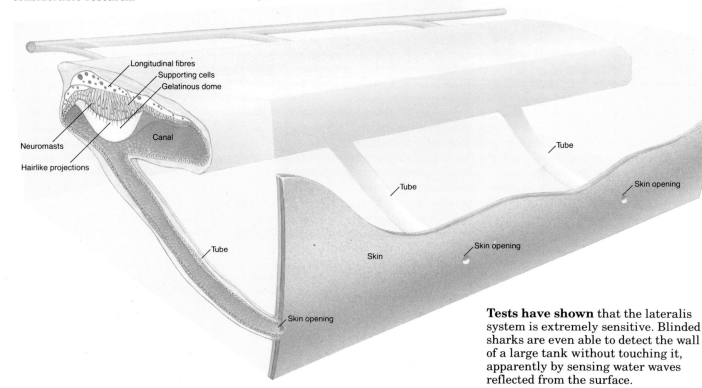

Lateral line canals

Longitudinal fibres
Supporting cells
Gelatinous dome
Canal
Neuromasts
Hairlike projections
Tube
Tube
Tube
Skin opening
Skin opening
Skin
Skin opening

Tests have shown that the lateralis system is extremely sensitive. Blinded sharks are even able to detect the wall of a large tank without touching it, apparently by sensing water waves reflected from the surface.

bottom-feeding dusky smoothhound *Mustelus canis* to 'home in' on live electrodes which were giving off weak electric (DC) pulses. The sharks ignored 'dead' electrodes and other stimuli. After observing this identical behaviour in hundreds of other dusky smoothhounds in their natural environment, Kalmijn and Rose concluded that the sharks can detect their prey at close range using only their electric sense.

So responsive are sharks to a very weak electric field that Kalmijn believes they may also be sensitive to the earth's magnetic field and can use this ability to navigate. The dusky smoothhound regularly migrates southward from the waters off Cape Cod, Massachusetts, for the winter months, and is apparently endowed with a good sense of direction. The ampullae of Lorenzini may

therefore provide the sharks with a very accurate internal electromagnetic compass.

During his experiments Kalmijn found that 'within the frequency range of direct current up to about eight hertz (cycles per second), sharks respond to fields of voltage gradients as low as a hundred-millionth of a volt per centimetre. That would be equivalent to the field of a flashlight battery connected to electrodes spaced 1000 miles [1600 km] apart in the ocean'! This remarkable electrical sensitivity is greater than that possessed by any other animal investigated so far.

Sharks have an acute vibration sense called the lateralis system which is located in their heads and bodies. It consists of several small canals that open at intervals to the surface through tubes to pores in

the skin. Each canal is filled with seawater and contains clusters of sensory cells, called neuromasts, on its inner surface. From each neuromast several hairlike projections, enclosed in a gelatinous dome, stick out into the interior of the fluid-filled canal. Vibrations that reach the shark's head and body are transmitted to the neuromasts and cause the hairlike projections to move very slightly, thereby triggering a nerve impulse to the brain.

More than half a century ago George H. Parker of Harvard University found that a dogfish that could not see or hear was still able to detect disturbances in the water as long as its lateralis system was undamaged. When he severed the nerves of the lateralis system, the shark ceased to respond.

In addition to the lateralis

Shark's ears have a number of primitive features which are still little understood. Both the endolymphatic duct and the macula neglecta have disappeared, or have been reduced, during the evolution of vertebrate ears. Shark ears have been particularly well studied because they have long been a favourite subject for dissection to test the skill of aspiring medical students – they contain the same basic structures that are to be found in the ears of all other vertebrates.

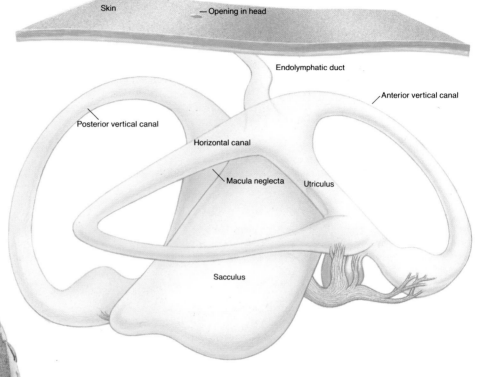

Skin — Opening in head

Endolymphatic duct

Anterior vertical canal

Posterior vertical canal

Horizontal canal

Macula neglecta

Utriculus

Sacculus

Opening to endolymphatic duct

Ear

A major function of a shark's ears, and indeed any fish's ears, is to provide the creature with information about its position and speed. In a watery world there are few visual clues to help with this task. The three semicircular canals are at right angles to one another and therefore detect movement in any one of the three spatial planes. Information of acceleration and deceleration is provided by the otoliths when they move, and liquid surging in the canals tells the shark's brain about the extent of a turn.

system, sharks also detect vibrations with their ears. The ears of a shark – one per side – are enclosed in its cartilaginous brain case, and are made up of the same basic components that are found in all vertebrate ears – three semicircular canals, the utriculus, the sacculus, and their related structures.

Recent evidence suggests that sharks can pick up low frequency sounds from great distances. Work by A.N. Popper and R.R. Fay in the 1970s showed that the shark's ear did this by detecting the movement of water particles, which carry vibrations, rather than from changes in sound pressure. The three fluid-filled semicircular canals in the shark's ear detect changes in the speed and direction of the shark's movement. Other organs in the sacculus and macula neglecta

contain otoliths – tiny granules of calcium carbonate – which move when the shark changes position, and send signals to the brain to tell it about the animal's attitude in the water. The macula neglecta is especially sensitive to vertical movements, and it can also pick up vibrations from the roof of the animal's skull.

Information from both the ears and the lateralis system may be used to locate the source of a sound quickly and accurately. It appears that the macula neglecta may be particularly important for doing this, a theory that is borne out by measurements made by J.T. Corwin. He examined the ears of a number of species of sharks and found that the macula neglecta was most elaborate in the grey reef shark, an active predator, less elaborate in the dusky smoothhound and nurse

shark, and still less elaborate in the rays, where directional hearing is of least importance for locating food.

Another curious feature of shark ears is a tiny duct – called the endolymphatic duct – which extends from the sacculus of both ears to small pores on the shark's head. The exact purpose of these ducts is as yet unknown.

Sharks also have one other sensory system which is still little understood. This consists of a large number of 'pit organs' scattered along the animals' bodies and around their lower jaws. These are usually protected by modified denticles, and closely resemble the taste buds of higher vertebrates. Opinion is divided on whether the organs have a taste function, whether they pick up vibrations, or even possibly sense movements in the shark's body.

INHABITANTS OF ANCIENT SEAS

*There were sharks in the oceans of earth long before the first animals had begun to colonise the land surface. Their history stretches back for at least 400 million years, a vast period of time which makes the 2-million-year-old history of humans (genus **Homo**) seem insignificant by comparison.*

The planet earth is at least 4500 million years old. The earliest signs of life date back 3000 million years, and by 600 million years ago quite complex animals and plants existed.

The story of the backboned (vertebrate) animals – the fishes and other forms that eventually led to humans – began about 600 to 500 million years ago. The first definite fossil of a creature with a stiffening notochord along its back was a Cambrian animal called *Pikaea*, which was discovered in 560-million-year-old rocks in Canada. The oldest complete fish fossil so far found came from central Australia, and was a jawless, armoured fish called *Arandaspis*, which dates from the early Ordovician period. This small filter-feeding or mud-grubbing fish lived in shallow coastal waters over 480 million years ago.

In the next 100 million years all the major fish groups that are found on earth today evolved, although their origins and relationships to one another are still uncertain. In the Silurian period – some 400 million years ago – the jawless fishes were the most numerous, although primitive bony and cartilaginous jawed fishes had begun to appear at about that time. Fossils of the so-called 'spiny sharks' – which had large fin spines – and of the earliest true sharks have also been found in Silurian rocks. By the Devonian period – about 30 million years later – fishes had diversified and spread into all parts of the world. By the end of the Devonian, some 25 million years further on, certain fishes had moved onto land. From these first amphibians evolved the four-legged animals, including reptiles such as dinosaurs, and eventually mammals.

The early evolutionary history of sharks and shark-like fishes is still poorly understood. Until recently scientists thought that there were no shark fossils to speak of in rocks older than those from the Middle Devonian. Now, however, it is certain that sharks did not appear suddenly at that time – it was just that researchers were looking for the wrong kind of evidence. Microscopic examination of ancient sediments has revealed fossilised remains of sharks which may push their origins back at least 50 million years further.

Traditionally, sharks have been regarded as primitive vertebrates – so-called 'living fossils' – but recent work suggests that they are highly specialised. Their complex biology ranks them with birds and mammals as highly evolved

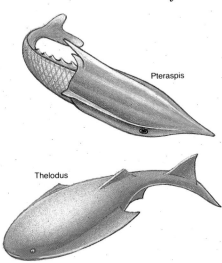

Two of the earliest backboned animals on earth. These ancient fishes, which lived in seas that covered the earth between 350 and 440 million years ago, had primitive, sucking mouths.

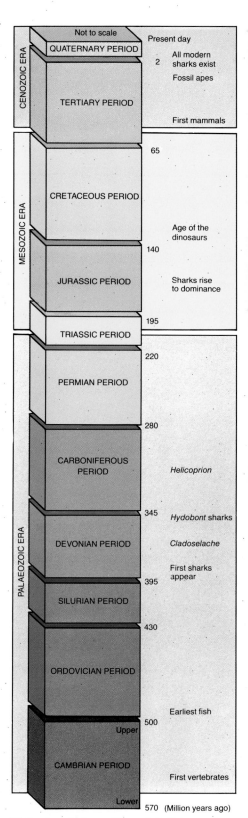

This chart shows the subdivisions of geological time, from the Cambrian period to the present day. The terms Lower and Upper are used to describe the beginning and end of a period.

Chart labels:

Not to scale

CENOZOIC ERA
- QUATERNARY PERIOD
- TERTIARY PERIOD

MESOZOIC ERA
- CRETACEOUS PERIOD
- JURASSIC PERIOD
- TRIASSIC PERIOD

PALAEOZOIC ERA
- PERMIAN PERIOD
- CARBONIFEROUS PERIOD
- DEVONIAN PERIOD
- SILURIAN PERIOD
- ORDOVICIAN PERIOD
- Upper
- CAMBRIAN PERIOD
- Lower

- Present day
- 2 — All modern sharks exist — Fossil apes
- First mammals
- 65
- Age of the dinosaurs
- 140 — Sharks rise to dominance
- 195
- 220
- 280
- Helicoprion
- 345 — Hydobont sharks
- Cladoselache
- First sharks appear
- 395
- 430
- Earliest fish
- 500
- First vertebrates
- 570 (Million years ago)

Image labels: Pteraspis, Thelodus

Complete, or almost complete, fossils of sharks are rare and therefore highly prized by scientists. This is a specimen of the genus *Stethacanthus*, which had a curious 'brush' on its back.

creatures. Even Devonian sharks, which were once considered to be the most primitive, are now thought to have been relatively specialised – with a longer evolutionary past than was once supposed.

The evolution of sharks remains unclear partly because it has been difficult to analyse particular characters – such as the shapes of braincases or fin structures – of modern sharks, which are an extremely diverse group, adapted to many habits and habitats. Any analysis of fossil sharks has had to rely almost solely on hard parts, such as teeth. Other features such as fins are only rarely preserved. Much more needs to be known about ancient sharks before any assessment can be made as to which characters were 'primitive', and which were 'advanced'.

All that is known about ancient sharks and their evolution has been gleaned from the fossil record. Fossil remains of sharks have been known for many centuries, although their true nature was not always recognised. Until the 17th century many scholars regarded such fossils as sports of nature, and thought that fossilised shark's teeth were bird's or snake's tongues. Some large fossil teeth, called glossopetrae (literally tongue-stones), were used as amulets to ward off evil and to protect against poisoning. It was not until about 150 years ago that the study of fossils, palaeontology, became a science, and the ancient remains of plants and animals were systematically classified.

Sharks are rarely found as complete fossils because their skeletons are made of cartilage. Normally only the hard parts, such as teeth, scales and fin spines, are found. However, under certain special conditions, complete fossil sharks are preserved, and these provide scientists with vital information. One such deposit, found last century in Upper Devonian Cleveland shales from the USA, yielded entire shark carcases which had been preserved in a bacteria-free environment so that even muscle and kidney tissue could be examined in the rock.

The very earliest signs of sharks are minute fossil scales and teeth which are found in rocks from the late Silurian to early Devonian

Fossil shark teeth embedded in a piece of Miocene limestone from Victoria in Australia. Detailed examination of such remains has enabled scientists to piece together the complex story of how life evolved on earth.

period (around 400 million years ago). It becomes more and more difficult, however, to identify shark scales in older rocks because they closely resemble those from jawless fishes called thelodonts, which lived at the same time. Only microscopic differences separate shark and thelodont scales, and the two kinds seem to become more and more alike the further one goes back.

A similar problem exists with ancient shark teeth, which did not seem to be present in rocks older than those from the mid-Devonian. It now seems that the reason for this was that scientists were not looking in the right places, and that early shark teeth were often very small. In 1986 teeth were found in Lower Devonian rocks from Spain which belonged to a group of sharks called xenacanthids.

What, then, were the origins of the shark-like fishes? One possibility is that different cartilaginous fishes (the group which includes sharks, skates, rays and chimaeras) evolved from placoderms (now extinct, bony-plated jawed fishes). Alternatively the placoderms and the cartilagenous fishes might all have shared a common ancestor at some time in the early Silurian period, some 430 million years ago. A third possibility is that the cartilaginous fishes and a group of primitive jawless fishes, such as thelodonts, both had a common ancestor. Thelodonts (now extinct) had a skeleton made of cartilage and were covered with scales, which may have lined their mouths as well. They also had paired fins and eight pairs of branchial structures for supporting their gills. One region where thelodonts evolved rapidly was around Tuva, in Siberia, which is also where the oldest known shark scales have been found.

The common ancestor of sharks and thelodonts (a fossil of which is yet to be found) would probably have been a small fish with a long slender body, one dorsal fin, no fin spines, paired pectoral fins and at least seven pairs of gill supports. Its mouth would have been either at the front of its body, or slightly beneath it, and the creature would have been covered with small scales which varied in size and shape according to their position on its

ANCIENT ANCESTORS OF MODERN SHARKS

Hybodus
The first hybodont sharks appeared during the Carboniferous period and members of this group only died out about 65 million years ago, at the end of the Cretaceous period. Specimens of *Hybodus* grew to around 2.5 m (7.5 ft).

Stethacanthus
This strange shark lived during the Carboniferous and Permian periods. The purpose of the brush-like patches of denticles on its head and back are unknown, but one theory suggests that they may have been used to simulate an open mouth which would have frightened away attackers. *Stethacanthus* grew to a length of about one metre (3.3 ft).

Cladoselache
The earliest complete fossil sharks so far found belong to this genus. They have very distinctive three-pointed teeth which first appear in rocks from the mid-Devonian period, and gradually disappear by the Permian period. Specimens range from 0.5 to 2 m (1.5 to 6 ft) in length.

Reconstructions of three ancient sharks, based on fossil remains and a knowledge of shark physiology. The colouring is entirely conjectural – fossils provide no evidence from which to draw conclusions on that subject.

body. Scales would also probably have lined its mouth.

The story of how sharks developed from these ancestral forms is complex and confused. Scientists do not have a set of fossil remains which show a smooth transition from species to species, connecting ancient forms to their modern descendants. Instead they have some isolated pieces from an immensely complex jigsaw. Some fossils are of evolutionary experiments which led nowhere and eventually became extinct. Others may have features which seem to explain gaps in our knowledge, but also have other features which raise more questions. Some new discoveries provide little information at present, but may

become vital when other pieces of the jigsaw are in place. Many theories exist to explain the evidence that is available, and these are constantly being modified as new information comes to light.

Although there is evidence of earlier sharks, the first complete fossils of shark-like fishes have been discovered in mid-Devonian rocks. Most frequently found are members of the genus *Cladoselache*, streamlined fish that grew to a length of about two metres (6 ft). Fortunately, complete specimens of *Cladoselache* have been preserved in the remarkable Cleveland shales, so quite a lot is known about them. They had five pairs of gill slits, a fin spine and all the same fins as modern sharks, except for an anal

fin. These spines, which become more common and elaborate in later sharks, and which still persist in some species today, were positioned in front of the dorsal fins and acted as cutwaters. *Cladoselache* had distinctive teeth with a large central cusp flanked by several smaller points, and apparently they lived on small fish – the remains of which have been found in the stomachs of fossilised specimens. These sharks are not now considered to be the main line leading to the modern species.

One important feature, however, was missing from *Cladoselache*, and most of its relatives in Devonian seas – claspers. These copulatory devices, which all modern sharks have, are only found in the

Shark teeth, together with scales and dorsal spines, are the three parts of sharks most often preserved in rocks. Both crushing teeth, for eating shellfish, and pointed teeth, for eating flesh, are included in this collection.

A chart showing the way in which the various groups of modern sharks might have evolved. Diagrams such as this are based on a study of fossil remains to see how ancient, as well as modern species are related. Fine details of the evolutionary tree change as new information becomes available.

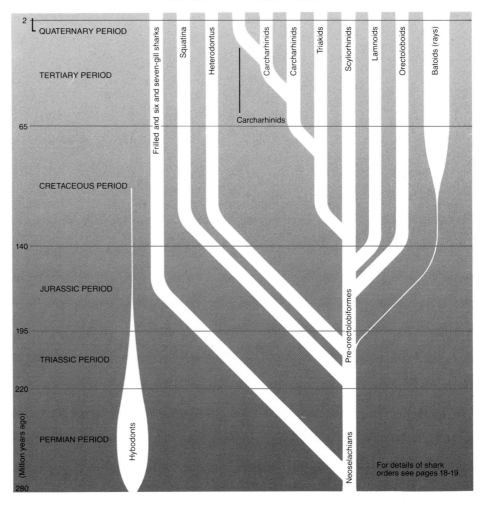

THE SHARK'S FAMILY TREE

ONE OF NATURE'S STRANGER EXPERIMENTS

Perhaps the most curious of all ancient teeth are those from the shark-like creature *Helicoprion*, which first appeared during the Carboniferous period, some 345 million years ago. Fossil teeth in the form of spirals or whorls are found in rocks worldwide and gave rise to many fantastic reconstructions before partially complete fossil specimens were found which enabled researchers to see how the teeth might have fitted inside the fish's jaws.

A whorl was created as new teeth, generated at the front of the creature's jaw throughout its life, rotated backwards as needed. Old teeth, instead of breaking off or falling out, disappeared into a special chamber inside the structure of the jaw, where they remained for the rest of the animal's life. Almost nothing is known about how these strange creatures lived, and there is even debate about whether they are related to the true sharks at all. Some scientists think that they belong in a special group of their own.

Fossil teeth (left) from Helicoprion.

Reconstruction (below) shows how teeth may have fitted into the jaw.

The curious teeth of a frilled shark *Chlamydosalachus anguineus* – one of the so-called 'primitive' sharks, which closely resembles some extinct species. This shark has some 300, three-pointed teeth, arranged in 27 rows, to provide it with about 1000 hooks with which to grasp the fish it eats.

stethacanthids and a few other groups of ancient sharks that lived at the same time as *Cladoselache*.

In the Devonian period a new group of sharks became common – the hybodonts. These became the dominant group during the Mesozoic era (from about 220 to 65 million years ago), when nearly all other shark groups died out. Although they were not as streamlined as modern oceanic sharks, and were probably not as accomplished as swimmers, they were nevertheless an advance on *Cladoselache*. A typical genus of this group is *Hybodus* which was found all around the world from the Triassic period to the mid-Cretaceous. This shark grew to at least 2.5 m (7.5 ft) in length, and had a blunt snout with an elongated body. The arrangement of its teeth – with sharp pointed ones at the front and blunt ones at the back – seems to suggest that it caught swimming prey as well as eating shellfish, such as molluscs.

Although sharks and shark-like fishes have a long history, the modern sharks (neoselachians) did not rise to dominance until after the Jurassic period, when, for some reason that is not yet clear, many of the more ancient forms had become extinct. Some Jurassic sharks are closely related to modern sharks, and this gives many present-day shark families histories which stretch back for 135 million years or more. The skates and rays, another group of cartilaginous fishes, also appeared in the mid-Jurassic, but they did not really come into their own until the Tertiary period, between 65 and 2 million years ago, when they were able to exploit a dramatic rise in the numbers of bivalve shellfish in the oceans.

The fossil record of modern sharks is fairly good, but again it normally consists only of hard parts such as teeth and scales. The appearance and relationships of present-day groups are well understood compared with the situation in the Palaeozoic and Mesozoic eras. Oceans in the Cretaceous period (140 to 65 million years ago) were dominated by goblin, sand, porbeagle, nurse, cow and angel sharks. Early sawfishes appeared and later evolved into the modern sawsharks. At the beginning of the Tertiary period (about 65 million years ago) the grey nurse sharks (odontaspididae) were found in large numbers. All modern forms of sharks were present in seas of the Miocene epoch (25 to 5 million years ago), including the giant *Carcharodon megalodon*, perhaps the most awesome of all sharks, now extinct.

Many researchers are working on the problems presented by ancient sharks, and recent discoveries have included some of the oldest shark fossils found. Among international research has been work in Germany which has concentrated on examining the fine structure of shark teeth and scales, and has revealed that the outer enamel on many teeth has three layers – a feature which can be used to identify certain groups of sharks. Other work, in the USA, has been delving into the nature of the supposedly primitive modern species – the frilled shark *Chlamydoselachus anguineus*, the Port Jackson shark *Heterodontus portusjacksoni* and the sixgill and sevengill sharks (family hexanchidae) – in an attempt to understand their relationships to other modern sharks, and to uncover any links with earlier fossil forms.

One particularly important recent discovery has been the recognition of a new class of fossil sharks called iniopterygians. Remains of this strange group have been found in Upper Carboniferous rocks from North America which are 300 million years old. Examination has shown that these creatures are a 'missing link', and that they combined certain characteristics of both elasmobranchs (sharks, skates and rays) and holocephalians (chimaeras or rattails). The life styles of these fishes remain uncertain, although their complex tooth plates seem to suggest that they lived on shellfish.

There has been an upsurge of interest in fossil sharks in recent years as more information has become available from new fossil discoveries, especially in the southern continents, and from a microscopic examination of existing fossil remains. In many cases these discoveries have helped scientists to understand some of the finds made last century. There are still few definite answers about the origins and relationships of all the known fossil, and some modern, sharks but progress is being made.

A TRUE MONSTER OF THE DEEP

In 1909 scientists at the American Museum of Natural History attempted this reconstruction of a megalodon *jaw. Modern experts consider it to be far too large, having been based on incorrect assumptions.*

Some 12 000 years ago, at about the time when mammoths became extinct, humans who ventured into the sea faced the possibility of meeting the largest flesh-eating shark that has ever lived – a close relative of the great white.

Estimates vary for the length of *Carcharodon megalodon* – as this monster has been named – but the most realistic seem to agree on a figure of between 12 and 15 m (40 and 50 ft), with a weight of around 20 tonnes.

Teeth from this giant shark – some measuring up to 152 mm (6 in) in length, and weighing 340 g (12 oz) – are commonly found in Palaeocene sediments from around the world. Many have also been dredged from the sea floor (see p 70).

Nobody can be sure exactly when *megalodon* became extinct, and some optimists have even claimed that isolated specimens may still exist in the ocean depths today. Most scientists, however, dismiss this possibility out of hand.

Two teeth from the giant extinct shark Carcharodon megalodon, compared with *that of a great white. The fossil teeth are large – probably as large as any found – and came from a shark that must have been at least 12 m (40 ft) long. The great white to which the single tooth belonged was around 3 m (9.8 ft) long. The enamel height on the largest* megalodon *tooth ever found is 115 mm (4.53 in), compared with a maximum for a great white of around 70 mm (2.8 in).*

SHARKS IN THE WILD

It is difficult to study sharks in the ocean, particularly the big predators, because they are almost impossible to watch for any length of time. Before techniques for tagging large sharks were developed, very little was known of their movements and migrations.

In the 1950s various tags were developed which could be inserted into fishes without removing them from the water. This is especially important with sharks because their organs are supported by membranes which tear when subjected to the full force of gravity.

The techniques for tagging large fishes were developed at Woods Hole Oceanographic Institute, Massachusetts, in the USA. Fish were caught with conventional sport fishing gear and a long pole was used to prod a sharpened tag into the shoulder of each animal before it was released.

Because this method proved to be most effective for catching and tagging large sharks, scientists took advantage of a growing interest in sport fishing, and issued tags to recreational anglers. This voluntary system has been so successful that many fisheries' programmes throughout the world now rely completely on the assistance of thousands of dedicated anglers.

By far the largest co-operative

A tagged copper shark *Carcharhinus brachyurus* about to be released off the New South Wales coast. The white tag can clearly be seen projecting from beneath the fish's dorsal fin.

shark tagging programme in the world is conducted from the National Marine Fisheries Service laboratories in Narragansett, Rhode Island, USA. The programme has been running for over 20 years, and in that time over 50 000 sharks have been tagged. Recreational anglers have carried out most of those taggings, the balance being done by scientists on board research and commercial vessels. The results have been outstanding and have helped in an understanding of the growth, movements and population structures of a number of species of large sharks.

Probably the most complete picture of migration patterns has come from the tagging of over 30 000 blue sharks *Prionace glauca*. Many transatlantic crossings have been recorded, by sharks starting from both sides of the Atlantic, as well as other long distance movements throughout the region. In 1985 the first blue shark tagged in the western Atlantic was recaptured over the equator in the southern hemisphere. Until then, it was thought that blue sharks in the north Atlantic were part of one stock, distinct from those in the south Atlantic.

Long distance movements have also been recorded by shortfin mako, tiger and sandbar sharks. The greatest distance recorded for a tagged mako was 2700 km (1690 miles) from Virginia, USA, to the West Indies. The fastest sustained trip for this species was made by a fish which, in just three months, swam over 2413 km (1500 miles) at a rate of 28 km (17.6 miles) per day. Of course, this is the minimum rate of travel for a straight-line journey. In reality, the shark would have covered a far greater distance.

A tagged tiger shark swam 2965 km (1853 miles) from New York to Costa Rica, while many sandbar sharks have been tagged off the eastern United States and

FITTING THE PUZZLE TOGETHER

The results of tagging studies are slow to realise. Only a small proportion of the fish tagged are ever recaptured, so many tens of thousands must be released before any pattern of behaviour will begin to emerge. In 1985 over 7000 sharks were released in the United States' programme, and only 256 sharks were captured with tags in them. The 256 tags were returned from 15 countries around the world, as far apart as Japan, Spain, Puerto Rico, Canada and Korea. Most of the recaptured fish (48 per cent) were caught by commercial long-line fishermen, with 36 per cent being caught by amateur anglers fishing with a conventional rod and line.

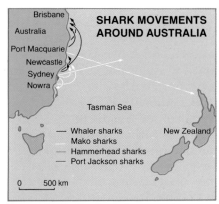

A mako holds the Australian record.

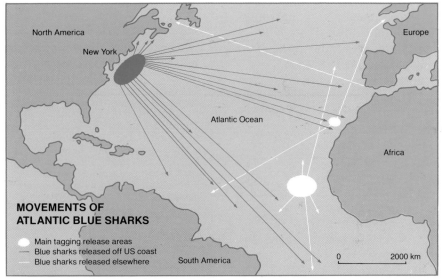

Blue sharks are the greatest travellers of all — some swimming 6000 km (3800 miles).

Sharks of these three species regularly swim 2700 km (1700 miles) or more.

recovered in Mexican waters, 2900 km (1800 miles) away.

Another co-operative gamefish tagging programme, modelled on the successful American example, started in Australia in 1973. This programme, with its headquarters at the New South Wales Department of Agriculture's Fisheries Research Institute in Sydney, seeks the co-operation of anglers to tag a wide range of gamefish including marlin, tuna and the so-called game sharks.

Over 40 000 fish have been tagged by volunteer anglers since the programme started, including around 3000 sharks. The whaler sharks (family Carcharhinidae) are the most frequently tagged.

Nearly two per cent of all sharks tagged in Australian waters have been recaptured. Most of those recovered were whalers, with makos second. All of the whaler sharks recaptured were found to the north of their release points. This is interesting because most sharks of this group tagged off the eastern United States migrated to the south. Sharks in both hemispheres seem to move towards the equator.

The longest movement recorded so far was by a mako shark which crossed the Tasman Sea from Australia to New Zealand, a distance of 2050 km (1285 miles). The fastest rate of travel was only 3.3 km (2 miles) a day for a whaler shark at liberty for 86 days. This is much less than the United States record, but similar results are expected as more tagged sharks are released each year.

Apart from providing information about migration

Scientists grapple with a small shark on the deck of a research vessel as they attempt to insert a tag. Even small sharks like this are surprisingly strong and can only be held down with some effort. The creature's razor sharp teeth could inflict considerable damage if it managed to break free.

RECORD TRAVELLERS

Dozens of blue sharks Prionace glauca *mill about in the water beneath a boat.*

The most travelled species of shark (and one which has been tagged in large numbers) is without doubt the blue shark. Tagging has shown that the species wanders throughout the north Atlantic Ocean.

Many sharks are popularly thought to be territorial, but tagging shows that most species do move around to some extent. Perhaps the least travelled group are the nurse sharks.

The record distance travelled by a shark is held by a blue which swam 5980 km (3740 miles) from New York State, where it was released, to Brazil.

The time record between tagging and recapture is held by two sandbar sharks. Both were tagged in the same week in 1965 off the eastern coast of the USA. Incredibly, they were both recaptured in the same week, 19.7 years later, over 1600 km (1000 miles) from where they were released, but only 160 km (100 miles) apart!

patterns, tagging programmes can also help in studying other aspects of the biology of sharks, such as growth rates and population structures.

It is important to know how sharks (and other fishes) grow and age so that replacement rates can be estimated. Only then is it possible to say how many sharks can be taken by fishermen without seriously damaging stocks. Because tagged sharks are actually measured when they are released and recaptured, often some years later, it has been possible to show that some species grow only a few centimetres a year. This, together with the fact that often very few young are produced in a season, means that such species can easily be over-exploited.

Tagging has also shown that some sharks keep close to the coast all of their lives, while others, such as blue sharks, may cross oceans and enter the fishing zones of other nations. This information is vital when 'ownership' of fish stocks are discussed internationally. Studies have also revealed that males and females of some shark species are often segregated for much of their lives, only mixing during the breeding season.

At present tagging can only show where a fish was released and recaptured, while the history of its actual day-to-day movements and activities remain a mystery. However, a new type of tag may help to provide this information. Known as the sonic tag, it is a small, battery-powered transmitter attached to a normal tag head. The

STUDIES THAT SHOW HOW SHARKS AGE AND GROW

Sharks, like other fishes, continue to grow throughout their lives. Early growth is usually fairly rapid in most species, tapering off after maturity, and eventually becoming very slow, but nevertheless still perceptible, throughout later life.

It is fairly easy to calculate the age of bony fishes, such as trout or perch, because scales and bones have annual growth rings. Sharks, however, have skeletons made up mostly of cartilage and only the core of the skeleton, the vertebrae, show any growth rings which can be used to estimate age.

To age a shark several vertebrae are cut from the animal's body and the central part is removed and treated in some way to expose the growth rings. This can be done by etching the bone with mild acid and silver nitrate, scorching or polishing. When it has been treated, the surface of the vertebra will usually show concentric rings, like those on a cut tree trunk – and in much the same way, the age of the shark can be estimated by counting these rings. In practice, there are usually many more rings than there are years that the shark has been alive, and

this is where tagging studies can assist scientists in deciding which rings to count.

If a shark is recaptured one, two or more years after being tagged, then its vertebrae can be used to count likely annual rings. This method is especially useful if very small sharks of known age (say less than one year old) are tagged, and subsequently recaptured several years later. The real annual rings can then be determined and these results applied to all other samples. For this reason, scientists are always excited when they receive the whole carcass of a recaptured shark that has been at liberty for more than one year.

Ageing studies of sharks have shown that some species are very slow growing, while others are much faster. The average growth rate of sandbar sharks *Carcharhinus plumbeus,* for example, has been found to be about 43 mm (1.7 in) per year, whereas the shortfin mako apparently grows at the much faster rate of about 280 mm (11 in) per year. Blue sharks grow even faster, at about 320 mm (12.6 in) per year. Individual sharks of the same species may also have very different growth rates (see below).

Growth rings in the vertebra of a female spot-tail shark (above).

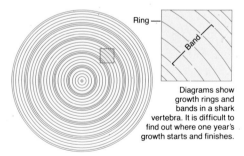

Ring —

Band

Diagrams show growth rings and bands in a shark vertebra. It is difficult to find out where one year's growth starts and finishes.

1 First capture 1140 mm

Growth in 5.1 years 260 mm

2 First capture 1290 mm

Growth in 5.1 years 180 mm

1 Second capture 1400 mm

2 Second capture 1470 mm

Two Galapagos sharks Carcharhinus galapagensis *tagged and recaptured off South Africa. Both had been at liberty for*

5.1 years, and had grown at quite different rates. The growth rate of the first shark had almost doubled that of the second.

Various chemical processes can be used to accentuate growth patterns in the vertebrae (spinal bones) of sharks. The patterns take the form of bands, each made up of a number of closely-spaced rings. Experiments are now being carried out to inject captured sharks with chemicals that are quickly deposited in bone. When sharks that have been treated in this way are recaptured, their vertebrae can be examined to show up the band of injected chemical, and any subsequent growth rings that can be counted will therefore have been formed over a known period of time.

device emits sonic pulses which vary with depth, and these can be tracked and recorded using a receiver on a boat.

The system has been used successfully on billfish and tuna, but only recently on sharks. One such experiment involved tracking a large white shark for two and a half days. In that time, it cruised at an average speed of 3.2 km/h (2 mph) and covered about 190 km (120 miles).

One possible problem with this type of experiment is that sharks may not behave normally for a while after being hooked and tagged. It has not been possible to track sharks for more than a few days, and it is during this period that their behaviour is most likely to be abnormal.

A number of different types of tags were used to mark sharks in the past, including internal plastic discs, plastic clips attached to dorsal fins, and even freeze-branding with very cold implements. Most modern shark tags resemble small arrows or darts, made from plastic, nylon and stainless steel. These are inserted into the shoulder muscle with a short jab using a tag pole.

Few sharks die after being tagged and released, and the process does not appear to upset them for long. There are many cases of tagged sharks being recaptured the same day that they were released, and even of freshly tagged sharks doggedly following the boat which released them!

Once the tag is embedded and fully healed, it is likely that it will stay in place for several years. Hooks are sometimes seen in the mouths or stomach linings of recaptured sharks, but because very few are found, it seems that they corrode and fall out soon after the fish is released. Only rarely do wounds become ulcerated.

The two main international tagging programmes in which sharks are included are detailed in the box (right). Programmes involving anglers also exist in Great Britain, South Africa, Canada, and other parts of the United States. The main species studied are the large predators, including the blue, mako, tiger, hammerhead and white sharks, and various species of the family Carcharhinidae. Most of these are distributed unevenly around the world and scientists hope that tagging will help to show if they are interrelated.

A fisherman uses a tagging pole to insert a tag in a small shark that has been hooked and is being held alongside the boat by another angler. This experience apparently causes the sharks no lasting harm.

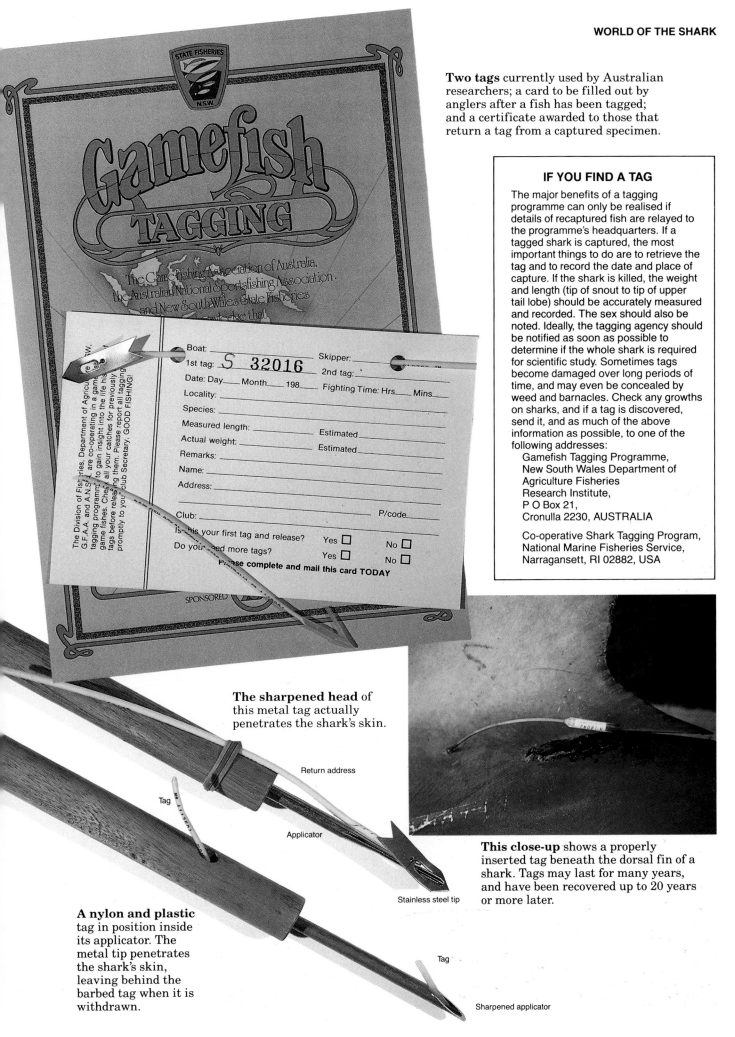

Two tags currently used by Australian researchers; a card to be filled out by anglers after a fish has been tagged; and a certificate awarded to those that return a tag from a captured specimen.

IF YOU FIND A TAG

The major benefits of a tagging programme can only be realised if details of recaptured fish are relayed to the programme's headquarters. If a tagged shark is captured, the most important things to do are to retrieve the tag and to record the date and place of capture. If the shark is killed, the weight and length (tip of snout to tip of upper tail lobe) should be accurately measured and recorded. The sex should also be noted. Ideally, the tagging agency should be notified as soon as possible to determine if the whole shark is required for scientific study. Sometimes tags become damaged over long periods of time, and may even be concealed by weed and barnacles. Check any growths on sharks, and if a tag is discovered, send it, and as much of the above information as possible, to one of the following addresses:

Gamefish Tagging Programme,
New South Wales Department of Agriculture Fisheries
Research Institute,
P O Box 21,
Cronulla 2230, AUSTRALIA

Co-operative Shark Tagging Program,
National Marine Fisheries Service,
Narragansett, RI 02882, USA

The sharpened head of this metal tag actually penetrates the shark's skin.

Return address

Tag

Applicator

Stainless steel tip

This close-up shows a properly inserted tag beneath the dorsal fin of a shark. Tags may last for many years, and have been recovered up to 20 years or more later.

A nylon and plastic tag in position inside its applicator. The metal tip penetrates the shark's skin, leaving behind the barbed tag when it is withdrawn.

Tag

Sharpened applicator

49

GREAT WHITE DEATH

Villain of a hundred stories, hated, abused, misunderstood, the great white shark **Carcharodon carcharias** *rose to prominence in films such as* **Jaws** *and* **Blue Water, White Death**. *It is therefore surprising to discover that, for all its fearsome reputation, very little is known scientifically about this huge fish. Few people have had more experience with them in their natural environment than the photographers Ron and Valerie Taylor, and here Valerie gives some of her own observations about these monsters of the deep.*

'In 1965 Ron became the first person to film a great white shark underwater. He did this by hanging unprotected from the platform at the back of a tuna boat. On board, along with shark victims Brian Roger, Rodney Fox and Henri Bource, was the world famous shark fisherman, Alf Dean. During the trip Alf caught five great whites and taught us how to attract them.

'It was the first and last time that Ron was involved with the mass slaughter of sharks. It was also the first and last time that he worked with great whites without the protection of a steel cage.

'We have been filming whites now for more than 20 years, and we still use Alf's original method of attracting them. Now, however, we have to use far more burley (fresh minced tuna, blood and fish oil), and there seem to be fewer great whites to attract. I believe that unless some protection is given to these beasts, they may be doomed to extinction.

'The great white shark, or white pointer, is the largest potentially

A curious great white shark closes in to inspect a potential meal. These sharks will repeatedly ram a cage in a search for something edible, their teeth tearing at the flimsy mesh. On more than one occasion badly shaken divers have had to be evacuated by their companions from damaged cages.

Three consecutive frames (below) from a movie film show the astonishing speed with which a great white shark seizes its prey. The photographs are only four-hundredths of a second apart. In order to attack, the shark changes the whole shape of its head so that the mouth moves to the front, and the snout bends up out of the way. After biting, the mouth moves back to its original position. Even a 5-m (16-ft) great white can easily tear a piece of blubber the size of a large dog from the tough hide of a dead whale.

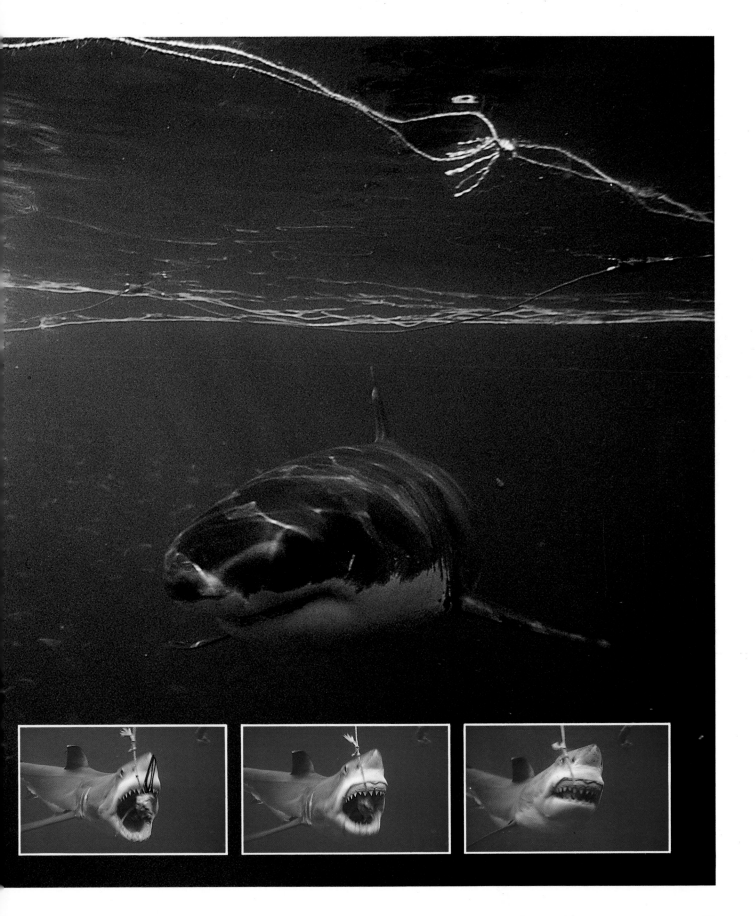

Teeth from the upper and lower jaws of a great white shark have razor sharp serrated edges, specially adapted for slicing through the toughest skin.

dangerous fish in the ocean. It tends to live in temperate waters, although it has been found in almost every ocean on earth.

'We believe that great whites are basically territorial, returning regularly to the same area year after year. The size of their territory may vary according to the richness of the feeding grounds and the number of other large sharks living nearby. On one occasion we tagged a shark which was subsequently caught six months later only 1 km (1.6 miles) away from the tagging site. We have also noticed that we see the same sharks year after year in the same areas. Not all sharks are easily recognisable, but some have unmistakable peculiarities that make them stand out. There seems to be little doubt that sharks remember past encounters with us. When they first come up against our steel cage they test its strength by biting it, trying to get at the diver inside. On a second meeting they hesitate to bite, apparently realising that the steel bars will break their teeth.

'Many sharks, because of their size, need large amounts of food. This is why great whites are often found around seal colonies, rather than near coral reefs.

'Very little scientific research has been carried out on great white sharks. They are not commonly seen unless attracted by baits. Because their diet occasionally includes humans, they can only be studied in their natural environment from a cage. In such circumstances it often seems that the observer, imprisoned

behind bars, has become the observed, while the sharks are free to come and go as they wish.

'Most of what we know about great whites is related to their feeding patterns. What they do when they are not looking for food is a matter for speculation. We can only guess as to where they breed, how large they are at birth, how often they eat and how far they travel under normal circumstances.

'Some facts have, however, emerged from our observations. Over the years we have noticed that adult great whites in some areas tend to live in groups according to their size and sex. At Dangerous Reef in South Australia, for

example, the average shark we see is a male 3 to 5 m (10 to 16.4 ft) long. Further west, around Streaky Bay, the average shark is a female around 5 to 6 m (16.4 to 19.7 ft) long. Juvenile great white sharks are not seen by divers, yet at certain times of the year they are caught in mesh nets off southern Queensland.

'Along the northern Californian coast, where great whites are very common, the sizes and sexes seem to be more mixed. In this area there are many islands that support a large population of seals.

'A few years ago it was believed that sharks, like most fish, were cold blooded – that their body temperature was the same as that

The monster contemplating this diver is around 3.5 m (11.5 ft) long. While record claims are confused and difficult to verify, it appears that great whites can occasionally reach an astonishing 9.1 m (30 ft) long, and may perhaps grow even larger.

Great whites are the only sharks that lift their heads clear of the water so that they can inspect objects on the surface. They will also emerge partly from the water to secure a good grip on an intended prey.

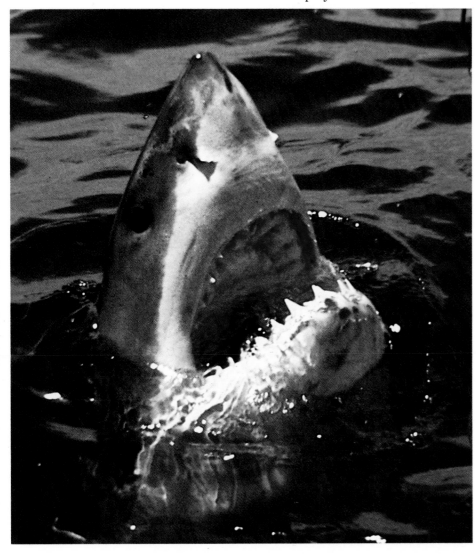

of the surrounding water. At the request of an American shark expert, Mr Thomas A. Lineaweaver, we always carried two large thermometers with us when diving. Mr Lineaweaver believed that large, fast moving fish and sharks, because of constant muscle action, may generate a body temperature higher than that of the surrounding ocean. He therefore asked us to take the temperature of a living great white shark.

'In January 1973, while we were filming for a television special, a large female great white, 4.3 m (14 ft) long and weighing around 700 kg (1540 lb), became entangled in the steel trace attaching our cage to the boat. This was a perfect opportunity. Once she was tired, we carefully dragged her into shallow water. She struggled half-heartedly, but the steel trace held fast. Ron drove a slender knife deep into her back, then inserted the thermometer. Her body temperature was 22.55°C, and at the time the water temperature was 20.5°C. When we measured the shark's temperature she had been practically motionless for about three hours, so muscle action could hardly account for her higher body temperature (see p.20).

'In 1965, when we first began working with great whites, I thought they were dumb brutes – all brawn and no brains. Now, after working with hundreds of these sharks, I know my original impression was false. Great whites may have small brains, but they seem to use them effectively. They can be taught simple tricks in about 20 minutes – such as to always approach the sunny corner of a boat for food (for filming purposes). Great whites can also see very well, and they are the only sharks to lift their heads clear of the water to inspect surface objects. It is quite unnerving to look up and find a shark watching your every move.'

SHARKS FOLLOW THEIR NOSES

Sharks have an extremely acute sense of smell, and are able to detect very small concentrations of some chemicals – particularly those that are important to them when hunting food. Some experiments carried out in the United States of America have proved sharks to be capable of responding to concentrations of certain chemicals in dilutions as low as one part per thousand million (for more details of this amazing ability see p.32).

Sharks are able to use smell to home in on a potential prey by adopting a very simple strategy: whenever they encounter the smell they simply turn into the current. By constantly swimming and turning upcurrent whenever the smell is detected (diagram right) they are able to find its source very rapidly. Humans and other land animals use very much the same method to find the source of an air-borne smell.

Source of smell

Water current

Shark

Path of shark

THE LARGEST FISH ON EARTH

Whale sharks and their relatives the basking sharks, are the largest fish on earth. However, while basking sharks are common enough to be hunted commercially for their livers, whale sharks, the larger of the two, are rarely seen.

Cavern like, the huge mouth of a 10-m (33-ft) whale shark dwarfs a diver. Fortunately for humans, these giant fish live almost exclusively on microscopic plankton, filtered from the water as they swim slowly along, just beneath the surface of the ocean.

A comparison between a whale shark and a medium-sized passenger car gives some idea of the fish's great size. Whale sharks are about the same size as sperm and humpback whales, but are considerably smaller than blue whales.

The name often causes confusion in the minds of laymen, but these gigantic fish are definitely sharks. The word whale merely refers to the creature's great size, and they have probably been mistaken for whales on many occasions. Whale sharks may grow to almost 18 m (59 ft) in length, and can weigh up to 40 000 kg (88 200 lb).

Because of their size, it is fortunate that they are plankton feeders. Humans have little to fear from these gentle creatures except for the possibility of having a boat bumped by one as it cruises along just beneath the surface of the sea.

Little is known about the lives of these giant sharks. They have two dorsal fins, a mackerel-shaped tail, small eyes and large gill slits. The body is ridged lengthwise and is decorated with a unique pattern of light spots with vertical and horizontal stripes on a dark background. Like several other species, such as the Port Jackson shark, whale sharks also lay eggs, the world's largest. One specimen trawled up from 57 m (187 ft) in the Gulf of Mexico measured 300 x 140 x 80 mm (12 x 5.5 x 3.2 in).

The embryo inside the egg was a well developed spotted replica of the adult. How fast newly hatched sharks grow, or how long they live remains a mystery. Only mature whale sharks have been observed, generally swimming slowly on the surface, their dorsal fins protruding from the water.

Whale sharks are found, although rarely, in most tropical waters. They are seen regularly near the Maldive Islands and the Seychelles in the Indian Ocean. At certain times of the year in the Gulf of Mexico charter boat operators can practically guarantee divers a swim with a whale shark.

The Gulf of Mexico is exceptionally rich in marine life. Plankton clouds the water, attracting all types of filter feeders, including whales and whale sharks. While plankton and small school fish seem to make up the largest part of a whale shark's diet, they have also occasionally been seen eating tuna, when both are sharing schools of bait fish. In each case, the sharks were feeding vertically, moving up and down through masses of small fish, their blunt heads periodically breaking the surface of the water. Tuna that were

feeding on the same fish were seen to be scooped into the sharks' enormous mouths, and although some jumped out, many were apparently eaten.

Whale sharks pay little attention to divers. Probably because of their size, they have little to fear in the ocean.

Since the discovery that they are common in the Gulf of Mexico, riding them has become a popular pastime with the lucky few. The sharks seem to tolerate humans hanging onto their dorsal fins, pectoral fins and tails without complaint. The diver's presence, provided it does not give discomfort to its host, probably causes no more inconvenience than sucker fish do to small sharks.

One group of American divers met a whale shark that actually appeared to like them. She was around 10 m (33 ft) long, and even when they had finished their dive, she followed the charter boat, apparently waiting for the divers to return. This amazing association continued for three days, after which the shark left. It is well known that whale sharks enjoy rubbing against floating objects, possibly to dislodge unwanted parasites. In this case, there were seven divers riding on the shark, so perhaps she simply enjoyed the constant handling.

Whale sharks are not often seen in Australian waters, but they are sometimes sighted. Diver and photographer Valerie Taylor described one such exciting encounter: 'We had our big thrill one bleak autumn day in the early 1970s. Ron Taylor, myself and a friend, John Harding, were returning from Seal Rocks, two miles [3.2 km] off Sugarloaf Point, New South Wales, when a huge fin broke the surface. At first, because of its size, we thought it might be a great white shark. I remember Ron saying, "No great white can be over 30 ft [9 m] long, it must be something else". We were all staring excitedly at the huge shape ahead of us. In those days, only two other divers had ever ridden and filmed a whale shark. Our delight at this incredible piece of luck made us forget the cold, dismal day and rough seas. This was our chance, and we certainly made the most of it. The shark was a large female, between 35 and 45 ft [10.7 and

THE STRANGE HISTORY OF WHALE SHARKS

This small whale shark was the victim of a collision in the Indian Ocean in 1932.

The first whale shark to be scientifically examined was harpooned in Table Bay, South Africa, in 1828. It was only a small specimen – a mere 4.6 m (15 ft) long – and the skin eventually found its way into a museum in Paris. Since then a number of whale sharks have been rammed by ships or stranded, but only a very few have been properly examined.

Over 20 collisions between whale sharks and ships have been recorded. These are apparently due to the fact that whale sharks are surface feeders, slow moving and

seemingly oblivious to danger. Both ships and sharks are damaged in these encounters, the sharks usually coming off worst. It is, however, interesting to note that the skin of a nine-metre (30-ft) whale shark was found to be 102 mm (4 in) thick – the thickest skin found on any living animal.

Various claims have been made for the largest whale shark ever sighted – some reaching an unlikely 20 to 23 m (65 to 75 ft). The largest properly measured specimen, caught near Karachi, Pakistan, in 1949, was 12.65 m (41.5 ft) long.

Clinging precariously to the pectoral fin of a huge whale shark, this diver was towed through the waters of the Gulf of Mexico at a comfortable 4 km/h (2.5 mph). Above her are the shark's giant gill slits.

13.7 m] in length, and we stayed with her for around three hours and travelled roughly 5 miles [8 km].

'She was heading steadily south at about 2 mph [3.7 km/h]. We turned her a few times, but she always swung back onto her original course. We were not using scuba diving equipment so could keep up with her if we swam fast, but our aluminium dingy was a problem. Fortunately the wind was pushing the 14-ft [4.5-m] boat in the right direction, but we still had to constantly pick it up and motor after our shark. Probably the most exciting moment, next to first seeing her, was when John and I rode on her tail. Being dragged through the water at tremendous speed as the tail swept to and fro in a 7-ft [2-m] cycle was a thrilling experience that I shall never forget.

'Eventually cold, failing light, and a strengthening wind drove us from the water. We last saw her, a large dark shape, disappearing through the white caps. Pounding into the worsening weather, we returned to our camp at Seal Rocks, the happiest divers in the world.'

A dwarf shark, barely 100 mm (4 in) long.

THE SMALLEST SHARK

In direct contrast to the whale shark, and shorter at sexual maturity than one of its giant eggs, is the spined pygmy or dwarf shark *Squaliolus laticaudus*. This tiny fish is the smallest known species of shark, reaching a maximum of only 250 mm (9.8 in). It is rarely seen because it lives on the ocean floor during the day, and travels 200 m (660 ft), or more, to feed near the surface at night. Dwarf sharks have numerous luminescent organs on their undersides which makes them more difficult to see from beneath, and therefore less vulnerable to predators.

Tab. VI

1

Tænia altera

2

Meer haub Tænia

Tænia Bellonÿ

3

Tænia falcata Imperati

4

Canis Carcharias

Großer Meer hun.

Canis Carchariæ species alia

ein ander art Meer oder Walhunds

5

Canis Carcharias alius

6

Part Two

2

Men and Sharks

At a time when
humans have little to
fear from the animal world
on land, sharks still reign
supreme in the oceans. Here is
the fascinating story of
man's relationship with
this most terrible of
all predators.

Illustrations of sharks
from Conrad Gesner's
Fisch-Buch, first
published in 1670.

'A MARVEILOUS STRANGE FISHE'

Human beings have known of the existence of sharks for as long as they have lived near the sea. To early humans sharks were only one of many dangerous and hostile animals that lived in the world around them. The encroachment of wild animals into the human domain was always alarming; at least sharks kept to the oceans.

Early societies saw the animals and plants around them in symbolic and religious terms. The natural world had no meaning or validity in its own right, but only in its resemblances and analogies to people, and sharks, like many animals, developed a role in various legends. Often they were the basis for the sea-monsters of mythology.

Although human societies knew enough about sharks to be afraid of them, there was no understanding of their natural history. Very little was known of the range of shark species, and there was no sense of classification. Sharks were known by many and changing names.

One of the earliest stories that may have involved a shark is the ancient Greek legend of Andromeda, the daughter of Cepheus, king of Ethiopia. Andromeda's mother boasted that her daughter was more beautiful than the Aegean nymphs known as Nereids. Poseidon, god of the sea, was angered by this and sent a sea-monster to ravage the coastline. The monster would only be placated by the sacrifice to it of Andromeda herself. Andromeda was then chained to a rock but was rescued by Perseus who slew the monster and married Andromeda.

The Biblical story of Jonah and the whale – if it can be taken literally at all – is now thought to refer to a shark rather than a whale. The original Hebrew version of the story uses the word *tanninum* which means any large sea animal. Traditionally this was thought to have referred to a whale because Saint Matthew, in the New Testament, mentions the story of 'Jonah and the whale'. Both whales and sharks were seen in the Mediterranean at that time.

There are a number of reasons why a shark, especially a great white shark, was more likely to have swallowed Jonah than a whale. The white shark has a less rigid diet than the largest toothed whales, such as the sperm, and is a more opportunistic feeder. They can also swallow large animals whole. One white shark was found to have an entire 50-kg (110-lb) sea lion in its stomach. The sixteenth century French naturalist Guillaume Rondelet reported finding a whole (and fully clad) sailor in the stomach of a great white. He believed that this shark was the 'fish' in the story of Jonah.

Some sharks also have a curious digestive system which allows them to store food in their stomachs for long periods without breaking it down. One tiger shark kept two intact dolphins in its stomach for over a month. Sharks can also regurgitate the entire contents of their stomachs at will.

The first historical reference to sharks is by the Greek writer Herodotus, known as 'the father of history'. His *Histories,* written in the fifth century BC, was the first great prose work of European literature, and described the struggle of the Greek city states against the Persian empire. In 492 BC, the Persian fleet was hit by a violent gale and Herodotus recorded that: 'a great many of the ships were driven ashore and wrecked on Athos [in northeastern Greece]. Indeed, the report says that

The 'great fish' that swallowed Jonah was more likely to have been a shark than a whale. Great white sharks are quite capable of swallowing a man whole, and there is even a report from 1758 of a sailor being swallowed by a shark which was forced to vomit him up, unharmed, shortly afterwards.

A mosaic from the Roman town of Pompeii, dating from about the first century AD, illustrates some of the life to be found in the Mediterranean Sea at that time. Included are two sharks (bottom left and top right).

something like 300 were lost with over 20 000 men. The sea in the neighbourhood of Athos is full of monsters so that those of the ships' companies who were not dashed to pieces on the rocks were seized and devoured.'

The first attempt to understand sharks as animals rather than mythologically was made by the philosopher and scientist Aristotle, who lived in Greece a century after Herodotus. His most important work on biology was the *Historia Animalium (Enquiry into Animals)* written about 330 BC.

Aristotle lived for many years by the sea in Macedonia and gathered a great deal of information about fishes and their habits from local fishermen. His knowledge of the fishes of the Mediterranean was greater than that of any other ancient writer and greater, in fact, than any naturalist until the sixteenth century. He was the first to describe the distinction between the bony and cartilaginous fishes. Although his fishes are described separately without any attempt at classification, Aristotle gathered the sharks and rays into a group he called *Selache,* a name still used in various forms by modern ichthyologists. He noted that sharks, unlike other fishes, have uncovered gills, and that, with some exceptions, they bear live young.

Aristotle was also the first to record that sharks mate by internal fertilisation (although he also wrongly assumed that other fish do so as well): 'All fishes with exception of the flat selachians [skates and rays] lie down side by side and copulate belly to belly ... Again in cartilaginous fishes the male, in some species, differs from the female in the fact that he is furnished with two appendages hanging down from about the exit of the residuum, and that the female is not so furnished.'

Although Aristotle was right

more often than he was wrong, he also started a myth about sharks that persists to this day. He noted that 'the mouths of sharks are placed not at the front but on the underside of the head ... so that these fishes turn on their back in order to take their food. The purpose of Nature in this was apparently not merely to provide a means of salvation for other animals, by allowing them opportunity of escape during the time lost in the act of turning – for all the fishes with this kind of mouth prey on living animals – but also to prevent these fishes from giving way too much to their gluttonous ravening after food ... an additional reason is that the projecting extremity of the head in these fishes is round and small, and therefore cannot admit of a wide opening.' Aristotle was wrong. Shark jaws are, of course, hinged to allow a near vertical gape and

A 4th century bust of Aristotle, whose observations of sharks and their behaviour, compiled in about 330 BC for his *Historia Animalium,* remained the most thorough study of the subject for almost 2000 years. Aristotle was also responsible for the myth that sharks must turn on their backs to attack.

sharks can and do bite right side up.

Over 400 years after Aristotle's *Historia Animalium*, another popular work on the natural world was compiled by Pliny the Elder, a Roman administrator and writer. In his encyclopaedic *Natural History*, written in about 77 AD, he described in colourful terms the dangers of dog-fishes, a general term for smaller sharks. 'Divers have fierce fights with the dog-fish; these attack their loins and heels and all the white parts of the body. The one safety lies in going for them and frightening them by taking the offensive; for a dog-fish is as much afraid of a man, as a man is of it.'

Other classical authors provided misinformation about sharks which persisted in some cases into the nineteenth century. Oppianus, a third century Greek

poet from Cilicia, wrote a long fishing epic called *Halieutica*. In it he developed a myth about blue sharks as ideal parents which is entirely inaccurate.

> 'Thus the Blue sharks, secure
>   from chasing foes,
> Within their widen'd mouths
>   their young enclose.
> Beneath the circling arch they
>   fearless hide,
> The bulky forms drive on the
>   rising tide.
> Of all oviparous kinds that
>   throng the seas,
> The fond Blue sharks in tender
>   care surpass.'

Sharks are, of course, found in all the world's oceans and other societies and cultures dealt with them in their own particular myths and practices.

The pearl divers of Sri Lanka,

to this day, place great reliance on shark-charmers, a custom that was first noticed by the Venetian traveller Marco Polo in 1298. 'There are moreover in that bay of the sea [the Gulf of Mannar] a multitude of great fishes,' he wrote, 'which would kill the fishers going down to the sea. But provision against that danger is made by the merchants in this way. The merchants take certain magicians with them who are called braaman, who with their enchantments and diabolical art control and stupefy those fishes so that they can hurt no one. And because this fishing is done by day and not by night, those magicians make spells by day which they break for the following night; for they are afraid lest anyone go down by stealth without the leave of the merchants into the sea by night to take pearls.'

The power of the shark charmers was supposed to be hereditary. 'At one time the charmer used to be allowed a percentage of one oyster per day from each diver but this has been commuted to a

Three mythical sea creatures from the late fifteenth century – a sea-cow, a sea-dog and a sea-horse. Small sharks were given the name sea-dogs or dogfish simply because they have sharp teeth, and popular imagination made them the nautical equivalents of dogs.

money payment', reported an article in the *Cornhill Magazine* in 1866. 'Accidents have never been known to occur on the pearl divers from sharks, which is of course attributed by the superstitious natives to the wise charming of the charmer.'

In the Pacific Ocean, shark

fishing has always been important to the economies of the island communities, and as a result has been overlaid with religious symbols and ceremonies. In contrast to the European idea of sharks as evil monsters, Pacific islanders have had a more ambivalent attitude; in many parts of Polynesia, for example, shark worship is still common.

Hunting the *kapeta* or dog-shark by New Zealand Maoris was a ritual controlled by priests from the shore. Up to 1000 men would set out to hunt the sharks on two specified days of the year. Other shark species could be caught at any time. The Society Islanders, in French Polynesia, also worshipped one shark, the blue, at the expense of others. 'Temples to these sharks were erected,' reported the missionary William Ellis in the late nineteenth century, 'and offerings were presented to the deified sharks while fishermen and others, who were much at sea, sought their favour.'

There are a number of legends of humans reincarnated as sharks, and the Hawaiians tell the story of the *mano-kanaka* or shark men – sharks who take human form to create mischief on land. In Hawaii and on the Solomon Islands there is evidence that people were once sacrificed to sharks. In Tonga, shark hunters would go to great lengths to obtain occult support. They would be celibate the night before going to sea, and while they were away the whole village would have to remain totally quiet.

Although the arrival of

An Australian Aboriginal bark painting from north-east Arnhem Land shows a fresh water shark, probably one of the whalers (family Carcharhinidae). Sharks were important to the Aborigines – as they were to many native people around the world – as a source of food, and because of the valuable oil in their livers – which is shown in this painting.

For medieval Europeans, who were only just starting to explore the world, the oceans teemed with hostile monsters. Some of the strange creatures in this illustration, which dates from about 1500, were clearly based on hazy descriptions of sharks (such as those labelled K, S and N).

Christianity in the nineteenth century reduced shark worship in the Pacific, many features of it remain in the more remote islands today. In the 1930s, Hawaiian shipwrights would try to propitiate sharks during a ship's maiden voyage. This custom was common in east Africa as well, where boat-builders still anoint the wood of new vessels with hammerhead shark oil to bring a good wind and a successful voyage.

Sharks also occur in Japanese legend. One of the traditional Japanese deities is a storm god known as Shark-Man. In one legend Shark-Man was rescued by Totaro whom he then made very rich. Totaro, however, wanted more – to marry a girl named Tamara. He asked Shark-Man for jewels for his bride and Shark-Man, after reproaching him for his greed, wept blood into a dish. The tears crystallised into ten thousand rubies. Another Japanese legend involved a warrior who performed amazing feats of strength, one of which was to swim through the

ocean with a shark under each arm.

In India, the god Vishnu is sometimes represented as coming out of the mouth of a monstrous fish, probably a shark. Vishnu is revered for having saved the *Vedas*, the sacred religious texts of India, when the entire world was drowned – an obvious parallel with the legend of Noah.

Many American Indian tribes have given sharks a place in their folklore. Some tribes, reported the herpetologist Lawrence Klauber, referred to rattlesnakes as 'the little sharks of the woods'. The Tlingit Indians used shark crests as the curved emblems for tribal clans. In Central and South America shark images have been found on ancient Indian pottery, and figurines depicting shark attack scenes were also made.

After the close of the classical age in Europe, curiosity about geography and natural history waned, and few observations of sharks were recorded. Europe closed in on itself and took little notice of the world outside. Marco Polo

mentioned sharks in the seas around Ceylon in the account of his journey to China in the thirteenth century, but it was not until the great voyages of exploration beginning in the fifteenth century that European chroniclers took an interest in sharks once again.

On Christopher Columbus's voyage to the West Indies in 1502, his ships were at one stage surrounded by sharks. 'It was frightening, especially to those who believe in omens,' recorded his son Ferdinand in a biography of his father. 'For just as some say that vultures recognise the presence of a corpse by its smell many leagues away, so some believe that sharks have the same divinatory power.'

Ferdinand Magellan noted the presence of sharks on his voyage around the world between 1519 and 1522. Off the west coast of Africa during a calm he recorded that 'great fish called tiburoni [sharks] approached the ship. They have terrible teeth and eat men when they find them alive or dead in the sea. And the said fish are caught with a hook of iron . . . but they are not good to eat when large.'

Roger Barlow, an English geographer, agreed with Magellan in 1540 about the quality of shark flesh – 'the meete is very tough and unsaverie', he reported. However, Peter Martyn Anglerius, a Dutch navigator in the West Indies wrote in the 1550s that 'the leaste of these fyshes [sharks] are most holsome and tender. When they have slayne this fyshe they [sailors] cutte the body therof in smaule pieces and put it to drye, hangynge it three or foure dayes at the cordes of the sayle clothes.' Anglerius also noted how sharks 'coome furth of the sea and enter into the ryvers . . . they are very dangerous in certeyne washynge places or pooles by the ryvers sydes.'

Many unreliable legends still surrounded the European view of

The illustrator working on Sir Thomas Herbert's account of his voyages, published in 1638, managed to get two of the hazards facing unfortunate sailors into the same engraving – sharks and tornadoes.

sharks. Olaus Magnus, a noted Swedish historian, wrote in 1555 of the malevolent 'sea-Dogfish that will set upon a man swimming in Salt-Waters so greedily … that he will sink the man to the bottom, not only by his biting, but also by his weight; and he will eat his more tender parts, as his nostrils and fingers.' Magnus went on to describe how the ray (a cousin of the shark) will come to the rescue of the

FAITHFUL COPIES

By the end of the eighteenth century enough information had been gathered by European explorers to enable scholars to assemble the first comprehensive guides to the plants and animals of the world. The first major work on fish – which included the 15 species of sharks then known – was published in Germany between 1785 and 1795, under the title *A Complete Natural History of Fish.* Its author was Marcus Eliezer Bloch.

Bloch was born in Ansbach, near Nuremberg, Germany in 1723. He was the son of poor Jewish parents and received hardly any education as a child. At the age of 19 he could still not read, but despite this managed to become tutor to the household of a barber in Hamburg. While working there Bloch realized that he needed to educate himself and, with the help of relatives, he went to Berlin to study medicine. He eventually gained his degree in Frankfurt, and later returned to Berlin.

Bloch was fascinated by fish all his life, and eventually came to be regarded as the most important ichthyologist of the 18th century. Both of his major works – a four-part monograph on the fishes of Germany (1781) and the nine-part *Natural History* – were published at his own expense.

The *Natural History* contained 216 colour plates which became a standard source of reference for artists and publishers for many years afterwards. Even errors, such as the jaws of the great white shark which were shown upside down in Bloch's book, were perpetuated in dozens of other publications for many years afterwards.

The great white shark from Marcus Bloch's Complete Natural History of Fish *(1785-95).*

Bloch's shark transferred to a South Seas island setting.

The white shark's inverted jaws were faithfully reproduced in this copy.

Any comparison with a real shark would have revealed serious errors in the fin shapes on the white shark.

man and drive the shark away – another myth that survived into this century.

Until the mid-sixteenth century the word shark in English referred only to human low life. Small sharks were known as dogfish and large ones as *tiburon* – the Spanish word for shark. The current meaning of shark did not come into the language until 1569, after a specimen captured by the explorer and slave trader Sir John Hawkins was displayed in London. 'There is no proper name for it (a marveilous strange Fishe) that I knowe,' said one observer, 'but that sertayne men of Captayne Hawkinses doth call it a sharke.' Other words such as tiburon, haye, requiem and sea-dog continued to be widely used for many years.

Because natural historians had not advanced much further in the classification of sharks since Aristotle's time, new shark-like animals were discovered and described without any attempt at understanding their relationships with known fishes. They were always seen in human terms – normally unpleasant ones.

The French naturalist Guillaume Rondelet wrote in 1558 of a 'sea-monster' taken in Norway after a great storm which he named monk-fish since 'it had a man's face, rude and ungracious, the head smooth and shorn. On the shoulders, like the cloak of a monk, were two long fins in place of arms and the end of the body was finished by a long tail.' The fabulous creature described by Rondelet is today known as the angel shark.

The earliest reliably-documented shark attack occurred in 1580 somewhere between Portugal and India. A sailor fell overboard from his ship and an eyewitness described, as the sailor was hauled by a rope towards the ship, how 'there appeared from below the surface of the sea a large monster called Tiburon; it rushed at the man and tore him to pieces before our very eyes. That was a very grievous death.'

By 1600 the word shark had spread into fairly common English usage. Shakespeare used it in the recipe for witch's stew in *Macbeth* (written in 1606):

'*Scale of dragon, tooth of wolf Witches' mummy, maw and gulf of the ravin'd salt-sea shark.*'

Sharks and shark-related customs around the world were described by a growing and far-flung band of European travellers. Samuel Purchas in 1617 noted that along the Ganges delta in India there were 'many Fishes called Sea-Dogs. They which are weary of this world, and desire to have a quick passage to Paradise, cast in themselves here to be devoured of these Fishes.'

Twenty years later Sebastian Manrique described the customs of

---

THE FRUITS OF EXPLORATION

An oceanic whitetip shark Carcharhinus longimanus *drawn during Duperrey's Pacific voyage on the* Coquille, 1822-25.

During the eighteenth and nineteenth centuries interest in exploration rapidly turned into a fever. Ships from many seafaring nations – including France, Britain, Russia, Germany and the United States of America – explored, charted, mapped, claimed and colonised land in the furthest corners of the earth.

Most expeditions carried with them trained scientists and artists to document their finds. The published results of these great voyages – complete with exquisite illustrations of the plants and animals that they found – gave people in the western world their first accurate view of the creatures around which so many myths had once been woven.

Mermaids turned into dugongs, krakens into cuttle-fish and sea monsters into whales and sharks.

Hindu pilgrims at the mouth of the Hooghly River. 'As soon as they have made this solemn vow [to the priests] they enter the sea up to their breasts and are very soon seized and devoured by certain ferocious male and female sea-monsters which we call sharks.'

Gradually sharks ceased to be only fearsome monsters, and a growing curiosity appears in the literature. 'I was told in Batavia and elsewhere,' wrote Francois Leguat in 1691, describing a number of shark remedies, 'that the Brain of a Shark had a Virtue in it, which made Womens' Pains in Child-Bed not so racking to them as they generally are.' In 1730 Monsieur Pomet, Louis XIV's chief druggist, asserted that 'there is found in the Shark's head two or three spoonfuls of brain that is as white as snow, which being dried, reduced to powder, and taken in white wine, is excellent for the gravel [kidney stones]'.

Later Pomet went on to sum up the popular view of sharks – a view that has not changed much to this day: 'He is one of the most gluttonous animals in the world; nothing comes amiss to him; tho' it be a log of wood he will swallow it, provided it be but greasy, for he swallows without chewing. He is furious and bold, and will throw himself to the shore, and remain almost on dry land, that he may have the opportunity of catching the passengers. Sometimes he will bite at the very oars with his sharp teeth, for rage and madness that he cannot get at the men which are in the boat.'

From the eighteenth century onwards accounts of sharks start to show a gradual departure from the assumptions of the past. Naturalists were beginning to see animals as a field detached from the human, to be properly studied and documented in their own right.

In 1771 Peter Orbeck on a

Sailors feared and hated sharks with good reason. Sharks regularly followed ships in the hope of eating any garbage that was thrown overboard, and their presence must have been constantly at the back of every man's mind. Persistent myths reinforced the fear: 'But a far worse character attaches itself to the shark,' wrote one observer, 'which is his preference for human flesh: of all other food it is this that he prizes …' It is therefore scarcely surprising that shark fishing was a popular sport whenever there was little else to do on board. Even Napoleon Bonaparte (above) was treated to the spectacle of a captured shark while aboard the *Bellerophon* after his surrender in 1815.

Two of the *Challenger's* dogs look on in amazement as a shark is hauled aboard. Everything encountered during the expedition was subjected to intense scrutiny by scientists.

voyage to China reflected on the problems of studying sharks. 'We caught the dogfish today, which is reckoned the most voracious animal of prey. Authors have already described several kinds of them, though not very clearly. The reason thereof is probably that some sorts are nowhere to be found but in great seas, where they can be but seldom examined by inquisitive people: whence all sorts are called by the same name because they look alike at a distance. Very seldom does the opportunity offer of comparing several sorts together, that specific marks might be ascertained, which otherwise is difficult, as their fins do not constitute the only difference.'

Today there are thought to be about 344 species of sharks. At the end of the eighteenth century most of these were still unknown. The German ichthyologist Marcus Bloch (see box p 67) reported in 1795 that there were 14 or 15 known shark species. The largest shark of all, the giant but harmless whale shark, was not discovered until 1828.

Slowly and painfully a body of information about sharks was built up. The 1844 edition of Oliver Goldsmith's *History of the Earth and Animated Nature* (originally published in 1774) stated that there were 30 different species of sharks.

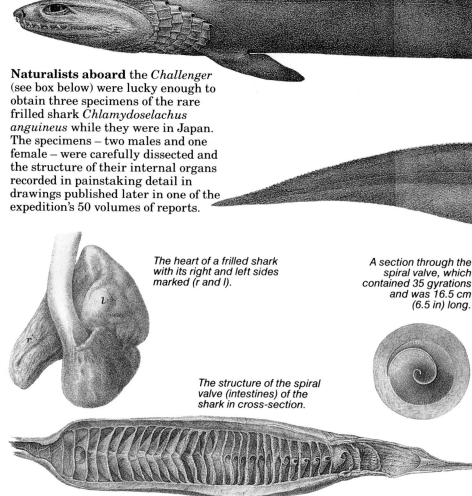

Naturalists aboard the *Challenger* (see box below) were lucky enough to obtain three specimens of the rare frilled shark *Chlamydoselachus anguineus* while they were in Japan. The specimens – two males and one female – were carefully dissected and the structure of their internal organs recorded in painstaking detail in drawings published later in one of the expedition's 50 volumes of reports.

The heart of a frilled shark with its right and left sides marked (r and l).

A section through the spiral valve, which contained 35 gyrations and was 16.5 cm (6.5 in) long.

The structure of the spiral valve (intestines) of the shark in cross-section.

A GREAT VOYAGE OF SCIENTIFIC DISCOVERY

By the second half of the nineteenth century most of the world had been mapped, and scientists had embarked on the vast job of systematically examining and classifying objects in the natural world. However, while much was known about plants and animals that lived on the land, almost nothing was known about those in the oceans. In about 1850 it was even possible for Edward Forbes, Professor of Natural History at Edinburgh, to state categorically that no life at all existed below 548 m (1800 ft).

All this changed in 1872 when HMS *Challenger* set sail from Portsmouth in England on a voyage that was to found the science of oceanography. For almost four years the *Challenger* cruised the oceans of the earth covering an astonishing 127 634 km (68 890 nautical miles). Many thousands of new species of marine plants and animals, including sharks, were discovered and carefully described.

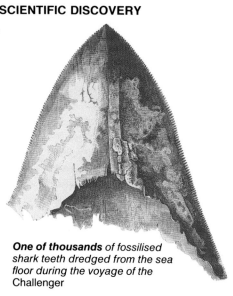

One of thousands of fossilised shark teeth dredged from the sea floor during the voyage of the Challenger

An external view of the claspers belonging to a male frilled shark.

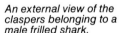

The skeleton of a clasper, showing the cartilaginous rod inside it.

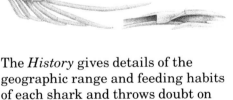

THE SHARK IN FICTION

The popular view of sharks, as cunning and malevolent, is expressed in this British comic.

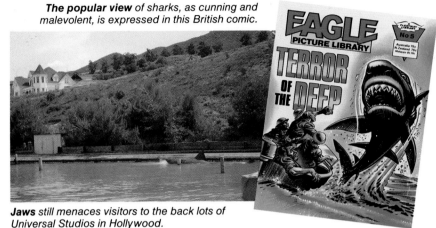

Jaws still menaces visitors to the back lots of Universal Studios in Hollywood.

Sharks have not featured greatly in western art and literature. Representing, as they do, the grisly and ugly, with no redeeming 'human' or interesting characteristics, they have been reduced to symbols of terror in comic books and popular fiction.

Herman Melville deals in passing with sharks in *Moby Dick*. 'De god what made de shark must be one dam injun', says Queequeg, the harpoonist. Mark Twain in *Following the Equator* tells the fanciful tale of how Cecil Rhodes founded his fortune after recovering a copy of the London *Times* from the stomach of a shark caught in Sydney Harbour. News in the paper of a rise in the price of wool, received 40 days ahead of the fastest steamer, allowed Rhodes to make a financial killing. In *The Old Man and the Sea* Ernest Hemingway describes a

mako, one of the sharks that destroys the old man's great fish.

Sharks appear in the writings of Melville, Twain and Hemingway as secondary figures, but in 1974 a novel appeared in which the main protagonist was a great white shark. Peter Benchley's book *Jaws*, and the film that followed, released a tidal wave of public concern about the 'shark menace', on a scale that had not been seen since the New Jersey attacks of 1916 (see p 120). Dozens of books and magazines on the subject appeared almost overnight. A second novel and two more films followed. For humans who have tamed and subjugated so much of the natural world, sharks obviously remain as one of the last of the fearsome unknowns – a peg on which to hang unconscious fears.

The *History* gives details of the geographic range and feeding habits of each shark and throws doubt on some persistent myths, such as the story of the blue shark protecting its young in its mouth. However it gives credence to other enduring myths: 'Along the coasts of Africa where these animals [sharks] are found in great abundance,' Goldsmith stated, 'numbers of the negroes who are obliged to frequent the waters are seized and devoured by them each year. The people of these coasts are firmly of the opinion that the shark loves the black man's flesh in preference to the white, and that when men of different colours are in the water together it always makes choice of

the former.' Other writers also asserted that sharks preferred Asian rather than European flesh. Shark researchers today give little weight to theories that sharks have a preference for any skin colour among humans.

Until the nineteenth century it was accepted that all animals had been created some time at the beginning of the world, and had remained unchanged in form since then. But even before Charles Darwin published his *Origin of Species* in 1859 the idea that animals changed over time, and that some species became extinct, was a widely discussed theory among naturalists. Today it is known that sharks come from an

ancient line of fishes and, due largely to their success within their ecological niche, have changed only slowly, if at all, over the last 300 million years.

Large areas of the natural history of sharks, however, remain a mystery even today. Many people are still obsessed by them – they are one of the few remaining creatures on earth that are outside the control of humans. Because creatures in the oceans are harder to study than those on land; because sharks are often hostile and dangerous; and because most sharks do not breed or behave naturally in captivity, many aspects of shark behaviour will remain a fascinating enigma for a long time to come.

A shark's eye view of the bathers at a beach. Although sharks generally prefer deeper water, most attacks at bathing beaches take place in water less than 2 m (79 in) deep, simply because that is where most people are found.

THE RISK OF ATTACK

Just what are the chances of being attacked by a shark? Some curious facts emerge from an attempt to answer this question. One of the most striking is the shark's apparently overwhelming preference for males – an astonishing thirteen males are bitten for every one female attacked.

The most authoritative analysis of shark attacks is the 1973 report compiled by Dr H. David Baldridge entitled *Shark Attacks Against Man*. In this report Baldridge makes a computer analysis of 1165 reported attacks, considering every possible aspect of shark attack. The 1165 cases make up what is known as the International Shark Attack File. This file was compiled as a result of a United States Navy sponsored meeting of 34 civilian scientists from all over the world. The meeting took place in New Orleans in April 1958 and its original purpose was to seek ways to develop better shark repellants.

Early in the meeting it became apparent that what was known about sharks and their behaviour was woefully inadequate. To help remedy this a group of six scientists was formed into what was called the Shark Panel, with Dr Perry W. Gilbert as chairman. The panel was affiliated with the American Institute of Biological Sciences and funded by the United States Navy.

The panel was to act as a clearing house for information and to promote basic research on sharks. With financial support received from the United States Navy the Shark Attack File was started with panel member Dr Leonard Schultz of the Smithsonian Institute in charge. In the 10 years of its existence (1958-67) Dr Schultz and his workers amassed records of 1652 attacks, some with much detailed information, but many, unfortunately, were only brief newspaper reports. This work ended in 1967 because Navy funding was stopped. Navy funding was available for analysis of data in the files, however, and in 1968 David Baldridge, a United States Navy officer, took the files to the Mote Marine Laboratory in Sarasota, Florida, where he began the task of analysing the data.

The attacks in the file were not

Lone swimmers in deep water stand the greatest chance of being attacked. The fact that more males than females venture into deep water near beaches explains the fact that the ratio of males to females attacked at distances greater than 65 m (213 ft) from the shore is an astonishing 31 to 1.

confined to the years between 1958 and 1967. Records from newspapers and other sources going far back in history were also included. The earliest attack reported was that on a sailor who fell overboard in 1580 while travelling from Portugal to India. Few details of this attack are known, not even the sailor's name, only that he was torn to pieces by a large tiburon - the Spanish and Portuguese word for a shark. Most of the attacks in the file, about two-thirds, happened after 1940, although none were reported from World War II. The reason for this is that Allied medical records list shark attacks as 'unspecified animal bites' and there is no possible way data on shark attacks can be identified. In 487 of the recorded attacks the information is so sparse and unreliable that serious doubt is raised as to whether an attack actually happened, and some hoaxes were found. Thus, only 1165 were analysed in the computer. In spite of this, much valuable information has been obtained from the file which enables the following basic questions about attacks to be answered in some detail.

Which is more likely to be attacked, a male or a female? Not too surprisingly the answer is male. What is surprising is the

Seals are a regular source of food for several shark species, including the great white and the tiger. Their resemblance to wet-suited divers is quite striking.

Surfboard riders, especially when silhouetted against the sky, could easily be mistaken for a seal or a turtle – both of which are eaten by some sharks.

A CASE OF MISTAKEN IDENTITY?

Several species of sharks – notably the great white, the tiger and the mako – are all known to feed on seals and sea lions. In some areas — such as off the southern coasts of Australia and northern California – seals are a major component in the diet of some sharks. Tiger sharks have also been known to eat large sea turtles, either whole or in pieces. The tough shell provides little protection against the sharp teeth and powerful jaws of this species.

Several researchers have pointed out a striking similarity between the shape of a wet-suited diver, complete with flippers, and that of a seal. They have suggested that attacks on divers, particularly in murky water, could simply be the result of a mistake on the part of the shark. The fact that a shark will often lose interest in a human

victim after the initial bite, despite the presence of blood, seems to support the theory.

In one Australian attack, the diver Henri Bource, clad in a wetsuit, was swimming with other people among a group of seals when he had his leg torn off. This attack was blamed on either a great white or a tiger shark estimated to be between 3.7 and 4.3 m (12 and 14 ft) long.

This theory has also been extended to explain attacks on surfboard riders. Viewed from beneath, a short surfboard, with its rider's flippers projecting from the back, and his head and arms from the front, could easily be mistaken for a seal or turtle. The noise of paddling, and also that made by the board's fins as they slice through the water at speed, may all help to attract the attention of passing sharks.

FACTORS THAT HELP TO DETERMINE THE RISK OF ATTACK

The seas that wash these beautiful, deserted beaches on the coast of southern Australia are home to many species of sharks, including the tiger and great white. While bathers here are no more at risk than they would be anywhere else in tropical or temperate waters around the world, the possibility of an attack still exists. The labels below summarise some of the findings that emerged from Dr David Baldridge's analysis of shark attack records which were gathered in the United States of America during the 1950s and 60s for the Shark Attack File.

Dr Baldridge reached a number of conclusions about the possible reasons for shark attacks, and these have been expressed in some simple precautions that can be taken by those who consider themselves to be a risk (see box page 81). In essence, the findings may be distilled into the following simple conclusions: Sharks are efficient predators and people who enter their realm run a risk (albeit slight) of being bitten. However, potential victims may draw comfort from the fact that sharks do not seem to be particularly partial to people as food.

Divers *seem to be particularly vulnerable to shark attack. Twenty-five per cent of the victims identified in the Shark Attack File were involved in some underwater activity, and of those, 43 per cent were free-diving, with or without a snorkel. The fact that diving takes people into deep water, and that enthusiasts are often handling bleeding and injured fish, obviously makes them attractive to sharks.*

What the victims were doing *at the time of an attack did not seem to be very significant. In 34 per cent of cases they were swimming; in 23 per cent diving; in 20 per cent wading and in 8 per cent surfing (either with or without a board). Splashing, playing around or unusually loud noises were only recorded in 14 per cent of cases. These percentages have been found to agree roughly with the proportions of people involved in these activities on any normal day at the beach.*

The background photograph *is of the western bays of Wilsons Promontory, on the southern coast of Australia. In the foreground is Oberon Bay, and in the far distance the shore curves around to Cape Liptrap.*

Water depth *is closely linked to the frequency of shark attacks, but only because most people are found in shallow areas. Sixty-two per cent of incidents in the Shark Attack File (in which water depth was recorded) took place in less than 1.5 m (5 ft) of water. Of the remaining attacks, 12 per cent took place in water from 1.8 to 3 m (6 to 10 ft) deep; 11 per cent from 3.3 to 6 m (11 to 20 ft); 5 per cent from 6.4 to 9 m (21 to 30 ft); 3 per cent from 9.4 to 12 m (31 to 40 ft); 6 per cent from 12.5 to 46 m (31 to 150 ft) with the remaining one per cent taking place in water more than 46 m (150 ft) deep.*

Water clarity *seems to have little influence on the incidence of shark attacks. An analysis of cases in the Shark Attack File, where water clarity was mentioned, showed that roughly half of the attacks took place in clear water and half in cloudy water.*

Nearshore waters *were the places where almost half of the recorded attacks took place. In cases where a note was made of position of the attack site in relation to breaking waves, the numbers were equally divided between those that took place just beyond the surf line and those that took place inside the surf line.*

Most bathers *at a beach stay close to the shore. Studies of people at beaches have shown that 90 per cent remain in water that is between ankle and neck deep, and that 81 per cent do not venture more than 30 m (100 ft) from the shore.*

Sea conditions *probably have more influence on whether people go into the water, rather than on the behaviour of sharks. The Shark Attack File showed that 69 per cent of attacks took place in calm water; 19 per cent in surf; 7 per cent in choppy water; 3 per cent in a swell and only 2 per cent in severe sea conditions.*

Human females *do not seem to be as attractive to sharks as males, although the reason for this is not at all clear. The ratio of males to females attacked is 13.5:1. Observations have shown that males are generally more active than females in the water, and this may be a factor in explaining the difference. It is also a fact that males tend to venture into deeper water than females.*

Distance from the shore *seems to play a part in determining whether a bather is at risk or not. The figures show that there is an increase in the proportion of bathers attacked the further one goes from the shore. Over half (51 per cent) of the recorded attacks took place less than 60 m (200 ft) from the water's edge, but this is to be expected because it is in this area that most bathers are found. Twenty-seven per cent of the remaining attacks took place between 60 and 1600 m (200 ft and one mile) from the shore – in a zone where there must be considerably less than half the number of bathers found closer in. The remaining 22 per cent occurred in open sea. There is no minimum distance for attacks – sharks have been known to beach themselves.*

Inlets *are often used by sharks as breeding grounds, and they are therefore potential attack sites – a claim that is borne out by the records. Eighteen per cent of recorded attacks took place in or near harbours, docks, wharfs, jetties, bays, rivers and river mouths. The fact that garbage is often found in these areas may also help to increase the risk.*

Channels *and areas where the water deepens suddenly are best avoided by swimmers. All such places allow sharks to stalk bathers without being seen themselves.*

0 – 15 m (0 – 50 ft) Thirty-one percent of attacks took place in this zone.

15 – 30 m (51 – 100 ft) Eleven per cent of attacks took place in this zone.

30 – 45 m (100 – 150 ft) Six per cent of attacks took place in this zone.

45 – 60 m (150 – 200 ft) Three per cent of attacks took place in this zone.

60

45

30

15

0

metres

overwhelming preference for males. The overall record shows 13.5 male victims for every female! If the data is limited to attacks along beaches the ratio drops to 9.1 males to 1 female. The old cliché about sharks being maneaters is almost literally true. But why is there this seeming preference for male victims? Casual head counts of beach populations show about equal numbers of males and females. Males do tend to be more active — swimming, diving and surfing — and they generally venture further from the shore. A possible related statistic is drowning deaths. It is the case, in the United States of America at least, that with drowning deaths in the range of ages that includes most shark attack victims (15-25 years), the ratio of males to females is 10.6 to 1. The similarities between these two ratios implies a relationship between the circumstances leading to drowning and shark attacks.

Is a person's race a factor in shark attack? All races have been attacked by sharks and there is no evidence that one race is more likely to be attacked than any other.

What about colour of clothing and bathing suits? Again there is no conclusive proof from the files that the colour of clothing was a factor in attacks. Laboratory tests with captive and wild sharks have shown that sharks are much more likely to approach bright, reflective objects for food than dark, dull ones.

Where do attacks occur? Shark attacks have occurred in every type of location where people go into the water and where sharks live. There are even reports of sharks stranding themselves in attempts to get at beach strollers. A large proportion of attacks occur at bathing beaches, in water less than two metres (79 in) deep, and within 65 m (213 ft) of the shore. This is because the largest number of bathers swim there.

Sharks generally prefer deeper water, only coming close to shore at night. About one-third of beach attacks occur at distances greater than 65 m (213 ft) from the shore, and the number of attacks is relatively independent of distance beyond that point. This can be explained if it is assumed that, while the number of people present decreases with distance, the number of sharks increases, thus the chance of an individual being attacked increases with distance from the beach. The chance of drowning also increases, since a swimmer is getting further from potential rescue. This is the probable reason for the high proportion of males being attacked. In observations made of swimmers at beaches, males are generally in deeper water than females, making their chance of encountering a shark that much greater. In fact the ratio of males to females attacked at distances greater than 65 m (213 ft) from the shore is 31 to 1, much greater than the overall ratio.

Are divers with air tanks and skin divers safer from attack than surface swimmers? It has been widely thought that divers have the advantage of being able to see an attacking shark and take evasive action. But only half the divers attacked reported seeing the shark before they were hit. About 10 per cent of reported attacks are on divers. Since the number of divers in the water at any one time must be much smaller than 10 per cent of beach bathers, the odds of being attacked must be significantly greater for divers. No doubt diving activities such as spear fishing and collecting abalone in turbid waters, in places where sharks feed on seals, add greatly to the chance of attack. The chance of encountering a shark in the deeper water frequented by divers is also much greater. There is

WARNING FOR THE WARY

NORMAL BEHAVIOUR

Side

Front

THREAT BEHAVIOUR

Lifted snout

Hunched back

Side

Lowered pectoral fins

Front

Body language among sharks has been little studied yet, simply because there are not enough people working with these animals. The value of such research, particularly to divers, is illustrated by the discovery of a threat display exhibited by grey reef sharks *Carcharhinus amblyrhynchos* in the Pacific Ocean (although not in those found around Australia). A solitary shark will sometimes confront a diver with its back hunched, its nose turned up and its pectoral fins pointed down at an abnormal angle. If the diver continues to approach the shark, he or she risks a quick, slashing attack before the shark flees. During experiments conducted by United States' researchers these sharks were even provoked into attacking a small research submarine.

evidence that one species of grey reef shark *Carcharhinus amblyrhynchos*, found around many reefs in the Pacific Ocean, is territorial and becomes aggressive towards divers if it feels threatened by the invasion of its domain. These sharks go through a threatening display of back-hunching and erratic swimming before attacking, so alert divers are forewarned.

What is the relationship of water temperature to the chance of attack? More than 20 years ago two scientists, Dr V. M. Coppelson and Dr D. H. Davis, suggested that there was a strong relationship between the chance of shark attack and water temperature. The chance of shark attack below a water temperature of 20°C (68°F) was supposed to be low. Taken at face value the data from the file supported this view. Almost 80 per cent of recorded attacks occurred at temperatures above 20°C (68°F). However, David Baldridge put forward the very reasonable and logical argument that the relationship between temperature and attacks is due more to the comfort and physiology of people than to shark behaviour. Studies of the ability of people to maintain their body temperature in cold water show that in water below 20°C (68°F) the average person cannot maintain body temperature, and within a few hours will probably die of exposure. In census counts made at two popular beaches it was found that only an average of nine per cent of those present would swim in water colder than 20°C (68°F) at a given time. This is indeed fortunate, because at one beach, in Florida, the shark population is known to be much greater at temperatures below 20°C (68°F) than at the more comfortable (for humans) water temperatures above 24°C (70°F). The conclusion to the argument is that the probability of attack is greater in warm water,

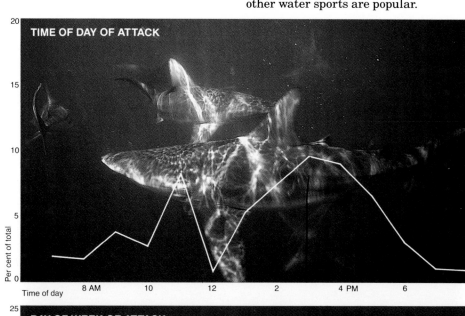

TIME OF DAY OF ATTACK

Per cent of total

Time of day 8 AM 10 12 2 4 PM 6

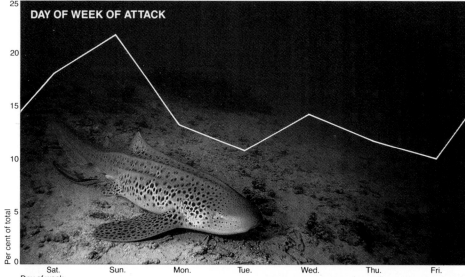

DAY OF WEEK OF ATTACK

Per cent of total

Day of week Sat. Sun. Mon. Tue. Wed. Thu. Fri.

COUNTRY OF ATTACK

Rest of the world 34 per cent of attacks

South Africa 8 per cent of attacks

Pacific Islands 12 per cent of attacks

United States of America 19 per cent of attacks

Australia 27 per cent of attacks

A silvertip shark among schools of fish on Australia's Great Barrier Reef. Sharks are obviously attracted to fish – particularly to large schools.

because the very large increase in bathers far exceeds the decrease in shark population. The chance of an individual being attacked in warm water is actually lower than in colder water. Wet suits, which allow people to go into colder water, and stay longer, are probably a factor in the relatively high incidence of attacks on divers, as well as the fact that the chance of encountering a shark is greater in deep water.

What days of the week and times of the day do attacks occur most often? By now it has been well established that there is a strong relationship between the number of bathers and chance of attack. It is therefore not at all surprising that more attacks take place on weekends than weekdays. In fact 65 per cent more attacks occur on weekends than weekdays. The time of day at which most attacks occur

is also strongly related to beach population. After dawn the number of attacks increases to a peak at about 11 am, drops to a minimum at noon, increases again to a broad peak in mid afternoon, between 2 pm and 4 pm, then decreases to another minimum after 6 pm. Baldridge found a similar pattern for beach population.

What circumstances may increase the chance of an attack? The presence of large numbers of fish, or fish behaving in an unusual manner, has been reported preceding many attacks. About 20 per cent of shark attack victims were associated with people pole fishing – they were either fishing themselves, netting fish, holding caught fish or simply standing or swimming nearby. In another 20 per cent of cases people were spear-fishing in the area of an attack. A

comparison of the number of people swimming to those fishing and spear fishing seems to show that those two pastimes have by far the highest risk of inducing an attack. Sharks are well known to frequent areas where refuse is dumped into the ocean. The presence of such material was strongly suspected to have been an important factor in about 25 per cent of the cases.

What are the characteristics of shark attacks? Individual sharks acting alone are believed to be responsible for 94 per cent of attacks. There was more than one shark involved in only 6 per cent of reported attacks. The shark was seen prior to the attack in only one-third of the cases. Practically all attacks were direct strikes on the victim. It was seldom that close passes were made before the attack, and in the majority of cases there

Humans are bitten by sharks mostly on the arms, hands, legs and feet. This is not surprising, because most attacks take place in waist-deep water, and the victim often tries to fend the shark off with the hands, if at all possible. The extent of wounds range from severe lacerations, which are the most frequently described injury, to the body being skeletonised in a small number of cases. Only on very few occasions has the victim been swallowed whole.

Head 2.4 per cent of attacks

Shoulders 3.8 per cent

Hands and fingers 20 per cent

Arms 23 per cent

Chest 5.5 per cent

Abdomen, stomach and waist 11.2 per cent

Back 3.7 per cent

Genitals 2.2 per cent

Buttocks 10 per cent

Thighs 33 per cent

Calves and knees 40 per cent

(Figures total more than 100 per cent because more than one body part was injured in some attacks.)

Feet and toes 23 per cent

THE DEADLY TRIUMVIRATE

Three species of sharks – the bull shark *Carcharhinus leucas* (top left), the tiger shark *Galeocerdo cuvier* (top right) and the great white shark or white pointer *Carcharodon carcharias* (bottom) – have been blamed for most attacks on humans. These three species were identified as being responsible for 80 attacks between them in the Shark Attack File, with the great white (32 attacks) as the clear leader. Other species classed as dangerous are the blacktip, blacktip reef, blue, Caribbean reef, copper, dusky, Galapagos, grey reef, lemon, nurse, oceanic whitetip, sand tiger, shortfin mako, sharptooth lemon, spinner, spotted wobbegong, tasseled wobbegong and tawny nurse sharks. All of these have actually attacked people or boats.

was only one strike. Few attacks involved numerous bites. This indicates that in many cases the attacking shark mistook the victim for a more usual kind of food, and did not attack any further when the error was discovered. It is fortunate that sharks, in most cases, do not consider humans to be suitable food. This information also refutes the long-standing notion that fresh human blood is a powerful attractant that excites sharks into a feeding frenzy. If this were so, the presence of blood would certainly have induced the attacking shark to strike the victim repeatedly. Most wounds occur on the appendages – the hands, arms, legs and feet. Lacerations of varying severity are the most common types of injury. About 25 per cent of attacks kill the victim. The most usual cause of death is shock, combined with a severe loss of blood.

What species of shark are most likely to be involved in an attack? In about one-quarter of the cases in the Shark Attack File the attacker was identified with varying degrees of certainty. Not too surprisingly the great white shark was blamed most often, with 32 attacks. The tiger shark *Galeocerdo cuvier* was

second with 27 attacks and the bull shark *Carcharhinus leucas* was third with 21 attacks. The rest are divided among about 30 other species known to attack people. The size of the attackers varied from under 500 mm (20 in) to over seven metres (23 ft) in length, with the average length being about two metres (6.6 ft). This is also about the average length of sharks caught.

What is the actual risk of being attacked by a shark? Other than saying that the risks are extremely low, it is very difficult to make quantitative estimates of the risk of attack. The true statement is often made that more people are killed each year by lightning than by shark attack. In the United States of America about 500 people are struck by lightning in a year. But the United States has a much greater incidence of lightning strikes than any other large country, and not everyone who is a potential shark attack victim is exposed to lightning, and vice versa. The only meaningful comparison that can be made is that between drowning deaths and shark fatalities along bathing beaches. There are at least some common factors among the victims in both

cases. The male to female ratio among victims is almost the same, being about nine or ten to one. In both cases the victims' ages have been in roughly the same range, between 15 and 25 years. If only drowning deaths along beaches where shark attacks have occurred are considered, together with the number of shark attacks in one year, it is possible to estimate the relative chance of drowning compared to that of being killed by a shark. For the United States including Hawaii, the chance of drowning is more than 1000 times greater than that of dying from a shark attack. Assuming all other factors to be the same, and taking into account the different population sizes and number of shark attacks, for Australia the chances are 50 to 1, and in South Africa 600 to 1. While these numbers indicate that the chances of being killed by sharks in Australia are considerably greater than in the other two countries, the chances are still really very small.

IF THE WORST HAPPENS

Ms Beulah Davis, Director of the Natal Anti-Shark Measures Board in South Africa, in collaboration with two physicians, has published detailed instructions for the treatment of shark attack victims. Their advice is summarised below.

Shark attack victims usually die from a combination of shock and blood loss. Therefore, the following things should be done as soon as possible:
● Remove the victim from the water as quickly as possible and place him or her head-downward on the beach slope to combat shock by increasing blood flow to the head.
● Control bleeding by pressing on pressure points, or by applying tourniquets. Efforts to stop bleeding should start while the victim is still in the water.
● Notify a doctor, paramedic or hospital. Take the victim's blood pressure and pulse

rate if possible for future reference by a doctor or hospital.
● Do not give the victim warm drinks or alcohol, only sips of fresh water. Protect the victim from cold by wrapping him or her in a blanket to minimise heat loss.
● Bring aid to the victim rather than take the victim to the aid. This is because movement can increase shock. The victim should not be moved unless he or she has recovered from shock and a doctor is present. Victims are better off left alone than moved unwisely or unnecessarily.
● Untrained people should not try to help the victim in any way, other than by carrying out the steps outlined above – more harm than good can result from well-meant but incorrect attempts to render aid. Experts think that this is one of the most important factors in determining whether a victim survives or not.

REDUCING THE RISK

Swimmers and divers can reduce the chance of being attacked by following a few simple rules: Never swim in areas where sharks are known to be common. If the area is unfamiliar you can find this out by asking local residents. If possible swim at beaches where there are life guards present. Never enter the water where people are fishing, either from the beach or from inshore boats.

If there are a number of people in the water do not separate yourself from them. There is safety in numbers. Avoid swimming near deep channels, or where shallow water suddenly becomes deeper. Do not swim alone, or at dusk or after dark, when sharks are feeding actively and likely to be closer to the shore. Do not enter the water, or if in the water leave immediately, if large numbers of fish are seen, or if fish seem to be acting strangely. Be alert for unusual movements in the water. Do not wear a watch or other jewellery that shines and reflects light. Do not enter the water with an open wound, and women should not swim during their menstrual periods.

Testing A New Theory

In the early 1970s an American scientist suggested that sharks were frightened of divers wearing black and white striped wet suits because they resembled giant sea snakes. This exciting possibility was tested some years later near Osprey Reef in the Coral Sea by diver Valerie Taylor.

'I was sceptical from the first about claims that sharks are frightened of banded sea snakes. The initial experiments had apparently been carried out around Lord Howe Island where sea snakes are rarely seen. On several occasions I had seen both sharks and banded sea snakes attracted to baits, but had never noticed any obvious animosity between them.

'I had dived with the three species of sharks that we encountered that day on Osprey Reef on many occasions. All could be tempted to approach a diver with an offer of food, but they were always cautious, and would never come close enough to touch. The banded suit, however, seemed to change all that.

'Three of us dived on the reef and positioned ourselves on a ledge about 25 m [80 ft] beneath the surface. Only I was wearing a banded suit. I opened the bait bag, sending blood billowing into the water. Immediately a whitetip reef shark [*Triaenodon obesus*] appeared from behind and pushed into me. It was followed by two more sharks

that pushed into my legs so hard that I could not open the bag to extract more bait. I held one steady by putting a flipper on its head, and wrestled more tuna from the bag.

'This violent tug-of-war provoked immediate action from the larger sharks further out. Eight grey reef sharks [*Carcharhinus amblyrhynchos*] torpedoed in. It was as though I did not exist. One moray eel, two grouper and dozens of other fish added to an incredible muddle. I snatched back the bait bag twice, tearing it from the mouths of sharks as they tried to drag it away. A bump in the side had me spinning away from a grey reef shark, which had charged in at my feet.

'More sharks joined the action. A whitetip forced its head between my legs from behind. I jammed them shut, ramming my (blunt) knife onto its head without effect. The small shark struggled forward, grabbing at the bag. As I wrestled with this shark a second hard, grey head pushed under my arm. I could feel the suit catching and stretching on their skins as the sharks jostled about me. No baits were visible, but

every shark knew they were there, and was trying to reach them. Then, as suddenly as it had started, the action stopped. Only an eel and a few stray whitetips remained.

'Further out the cat-eyed greys patrolled back and forth, sleek shapes in the deep blue ocean. A fat 2.5-m (8.2-ft) silvertip shark [*Carcharhinus albimarginatus*] moved in, but for all its size and speed it lacked the courage of its brothers and sisters, and did not come closer. I sensed that the other divers were the deterrent, not me.

'Six months later at Great Detached Reef, further north, I tried again. I had been told that the stripes on my first suit may have been too wide, so I had had a second suit made with narrower bands. The results, however, were the same.

'After fairly extensive tests I feel sure that black and white striped suits do not deter sharks at all. In over 30 years of diving I have never had to push grey reef sharks away. It was only when I was wearing the striped suit that they treated me without respect, almost as if they could not see me.'

Some banded sea snakes are highly venomous, and can be dangerous to humans. This observation led to the development of the theory which claims that sharks are frightened of banded sea snakes, and that divers wearing black and white striped wet suits should be safe from attack. Sceptics questioned the reasoning, pointing out that not all black and white sea snakes are venomous, and that some sharks have been known to eat sea snakes as part of their normal diet.

Wary, and clutching a knife for protection, Valerie Taylor watches as a grey reef shark and a whitetip close-in on her. Rather than deterring the sharks, as it was supposed to do, the striped suit actually seemed to make the sharks less cautious in her presence.

A diver despatches a mortally wounded grey nurse shark. Despite the lurid stories, sharks have far more reason to fear humans that humans have to fear sharks.

TALES OF TERROR AND BRAVERY

There is little to say about the moment of crisis in an attack – the actual bite. Sharks are efficient predators with sharp teeth and powerful jaws – the outcome of an attack is a foregone conclusion. The real interest revolves around the amazing feats performed by humans in extreme circumstances, as they cling desperately to life, and the bravery of those who go to their aid.

A near-straight five-kilometre (three-mile) stretch of sand from Aldinga Beach to Cactus Canyon is a highway on the South Australian coast for cars towing boat trailers; a boat-ramp sign puts the 'beach speed limit' at 25 km/h (15 mph). Off Snapper Point, a wide sea-level reef pushes out into an aquatic reserve: fishing is prohibited.

Fishing was not prohibited on Sunday 12 March 1961 when Brian Rodger took to the water. Rodger, 21, his body trimmed by a summer of exercise and diet, was competing in the annual spearfishing competition conducted by the Cuda Spearfishing Club and the Underwater and Photographic Association, of which he was president.

After four hours in the water, Rodger had an impressive take: he was missing only a herring kale to complete a catch of all the common species. He headed for a deep ledge one kilometre (1100 yds) off the sand highway, speared two kale and a morwong and, feeling well pleased with himself, headed back to shore.

As two huge kingfish passed beneath him, he thought idly that the sight was unusual, perhaps he might even sight a big shark. He had never seen a really big shark, and marked it as a gap in his diving experience. (Everything is relative: the week before, Rodger had seen a 2.7-m (8.9-ft) whaler shark, and a companion had lost 23 kg (51 lb)

Diver Valerie Taylor rests on the deck of a boat while she waits to be taken to hospital for treatment after a shark bite. In over 30 years of diving – much of the time with large sharks – she has only ever received minor injuries.

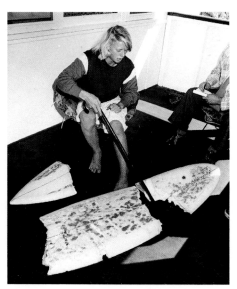

Philip Horley, aged 17, points to damage caused to his surfboard by a great white shark. The incident occurred at Cactus Beach, Western Australia, in August 1977 when Horley was surfing with friends about 270 m (300 yds) offshore. He was flung from his board by the shark and was lucky to escape with severe gashes to his thigh and knee. It is surprising, considering the popularity of surfboards and the fact that surfers take pleasure in ignoring the danger, that more riders are not taken by sharks.

A Javanese native being harrassed by a strange furry shark. The artist seems to be in two minds as to whether he is illustrating a shark or a seal. Many species of sharks, including all the dangerous ones, are found throughout the tropical regions of the earth. The native inhabitants came to terms with their presence long ago. However, despite the worship of shark gods, and elaborate rituals designed to ward off attack, fishermen were regularly attacked, and sometimes killed.

of fish and a pair of plastic shoes from his float. Rodger was mildly irritated: they were his shoes.)

He breathed deeply through his snorkel, preparing to dive after the kingfish. Suddenly something sharp and ragged seized his leg and hip and shook him; he twisted and saw a 3.6-m (11.8-ft) great white shark. As his body contracted in a spasm of pain and fear, his left arm jabbed for the shark's black eye. He missed. The teeth on the shark's upper jaw slashed his left arm to the bone. Unaccountably, the shark released him.

Rodger, superbly fit, at home in the water, and psychologically comfortable with the risks of shark attack – as all experienced divers are – did not panic. He was a competitive killer of fish, and as the shark turned around him in a tight, fast circle, the thought struck him

that he would have to be good to get out of this. For the first time he saw the shark's full size and sensed its enormous power.

He speared the shark on the top of its head, about 70 mm (2.8 in) behind the eye. It stopped its charge – and shook out the 1.5-m (4.9-ft) stainless steel spear. Rodger, badly hurt and bleeding profusely, felt elated. 'It was quite irrational, but for a moment [the spear hit] was all that mattered.'

Then the spade tail flicked away and Rodger, suddenly alone, realised how desperate things were. He was more than 700 m (765 yds) from shore. His leg and arm were cut to the bone, pumping inky clouds of blood into the water.

Tentatively, he tested his lacerated leg and found to his surprise that he could still move it. His vital organs were untouched: if

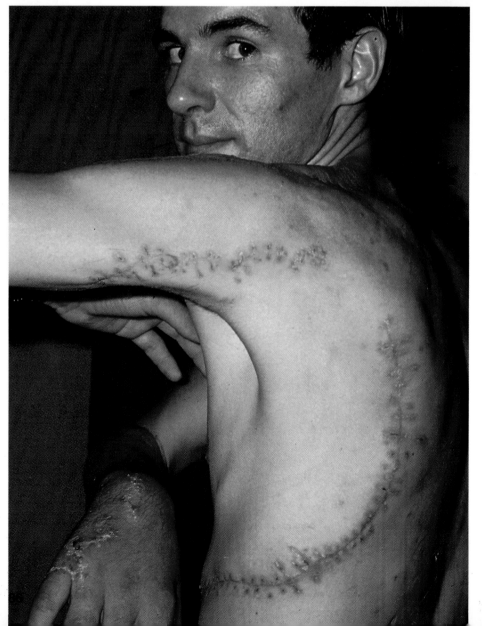

Rodney Fox, an award-winning Australian diver, must be one of very few people to have experienced and survived the bite of a large shark. The attack exposed his stomach, lungs and rib cage; the flesh on his arm was stripped to the bone and his ribs were crushed – one of them puncturing his lung. Fox spent four hours on the operating table in Adelaide (above) and he was lucky to be attended by a surgeon who had just returned from a course in England on chest operations. The wounds needed 462 stitches. Not long after the attack, Fox was back diving again, and a year later he was part of the team which won the Australian national championship. He will carry the scars (left) of his awful encounter for the rest of his life.

he could reach the shore he could survive. He began the agonising swim, worrying about his loss of blood, then realising he could make a tourniquet from his spear-gun rubber. He twisted the rubber tight around his upper thigh, using his knife as a windlass, and secured the knife handle under the bottom edge of his wet suit jacket.

The tourniquet reduced the blood flow, but Rodger felt his strength draining dangerously. He released his speargun, lead belt and the float with all his fish, bitterly regretting it. He thought later how absurd it was, longing to keep a few dollars worth of equipment and a

HEADLONG INTO DANGER

Two pearl divers have had miraculous escapes in strangely similar attacks. In both cases the shark grabbed the diver by his head, and was forced to let go when the victim struggled and gouged at the shark's eyes. The first incident took place in about 1913 in Torres Strait, between New Guinea and Australia, with the second 24 years later in the same area.

The first victim was a young Thursday Islander named Treacle. He dived straight down from a pearling boat into the open jaws of a large tiger shark, which almost succeeded in tearing his head from his body. Deep gashes in Treacle's neck exposed his jugular vein and his head and shoulders were also badly cut.

The 38-year-old victim of the 1937 attack, Iona Asai, recounted his experience: 'First time I went down I found one pearl shell and put it on the deck. Then I went down again the second time and found another pearl shell. The third time I dive and walked on the bottom. I was behind a little high place, the shark was on the other side. I never saw him and he never saw me. I saw a stone like a pearl shell on the north side, and when I turned I saw the shark six feet [1.8 m] away from me. He opened his mouth, already I have no chance of escape from him. Then he came and bite me on the head. He felt it was too strong to swallow and put his teeth around my neck. Then he bite me and I felt his teeth go into my flesh. I put my hands around his head and squeeze his eyes until he let go me, and I make for the boat. The captain pulled me into the boat and I faint. They get some medicines from a school teacher.'

Iona Asai survived an attempt made by a shark to bite his head off.

few fish for points in a competition when he might die, but he had to force himself to let them go.

The swim seemed to take forever. He found breathing through the snorkel difficult and turned on his back. He raised his arm, waved and shouted 'shark' but the families on the beach did not react. He subsided, cursing the waste of energy, when a small rowing boat manned by two furiously paddling spearfishermen approached. It was obvious the two-metre (6.6-ft) boat would not hold the three of them; one jumped into the bloodied water, helped to heave Rodger into the boat, then swam behind to push it.

A dozen divers ran across the reef, lifted the boat from the water and carried it to shore, where a St John's Ambulance man tended Rodger while the divers prepared an old door as a stretcher and carried him up the steep rise backing the beach to the ambulance. Police escorted the ambulance in the 55-km (34-mile) dash to the Royal Adelaide Hospital.

Doctors inserted 200 stitches in Rodger's wounds in a three-hour operation. He had lost four litres (7 pints) of blood. He resumed skindiving less than three months later, and before the end of the year set a new Australian record by reaching a depth of 45.4 m (148.9 ft) in a lake without air tanks.

While Brian Rodger fought off the great white, Rodney Fox, another spearfishing competitor, cruised the bay nearby. Fox knew nothing of the drama until he came ashore – but he too had a brush with a great white shark, a huge brute which circled him ominously and occasionally came so close he could have reached it with his speargun. Fox repeatedly dived to the bottom, moving cautiously shorewards and after 10 minutes the shark lost interest and moved off. Later, when he talked about the attack with Rodger, they agreed that all you could do with a shark was go for the eyes, that was the only vulnerable spot.

Two years and eight months later, on 8 December 1963, Fox was competing in the South Australian Spearfishing Championships, having won the title the previous year. The scene was again Aldinga Bay – although this time the divers were not using fish floats: competition boats picked up the catches.

Fox was in superb form, drifting, gliding, spearing his quick elusive targets with the practised ease of a born competitor. With an hour left, he looked likely to win the title again. He was one kilometre (1100 yds) offshore, drifting in for a shot at a dusky morwong, sure of the kill, his finger tensing on the trigger, when something huge hit his left side – 'it was like being hit by a train' – knocking the gun from his hand and tearing the mask from his face. His next impression was of speed, surging through the water faster than he had ever done, a gurgling roar in his ears, and of the easy, rhythmical power of the shark, holding him as a dog does a bone.

With his right arm he clawed for the shark's eyes; it released its grip and Fox instinctively thrust out his right arm to ward it off. The arm disappeared into the shark's mouth, lacerating the underside on the bottom row of teeth. As the horrified Fox jerked it out, the arm caught the upper jaw. In extremity men do amazing things: Fox, terrified of the open maw, tried to bear-hug the shark, to wrap his arms and legs around the abrasive skin, to get a purchase away from the teeth. It did not work – the

Continued on page 90

THE PERSISTENT SHARK

Few of the victims of shark attacks get more than a fleeting glimpse of their assailant. However, in February 1966 – in a unique incident – a young Sydney boy was badly mauled by a shark that refused to release him, even when it was carried ashore.

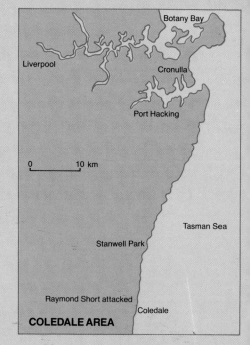

One of the Coledale lifesavers who helped in Raymond Short's rescue holds open the mouth of the attacking shark. A healthy great white of this size could easily kill an adult human.

It was a warm Sunday afternoon, typical of late summer. At the small seaside town of Coledale, 64 km (40 miles) south of Sydney, a crowd of holidaymakers were enjoying the last of a fine weekend. From the beach, lifesavers watched as about 60 people swam, paddled and played in the stretch of warm, shallow water between the patrol flags. Just outside the flags a few surfboard riders made the best of the day's small waves.

About 27 m (30 yds) offshore, still only in chest-deep water and well within the patrolled area, 13-year-old Raymond Short was swimming just inside a sandbar which ran parallel with the beach. He was down from Sydney with his parents for the weekend, staying in a caravan park near the waterfront.

None of the swimmers in the water, Raymond included, took much notice of the patches of weed drifting in with the tide. There had been weed in the water – which was slightly cloudy – for the past couple of days. One of the lifesavers on duty that day, Eddie Patmore, remembers glancing idly at what

looked like a particularly large clump drifting among swimmers and heading towards Short, but he, too, ignored it.

Suddenly the afternoon peace was shattered as Short screamed out in panic, shouting for help at the top of his voice, as the water around him turned pink with blood.

At first lifesavers thought that Short had become entangled in seaweed, but as the swell rose they could see a shark wallowing in the water beside him. Immediately the shark alarm was sounded and six lifesavers dashed into the sea, struggling to run through the water as they converged on the boy.

When they reached Short he was in chest deep water beside the sandbar. The shark was nowhere to be seen, so they started pulling him towards the beach, hampered by the small waves that were breaking over them. They were quickly joined by a nearby surfer who offered his board as a stretcher.

As the lifesavers half-lifted, half-dragged Short through the water he kept screaming out 'It's still got me. Get it off. Get it off.'

Incredulous, one of the lifesavers, Raymond Joyce, thrust his hand into the murky water. To his horror, his fingers touched the snout of a shark, its jaws still firmly clamped onto the boy's leg.

Four more lifesavers now joined the struggling group, and as two continued to help Short towards the beach, the rest lifted the 2.4-m (8-ft) shark bodily from the water and carried it ashore.

Near the beach the shark still stubbornly refused to open its jaws. In desperation one of the lifesavers grabbed a nearby surfboard and smashed it down repeatedly on the shark's head, but without any noticeable effect. Another lifesaver, who lived nearby, rushed home to fetch a rifle, and while he was gone the rescuers renewed their

Raymond Short (fourth from left), and the seven Coledale lifesavers involved in his rescue, at Government House in Sydney on 18 November 1966. The men, who all received the Queen's Commendation for brave conduct, are (l to r) Raymond Robertson, Clarence Taylor, Brian Joyce, (R. Short), Warren Haberley, Dallas Haberley, Lessley Kennedy and Raymond Joyce.

*Map caption:*
Botany Bay
Liverpool
Cronulla
Port Hacking
0 — 10 km
Tasman Sea
Stanwell Park
Raymond Short attacked
Coledale
COLEDALE AREA

desperate assault on the shark, which finally released its grip.

Immediately towels were packed around Short's lacerated legs, and he was rushed from the beach to a nearby hospital.

The boy was in the operating theatre for two hours while doctors repaired the damage to his badly mauled legs and hands. He received a massive transfusion of blood, and was in a critical condition when he left the operating theatre.

The shark was identified as a female great white, which weighed about 136 kg (300 lb). A close inspection showed that it had long, deep gashes down its sides near its tail, as well as numerous teeth marks elsewhere on its body. The wounds were only partially healed, and experts later suggested that the shark may have been weak and unable to catch its usual food. In desperation it had attacked a swimmer instead.

Doctors in the hospital watched anxiously as Short's condition gradually improved over the next couple of days. At one stage it had seemed possible that his right leg might have to be amputated, but this was not necessary. A few days later he returned home, and eventually recovered completely.

The jaws were removed from the shark, cleaned and offered to Raymond as a memento of his brush with death. Instead he insisted that they be presented to Coledale Surf Life Saving Club, as a tribute to the bravery of its members.

Desperate moments as helpers try to stem the flow of blood from Henri Bource's severed leg. Bource was attacked by a great white shark off the southern coast of Australia in November 1964.

shark was too big for him to hug.

He suddenly realised another need even more urgent than fending off the shark – air. He pushed away, kicked for the surface, gulped one breath and looked down on a scene that burnt itself into his memory. His mask gone, his vision blurred, he floated in a pink sea, and a few metres away was a pointed nose, and a mouth lined with razor sharp teeth, coming at him.

In desperation, Fox kicked with all his force at the shark. It was a terminal gesture, pointless, useless – but it worked: the shark turned from Fox, lunged for the buoy tied to his belt, swallowed it whole, then plunged for the deep. Fox, his ears roaring, reached for the quick-release clip on his belt. He could not find it. He realised the shark must have wrenched the belt around his body: the clip must be at his back. His lungs drained of air, his mind becoming fuzzy, he thought: that's it.

Then the impossible happened: the buoy rope snapped. Fox realised later that the shark must have bitten the rope when it attacked him. He floated to the surface, where his friend Bruce Farley and another man who had seen blood in the water pulled alongside in a boat. Fox's arms were so lacerated he could not raise them, so his friends gripped his wet suit and rolled him into the boat. Blood was pouring from his wet suit. Farley ran the

boat onto the horseshoe reef. As they lifted Fox from the boat, loops of his intestines emerged from the hole in his belly; a bystander who had studied first aid for the police examinations pushed them back with his fingers. Fox was bundled into a car, straining to breathe – his left lung had collapsed. As the car sped for Adelaide, a friend, sick with anxiety, talked him on: 'You've got to keep breathing. Come on, keep trying, Rodney. Think of Kay and the baby. Keep going.' While his collapsed lung gurgled and he heaved the air into his chest, his most vivid sensation was of swaying in the back of the car as it reached 150 km/h (95 mph). An ambulance dashed to meet them, and Fox was in hospital in Adelaide within an hour of leaving the water.

Later, his wet suit removed, the extent of his wounds apparent, he heard someone suggesting that this man was near death, they should call a priest. He still had the energy, blood gurgling in his throat, to say: 'But I'm a Protestant!'

He recovered completely, and in 1964 Fox, Rodger and Farley won the Australian Spearfishing Championship team's event.

Attacks on skindivers generally follow a pattern: the strike is quick, the shark unseen, the diver's first impression being of the shark's weight and power. Then the instinctive reaction – gouging the shark's

eyes, kicking, anything to stay away from the teeth. In these first frantic seconds, divers commonly experience a curious detachment, fighting for their lives at one level, and with another part of themselves seeing the deadly encounter calmly and analytically. Because divers are physically at home in the sea and familiar with the presence of sharks, their reactions maximise their chances of survival. After the shark breaks off the attack, their ease of movement, ability to think rationally and above all their level of physical fitness are the factors that decide whether they reach shore alive or not.

With swimmers, bodysurfers and board riders the pattern is different. Most attacks take place in waist-deep water, and the first bite is usually to the most accessible parts of the body – the legs or feet. Many victims experience a bump or brush, then the brutal realisation that it is a shark, followed by a scream of fright, a frenzied struggle to escape and often, at the moment of safety, the first experience of pain and the discovery that a leg, foot or hand is missing.

Although most near-shore attacks take place in water only one to two metres (39 to 78 in) deep, some occur in water so shallow that the shark is in danger of being beached. In 1933 a man sitting in less than one metre (39 in) of water

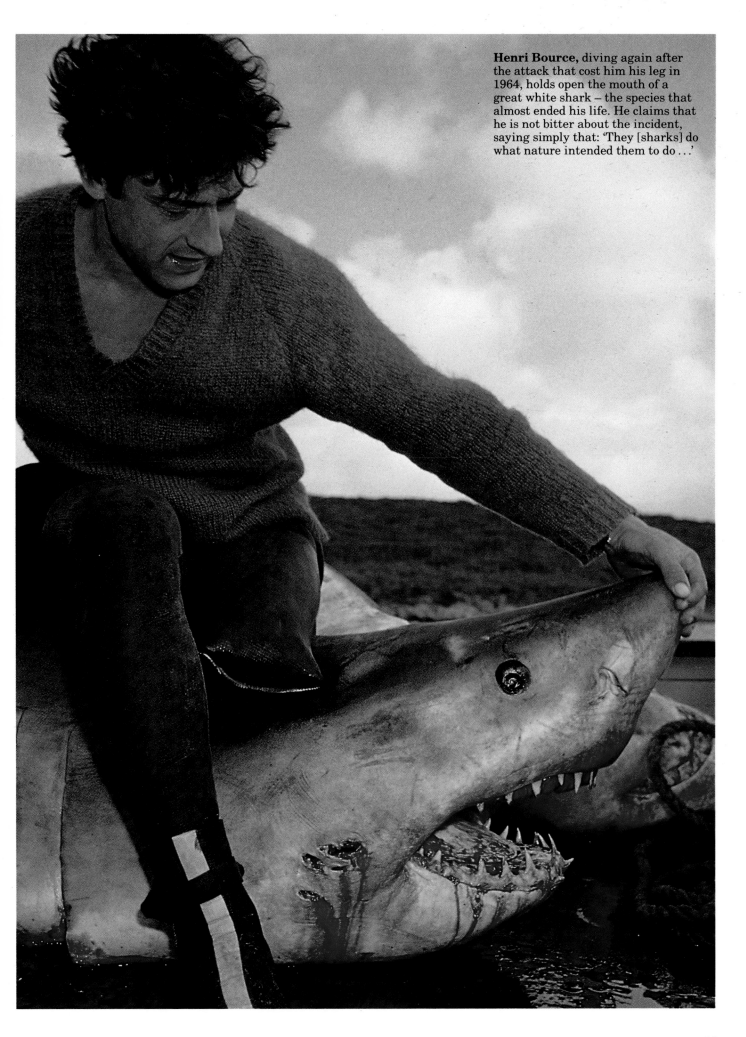

Henri Bource, diving again after the attack that cost him his leg in 1964, holds open the mouth of a great white shark – the species that almost ended his life. He claims that he is not bitter about the incident, saying simply that: 'They [sharks] do what nature intended them to do . . .'

91

A native boy disappears in a flurry of water as he is seized by a shark. It is impossible to verify the authenticity of this photograph, taken in 1901, but the attitudes of the other people seem to suggest that it may be genuine.

at the mouth of Charleston Harbour in the United States of America, had his right knee seized by a 2.4-m (8-ft) lemon shark. When he lashed out with his left leg, that too was bitten. In 1961 a 13-year-old boy was standing on a submerged rock, also in water less than one metre (39 in) deep at Winklespruit beach near Durban, South Africa, when he felt something touch his right foot. He reached down with his right hand which was promptly bitten. Lifesavers carried him ashore, followed by a two-metre (6.6-ft) shark. His right foot was missing and his hand deeply bitten. An even more remarkable case occurred in 1966 when an 8-year-old boy and his mother were walking along a beach

in Florida. The boy was splashing around in about 30 cm (12 in) of water near the shore when his mother spotted a 'grey form' out of the corner of her eye. As she grabbed the boy, lifting him clear of the water, a shark rushed past so quickly that it was carried up on to the sand. It lay exposed for a few minutes before a wave carried it struggling back into the ocean. The pair continued their walk, now well back from the water's edge, and were followed by three or four sharks a short distance offshore.

Less than one kilometre (1100 yds) from the attack on the 13-year-old boy near Durban, Damon Kendrick, aged 15, reported a strange phenomenon when he was

attacked while bodysurfing after a lifesaving championship on 13 February 1974. A friend with him shouted a warning. As the shark bit into Kendrick's right leg, he heard 'a growl, best described as [the sound made by] a father who wants to amuse his child in a swimming bath, growling and blowing into the water at the same time'. Experts agree that sharks do not growl: perhaps what Kendrick heard was the commotion of the water and the shark's teeth grinding through his shinbone. The bite lasted two seconds and then a wave washed Kendrick ashore. Holding his injured leg up in front, he pushed himself backwards up the sloping beach, watching a 'river of blood'

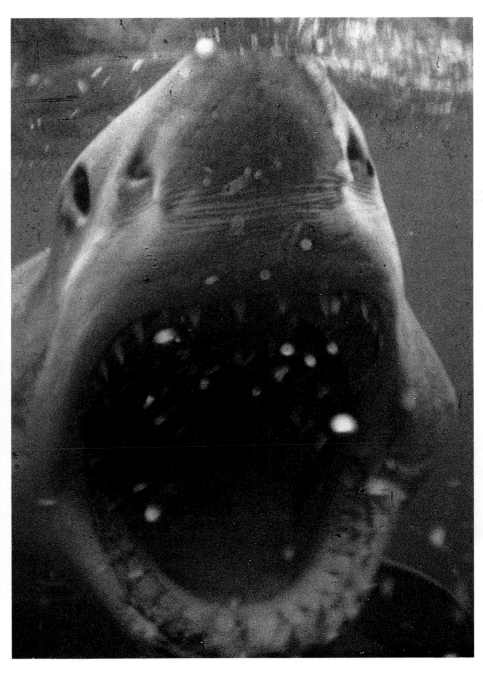

The awesome size and power of the jaws of a great white shark are clearly conveyed in this view of an approaching monster. Even the bite of a two-metre (6.6-ft) shark has been measured at 3 tonnes per sq. cm (21 tons per sq. in).

companion towards three yachts and a powerboat moored 250 m (273 yds) off Fourth Beach, Clifton, South Africa. Halfway there, Spence stopped and, joking to his companion, re-enacted the struggles of the girl shark victim in the film *Jaws*. They then swam seawards for three minutes and trod water near the yachts. Spence later reported 'a hard thump on my side and I felt a vice clamp on my chest'. The shark quickly released its grip, then swam in front of him. Spence saw the open mouth as the shark appeared to be looking at him. Then its back and dorsal fin broke the surface and it disappeared. A dinghy quickly picked Spence up and took him ashore where doctors attended him. His wounds were superficial and he recovered completely. It seemed the shark, perhaps attracted by the vibrations caused by Spence's *Jaws* imitation, may have mistaken him for a fish in trouble.

Not all shark attack victims are as lucky as Geoffrey Spence. In about 35 per cent of attacks the victim dies – either as a direct result of the bite, later through blood loss, or from shock or drowning.

The most frequently reported serious injuries are the loss of hands, feet, arms or legs – in 26 per cent of attacks these were bitten off directly, or were so badly mauled that they had to be surgically removed later. In some seven per cent of reported attacks the body cavity was opened by a bite, and in just over two per cent the trunk was severed, or the victim was swallowed whole.

One rare eyewitness account of a man being almost eaten whole by a shark is that reported by Gerald Lehrer. In midsummer, 14 June 1959, Lehrer and his friend Robert L. Pamperin, were diving for abalone in La Jolla Cove, near San Diego in the United States of America. They were near underwater rocks, less than 100 m (110

run from his leg. 'I have never seen so much blood before, and what scared me most was that it all came from me,' he said later. He survived, although his leg had to be amputated below the knee.

Five weeks later James Gurr was riding a surfboard just south of Inyoni Rocks, also on the Natal coast of South Africa, when he saw a shark's fin heading straight for him. He lifted his legs. The shark hit the surfboard, spilling him into the water. As he was remounting he felt a 'violent shove' from the shark under his arm. He panicked and paddled madly shorewards, feeling he had 'unbelievable strength'. Again he was bumped from his board by the shark,

but he remounted and paddled furiously as the shark zig-zagged in front of him. He caught a broken wave over the top of the shark, hit the beach, and sprinted away from the water. A friend later retrieved the board, which had teeth marks in the fibreglass.

The nature and outcome of many attacks seem to confirm the theory that at least some shark attacks are the result of mistaken identity. Once the shark realises that its human victim is not a seal or a large fish it loses interest and swims away. This appears to be what happened in the case of Geoffrey Spence.

On 27 November 1976 Spence, aged 19, was swimming with a

Many grisly remains have been removed from the stomachs of captured sharks. In 1886 this shark was caught in Sydney Harbour, and when cut open was found to contain several bones (including the lower portion of a human backbone), pieces of flesh, the leg of a pair of grey tweed trousers (the pocket of which still contained a penny) and the buckles belonging to a pair of braces. Simple detective work led to the trousers being identified. Their owner had not been seen since heavy seas had swamped his boat some days before the capture of the shark.

yds) from shore, and dozens of other swimmers were splashing in the water nearby.

Lehrer surfaced and looked towards Pamperin, a few metres away. Suddenly he saw a black dorsal fin slicing towards Pamperin. Lehrer screamed a warning and pointed to the fin. As he did so, Pamperin rose high in the water, as if he had stepped onto a submerged rock, then plunged back, threshing his arms. Lehrer, ducking his face beneath the surface, saw a shark about six metres (20 ft) long with Pamperin's upper body protruding from its jaws. Pamperin's mask was gone, his eyes were open and staring upwards. Lehrer could not tell if he was alive. He swam for shore and shouted a warning to the other bathers. Lifeguards in boats, a Coast Guard helicopter and divers

searched the area for hours, but no trace of Pamperin was ever found.

The attack on Pamperin gave him no chance at all of survival: a bite through the torso means either instant, or very quick death. Many survive bites to the arms or legs, although shock and blood loss are often fatal.

On 25 July 1936, 16-year-old Joseph Troy was swimming in Buzzards Bay, Massachusetts in the United States of America with Walter Stiles, an older man. They were about 130 m (143 yds) off-shore and about three metres (10 ft) apart. Suddenly both saw the familiar black fin alongside Troy. It disappeared, and then the shark struck the boy and dragged him under. Stiles dived and saw Troy, his left leg between the shark's teeth, kicking and struggling to break

ATTACKS THAT NEVER WERE

Such is the public fascination with sharks and shark attacks that any spectacular photographs of incidents involving people always have a ready market. It is inevitable, therefore, that enterprising divers are tempted to fake attacks.

In 1968 *Life* magazine ran a series of dramatic photographs in a story entitled 'Shark Kills a Diver'. In a sequence of five gory photographs a diver was shown being fatally bitten by an attacking great white. The story told how 32-year-old stuntman José Marco was acting out a scene involving a drugged bull shark when a great white broke through a net surrounding the underwater movie set and mauled him. Only later was it revealed that the photographs were fakes – somehow publicity stills had been circulated to various magazines as genuine shots.

In the 1960s a bizarre competition developed between two Australian underwater photographers as they attempted to outdo one another with dramatic photographs of underwater attacks. No sooner would one manage to have a (faked) photograph published of a diver fending off an attacking shark with a spear, than the other would immediately set about constructing an even more dramatic scene with a larger shark and a thinner spear. An imaginary diver, Ron Thomas, became the hero of these increasingly unlikely incidents, and for a time he was much sought after by television channels.

Intrepid diver Ron Thomas defends himself with a pitifully inadequate spear. It is fortunate that the shark in this faked photograph is dead.

Enterprising photographers were naturally willing to try and satisfy an insatiable demand for scenes of attacks – even if the sharks had to be dead before they would cooperate properly.

free. He did so and rose into Stiles' arms. Stiles, with Troy beneath one arm, sidestroked for shore. A man in a rowing boat who had seen the commotion and heard the screams picked them up – observing, as he did so, a large great white shark cruising about as if considering whether to make another attack.

Troy, parts of his left leg stripped to the bone, was rushed to a New Bedford hospital, but he died five hours later.

Another swimmer who, like Joseph Troy, had a heroic companion but was cruelly out of luck, was Albert Kogler.

On 7 May 1959, Kogler, aged 18, was treading water with a girl friend, Shirley O'Neill, 50 m (55 yds) off Bakers Beach outside San Francisco's Golden Gate. Suddenly he screamed and thrashed his arms,

and Shirley saw the upthrust of a monstrous tail. 'Go back! Go back!' Kogler screamed. Shirley hesitated. 'It's a shark – get out of here'. Shirley swam into the reddening water and reached for Kogler's arm. She found it barely hanging from his shoulder. Shirley put her arm around him as he floated on his back and both struggled shorewards, with Kogler kicking feebly. On the beach, his left arm almost detached, his neck and back deeply lacerated, Kogler lost consciousness. Two hours later he died in hospital.

Death came more rapidly to another youngster, 16-year-old Jeff Corner, while spearfishing with a friend, Allen Phillips, at Caracalinga Head on the South Australian coast on 10 December 1962. Corner was the state junior spearfishing champion and the pair

were about 180 m (197 yds) offshore while taking part in a competition. Phillips was pleased when, surfacing after a dive, he saw a commotion in the water around Corner, thinking 'Jeff's got a big one'.

Seconds later, he saw a large shark's tail break the water and thought 'it's probably pinching fish off the float'. He swam over to his friend and found himself in a cloud of blood. Sick with horror, he swam for their surf ski and paddled over. He tried to pull his friend onto the ski, but realised that the shark still had him in its grip. Corner disappeared beneath the ski and emerged on the other side. Phillips caught him by the shoulders and, still feeling the shark's grip, smashed at it with the ski paddles. Suddenly it let go. Phillips pulled

Continued on page 98

A Bolt
From The Blue

Most shark attacks are over before bystanders realise what has happened. Few people have the misfortune to see one at close quarters. Fate decreed that Lee Warner should watch, helpless, as a friend was savaged in the most terrible way.

Hundreds of kilometres of lonely coast stretch north from Perth, fringing one of the remotest and least populated parts of Australia. The few tiny settlements scattered along its length survive on fishing and a small seasonal influx of holiday visitors. Waves rolling on to its beaches from the Indian Ocean might have travelled unchecked across almost a third of the globe – the nearest land to the west is Africa, 8600 km (5300 miles) away.

In August 1967, on a bleak Saturday in winter, two divers arrived at Jurien Bay on this remote coast, 210 km (130 miles) north of Perth. They were Lee Warner, 26, a professional fisherman, and his 24-year-old companion Bob Bartle. Both were highly experienced divers and, as Western Australian State pairs spearfishing champions, they planned to enter the national championships to be held four months later at Busselton. The pair were at Jurien Bay that day for a minor competition that was to be held on the following Sunday. This

was to be the practice day, an attempt to find the best spots, and to assess local conditions.

From the top of North Head, parked among cars owned by other divers, they could look along the sand- and scrub-covered coast to the distant township of Jurien, 10 km (6 miles) away as the crow flies across the bay. Out to sea islands and reefs were picked out in white as winter waves broke around them.

The two men donned their wet suits and sorted out their equipment beside the car. Warner was wearing a full black wet suit, and Bartle a black suit with yellow seams and black flippers. Bartle's legs were bare, and both men wore hoods that covered their heads.

They entered the ocean below the headland and swam easily seaward into deepening water, heading for reefs about 1.6 km (one mile) offshore. The water was cold

Jurien Bay's brilliant, clear water looks benign on a calm morning. However, sharks – including great whites – frequent this area, and have been known to feed on seals nearby.

and slightly murky, although the weed-covered sea floor was visible about eight metres (26 ft) below.

After they had been swimming for about 20 minutes they reached a small dip in the sea bed about 700 m (760 yds) from the shore. The overhanging rocks fringing the depression looked like a promising spot for fish so Bartle dived down to check. There was nothing there, so Warner turned to continue seaward. Suddenly a huge, black shape shot past him, just beneath his flippers. Warner later recounted the events of the next few moments:

'The shark came from the opposite way and went straight under me about 8 ft [2.4 m] down. It came out of the blue like a rocket and grabbed him [Bartle]. It moved so fast that by the time I looked back it had Bob in its mouth and was shaking him like a leaf. I rolled over immediately, dived and placed a spear in its head. It broke Bob in

half and rose up at me with Bob's legs and flippers sticking out of its mouth. Bob's upper half floated to the surface. The shark began circling slowly. It made one pass at me, and I poked my spear gun in the direction of its eye. The gun struck behind its right eye, and a membrane appeared to cover its eye in a lateral plane. Realizing I was helpless, I retrieved Bob's gun which was floating near his body. As the shark passed by once more, I endeavoured to spear it in the eye. However, the spear passed over the shark. In his circling motion, he tangled this spear around Bob's float line and my spear line. I moved from the pool of blood and watched for some movement. The shark did not appear to be feeding. Bob's feet and flippers were still projecting from its mouth. The jaw must have been 2.5 ft [76 cm] wide. As there was nothing further that could be done, I swam towards shore...'

Warner now began a desperate swim back to the beach, 700 m (760 yds) away, glancing back constantly to check that the shark was not following him. As he struggled ashore he looked out to sea where the floats of other divers bobbed about on the surface, their owners unaware of the terrifying events that had just happened so close by.

Warner ran to the cars on the top of the headland and drove frantically down 8 km (5 miles) of bumpy track to Sandy Point, a tiny fishing settlement to the north. There he convinced Harry Holmes, a crayfisherman, to take him back to North Head in his boat.

Ninety minutes later, off the headland, they found the shark still tangled in the float line. An attempt was made to spear it again,

An aerial view of the Western Australian coast at Jurien Bay, north of Perth. Bob Bartle was taken 700 m (760 yds) off North Head, which juts into the ocean in the middle distance.

COAST OF WESTERN AUSTRALIA

Jurien

Cervantes

Indian Ocean

Western Australia

0   50 km

Lancelin

JURIEN BAY AREA

Sandy Cape

Bob Bartle attacked

North Head

Jurien Bay

Whitlock Island

Jurien

Escape Island

Indian Ocean

Yanchep

0   10 km

Perth

but it broke free and disappeared. They retrieved the upper half of Bob Bartle's body, which was floating nearby. It was unmarked, and an autopsy later revealed that there was still air in his lungs. Death must have been instantaneous.

Later, attempts were made to find out which species of shark had been responsible for the attack, but Lee Warner was unable to recall any details of its appearance. His entire attention had been riveted by the ghastly contents of its mouth. Experts thought that only a tiger or great white shark would have been large and powerful enough to have carried out such an attack. The fact that Warner saw a membrane cross the shark's eye seemed to rule out a great white – the most likely culprit – because they do not have a nictitating membrane. However, others have pointed out that the great white does roll its eye – displaying the white of the eyeball – just before it attacks. This is not, however, the question that is uppermost in Lee Warner's mind. To this day he still asks himself 'Why Bob?' Why did the shark pass him to attack Bartle?

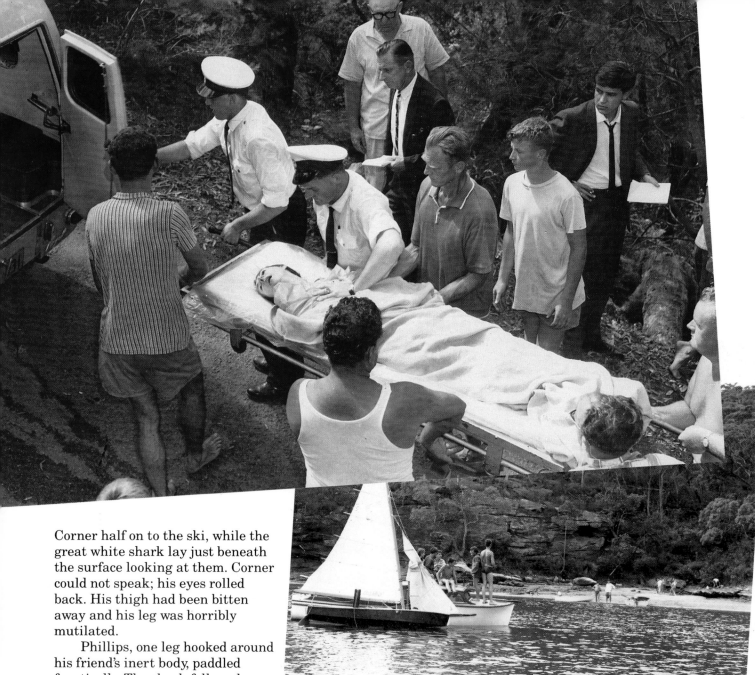

Corner half on to the ski, while the great white shark lay just beneath the surface looking at them. Corner could not speak; his eyes rolled back. His thigh had been bitten away and his leg was horribly mutilated.

Phillips, one leg hooked around his friend's inert body, paddled frantically. The shark followed. Another spearfisherman, Murray Brampton, paddled across and struck at the shark with his paddle.

Jeff Corner was dead when they reached the shore. His parents, and Phillips' wife and child, were among the hushed, horrified crowd.

Eyewitness accounts of shark attacks sometimes have the ring of authenticity – victims often report vivid details – but how much of the detail is true? Do eyewitnesses sometimes subconsciously persuade themselves that they have seen what they think they should have seen? Does terror play tricks on both perception and memory?

At Portsea, Victoria, on the Australian south coast, on 4 March 1956 six surf lifesavers went bodysurfing after a day's competition in surf rescue and swimming routines. All were young, fit and strong swimmers. Among them were John Wishart, 27, a plumber; Jack Hopper, 31, Captain of the Portsea Surf Life Saving Club; Gregory Warland, a sergeant at the Portsea Officers' Training School for the Australian Navy; and Richard Wright, 20. Two hundred metres (217 yds) off the beach, they trod water and waited for a wave.

This is Hopper's account of what happened next:

'Suddenly an enormous black shape coming from behind us darted between Wright and myself. He swirled in front of me close

Actress Marcia Hathaway (top) is carried to an ambulance shortly after being attacked by a shark on 28 January 1963. She died before reaching hospital from shock and loss of blood. The location of the attack, at Sugarloaf Bay (above) in Sydney Harbour, is notorious for sharks, and there have been five deaths near there since 1942. Miss Hathaway was with a number of other people wading in water only 76 cm (30 in) deep when a shark bit her below the calf. In a second lunge the shark almost tore her leg off as it sank its teeth into her upper thigh. Her horrified fiancé, who was standing beside her, fought the shark off and carried her to shore. The culprit was never found, despite an extensive hunt by fishermen.

The fate of this young girl, mauled
during a boating trip from Trieste,
present day Italy, in 1908, is not
recorded. The Adriatic Sea holds the
record for being the site of the world's
most northerly recorded unprovoked
attacks on humans.

enough to be touched and dived
diagonally at John Wishart. Next
instant there was a terrific crash as
he took Wishart on the way down.
The whole thing happened in a
second. I imagined the brute
brushed me with its tail, but it was
the force of water as it swerved that
hit me in the stomach.' He thought
the shark was a whaler or tiger
three to four metres (10-12 ft) long.
Hopper swam madly for the shore.

This is Warland's account:

'Suddenly there was a splash
and I could see the shark's jaws
come out of the water. Then it
seemed to splash down on top of
Wishart. It was about four yards
[3.6 m] away. There was swell in the
water, then nothing. Hopper and
myself first thought we could help,
and tried to see Wishart. Then we

realised it was useless and swam
madly for the shore.'

Here are two basically
consistent accounts by eyewitnesses very close to the tragedy.
Mrs G. Bell, however, was watching
from a small bluff behind the beach
where Wishart's mother and sister
were sitting. Mrs Bell saw 'five of
the men catch a big wave and ride it
to the shore. But the poor sixth man
missed it by about two feet [0.6 m].
He appeared to be waiting for the
next breaker when he suddenly
threw up his arms and disappeared.
Then he began to thrash his arms in
and out of the water. We then
realised that he was being attacked
by a shark. We saw a large dorsal
fin break the water and a pool of
blood spread over the surface . . . The
man in the water must have been

one of the bravest men that ever
lived, the way he fought off the
shark for four minutes.'

None of the accounts sound like
verbatim tape transcripts, and it is
possible some of the inconsistency
arose from reporters condensing the
eyewitnesses' interviews. Even so,
how did Mrs Bell see a four-minute
struggle by a lone surfer, when two
surfers saw one man plucked from a
line of surfers by a single strike?

Three days after the attack,
a 227-kg (500-lb) shark swallowed
a bullock's liver bait on a line from
a floating oil drum. Fishermen in
a 5.5-m (18-ft) skiff killed it with
a twelve-bore shotgun and five
bullets from a .22 rifle. Taken
ashore at nearby Sorrento Beach,
it was raised and disembowelled as
a crowd of 1200 watched. The

stomach was empty. John Wishart's remains were never found.

With their wet suits for protection against grazing, facemasks that give clear underwater vision, flippers for speed, spearguns as weapons, and a psychological ease in the ocean, spearfishers have the best protection against sharks. Board and body surfers and beach swimmers are more vulnerable – with no weapons and no protective equipment – but at least they are usually close to the shore, to help in the water, and to medical attention on the beach.

Survivors of aircraft crashes or shipwrecks are by far the most vulnerable of all potential shark attack victims. They may enter the water shocked, concussed, with broken bones, and they may be bleeding. Land, and safety, may

be 1000 km away. They will have neither spearguns, nor masks, nor wet suits. If the sharks spare them, they may meet death by drowning, exposure, shock, starvation or a failure of the will to live. Common to all of them is the knowledge, rare in the most extreme human crises, that they are utterly helpless.

A United States' study of 2500 World War II air crash survivors' accounts revealed that there were only 38 shark sightings and 12 attacks, but the fear of shark attack was a common theme in every survivor's story.

Airmen surviving an ocean ditching were typically left with only inflatable lifejackets for support. They often discarded their heavy waterlogged boots so they could move easily, leaving their naked feet dangling like bait from beneath a lifejacket which prevented

them from diving or moving quickly if any sharks came.

United States Navy pilot Lieutenant A. G. Reading, with airman E. H. Almond, the radioman, ditched in the central Pacific Ocean in the mid-1940s, more than 100 km (62 miles) east of Wallis Island. Their reconnaissance plane had developed engine trouble. The impact of the crash knocked Reading unconscious. Almond pulled him from the sinking aircraft and inflated his lifejacket, ripping his own trousers off in the frantic struggle to get free of the cockpit. Reading recovered consciousness in the water.

Within 30 minutes they were being circled by sharks, although nothing happened for about an hour. Then they heard the sounds of aircraft. Reading reported later: 'I said to Almond, "Let's kick and

Gulf Stream, Winslow Homer's famous painting, raises many questions in viewer's minds. Homer is reported to have said: 'Tell them it is all right; the tornado does not hit him and he is picked up by the ship.'

This dramatic scene — which seems to owe something to Géricault's *Raft of the Medusa* — appeared on the cover of a Paris magazine in March 1906. The actual circumstances of the event it depicts are unknown, but presumably some of the sailors survived to tell the tale of their ordeal.

Dix-Huitième année. — N° 903.

Huit pages : CINQ centimes

Dimanche 27 Mai 1906.

Le Petit Parisien
SUPPLÉMENT LITTÉRAIRE ILLUSTRÉ

TOUS LES JOURS
Le Petit Parisien
5 centimes

CHAQUE SEMAINE
LE SUPPLÉMENT LITTÉRAIRE
5 centimes

DIRECTION: 18, rue d'Enghien (10°), PARIS

ABONNEMENTS

PARIS ET DÉPARTEMENTS
12 mois, 4 fr. 50. 6 mois, 2 fr. 25

UNION POSTALE:
12 mois, 5 fr. 50. 6 mois, 3 fr.

TERRIBLE DRAME EN MER. — NAUFRAGÉS ATTAQUÉS PAR DES REQUINS

splash around to see if we can't attract their [the aircraft's] attention." It failed, but suddenly Almond said he felt something strike his right foot and that it hurt. I told him to get on my back and keep his right foot out of the water, but before he could the sharks struck again and we were both jerked under the water for a second. I knew that we were in for it as there were more than five sharks and blood all around us. He showed me his legs, and not only did he have bites all over his right leg, but his left thigh was badly mauled. He

The predicament confronting these two unfortunate mariners will be familiar to a modern generation of comic readers. In 1860, when this engraving was published, artists often had to reconstruct scenes of events in farflung parts of the world from only the haziest of descriptions.

101

wasn't in any particular pain except every time they struck I knew it and felt the jerk. I finally grabbed my binoculars and started swinging at the passing sharks. It was a matter of seconds before they struck again. We both went under, and this time I found myself separted from Almond. I was also the recipient of a wallop across the cheekbone from one of the flaying tails of a shark.

Attacks on boats are common, and occasionally large pieces have been torn out of hulls and oars by sharks. The motives for such attacks are unclear, but it may be that sharks are attracted by flashing metal, or are simply curious and explore unfamiliar objects by biting them to see if they are edible. On one occasion the teeth of a giant shark were found embedded deep in the copper-clad hull of a large schooner when it was pulled from the water for routine maintenance. The strange looking shark attacking the rowing boat (above) dates from 1820, while the great white biting the stern of a power boat (left) was photographed in the early 1980s. The most terrifying incidents involve sharks that actually leap from the water into open boats. In December 1949 a 2.6-m (8.5-ft) grey nurse shark landed on top of a seasick fisherman who was resting in the bottom of a boat off Seaholme in southern Australia.

Almond's head was under water and his body jerked as the sharks struck it. As I drifted away ... sharks continually swam about and every now and then I could feel one with my foot.' At midnight Reading sighted a navy boat, called for help and was rescued unhurt. The fact that Almond lost his trousers as he pulled Reading from the cockpit may have made the fatal difference.

An Ecuadorian flight officer survived a similar tragedy in June 1941, after his plane ran out of fuel and he was also forced to ditch in the Pacific. The three survivors, supported by lifejackets, swam towards the nearest land through rough seas, but after five hours one man, weakened by the crash, the huge waves, and having swallowed a lot of salt water, died. The flight

officer, hoping to bring the body ashore, pushed the dead man ahead of him. A short time later something dragged the body from his grasp. After another five hours, the second survivor died in his lifejacket, and again the flight officer pushed the body ahead of him. Now, by the light of the moon, he saw dark shapes in the water and discovered that parts of the corpse's legs were missing. After two more strikes, the great black fish brushing against him as they bit into the corpse, he let it go and saw it quickly dragged away. At daylight he saw sharks following him closely. When he stopped to rest, his feet touched the backs of them swimming directly beneath him. But, although they followed him all that day, they did not attack

again. Thirty hours after the ditching he waded ashore. It was as if these sharks, on that occasion, would attack only the dead.

That was not always the pattern. At dawn off Guadalcanal, in the Solomon Islands, on a night in 1944, Lieutenant Commander Kabat, afloat in a lifejacket, felt a scratching sensation in his left foot and found it was gushing blood. A 'great fish' with a brown back was swimming away. It turned, breaking the surface in a steady line and came at the Lieutenant. He kicked and splashed in a frenzy and the great fish veered away. It came again. Kabat thrashed about and punched the shark, which again veered away, although he discovered it had taken a piece from his left hand. The shark attacked repeatedly at intervals of 10 or 15 minutes, biting Kabat's heel, elbow, hand and calf. But he found the salt water minimised the blood flow, and that he had no consciousness 'of great pain'. When he saw a passing ship and shouted for help, the shark bit his thigh to the bone. Men on the ship fired at the shark until Kabat screamed at them to stop, terrified that having survived repeated attacks he might be killed by a bullet within reach of safety. After months in hospital, he recovered.

Kabat's experience showed that even an utterly exposed and effectively helpless man could, against all odds, survive repeated attacks. Some survivors' experiences suggested that there was safety in sticking together. In September 1955 the four-man crew of a ditched DC-4 fought off sharks for nearly 44 hours between Wake and Johnston Islands in the Pacific by staying together in a square of marker dye and shark repellent. Although the repellent did not bother the sharks, the men stayed in a tight group slapping the water and yelling. Two of the four were not wearing shoes and their feet were constantly bitten. Eventually one man, who lost a thumb to a shark, died of exhaustion and loss of blood. As a rescue ship approached, another lagged behind his two companions and was killed by repeated, aggressive attacks. It seemed that four men together cause enough noise and confusion to intimidate a shark pack which would kill an individual in minutes.

On another occasion, in July 1958, three men from the crew of a United States Air Force mail carrier survived for three days in shark-infested waters between Hawaii and Wake Island. They kept together beside a 'raft' of mail bags too small to support any one of them. When the sharks attacked, they all tried to climb onto the raft, kicking, splashing and screaming. Two other men who drifted away from the raft were killed.

Perhaps the worst loss of life to sharks in a single incident occurred when a German submarine torpedoed the British steamship *Nova Scotia* off the South African coast on 28 November 1942. The *Nova Scotia* carried 900 men, 750 of them Italian prisoners of war. Giant sharks tore into the shrieking survivors in what one of them described as a 'feeding frenzy'. Clinging to rafts, oars and floating debris, the survivors remained for 67 hours in shark-infested waters. Eventually a Portuguese sloop picked up 192 men, the Portuguese sailors fending off sharks with boathooks during the rescue. There is no way of knowing how many of the 700 who died were shark victims, but the incident horrified the public in Britain.

In the United States of America, the Office of Scientific Research and Development, and later the United States Naval Research Laboratory, responded to this threat to morale in the allied navies and air forces, by conducting urgent research to develop a chemical shark repellent. Although a repellent was produced it was not effective and gave only peace of mind to those who used it. No effective repellent has ever been found, and work on the problem has virtually halted.

THE SAILOR'S REVENGE

From the earliest times sailors hated sharks and took pleasure in inflicting great suffering on any they caught.

In 1593 Sir Richard Hawkins — the first person to bring a shark back to England — made these observations during a voyage: 'Every day my company tooke more or lesse of them [sharks], not that they eat of them (for they are not held wholesome; although the Spaniards, as I have seene, doe eat them), but to recreate themselves, and in revenge of the injuries receiveth by them; for they live long, and suffer much after they bee taken, before they dye.

'At the tayle of one they tyed a great logge of wood, at another an empty batizia [small cask], well stopped; one they yoaked like a hogge; from another they plucked out his eyes, and so threw them into the sea. In catching two together, they bound them tayle to tayle and so set them swimming...'

Sailors 'punish' a shark for the misdeeds of its species in this 1840 engraving.

THE FINAL PARADE

The story of the wreck of the **Birkenhead** *is notorious in the annals of shark attacks. No one can say for certain how many of the 455 who died were taken by sharks.*

At 2 am on 26 February 1852 the paddle frigate *Birkenhead,* carrying 490 soldiers of the British Army, with 25 of their wives and 31 children, together with a crew of 134, struck a reef about 1.6 km (1 mile) off Danger Point near the southern tip of Africa.

In the first few minutes following the collision, confusion reigned. Seamen, soldiers and passengers struggled onto the deck to escape water rapidly filling the ship as she settled at the bow.

On deck the officers moved quickly to establish calm, ordering the men to fall in on the poop. Lieutenant Colonel Alexander Seton, the senior army commander aboard, called his officers together and calmly requested them to make sure that any orders given by the ship's captain – Robert Salmond – were instantly obeyed.

Captain Salmond ordered the women and children into a lifeboat, detailing an ensign and a sergeant to forcibly separate women who

THE *BIRKENHEAD* DISASTER

South Africa

Cape Town

Cape of Good Hope

Birkenhead went aground

Danger Point

Cape Agulhas

0   100 km

clung desperately to their men. A second lifeboat with 30 men aboard was lowered into the swell. For the 600 remaining aboard the dangerously listing ship there were no lifeboats. Many trapped below decks had already drowned. Many more had been killed by falling wreckage or swept overboard. From the water came terrified screams as floundering swimmers were dragged down by packs of sharks that cruised around the doomed ship. The 200 survivors still able to stand, supporting those who were not, stood fast on the poop deck.

Salmond climbed a few metres up the mizzen rigging and shouted to the men: 'Save yourselves. All those who can swim jump overboard and make for the boats. That is your only hope of salvation.' Lieutenant Colonel Seton, was appalled. The lifeboats were already dangerously

full. If 200 soldiers tried to board them, the boats would be lost.

Seton raised his hand above his head and shouted: 'You will swamp the cutter containing the women and children. I implore you not to do this thing. I ask you all to remain where you are.' Some survivors later said that three men went over the rail, but of the rest of the 200, not a man moved. They stood rigidly to attention. Moments after Seton's command, the *Birkenhead* broke its back, the bow slid beneath the water and the stern reared up. A surviving officer wrote later: 'Every man did as he was directed and there was not a cry or a murmur among them until the vessel made her final plunge... [The officers] had received their orders and had carried them out as if the men were embarking instead of going to the bottom of the sea.

This engraving of the *Birkenhead's* last moments was executed by an artist at the *Illustrated London News*, using instructions supplied by one of the men who survived the disaster.

THE "BIRKENHEAD" NEARING THE SUNKEN ROCK.

STRIKING THE ROCK.

BREAKING.

THE WRECK.

Four contemporary engravings show the sinking of the *Birkenhead*. Fifty survivors clung to the rigging on the mainmast after the ship sank. When the schooner *Lioness* reached the scene at dawn on the following day only 30 were left, the rest had died from cold and exhaustion. News of the disaster reached London in the second week of April 1852, and these engravings appeared in the *Illustrated London News* on the 10th. The same issue carried a melancholy list of those who had perished, but only passing mention was made of the sharks.

There was only one difference – I never saw any embarkation conducted with so little noise or confusion.'

The *Birkenhead* went down just 30 minutes after striking the rocks. Within a short time all but a handful of those that had survived the sinking were dead. On the surface of the water, stained crimson with blood, floated the barely-recognisable remains of those torn apart by the sharks.

Lieutenant Frank Girardot later described what happened in a letter to his father. 'I remained on the wreck until she went down. The suction took me down some way and a man got hold of my leg, but I managed to kick him off and came up and struck for some pieces of wood ... I was in the water about five hours ... the surf ran so high that a great many were lost trying to land. Nearly all those that took to the water without their clothes on were taken by sharks; hundreds of them were all around us and I saw men taken quite close to me, but as I was dressed ... they preferred the others.'

More than 60 men made the 1.6-km (one-mile) swim to shore and safety – though most of the men aboard the *Birkenhead* could not swim, including Alexander Seton who drowned. Captain Salmond was thrown overboard and died in the water when struck by a piece of falling wreckage. The wreck claimed 455 lives, but the proportion claimed by the ship, the sea and the sharks is one of the mysteries of that dreadful night. One of the survivors, Captain Wright, said later that, but for the discipline of the men, the loss of life would have been still higher.

WHERE SHARKS ARE GODS

Sharks play an important part in the lives of many of the island peoples of the Pacific Ocean. Shark gods and goddesses are still worshipped, although human sacrifices are no longer made to them. The strange practice of shark calling was also widespread, and still takes place today. Here author Olaf Ruhen describes his experiences in the Pacific.

Numerous magic rituals accompany any attempt at shark calling. Gifts must be made to the appropriate gods, and the fish-magic man will be called upon to bless the dangerous enterprise.

In the reign of Edward II, King of England from 1307 to 1327, and throughout the following centuries the sturgeon, comparatively rare in English waters, was proclaimed a Royal Fish: it belonged to the King when captured. In the waters surrounding the Trobriand Islands, in the Solomon Sea, a similar distinction was accorded the shark. Any ambitious lad, eager for acclaim or privilege, would set out to catch a major shark and deliver it to the king at his village of Omarakana on the island of Kiriwina. If he did this successfully he certainly proved himself a man to watch. It was the crowning achievement of his adolescence.

It was by no means an easy accomplishment, for tradition ruled that the catcher had to follow certain routines and that he had to be alone in his canoe. About 1954, my wife and I were staying with the almost legendary island trader Mrs

Amy Lumley in her house at Gusoweta on Kiriwina's southern coast, when village gossip brought the news that a lad named Benia had the enterprise under way, and I went to see his preparations, which centred on a small one-man outrigger canoe. Besides the regular equipment of paddle and bailer shell it held a cane hoop one metre (3.3 ft) in diameter, on which were threaded nearly 20 of the hard shells of coconuts, in random order, but moving freely on the cane.

There was also something that at first glance gave the impression of a two-bladed aircraft propeller, carved from a large branch of the native hibiscus, a tough pale wood as light as balsa, and rather more than two metres (6.6 ft) long. The paddle ends were not designed to work in any reciprocal or complementary rhythm. The thickening at what would have been the boss had been pierced and threaded with

about four metres (13 ft) of rope laid up from pandanus-root fibre.

The fish-magic man had taken time from his regular employment in the mission garden and was in process of blessing the enterprise, chewing up the words he addressed to the gods and ancestors with a piece of ginger root that lay in a cup of calophyllum leaves he pressed close to his lips, and expelling the abundant saliva that resulted in a fine spray directed at the canoe and its contents. This, without explanation, was all I was permitted to see at this time, but I noticed the gifts of betel nut and cooked yam that the lad had made to the gods.

Rather shaky deduction assisted by luck afforded me a view of the more active stages that came later, not a good view, for I watched from the top of a low coral cliff.

Benia had the cane hoop half submerged in the water and was holding it by the top to shake it

The shark caller's equipment. The rattle is made from a cane hoop, about one metre (39 in) in diameter, threaded with some 20 discs cut from the hard inner shells of coconuts. Held half submerged in the water, it is shaken vigorously so that the noise will attract a shark's attention.

A shark's eye view of the source of the strange vibrations that have attracted its attention. The fish lure invites the shark to puts its head through the rope noose. To grapple, bare-handed, with an immensely powerful, three-metre (9.8-ft) shark from such a small craft is obviously highly dangerous, and sometimes leads to the death of the would-be hero.

vigorously. After only a few minutes a stiffening of his body announced that he had seen the target, and a moment later I saw it too: a good sized shark, its dorsal fin occasionally breaking the surface as it changed direction, half-right, then half-left but closing in on the canoe with some speed. Along the side of the canoe, half-obscured by Benia's body, the propellor shape was secured by a fragile lashing to the protruding tops of the ribs. When the shark was committed to its final charge Benia pulled the hoop rattle inboard and tossed it over the lashings of his outrigger, out of the way. He had made a slipknot of most of the rope attached to the float and now it opened in a big circle in the water beneath him, and he took up his lure, a fish fastened to a short pole.

The shark, now near the canoe, continued what must have been its questing investigation into the cause of the surface disturbance and underwater sounds that had brought it up, and Benia thrust his fish-on-a-stick through the loop, keeping that open with a light pressure on the slipknot.

I would have given much for a closer look at the action of the next minute or so – it took most of Benia's ingenuity and a share of his patience to inveigle the shark, but eventually the big fish thrust through the loop, Benia pulled it tight over the slatted gills and then the action exploded.

The float took erratic life. It twisted back and forth against the panicky struggling of the shark, ever coercing it to the surface. Benia's task was now nothing more than to keep the canoe free of the turmoil and watch his prey as it tired. An hour passed like a minute before the lessening spasms of frantic fury subsided altogether and the shark remained under the surface. Benia paddled carefully up to the float where it now lay on the surface, twitching only occasionally. He exchanged the paddle for a shark club and, pulling the head out of the water, though with a great deal of caution, despatched the great beast with a few well-aimed blows. My imagination had to supply the yells of victory – I could see the action but the sound did not carry to the cliff. The shark was a good one, a grey nurse, three metres (9.8 ft) long, longer anyway than the canoe from which Benia, un-aided, had encompassed its defeat.

This capture of sharks after calling them in occurs in several other locations: the St Georges Channel, for example, that separates New Britain and New Ireland. It has been reported from Kiribati and Tonga, and certainly there will be many communities from which the bold and vigorous youths take chances against the frequent ferocity of certain sharks, notably the wide ranging tiger.

In other island groups the shark was actually worshipped. In Savo Island in the Solomon group he was regarded as a beneficent deity and in the northern districts of Malaita, as well as nearby in Gizo, and in the Roviana Lagoon to the north there are many tales of sharks having come to the rescue of fishermen who had had ill-luck with their craft. In the coral-enclosed Langalanga and Lau lagoons on Malaita the shark is revered too, although the main gods are the ancestors. These people share with the Tongans and some others the comfortable belief that sharks will not eat them. Though Benia's shark, like the English sturgeon, came rightfully to the King's table, respect for the divine element in the shark's body was sometimes so extreme as to forbid the eating of the flesh.

In the Fijian theogony, chief of the gods was Degei, who was also an ancestor and historically a leader of the tribes that first settled the islands. He is known as 'the origin of the people' and he is envisaged as a huge snake who lives in a cave in the northernmost peak of the Kauvadra Range in the north of Viti Levu. The Reverend J. Waterhouse, writing about 1860, noted that by extension all snakes were known and honoured as 'the offspring of the origin'. But Degei's existence was nothing more than an orgy of sleeping and eating, and he took no interest in human affairs.

The executive gods were seen as Degei's sons and were recognised in different animals or different features of the landscape, commanding some reverence. But none exercised a greater puissance than Dekuwaqa, who was seen in a large shark rumoured to live in a sea-cave under the temple erected on Benan Island.

In Taveuni, Fiji's 'Garden

Coir armour worn by Gilbert Islanders while fighting with shark-tooth swords (Kiribati).

Sword studded with shark teeth (Kiribati).

Sword studded with shark teeth (Kiribati).

Coir helmet worn by Gilbert Islanders (Kiribati).

Island', he was recognised in a basking shark 13 m (42.6 ft) or more in length that used the rocks at the north end of the island as scratching posts to rid itself of barnacles. The people of Natewa and Cakaudrove were concerned to keep on friendly terms with him. In the old days he piloted them on night raids, the canoes following the phosphorescence of his wake, and for this reason he was also called Daucina 'the giver of light', the name by which he was known at Levuka and Kadavu. He was the chief god of fishing and seafaring communities, and from his love of fair women he was also noted as the god of adulterers.

In his honour the eating of

A group of objects, collected from various parts of the Pacific, that are either involved in shark worship or incorporate the parts of captured sharks. Some objects, such as swords edged with shark's teeth, can still be purchased today, although they are not as elaborate as the original weapons intended for use in battle.

Shark lure (Gulf Province, Papua New Guinea).

Coconut shell rattle used to attract sharks (New Britain).

Wooden float, with rope attached, to prevent captured shark from diving (New Britain).

Carved shark inlaid with pearl shell (Solomon Islands).

Shark-tooth knife (Kiribati).

Shark-catching charm (East Sepik Province, Papua New Guinea).

Lau) on the death of the previous incumbent, Ratu Pope. Two days before that event he was at sea and he made what might have seemed an innocuous entry in his diary:

'Soon after 11 am a specie of hammerhead shark (seven foot) [2.1 m] seen astern. He stayed over an hour alongside, six or seven times allowing himself to be touched, patted and pulled.'

Dr S.M. Lambert, who wrote the book *A Doctor in Paradise*, recorded that Ratu Sukuna told him that he knew at once that Ratu Pope was dead, or would soon die.

In his biography of Ratu Sukuna, Deryck Scarr commented: 'I joked about synthetic pillars of the Church who still believed in the heathen temples. Nonetheless the enormous satisfaction he drew from administering the land of Fiji could hardly have been separable from at least a sympathetic feeling for the spirits of the land. He was culturally enriched by remembering the places where spirits dwelt as also by the legends of Dekuwaqa.'

It seems doubtful whether tributes to Dekuwaqa amounted to a true worship or anything much more than a recognition of the commmon ground shared by all life – animal or vegetable. The latter is represented by the sacred groves of Ivi trees *Inocarpus edulis*, the Tahitian chestnut, or the ironwood which is very often grown in plantations around graves. Or perhaps these things are simply reminders of such spiritual power as rules humans too.

Fear is a motive for establishing a god, and man has worshipped at one time or another most of the living things he fears. History gives few examples of the deification of a fish. In the middle-east a notable exception was Dagon, the national god of the Philistines, a fish with the hands and face of a man for whom there were temples built at Gaza and Ashded, and who later

sharks was tabooed. Sometimes in the tidal fish-traps a shark was taken with markings on its belly claimed to be the tattoos of Dekuwaqa. Such a fish was freed into the open sea. When Fijian vessels passed over areas of sea that he was known to frequent the crews poured libations into the water, and accompanied this with offerings of cooked food. Remnants of this custom still persist.

The wholesale conversion of the Fijians to Christianity did not eliminate such deference to the old gods. Ratu Sir Lala Sukuna, one of the most distinguished Fijians of the twentieth century, an avowed Christian with an Oxford education, became Tu'i Nayau (the Lord of the gained a following in Phoenicia and parts of South Palestine. But Dekuwaqa seems his only rival in the records of history. Perhaps he gained a hold because of the scant population dependent on his share of ocean, and the few other living threats those people found to menace them there.

It is certain that the introduction of other religions tended to drive the shark gods from their sphere of influence. They had considerable power less than a score of years ago, particularly in the heart of the Solomon Islands. At that time shark gods commanded a majority of the Savo Islanders, who lived on the flanks of a graceful volcanic cone about halfway between Guadalcanal and Tulaghi in the middle of New Georgia Sound. Here I heard tales in abundance of this kindly swimming god who rescued the islanders from shipwreck, towed them home as they clung to its dorsal fin, rescued children who fell overboard unnoticed late at night – and was selective enough to destroy its worshippers' enemies.

Shark worship has become much less popular on Savo, a circumstance attributed to the number of corpses that had come the way of the local sharks during naval battles in World War II. It still persisted on Tulaghi, on the northern parts of Malaita and apparently in many other remote places. Some women with whom I travelled from Bellona Island in the far west of the Solomons had dark tattoos between their breasts, and in these sharks shared honours with frigate birds. Bellona gods had no competition at all from the missionaries until the 1940s, but I was told that shark worship was hale and hearty in the village of Laulasi in the Langalanga Lagoon.

This was actually two villages, crowded onto artificial islands built on the reef or in the shallow waters of the lagoon by the industrious hands of their inhabitants. One island was Christian, one heathen, but both were alike in their hordes of laughing children, most of whom could swim and handle a small canoe before they could walk.

In the heathen village the women all faced the one way, and were very pernicketty about it too, walking backwards or sideways if they wanted to go anywhere else. Not one faced the northern end of the village where, in carefully stencilled letters, a prominent notice proclaimed: PERSONS IN BLACK CLOTHING NOT PERMITTED IN THIS AREA. The

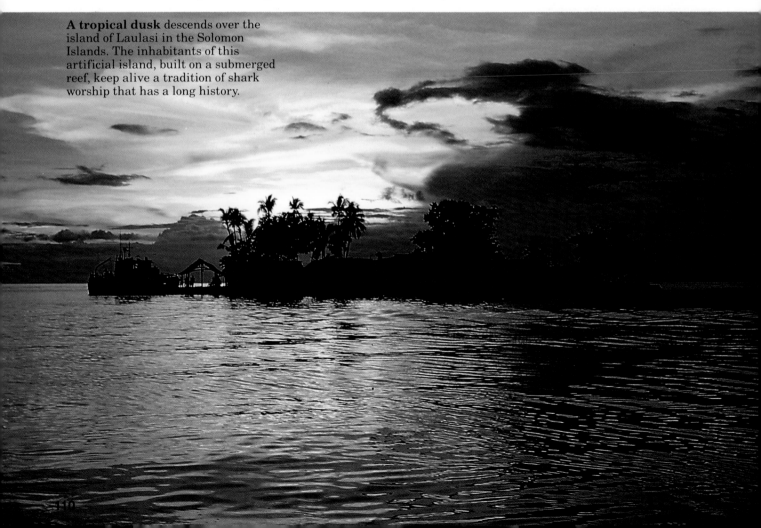

A tropical dusk descends over the island of Laulasi in the Solomon Islands. The inhabitants of this artificial island, built on a submerged reef, keep alive a tradition of shark worship that has a long history.

forbidden tract contained three large communal houses, each with a notice painted on its gable. They read: HEADMASTER RU GOLA, HEADMASTER MAEMADAMA, HEADMASTER MOUSI. These named individuals had nothing to do with schools, but were pagan priests controlling the 'spirit houses'. Maemadama, in a short wraparound skirt and wearing a flower in his hair, gave me permission to enter the one marked with his name.

The narrow doorway barely admitted enough light for vision. White wood ash around a central fireplace testified that a large congregation had gathered the night before. When I moved towards a big collection of leaf-wrapped shells tidily disposed in niches, Maemadama restrained me.

Indeed I was glad enough to return to the sunny exterior, where hordes of children bobbed about the lagoon surface in tiny canoes with only a few centimetres of freeboard, and gossiping women sat over their chores in the narrow passageways between the huts in their bright cladding of pandanus leaf. I had noted that although the overt worship was directed to the ancestors, these, in some mysterious way, also represented the sharks.

Now that there is no longer any mystique attaching to factory-made goods, the headway of the imported religions too is diminishing. The Christian community has enjoyed advantages from its conversion – health, education, and a boat-building school which concentrates on the techniques of repair – but such benefits have also come the way of the heathen by a process of osmosis. And perhaps the heathen have had to do more thinking for themselves, without missionaries to provide instruction.

Wade Doak, in his book *Sharks and other Ancestors*, reports on a visit to Laulasi a decade after mine. The shark worshippers had formed a company 'Laulasi Adventure Tours', properly constituted with seven directors and fifty shareholders in the village. They charged the tourist $19 a day to visit, and they provided transportation from the Malaita capital of Auki in outboard-propelled canoes. And they gave good value for the money. It seems the shark gods had no argument with modern ways.

Through the medium of these skulls – the remains of long-dead ancestors – shark priests on Laulasi call up the spirit sharks. Few, if any, Europeans have been allowed to witness the rituals associated with shark worship.

THE SHARK PAPERS

*The strange story of the capture of the **Nancy**, and the undoing of her captain, is a testament to the extraordinary appetites of sharks. This is the first of two occasions (that concerning the Shark Arm Case is told on p 114) in which sharks have been instrumental in bringing human villains to justice.*

The jaws of the shark which swallowed the *Nancy's* papers were preserved, and for a time were on display in a London museum. The shark involved was probably a tiger – a species renowned for its remarkable appetite (see p 117).

The *Nancy,* a brig owned by German-American Maryland traders, left Baltimore on 3 July 1799 bound for Curaçao and Haiti with a cargo of German dry-goods, food and timber. She was commanded by Thomas Briggs, a resourceful sailor, and one of the unluckiest in the history of the United States merchant marine.

Briggs delivered his goods to Curaçao and was on his way to collect the return cargo of coffee at Port-au-Prince, Haiti, when on 28 August the *Nancy* encountered the British cutter, *HMS Sparrow,* part of a blockade of Haiti effected by the British Navy. The United States and Britain were at war at the time.

Briggs immediately crowded sail onto the two-masted, square-rigged *Nancy* and fled. The *Sparrow* gave chase, put a shot across the *Nancy's* bows and boarded her – but not before Briggs had dumped the ship's papers overboard and replaced them with Curaçao-made forgeries stating that the *Nancy* was Dutch-owned, and therefore free to pass through the blockade.

The *Sparrow's* Commander, Lieutenant Hugh Wylie, was not impressed by the forgeries, or by Briggs' threat of legal action. He told Captain Briggs that he, the *Nancy* and her crew were now a prize of war. He ordered his men to sail the *Nancy* to Port Royal, Jamaica, where Briggs could put his case that the seizure was unlawful to the Vice-Admiralty Court.

A suit for salvage was brought on 9 September against 'a certain Brig or Vessel called the *Nancy,* her guns, tackle, furniture, ammunition and apparel, and the goods, wares, merchandize, specie, and effects on board her, taken and seized as the property of some person or persons being enemies of our Sovereign Lord the King ...' On 14 September, Briggs put his case for dismissal of the suit with costs, backing it with an affidavit in which he swore that 'no papers whatever were burnt, torn, thrown overboard, cancelled, concealed, or attempted so to be... all the papers on board [the *Nancy*] were entirely true and fair.'

A bizarre event at sea 15 days previously – the day after the seizure of the *Nancy* – was about to undo Briggs. On that day, another British ship, *HMS Ferret,* encountered a dead bullock in the sea near San Domingo Island. It was surrounded by sharks tearing at the carcass. The *Ferret's* commander, Lieutenant Michael Fitton, had a taste for shark fishing, and hooked the biggest of the sharks. When they decked and opened it, Fitton's men discovered inside the shark the wholly preserved ship's papers of the *Nancy,* tied in string. Fitton dried them in the sun on deck. By coincidence, Lieutenant Wylie, the *Sparrow's* Captain, had been invited for breakfast aboard the *Ferret* that very morning. The astounded Wylie, together with Fitton, immediately

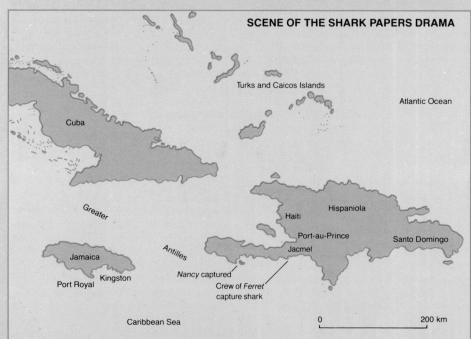

SCENE OF THE SHARK PAPERS DRAMA

Turks and Caicos Islands

Atlantic Ocean

Cuba

Greater

Antilles

Haiti

Hispaniola

Port-au-Prince

Jacmel

Santo Domingo

Jamaica

Kingston

Port Royal

Nancy captured

Crew of *Ferret* capture shark

Caribbean Sea

0   200 km

The *Nancy's* original papers, bound in string, and Lieutenant Fitton's affidavit which detailed the strange way in which he obtained them. Among the papers are a number of letters written in German from the ship's owners instructing their agent on board, Christopher Schültze, on what to do in certain circumstances. The compromising nature of these letters – which proved that the ship was American property, and that there was a conspiracy to conceal her identity – made it essential that they did not fall into British hands. Wrapped around the papers is a note signed by John Fraser, an official at the court in 1799, certifying their authenticity. These documents are now preserved in Kingston.

turned for Port Royal. On 24 September, Fitton's affidavit, giving his account of the shark's capture and the discovery of the papers and his supposition that 'the papers so found as aforesaid might be useful at the trial of the said vessel called the *Nancy* hath caused the same to be sealed up and delivered' was sworn in the Vice-Admiralty Court. The resourceful Briggs' perjury was exposed. The *Nancy* became a lawful prize of war. British justice had prevailed over an American ship running a blockade of Haiti in a court sitting in Jamaica – with the help of a freakish stroke of luck and a shark.

The *Nancy's* papers are exhibited in the Institute of Jamaica at Kingston. The shark's jaws were, for a time, set up ashore in Jamaica where they carried the inscription: 'Lieutenant Fitton recommended these jaws as a collar for neutrals to swear through'. Until recently they were held by a small museum in London, but the collection has now been dispersed, and the jaws have disappeared.

Shark Arm Mystery

The Shark Arm Murder is still one of the great unsolved riddles of Australian criminal history. It was only through the fateful intervention of two hungry sharks, and an extraordinary series of coincidences, that the police even knew a serious crime had been committed.

On 25 April 1935, at 4-m (13-ft) tiger shark was listlessly cruising in the Coogee Aquarium, Sydney, under the fascinated gaze of 14 holidaymakers. Suddenly the shark, which had been tired and languid for three days, lashed its tail, bumped hard against the white tiled pool wall, swam towards the shallow end, turned in three irregular circles and vomited up a bird, a rat – and a muscular human arm. A cloud of evil-smelling brown fluid spread over the pool floor.

When he answered the telephone at the Randwick Police Station a few minutes later, Detective Constable Frank Head heard the outline of an interesting, but fairly routine, mystery. The central questions – whose arm was it, and how had it found its way into a tiger shark's stomach? – might be quickly answered. It might be the arm of a suicide who had ended his misery in the harbour. It might be part of the torn remains of a derelict who had stumbled off a rocky cliff.

At the aquarium, Head got his first intimation that the case might not be routine: a rope about 600 mm

A "*Truth*" in Every Home: Nett Sales Per Issue Largest in ...... Hemisphere

Truth

FORECAST: Mostly fine. Cold night. Variable winds.

SYDNEY, SUNDAY, MAY 5,

THE PUBLIC LIBRARY
7 MAY 1935
132 PAG
OF NEW SOUTH WALES

No. 2365.   Registered at the General Post Office, Sydney, for transmission by post as a Newspaper.

WHAT SICK SHARK REV

MR. BERT HOBSON and his son Ron, who captured the shark. Above is the monster, and on the right the shark is seen in the Coogee Aquarium Baths.

Murder

BY one chance in a million — the fact that little more than a week ago a sick shark in captivity at Coogee Aquarium disgorged a tattooed human arm — some of the best brains of the Sydney C.I.B. are convinced that Fate has revealed a cold-blooded murder, which like the case of the Albury Pyjama Girl, may prove to be another perfect crime. The victim of this mysterious death drama is James Smith, of Gladesville, former billiards marker at City Tattersall's Club, a well-known suburban billiards saloon keeper, one-time promising lightweight boxer, and a man with seemingly not an enemy in the world.

"Truth," which played an outstanding part in the identification of Smith, knows that the dead man's relatives have expressed grave fears as to how he came to meet such a shocking fate.

They scoff at all theories of suicide. Instead, openly they have expressed the opinion that Jimmy Smith was murdered.

The finding of the arm opens up theories as to how he could have met such a fate.

Smith was either the victim of a quarrel while on a fishing excursion, and after being clubbed into unconsciousness, was securely bound and tossed into the ocean's depths, or—the dastardly deed was committed on dry land, and the brain of the human monster responsible conceived the idea of covering up traces of the crime by sending him to a watery grave.

TATTOO MARK.

The police were impressed and there was much to make them interested.

After the arm was disgorged by the giant tiger shark which for a week had lazed about in the clear waters of Coogee Aquarium, detectives discovered a vital clue. The limb bore a crude but discernible tattoo mark, and a knotted rope still hung from the wrist.

The tattoo mark was a distinctive one—that of two boxers sparring up to each other. It was so distinctive indeed that, when the description appeared in last week's "Truth", Jimmy Smith's brother went along at once to Randwick police station, and informed Detective Head that he was certain that the arm was that of his former boxer brother.

Until that moment, the police (not unnaturally) had believed that the shark's victim was a suicide, someone who, with nothing to live for, had deliberately drowned himself, and had then been swallowed by the tiger of the seas.

But Jimmy's brother soon enlightened them on that score. Jimmy was no coward to take an easy way out . . . and what was much more to the point,

THE TATTOOED BOXERS of Smith's arm.

Jimmy Smith had everything to live for.

Then the police began to make inquiries—inquiries that have been carried out with amazing secrecy, so much so that all the dead man's relatives have been ordered to say nothing at all about the matter. Just how much the authorities regard the crime is borne out by the fact that Detective-Inspector Quinn, Detective-Sergeant Matthews, Detective-Sergeant Allmond (who with Detective-Sergeant McRae) has been for months working on the Albury culvert horror, and Detective McDermott have been assigned to the case.

Every single belonging of the dead man has been temporarily taken by the police in the hope that it will yield some clue to the mystery . . . a mystery made all the more remarkable by the fact that five days after he had left home for the last time, Jimmy

Smith's broken-hearted widow received a telephone message.

That message was delivered by a voice she had never heard before. "Don't worry," said the mysterious caller . . . "Jimmy will be home in three days' time".

The caller rang off . . . Mrs. Smith had not the slightest idea then that anything was seriously wrong. Only when the shark, by an act of Providence, was netted, and after being put into the Aquarium (instead of, as it might well have been, killed as soon as it had been dragged ashore) gave up its grisly clue, later to be identified by the dead man's brother, did she realise that the mystery caller must have known full well that Jimmy Smith would never come home again.

Behind their veil of secrecy, the police are hunting . . . hunting . . . but "Truth" to-day is able to tell the exclusive story of the facts that led up to this astounding tragedy—a tragedy such as Edgar Allan Poe never dreamed of in his weirdest fiction . . . a tragedy that is without parallel in the history of crime the world over.

A little more than a fortnight ago, Mr. Bert Hobson, genial proprietor of the popular Coogee Aquarium Baths, set out with his boy Ron in their small boat, coming to anchor about a mile and a half off Coogee Beach.

An expert at landing sharks, Mr. Hobson set one of his big lines. He didn't have to wait long before he got a bite. In no hurry to land the shark, the fisherman played him, but it soon dawned on him that something was amiss.

Away went more line so Mr. Hobson decided to haul in. He has rarely had such a hectic battle and he soon learned the reason. On getting his catch to the top he found that the shark he had hooked had been eaten practically away and tangled, but securely held, in the line was the hungry attacker—a 15 foot Tiger shark, fearless and savage member of the species.

The million to one catch, Mr. Hobson described his feat.

(Continued on Page 24)

The lurid front page of the Sydney *Truth* gave a full description of the arm, together with a drawing of the tattoo found on it. On the following day the victim's brother, Edward Smith, came forward to identify it.

A sinister shape cruises around the perimeter of the pool at Coogee aquarium. Eight days after its capture this 4-m (13-ft) tiger shark vomited up a human arm with a length of rope attached to it.

Bert Hobson (left), a Sydney fisherman, caught the tiger shark when it became entangled in a fishing line he had left overnight about 1 km (1100 yds) offshore. He towed his prize to the aquarium at Coogee where it was put on display by his brother Charles (right).

(24 in) long was tied around the wrist. The knot, he noted carefully, was a clove-hitch. But at least identifying the person from whom the arm had been severed should not be too difficult: on the forearm was a distinctive tattoo of two boxers in red trunks shaping up.

Nor did Head have any difficulty discovering when and where the shark was caught: Albert Hobson, whose brother Charles owned the Coogee Aquarium, explained that eight days previously on 17 April, he had been shark fishing about 1 km (1100 yds) off Coogee Beach, and had left a baited set line overnight. When he returned next morning he

discovered he had caught not one shark but two: a small shark had taken the bait and hook, and the 4-m (13-ft) tiger, in the cannibalistic way of the species, had eaten its unfortunate brother – and then itself become tangled in the line. Albert towed it to the aquarium.

The answer to the next question – had the shark bitten the arm from a suicide or from the body of a drowned man, or from a live swimmer? – dramatically deepened the mystery. Dr Arthur Palmer, the Government Medical Officer for the City of Sydney, examined the arm the day after the shark disgorged it and said it had been severed at the shoulder by a sharp instrument,

probably a knife. But it was not the work of a surgeon – there were none of the skin flaps a surgeon would have left after an amputation. Although it was remarkable what terrible wounds lunatics could inflict on themselves, he thought it 'extremely unlikely' that the man could have cut off his own arm. Dr Palmer said he 'could not deny' the possibility that the man from whom the arm had been severed was still alive, but 'I could hardly conceive that he would be'.

The *Truth* newspaper, which specialised in lurid coverage of bizarre crimes, published a photograph and description of the tattooed arm at the end of April. An

The victim, James Smith, whose body was never found. His partially dismembered corpse had apparently been dumped into the sea somewhere off the coast of Sydney.

Sydney's convoluted coastline was the scene of the shark arm drama. The aquarium which housed the shark was at Coogee, an outer suburban beach, and Brady's cottage was at Cronulla, a popular resort on the southern outskirts of the city.

English-Australian, Edward Smith, went to the Randwick police station and said he recognised the tattoo and that the arm was that of his brother, James Smith. The crucial tattoo evidence had survived by the million-to-one chance of the small shark being hooked before it digested the evidence, and then the 4-m (13-ft) tiger shark which ate it becoming entangled in Albert Hobson's line.

The Sydney police quickly confirmed Edward Smith's identification of the arm: James Smith's fingerprints were on the police files from his arrest four years previously on a charge of illegal starting-price betting.

Smith, a tall, well-built Englishman who arrived in Australia when he was 20, had had a varied career in Sydney, trying his hand as a bartender, billiard marker, amateur boxer, sports club manager, bookmaker, builder and boat caretaker. Smith had left his Gladesville home on 7 April, 18 days before his arm floated into view at the aquarium pool. He told his wife Gladys that he was going fishing at Port Hacking, on the southern outskirts of Sydney, for a few days with a friend called Greg Vaughan and 'a rich man from interstate'. Smith did not go to Port Hacking. He visited Vaughan, then went to a cottage at Cronulla where

he visited another friend, Patrick Brady, a forger.

Smith and Brady met the year before the 'shark arm' appeared, when Smith was employed as caretaker of the luxury yacht *Pathfinder*, owned by Reginald Holmes, a wealthy boatbuilder and engineer. When Holmes bought the yacht it was insured for $4000. He increased the insured value to $7000 and then connived with Greg Vaughan, who became the nominal owner, to bump it up to $17 000. Brady visited Smith aboard the *Pathfinder* in Broken Bay. The broke former builder and the forger found they had much to talk about, and while the waves of Broken Bay

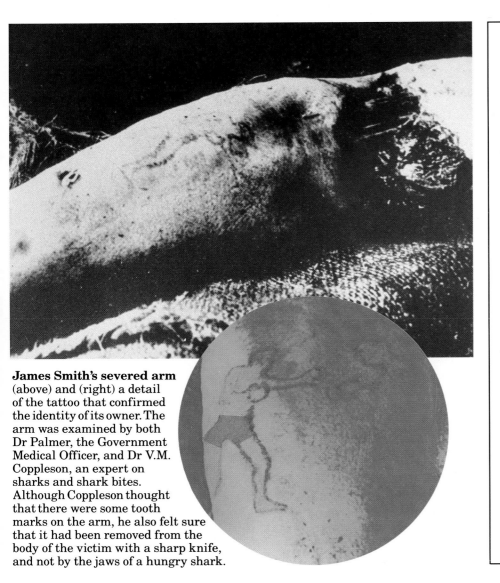

James Smith's severed arm (above) and (right) a detail of the tattoo that confirmed the identity of its owner. The arm was examined by both Dr Palmer, the Government Medical Officer, and Dr V.M. Coppleson, an expert on sharks and shark bites. Although Coppleson thought that there were some tooth marks on the arm, he also felt sure that it had been removed from the body of the victim with a sharp knife, and not by the jaws of a hungry shark.

A distinctively-patterned tiger shark.

THE CURIOUS EATING HABITS OF TIGER SHARKS

The tiger shark is one of three species most frequently named as being responsible for attacks on humans. Voracious eaters, they will swallow almost anything they encounter in the sea. At various times the stomachs of captured specimens have been found to contain an astonishing variety of objects including: a coil of copper wire, nuts, bolts, lumps of coal, boat cushions, clothing, a tom-tom, an unopened can of salmon, driftwood, birds, other sharks, seals and the head of a crocodile.

Sharks can regurgitate the contents of their stomachs at will, and some can apparently store food undigested. Sir Edward Hallstom, honorary director of Sydney's Taronga Park Zoo, once observed this phenomenon in a tiger shark that lived for a month at the zoo in 1950. On two occasions during its captivity the shark was fed on horse meat which it regurgitated. After it died the shark's stomach was cut open and was found to contain two undigested dolphins, eaten before its capture.

---

gently lapped the *Pathfinder*'s sleek hull, their conversation often turned to money, and to schemes which would make them rich men.

They planned to go to Hobart in Tasmania together. Brady went first, looking for buyers for Reginald Holmes' speedboats – but their joint Tasmanian ventures were aborted when Brady forged a cheque for $1000, was arrested and charged – and jumped bail. He returned to Sydney, where he rented the Cronulla cottage. Years later, Brady told a Sydney crime reporter, Vince Kelly, that he and another man had loaded the *Pathfinder* with rocks. On 9 April 1934 a coal ship saw the *Pathfinder* sinking in the

sea off Broken Bay and a man rowing towards the shore. When Vaughan reported the loss to the insurance company, the company called the Criminal Investigation Bureau – and Vaughan dropped the claim. The police suspected Smith's death involved some falling out among the conspirators who had attempted to defraud the insurance company, but could prove nothing.

Gladys Smith was used to her husband's unconventional lifestyle, but by 20 April, when he had been gone nearly two weeks, she was getting worried. She called one of his hangouts and was told James had been there a few days earlier. Four days later, with still no word,

she called Greg Vaughan. Vaughan told her that James had said he was taking a boat to Cronulla.

The police focused on Brady: he was a man with form, a criminal record, and Smith had been with him in the Cronulla cottage at about the time he met the violent death which delivered his left arm to the maw of a tiger shark. On 3 May, Gladys Smith received a letter in James' handwriting, addressed to their son Raymond. 'Keep your mother quiet,' it said. 'I am in trouble. But everything will be all right. Tell your mum I'll have plenty of money soon. They want me. Something in town. Never mind, be a man for me.' It was signed 'Your loving father Jim Smith', and added: 'Destroy this'. The police believed Brady, a gifted forger, had written the note.

When the police questioned Brady, he showed the style detectives expect from guilty suspects: he lied. He had not seen Jim Smith since he returned from Tasmania, he said. He had not been living at the Cronulla cottage.

The police theory was that Brady had murdered Smith, tried to fit the body into a tin trunk, discovered that it would not fit, then severed Smith's left arm, tied it to the trunk and dumped the trunk at sea. There a hungry small shark had taken the arm with the rope, and an even hungrier tiger shark had intervened, like fate, and later coughed up the evidence at Coogee.

The difficulty that the police had, was that although they had an arm in a condition suggesting that

murder was the only explanation, they did not have a corpse. A dead body is usually the starting point for a murder investigation. When the City Coroner began his inquiry into the cause of James Smith's death, Brady's barrister, Clive Evatt, insisted that the law required a body before the inquiry could proceed. The point went to the Supreme Court, where Evatt ridiculed the idea of having an inquest into an arm. What if one arm surfaced at Newcastle, 171 km (106 miles) north of Sydney, and another in Sydney? he asked. Would two different coroners have two different inquests, with perhaps two different verdicts, on the same corpse? Mr Justice Halse Rogers found Evatt convincing: an arm was not enough, he said, there must be a body, the inquest could not go on.

The police had an even more serious difficulty than the lack of a

body – the murder of their principal witness, Reginald Holmes.

On 20 May water police on Sydney Harbour spotted a powerful speedboat careering erratically near Pinchgut Island. When they finally overhauled the speeding boat they discovered Holmes at the wheel, a bullet wound in his forehead, and an empty brandy bottle behind him. 'They say I've been squealing', Holmes gasped, 'but you know I haven't. But I'm going to tell you all about it now.' Holmes was in hospital under police guard for four days while surgeons removed a .32 bullet from his forehead. When he left hospital he went straight to CIB headquarters and made a statement which, if a jury believed it, would send Patrick Brady to the gallows.

Brady had been extorting money from him, Holmes said. Early in April, Brady telephoned

It was at this small rented cottage in Cronulla that James Smith was last seen alive. The police suspected that Patrick Brady had murdered Smith there, and had then dumped his body at sea in a trunk.

Patrick Brady, a forger and small-time crook, was the chief police suspect in the case of Smith's murder. In September 1939 he was tried and acquitted, and he maintained his innocence to the end of his life.

Reginald Holmes, a key witness in the police case against Brady, was murdered on the morning of the Coroner's inquest into James Smith's death. Although two men were later charged, the identity of his murderer, and that of James Smith's, remain unknown to this day.

and said he was coming to see him on an urgent matter. When he arrived, Holmes gave him a brandy, and Brady, dirty, unkempt and distressed, said: 'I had a row with Smith and I have done him in.'

Holmes: 'What are you saying?'

Brady: 'I have killed the bastard. I put his body in a tin trunk and sank the trunk out at sea outside Port Hacking Heads. If you tell the police I've done this, I'll murder you too. And if I can't murder you, one of my mates will. I want you to remember this: if anything comes out about Smith, I know nothing about him. And I don't know you at all.'

Holmes, who had denied knowing Brady in an earlier interview, said he had done so because 'this was what Brady had told me to say; I was terrified about what might happen to me.'

At 1.10 am on 12 June, the day

the Coroner's inquest started, a police constable patrolling an area near Sydney Harbour Bridge noticed a car parked with its headlights on and the near-side front door open. The driver, slumped over the wheel, his hat on the back of his head, was Reginald Holmes. He had been shot in the chest from a distance of 300 mm (12 in) with a .32 calibre revolver.

Patrick Brady was charged with James Smith's murder. When he was committed for trial he stood in court and said 'Jim Smith is one of my best friends...If he is dead I didn't kill him.' At the end of the evidence in the Supreme Court trial, the judge directed the jury to acquit Brady, saying 'if the accused was convicted on the evidence we have heard, the conviction would not be allowed to stand.'

When he spoke to crime reporter Vince Kelly in 1962, Brady

argued that since he was acquitted of murdering Smith, and could never be charged with the murder again, even if he confessed, why should he lie now? 'The doctors tell me I haven't got much longer to live, so I want to tell you all I know about the case. But with my dying breath I repeat: I didn't do it.'

Two men were twice tried for the murder of Reginald Holmes. The first trial resulted in a hung jury; in the second, the jury acquitted both men. Patrick Brady died on 11 August 1965. Vince Kelly went to see his widow the next day and she told him: 'Pat was a weak man, but he wasn't a killer.'

The tiger shark remained sick and lethargic in the white Coogee Aquarium pool for three days after its digestive system revealed the gruesome mystery; then the Hobson brothers killed it. Its stomach contained nothing else of interest.

Death In New Jersey

In 1916, in the middle of World War I, an extraordinary series of shark attacks in the United States of America left three men and one boy dead, with a second boy badly injured, in the space of just 12 days. The sleepy towns on the New Jersey coast, just south of New York, were suddenly the focus of national interest, and the 'shark menace' even claimed the attention of President Wilson and his cabinet.

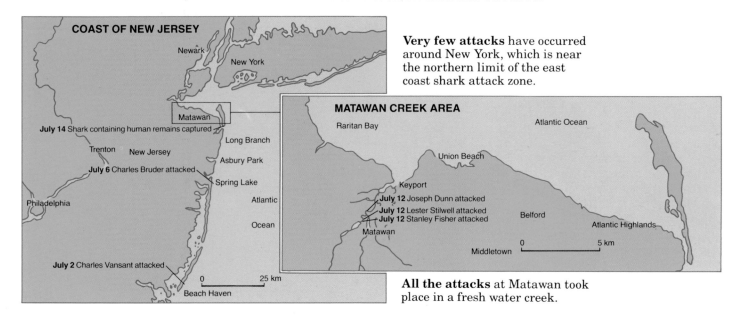

COAST OF NEW JERSEY

Newark
New York
Matawan
July 14 Shark containing human remains captured
Trenton   New Jersey
Long Branch
Asbury Park
July 6 Charles Bruder attacked
Spring Lake
Philadelphia
Atlantic
Ocean
July 2 Charles Vansant attacked
0   25 km
Beach Haven

Very few attacks have occurred around New York, which is near the northern limit of the east coast shark attack zone.

MATAWAN CREEK AREA

Raritan Bay
Atlantic Ocean
Union Beach
Keyport
July 12 Joseph Dunn attacked
July 12 Lester Stilwell attacked
July 12 Stanley Fisher attacked
Belford
Matawan
Atlantic Highlands
Middletown
0   5 km

All the attacks at Matawan took place in a fresh water creek.

The panic came slowly. On 1 July 1916 a 25-year-old Philadelphia fine arts graduate, Charles E. Vansant, was swimming 15 m (16 yds) from the shore at Beach Haven, New Jersey in the United States, when people on the beach saw a black fin slicing towards him and shouted at him to get out. Vansant splashed madly for the beach. As the shark closed on him, he screamed for help, then went under. An Olympic swimmer on the beach dashed into the water and pulled the badly mauled Vansant ashore. He died in hospital the following night.

The tragedy stirred no great unease along the Jersey shore, and still less in Manhattan, where the editors of the *New York Times* placed a two-paragraph report of the attack on page 18. It was one of the minor tragedies of summer, like a swimmer hit by lightning.

Five days later the level of anxiety on the Jersey shore made a

quantum leap upwards. On 6 July, Charles Bruder, a bellboy at a Spring Lake, New Jersey hotel, was attacked while swimming beyond the lifelines. A woman on shore cried that she saw a red canoe beneath the waves, but the 'canoe' was pumping from Bruder's severed legs. He died on the beach. Lifeguards and old Spring Lake residents told a *New York Times* reporter that this was the only shark attack death at the resort that they could remember. The *Times* editors placed the story, with details of women 'fainting' and 'panicking', on page one. Spring Lake hotel staff raised $1000 to send to Bruder's mother in Switzerland.

Although Bruder's death kept swimmers close to shore at Spring Lake the next day, even this elementary precaution extended no more than a few kilometres away. But the businessmen of the local resort towns, naturally assuming that

news of shark attacks would not help to attract summer holiday-makers, wanted reassuring official action – and Spring Lake Mayor, Oliver H. Brown, immediately established a motor boat patrol. The boats dragged bleeding quarters of lamb as bait while marksmen with rifles stood ready to shoot should a fin materialise. None did. The Mayor also ordered the beach bathing area enclosed in a sharkproof wire net, a precaution also taken by the nearby resort of Asbury Park.

Fishermen and surfers ridiculed these precautions, pointing out that no shark had ever been sighted off Asbury Park. Academic experts were also reassuring: Dr A. T. Nichols, the American Museum of Natural History's shark expert, said that there was 'very little chance' of a shark ever attacking anyone. The museum's director, Dr Frederick A. Lucas, said there was more chance of being struck by lightning than being attacked by a shark, and in any case, sharks' jaws were not powerful enough to bite through a human legbone. The captain of a trans-Atlantic liner said he was 'astounded' to learn of a man-eating shark off the New Jersey coast: this was the first time he had heard of one north of the Bahamas. A report in the *New York Times* of 11 July said 'Tiger sharks will hold but little terror for bathers in the waters hereabouts within the next few days' because of the netting at Asbury Park.

It was a classic piece of predictive journalism: within 24 hours sharks were part of every conversation on the Jersey shore.

July 12 brought tropical heat and humidity to Matawan, New Jersey, a small town 17 km (11 miles) west of the Atlantic shore, linked to the ocean by a meandering tidal creek. At 2 pm Lester Stilwell, a 12-year-old boy employed at the town's sawmill, was given the afternoon off because of the stifling heat. With four friends, he headed for the Wyckoff Dock, a dilapidated old steamboat pier on Matawan Creek which was the town's most popular swimming hole – throughout the summer naked boys would liberate themselves from heat and boredom by playing on the exposed dock pilings.

Shortly before Lester and his friends headed for the creek, Captain Thomas Cottrell, a retired sailor, was walking across a new Matawan Creek bridge about 750 m (833 yds) downstream from the swimming hole. He saw beneath the sparkling creek surface a huge black shadow moving quickly upstream with the incoming tide. Cottrell did not stop to tell himself that no shark could be that far upstream, he ran for a telephone and called the town's barber, John Mulsonn, who was also the chief of police. Then he ran to Main Street telling groups of boys headed for the creek,

It was near this spot on Matawan Creek that Captain Cottrell saw the shark. People in the town who scorned the idea that a shark would enter such a narrow waterway, and swim nearly 16 km (10 miles) from the sea, were tragically wrong on this occasion.

Searchers probe the muddy bottom of Matawan Creek in a vain attempt to find the body of 12-year-old Lester Stilwell. The boy's body eventually came to the surface three months later.

merchants and their customers: 'There's a shark in the creek!' People thought he was crazy: a shark? in a creek 10 m (11 yds) across at its widest? Clam diggers worked the shallows at low tide: poor old Tom's eyes must have been playing tricks on him. As Chief Mulsonn stropped his razor he reflected that people tell policemen some crazy stories.

Lester Stilwell, who suffered from 'fits', was a strong swimmer. He was floating further away from the pier than his friends when they saw him suddenly disappear, re-emerge, scream, then disappear in a flurry. His friends sprinted into Matawan shouting that Lester had had a fit in the creek and had disappeared in the water.

Stanley Fisher, a likeable, popular man of 24, who had just started a dry-cleaning business, was one of the many who heard the boys' shouts. Stanley, a 95-kg (210-lb)

blonde giant, had recently been mocked by his friends for accepting a $10 000 life insurance policy instead of cash in payment for a suit. He was nuts, they said. You? Life insurance? At 24? You must be joking. The good-natured Stanley just smiled quietly.

As Fisher ran for the creek, he passed a woman acquaintance, a Matawan teacher, who shouted: 'Remember what Captain Cottrell said. It may have been a shark.' Fisher barely paused. 'A shark here?' he said. 'I don't care – I'm going after that boy.'

Men, women and children were streaming from the town to the pier, among them Lester Stilwell's parents. As Fisher yanked on his bathing trunks and plunged into the creek about 200 people lined the banks while men in rowing boats poled for Stilwell's body.

The urgency of the action, the

need to do something – anything – in the face of tragedy must have driven Stanley Fisher, for in his rational mind he surely knew that if Lester was still beneath the creek he must have drowned, or worse. But the urgency of the moment was very powerful: several other men were also in the creek, making repeated dives, clawing along the mud for the boy's body. After several midstream dives, Fisher surfaced and shouted to the watchers on the bank: 'I've got it.' He had a grip on Lester's body and struck out for the nearer shore opposite the pier, followed by two men in a motorboat. He stood up in waist-deep water near the bank, then staggered, cried out, and dropped into a crouch. From the motorboat, Detective Arthur Van Buskirk saw Fisher with both hands clamped around his right leg – the outside of his thigh, from hip to knee, was missing. Van Buskirk

Townsfolk of Matawan gather on the banks of their creek to do battle with the shark. Dynamite, shotguns, handguns, harpoons and pitchforks were all used in the search for the killer.

pulled him into the boat. On the dock men improvised a stretcher from planks and carried him, still conscious, 250 m (273 yds) to the Matawan railroad. He was placed aboard the 5.06 train from Long Branch. At 7.45, as he was being wheeled into the operating theatre of the Monmouth Memorial Hospital, he died. The townspeople – frightened and angered by the monster which had killed a boy just on the verge of leaving childhood, and one of Matawan's most personable young men, in one unbelievable afternoon of horror – collected dynamite and set underwater charges by the pier. They had two hopes: the blasts might kill the shark and they might force Stilwell's body to the surface.

Just as the charges were ready for blasting, a motorboat roared upstream to the pier with another shark victim. Joseph Dunn, a

14-year-old from upper Manhattan, had been swimming with several other boys off a dock 800 m (867 yds) downstream from the Wyckoff pier when someone ran up with a warning: 'There's been two shark attacks upstream – get out of the water!' The boys struck out quickly for the dock. Joseph, the last out, was on the ladder when the shark seized his right leg. 'I felt my leg going down the shark's throat – I thought it would swallow me,' he said. At first Dunn would not give his name because he was afraid his mother would worry about him. Seriously injured, with much of the flesh below the knee stripped from his leg, he was rushed to St Peter's Hospital in New Brunswick.

While a surgeon cleaned and stitched Joseph's severed tendons and lacerated leg muscles, Matawan Creek boiled and spurted geysers as if a primal force had been let loose

---

CHARMED LIVES

Stanley Fisher was one of very few people to have been injured while going to the aid of a shark attack victim.

It is a remarkable fact that on many occasions people have ventured, unarmed into blood-filled water to rescue victims — often wrestling them from the jaws of attacking sharks — without being bitten themselves. The comments made by John Barrett who rescued a fatally injured man from the surf near Sydney in 1935 are typical: 'I didn't stop to think, but dashed straight into the surf. The water was stained deeply red, but my only aim was to reach that poor fellow … All the time I was acutely aware that the shark must still be with us and I'm not going to hide the fact that I had "the wind up", but I was determined to get him ashore.'

In 1922 two other young Australians, Frank Beaurepaire and Jack Chalmers also went to the aid of an attack victim near Sydney. The victim died, but the two rescuers received an award and £500 each. Beaurepaire used his prize money to start a business which eventually became a multi-million dollar industry, still thriving today.

between its tranquil banks. As indeed it had. In the grip of anger fuelled by fear, the men of Matawan purchased all the town's dynamite in a few hours. Before the sun set the town was also out of ammunition: hundreds of men lined the creek banks armed with handguns, rifles and shotguns. Those without guns brought pitchforks, knives, boathooks, antique harpoons ripped from living-room walls – even hammers. A small army of newspaper reporters and photographers descended on the creek, while newsreel cameramen filmed the vengeful fury and sometimes added to it – especially large charges pushed white geysers high above the creek for the benefit of the newsreels. Shark sightings, and sightings of shadows, were as common as the clams in the low-tide ooze, especially by lanternlight. With the incoming tide, sightings abounded; with the outgoing tide, escaping sharks abounded. A chicken-wire net was strung across the creek just above Wyckoff Dock, and a strong fishnet across the bridge where Captain Cottrell sighted the black shadow. But two days after the tragedy the orgy of vengeance had yielded nothing, and Lester Stilwell's body had still not been recovered.

While the men who sought relief in action shot and dynamited the creek, others who sought the relief of understanding tried to answer the questions: what sort of shark was it, and why these unprecedented attacks at this time?

Dr A. T. Nichols, at the American Museum of Natural History, believed a single shark was responsible for all the attacks. He thought it was a great white or tiger shark which had got out of the Gulf Stream, could no longer find the green turtles which were its staple diet, and had developed a taste for human flesh after the attack on Charles Vansant.

Some local fishermen blamed the Germans: World War I had reduced the number of passenger ships entering New York Harbour which tossed refuse overboard, so the sharks were naturally looking for an alternative source of food.

Although the *New York Times* loftily opined from the safety of its office on West 43rd Street in Manhattan that 'sharks have a much better right to kill us than we have

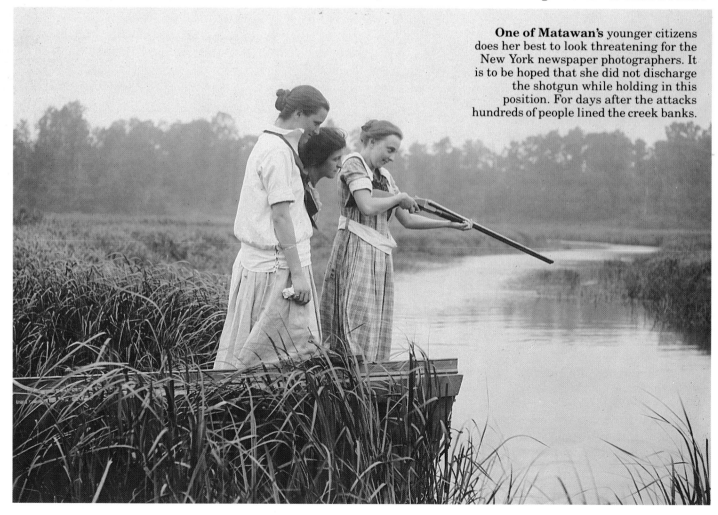

One of Matawan's younger citizens does her best to look threatening for the New York newspaper photographers. It is to be hoped that she did not discharge the shotgun while holding in this position. For days after the attacks hundreds of people lined the creek banks.

A charge of dynamite sends a huge geyser of water 7.5-m (25-ft) into the air over Matawan Creek. On the opposite bank newspaper photographers and a movie cameraman record the satisfying blast for a public agog for the latest news on the New Jersey horror.

to kill them', dozens of sharks were being hooked, shot and dynamited. On 14 April, funeral services for Lester Stilwell, whose body had not been recovered, and Stanley Fisher were conducted in Matawan. The same day, a Manhattan taxidermist, who had caught a 2.4-m (5-ft) shark off New Jersey, exhibited two bones found in its stomach – one of them identified by physicians as a boy's shinbone.

Joseph Dunn survived. Fifty-nine days after the attack, he left St Peter's Hospital. His leg would always bear the purple scars, but he was able to walk away.

Lester Stilwell's body was eventually found 100 m (110 yds) upstream from the Wyckoff Dock three months after the attack; it was marked by seven bites. On the same day, President Woodrow Wilson's cabinet met in Washington and devoted much of the agenda to the shark menace. The Treasury Secretary promised to instruct the Coast Guard to 'use every means for driving the sharks away or killing them', although he acknowledged that the Coast Guard 'really couldn't do too much about man-eating sharks anyway'.

The Director of the Museum of Natural History, Dr Lucas, offered newspaper reporters the insight that the reason for the attacks was that '1916 is a shark year, just as we have butterfly years and army-worm years.'

Three days after Lester Stilwell's body was found, the mayors of 10 New Jersey coastal resorts issued a statement protesting about news reports which 'cause the public to believe the New Jersey seacoast is infested with sharks, whereas there are no more than any other summer'.

The resort business, the mayors said, had been 'hurt without cause' by the news focus on sharks. Their towns lost an estimated $1 million in holiday cancellations.

QUEST FOR A CULPRIT

There was a lot of conjecture, both at the time and later, about which species of shark was responsible for the attacks at Matawan.

Experts at the Museum of Natural History in New York thought that either a great white or tiger shark was to blame. Indeed, a 2.6-m (8.5-ft) great white shark was caught in Raritan Bay, two days after the attacks at Matawan, with human flesh and bones in its stomach. Clearly it had eaten parts of at least one person, but whether it was Charles Vansant, Charles Bruder, Lester Stilwell or Stanley Fisher could not be determined.

When the wounds on Stanley Fisher's leg were examined and measured it was found that the distance between teeth on opposite sides of the shark's jaws was about 35.6 cm (14 in). Comparisons seemed to indicate that a shark with jaws that size was probably longer than the 2.7-m (9-ft) specimen that witnesses reported seeing in the creek.

The puzzle is that great white and tiger sharks rarely venture into fresh water. The one shark that is commonly found in fresh water, however, is the bull shark *Carcharhinus leucas*. Bull sharks have been found in the Mekong, Zambesi and Mississippi Rivers, as well as in Lake Nicaragua and as far as 4600 km (2600 miles) from the mouth of the Amazon.

NOT ALL SHARKS ARE KILLERS

Few people have a kind word to say about sharks – to most they are simply voracious and indiscriminate killers. Yet not all experienced divers share this view. Here Valerie Taylor, who has more experience with sharks than most divers, attempts to balance the popular image.

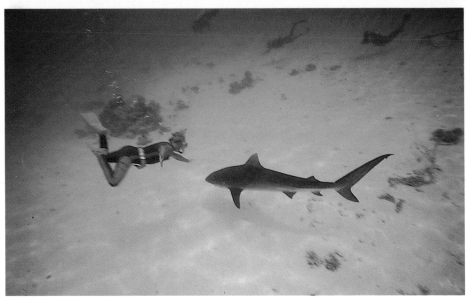

With graceful ease a large tiger shark *Galeocerdo cuvier* snaps a bait fish in half and swallows it in one gulp. This 3-m (10-ft) specimen carries the distinctive markings that gave the species its common name. Tiger sharks are most prominently marked when they are very young, after which the patterns gradually fade, becoming almost invisible when they are older. Tigers are oceanic sharks and are found worldwide in warm seas.

Cameraman Ron Taylor (far right) films a tiger shark during the making of the New Zealand feature film *The Silent One*. In the foreground his assistant shepherds the shark back towards the camera. Sessions like this had to be kept brief. The shark soon became tired and distressed and would need to rest before work could continue.

'Except for the tiger shark, I was alone in the lagoon. It was Sunday, my day off, and I was taking stills for my photographic library. I floated against the steel mesh fence that separated the lagoon from the open water. The shark had passed me twice in 30 minutes. Each time I had managed to take two photographs. It was going to be a long day, but the water was warm and some good tiger shark shots would be well worth the effort.

'I first met this particular tiger shark late in the afternoon of 10 October 1983. He was fat, 3.5 m [11.5 ft] long, and no doubt bewildered by what had happened to him. He had been caught some days before by a local diver, and the hook that had penetrated his cheek had been removed. The night of his capture he ate two large tuna, proving that he was in good condition and that his confinement in the lagoon had not spoilt his healthy appetite.

'In the past, Ron (my husband) and I had rarely worked with tiger sharks, mainly because they are not easy to find. Our modest experience suggested that they were calm, easy-going, and not threatening to divers, even when there was food in the water. They were also unafraid of humans, which to anyone not used to sharks can be very unnerving indeed.

'This shark was to appear in a major New Zealand feature film called *The Silent One* which told the story of a young deaf boy who had a giant turtle for a friend. We were working in a lagoon between two coral islands, and by using food, had attracted many marine animals into the area. The shark was needed to add an element of drama and excitement to the plot.

'Using tiger sharks in a feature film is not new: Hollywood is an old hand at it. However, Hollywood sharks always appear to be drugged and half dead, which in fact they usually are. We have never drugged or damaged any shark we wanted to work with, even though critics in the past have wrongly accused us of doing so. Sharks are intelligent creatures, and if coaxed with food quickly develop an understanding of what is expected of them – an understanding which lasts just as long as their hunger.

'Ron insisted that our shark should not be tampered with and the film's producer agreed. The actors and divers quickly became accustomed to working with the shark around, and eventually became quite fond of him. The shark endeavoured to ignore all human activities. Although the lagoon was large and full of natural marine life, he only thought of one thing – escape. A creature of the open water, he circled the lagoon constantly. That is how I knew I would see him every 15 minutes or so, simply by staying against the steel mesh. The beast knew freedom lay just beyond the slender wire and always passed it slowly, searching constantly for a way out.

'I had been in the water some 80 minutes, when I noticed a large sole trying to squeeze through the spaces in the wire mesh. It tried everything, curling up its sides,

The warm tropical and subtropical waters of the Pacific Ocean – with habitats ranging from coral reefs to deep water – are home to many dozens of species of sharks. Valerie Taylor's encounter with a tiger shark, described here, occurred while filming in a lagoon on the fringing reef near the island of Aitutaki, in the Cook Islands, about 2700 km (1680 miles) north-east of the North Island of New Zealand.

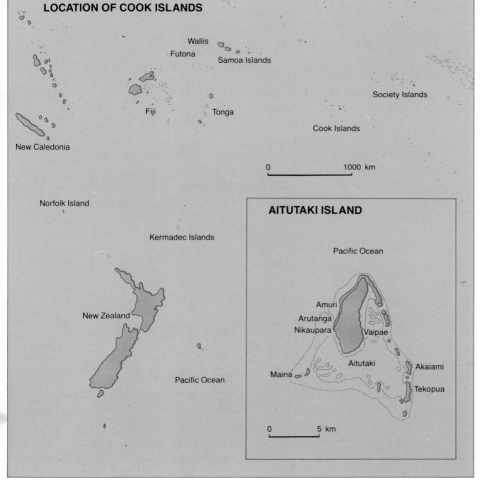

LOCATION OF COOK ISLANDS

Wallis
Futona
Samoa Islands
Society Islands
Fiji
Tonga
Cook Islands
New Caledonia
0   1000 km

Norfolk Island

Kermadec Islands

AITUTAKI ISLAND

Pacific Ocean

Amuri
Arutanga
Nikaupara
Vaipae
Aitutaki
Maina
Akaiami
Tekopua
0   5 km

New Zealand

Pacific Ocean

corner to corner, and finally every square all the way to the surface. Eventually it sunk to the sand and lay with its nose against the mesh. Feeling sorry for the fish, I swam down and began to scoop away sand from the base of the wire.

'Immediately it took a great interest in my efforts. Eventually I had an opening 80 mm [3 in] deep and about 500 mm [20 in] long. The sole immediately swam under and away. I returned to my post just as the tiger reappeared. He passed, black eyes missing nothing. I took my usual two shots. Suddenly, when he was about 5 m [16 ft] past me, the shark stopped, swung back fast and zoomed down to my excavation under the steel mesh. To my amazement, the great fish gently pushed his blunt snout into the gap, and bracing against the bottom, tried to lift the barrier. Three times he tried, each time exerting greater effort without the desired result, then, as though nothing unusual had taken place, the fish continued

patrolling the boundaries of his temporary prison.

'While working with our tiger shark we treated him gently at all times, but still he became distressed if forced to perform for too long before the camera, and would have to be given a rest. Eventually, when the filming had been completed, he was returned to the ocean unharmed by his experience as a film star. For Ron and I his behaviour confirmed what we have known for many years: that sharks, even the so-called dangerous ones, are far more intelligent than is generally believed. If handled in the right way, they will perform in a manner that shows that they have at least as much ability to comprehend a situation as many land animals do.

'My first experience with a tiger shark had taken place some years before, in a channel near Heron Island at the southern end of the Great Barrier Reef. I was snorkelling, gathering shells with

Ever watchful for a way out, the captive tiger shark cruises slowly around the perimeter of his temporary cage. The wound made by the hook used to catch him can still be seen at the corner of his mouth. The tail of a recent fish meal protrudes from one of the shark's gill slits.

two other divers in 5 m [16 ft] of water. It was a beautiful day, and we had been out for about an hour when I sensed something swimming very close to me. Thinking it was one of the other divers I looked around – straight into a large black eye. Little electric shocks seemed to shoot through my body, but even as I swung away I knew instinctively that the shark was not going to harm me. If it was going to bite, it would have done so before I saw it. The fish flowed gently past, huge, beige-coloured, silent. I looked around for the other divers and all three of us swam up over the coral into about 1 m [39 in] of water, and headed towards the island. There was no panic, although my heart was beating wildly. When

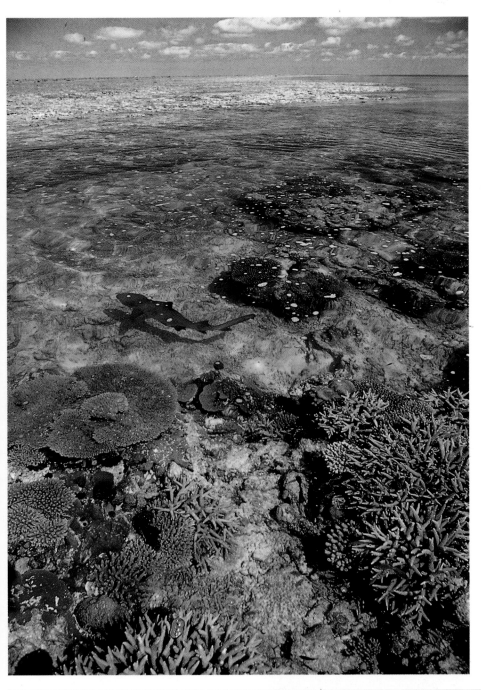

A small whitetip reef shark *Triaenodon obesus* searches for food in a tidal pool on the reef at Heron Island – part of Australia's Great Barrier Reef.

confronted by such a creature all defensive action seems useless.

'Back on the island I discovered that the shark was a female tiger, about 4.5 m [14.8 ft] long. She had often been seen by fishermen, and had even helped herself to a few hooked fish. She was probably simply passing by, sensed something unusual in her territory and had cruised over to investigate. This particular shark may have been caught two years later by a fisherman who frequently laid set lines in Shark Bay on the southern end of the island. Now all marine animals, including sharks, are protected around Heron Island, so perhaps one day another big tiger shark will move in to thrill visitors to the reef.

'When I first began diving, 30 years ago, fear of shark attack was my constant companion. The media with its lurid and often inaccurate accounts of shark attacks had conditioned me, along with everyone else, into believing that sharks were monstrous killers. 'The only good shark is a dead one', was the popular saying, and whenever I encountered a shark I always felt it was either it or me.

'Now I look back in wonder at

TIGER SHARK RECORDS

Record sizes for sharks are difficult to confirm. Estimates of lengths are almost always exaggerated, and the actual method of measuring of captured specimens may vary.

What is believed to be the largest tiger shark taken by a diver – a 4.0-m (13-ft) specimen – was killed by Wally Gibbons near Heron Island, Queensland, in 1963.

The record for a tiger shark taken on a rod and line stands at 4.23 m (13.9 ft), although unconfirmed reports have claimed rod and line records of 5.64 m (18.5 ft) near Port Jackson in NSW, and 6.23 m (20.75 ft) in the Gulf of Panama in 1922.

Two 6.4-m (21-ft) specimens have been captured in shark nets – one near Newcastle, NSW, in 1964, the other off Mackay in Queensland in 1980.

Diver Wally Gibbon *with a 3.4-m (11.2-ft) tiger shark he killed using a powerhead.*

my stupidity, but unlike today's divers, who can learn in 10 minutes from a book what probably took us 10 years of diving to discover, we had no one with experience to advise us. The Austrian diver Hans Hass was filming sharks in the Mediterranean – he did not even have flippers in those days – but we thought that he was crazy and would probably be eaten before too much longer. In Australia Ron Taylor was filming sharks in black and white for Movietone News theatrettes. The most popular footage always showed sharks being hunted, and the audience would cheer every time a shark was seen threshing its life away at the end of a barbless spear. Divers who hunted sharks were popular heroes, and when my turn came I eagerly joined their ranks.

'My attitude towards the sea and its inhabitants has now changed completely, particularly where sharks are concerned. What I once feared, I now respect. It always grieves me to see sharks caught and killed for sport or fun.

'My experience with whitetip reef sharks *Triaenodon obesus* confirms my belief that most sharks are not generally aggressive towards humans. If they attack there is usually a very good reason for them to do so.

'Whitetips are found throughout the Indo-Pacific region. They have little fear of man, and although not normally considered dangerous, are certainly large enough at 1.5 m [4.9 ft], and have sharp enough teeth, to inflict a nasty bite if they wished to. In the presence of food they can become uncontrollable.

'I know of only two attacks on humans by whitetips. On both occasions the victims were spearing fish. Neither attack was fatal, although one, a bite on the shoulder, required extensive surgery. I was told that the diver was holding a bleeding coral trout to his chest at

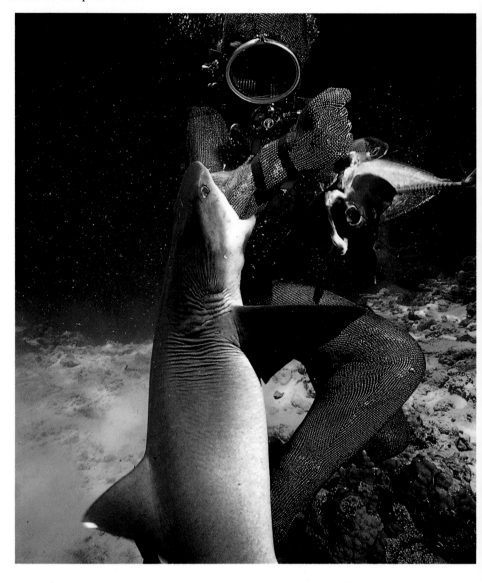

the time, so the reason for that attack seems quite obvious.

'My own experience with a whitetip attack occurred while Ron and I were carrying out tests on a chain mail suit [see p. 146] to see if it was effective against a shark attack. To coax the shark to bite I had to stuff fresh tuna pieces under the mesh, and then had to attract its attention by waving a whole fish in front of it. After one good bite, usually with a lot of shaking, each shark we experimented with was generally reluctant to try again. Instead it would nuzzle me, trying to find a gap in the mail.

'Far from being aggressive, the

whitetips, once fed, would hang around like friendly puppies, begging for more food. After a while they became a positive nuisance, eating all the bait we put out and swimming around in front of the camera lens.

'However, it was always easy to chase persistent whitetips away. A few smacks on the nose solved the problem. They are quick to recognise aggressive behaviour, and once they had learnt to associate humans with physical pain they would never come within arm's length again – a fact that potential shark attack victims might do well to remember.'

Hungry sharks can be induced to perform for the camera – like this whitetip about to grab a quick bite from a hand-held bait. Divers who hand feed small sharks can generally rely on their being able to distinguish between them and the food. Accidents usually occur when the shark confuses a potential meal – such as a struggling or bleeding fish – with the diver's body. However, only experience can tell a diver which sharks can safely be allowed within attacking distance.

These young divers are sharing the waters of a tropical lagoon with a large tiger shark – one of the three species that has been blamed for most attacks on people. A well-fed shark seems to pose little danger to humans, and would apparently prefer to avoid having anything to do with them.

THE SHARK AND THE LORD MAYOR

The strange story of Sir Brook Watson's encounter with a shark in Havana Harbour in 1749 owes its fame to a unique painting that he commissioned many years later from the American artist John Singleton Copley. Copley's painting is made even more remarkable by the fact that he had probably never even seen a live shark.

Brook Watson, the orphaned 14-year-old son of an English master mariner, was swimming in Havana Harbour, Cuba, in 1749 when a large shark bit off his right leg below the knee.

Watson's prospects, to say the least, were marginal. Not only were the Cuban surgeons obliged to work without anaesthetic – three burly 'assistants' held amputees down while the saw did its work in those days – but infections were regarded as a matter of course and survival was, by modern standards, little short of miraculous. Watson, however, survived not only the shark attack, but also the surgery. With his new wooden leg, he returned to Boston, Massachusetts, where a distant relative had been taking care of him – only to discover that the relative was bankrupt. The young Brook moved to Nova Scotia, Canada, and served as a commissary (concerned with supplying provisions) on the British side in the war between British Canadians and the French. He then helped evacuate British loyalists from the United States during the American War of Independence. Brook Watson's head was not filled with dreams of justice and republicanism. He believed in the established order, not in the ideas of visionaries and agitators.

He established himself as a merchant in London and became an able defender of the merchants' faith that progress for humanity lay in trade and commerce, and the laws and order which made commerce both possible and

---

DETAILS OF A DEADLY BITE

The shark in John Copley's painting most closely resembles a tiger shark, a species found in Havana Harbour. It seems unlikely that Copley ever saw a live shark, or even a complete dead specimen, but he may have had a set of shark's jaws to use as a model. The director of the New England Aquarium, John Prescott, has suggested that the finished work is a combination of features from various sharks, with two kinds of teeth and imaginary lips.

The lips on Copley's shark are interesting when compared to the mouth of a live attacking shark. When a shark, such as a tiger or a great white (bottom right), is about to attack it changes the whole shape of its head. The head and snout are lifted, and the upper jaw is pushed forward so that it protrudes from the mouth. Once the prey is securely impaled on the teeth of the lower jaw, the upper jaw closes and the shark swings its head and the front of its body violently from side to side, sawing the sharp upper teeth, which are often serrated, through the flesh until a large chunk has been gouged out.

Copley's curious shark in close-up.

A great white shark seizing a bait.

John Singleton Copley's dramatic reconstruction of the awful events in Havana Harbour in 1749 was in fact painted almost 30 years after it occurred. The work was exhibited at the Royal Academy in London in 1778 where it created a minor sensation and lively debate over its accuracy.

profitable. In 1779 he took a leading part in the formation of the Light Horse Volunteers who helped to suppress the riots fuelled by the fury of the dispossessed poor in London in 1780.

He was elected to the House of Commons for the seat of the City of London in April, 1784 and held the seat for nine years, becoming in the meantime a director of the Bank of England. He resigned the seat in 1793 to become commissary-general to the Duke of York's army in Flanders, and he served with the army until his return to England in 1795.

The wooden leg became Watson's symbol. In the Britain of the 1790s, the image of the bold adventurer, savaged in childhood on the exotic Caribbean island of Cuba by the tiger of the deep, was politically potent, and Watson exploited it to the full.

He was elected Lord Mayor of London in November 1796 – the culmination of a career with a fairy-tale quality to rival that of Dick Whittington. When visitors to the Lord Mayor's office had not heard the story of the most famous wooden leg in Britain, he delighted in mystifying them, saying baldly in response to questions that the leg 'was bit off'.

As part of his exploitation of the shark attack, Watson commissioned the American artist John Singleton Copley in 1778 to paint the incident. Copley, a self-taught Boston artist, moved to London in 1775 to escape the artistic provincialism of New England, and the trouble being stirred up by those notorious agitators George Washington and Thomas Jefferson. The American War of Independence broke out a year later, in 1776.

Copley's painting, which one critic said 'stands alone in its age', tells a vividly symbolic story. Its broad theme, the struggle between mankind and the wild, is as old as art itself. But Copley's painting had

Watson was made a baronet four months after this engraving of him was published in a London journal. He was 68 years old at the time. He lived only for a further four years and died at East Sheen, Surrey, on 2 October 1807. A contemporary obituary described him as: 'a diligent, zealous and faithful servant; a firm, upright and merciful magistrate; to his wife, a most affectionate and tender husband.'

Watson's remarkable coat of arms
was granted in 1803 at the time he was
made a baronet. He specially requested
'such Arms as may contain an allusion
to an awful event in his life, and be a
memorial of his gratitude to Heaven for
his signal preservation on that
occasion.' The letters patent granting
the Arms duly specified, among others,
these features: 'a human leg erect and
erased below the knee' and a gold-
crowned Neptune 'repelling a shark in
the act of seizing its prey proper'. The
Latin motto, *Scuto Divino*, could be
loosely translated as meaning 'Under
God's protection'.

broader themes: art critics saw in
the figure of Watson a neoclassical
allusion, man as eternal being, and
for some, the sailors reaching
towards Watson were like the
images of Christ's disciples with a
fishing net in a famous Raphael
tapestry entitled *The Miraculous
Draught of Fishes*.

The contrast between the
anguish and terror on the boat, the
furious energy of the thrusting
spear and the deadly movement of
the shark with open jaws, with
Watson's pale body floating
languidly in the face of primal
terror focuses attention on the 'man
versus beast' theme – and on
Watson as larger-than-life. When
the painting was exhibited it caused
an uproar. Nit-picking critics
questioned the accuracy of some
nautical details, and wondered
about the authenticity of the shark.
However, despite the fact that
Copley had never visited Havana,
his background details of the
harbour and town are historically
accurate. But the *St James
Chronicle* was not among the nit-
pickers. Copley's painting, the
Chronicle said in 1778, showed he
was 'a Genius who bids fair to rival
the Great Masters of the Ancient
Italian Schools.' He was elected to
full membership of London's

prestigious Royal Academy the
following year.

Outside the art world, not all
were lost in wonder at the portrayal
of a wealthy, powerful Tory
politician as a mythical figure of
heroic proportions. After the 1784
election, a satirical series in the
form of reviews of an imaginary
epic called *The Rolliad* were
published by reformist Whig
writers. One of them, John Wilkes,
was unkind enough to suggest that
had the shark torn off Watson's head
instead of his leg, a wooden head
would have done as well for him as
the wooden leg had.

The verse satirised both
Watson's famous accident and his
manner of speech:

'One moment's time may I
    presume to beg?'
Cries modest Watson, on his
    wooden leg;
That leg; in which such
    wond'rous art is shown,
It almost seems to serve him
    like his own;
Oh! had the monster, who for
    breakfast eat
That luckless limb, his noblest
    noddle met,
The best of workmen, nor the
    best of wood,
Had scarce supply'd him with a
    head so good.

POWERFUL SYMBOLS

Almost every conceivable object has been
used on a coat of arms at one time or another,
and both dogfishes and sharks have
occasional appearances.

The families of Jessie and Harrie both have
three dogfishes on their arms (left), and several
English and Irish families have adopted the
device of a shark's head swallowing a man
(right). A curious fastidiousness made the
creator of the arms show the unfortunate victim
as a negro – apparently to avoid offending
European sensibilities.

It is perhaps hardly surprising that sharks
have not been popular on national flags. One
notable exception, however, is the Solomon
Islands which became independent on 7 June
1978. On that occasion a new green and blue
flag was flown for the first time which featured
two frigate birds, a crocodile and a shark.

KEEPING SHARKS AT BAY

Is there any really effective protection from shark attack?
Jim Stewart, at the Scripps Institute of Oceanography, and
himself a shark attack victim, has a terse answer to this
question: 'Yes, the shade of an oak tree'. The only way to avoid
shark attack is to stay away from the water.

Swimmers and bathers are the most frequent victims of shark attack and a great deal of effort has been expended over the years in protecting beaches. One way to do this is simply to build a fence around the area. This has been done in South Africa, Australia, the Panama Canal zone and in other places around the world. While unsightly, these structures are effective if properly maintained. The reason they are not used more is that the initial costs are high, and so is the cost of maintenance and repair. The pounding that the fences receive from the ocean quickly damages them, and they must be constantly inspected for holes and gaps.

When Richard Nixon was President of the United States he had a house on the Atlantic Ocean near Miami, Florida. His private bathing beach was protected by a fence. One day the Secret Service was embarrassed to find sharks swimming inside the enclosure. It turned out that there was no plot against the president's life, it was simply that a hole had developed in the fence. After the hole was fixed and the sharks removed, navy frogmen were given the task of inspecting the barrier.

A system of protection used in

A large scalloped hammerhead, entangled in a meshing net off a Sydney beach. The numbers of sharks caught in these nets has declined in recent years.

Australia and South Africa simply involves catching as many sharks as possible in popular bathing areas, using a method called meshing. Meshing consists of setting nets at intervals along beaches. The nets are set in deep water parallel to the beach line. Sharks swimming either towards the beach, or away from it, usually at night, become entangled in the nets and die. By drastically lowering the number of sharks the chance of attack is greatly reduced, and this method has proved to be

Shark-proof enclosures, provided they are properly maintained, offer the best protection against attack. This enclosure is at a beach in Sydney Harbour where it is not exposed to the full force of ocean waves. Enclosures on ocean beaches are generally quickly damaged or destroyed by large seas.

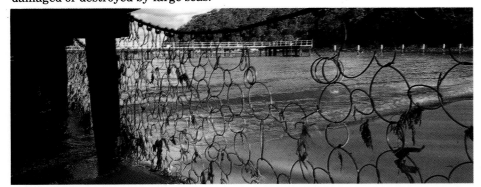

Shark fishing contests, which offer large prizes to successful anglers, have been effective in controlling shark numbers in some parts of the United States of America. However, some researchers fear that the large-scale slaughter of sharks will permanently affect populations of rarer species.

quite effective. The disadvantages of meshing are the relatively high cost involved, and the large number of harmless sharks, large fish, and even marine mammals that are killed unintentionally.

Along the coast of the United States bordering the Atlantic Ocean and Gulf of Mexico, shark fishing tournaments are becoming very popular, and this has proved to be an inexpensive method of reducing shark populations. Entrants pay a fee of between $25 and $100 for the chance to win total prizes of up to $50 000. The illegal, but inevitable, side bets can run into hundreds of thousands of dollars for the person who catches the largest shark.

Sharks have always been exploited for food in the Orient, and now their popularity is slowly spreading to other parts of the world. The number of sharks landed by fishermen in the United States has increased dramatically since 1980. Surprisingly this interest in sharks as food fish has not spread to Australia and New Zealand. The meat of the great white shark is exported from New Zealand to the United States where it is considered a delicacy rivalling swordfish.

Shark fins were being sold for about $(US)16 per kilo (2.2 lb) in 1985, and a bowl of shark fin soup in a restaurant could command up to $(US)20. Shark meat is lower in cholesterol than any other fish, and restaurant servings of great white and mako flesh brought $(US)3.50 per 100 g (3.5 oz). Apart from being

used for food, sharks also provide other products which are much in demand. A set of large shark jaws may fetch $(US)400. Leather made from shark skin is more durable than cow or pig hide, and boots, wallets and other items made from shark leather command high prices. Shark-eye corneas have been used for human transplants, and shark tissue to make artificial skin for burn victims.

Research on electrical shark barriers has been conducted in South Africa for more than 20 years. In this system current-carrying cable are located off beaches, outside the surf zone. Pulses of electric current are passed through the cables creating an electric field in the water. If the field is strong enough, sharks will not swim across the cables, and are repelled. This system has been successfully tested, but has not been put into use because of the high cost of operating and maintaining the equipment. Research is continuing, however.

Another system for repelling sharks that was widely publicised was the bubble-curtain. To produce a curtain or wall of bubbles a perforated length of hose was laid at the bottom of a tank and air was pumped through it. However, Dr Perry Gilbert and his colleagues tested the bubble curtain on 12 large tiger sharks at the Lerner Marine Laboratory in the Bahamas. They found that 11 of the sharks swam freely through the curtain of

bubbles; only one of the sharks was repelled by it. These results point up one very important feature of shark countermeasure tests. Tests must be done, not only on many shark species, but also on a large number of the same species to ensure that the results are accurate and consistent.

Experiments using sound to repel sharks have been conducted both in Australia and the United States. Very intense sounds were found to frighten sharks away

---

A SUCCESS STORY

Meshing was first introduced in Sydney in 1937. In the 18 years before that date there had been 14 attacks on Sydney's 20-odd ocean beaches, and 15 inside the harbour. Since 1937 there has not been a fatal attack on any ocean beach, although there have been some incidents. The number of attacks in the harbour has been reduced to seven.

The meshing is carried out by contractors who lay nylon gillnets 150 m (490 ft) long and 6 m (20 ft) deep, parallel to the beach and about 300 to 500 m (330 to 550 yards) offshore. Each net is suspended from floats and is anchored to the bottom by lead weights. Nets must be laid at each beach at least four times a month, and they must remain in place for a minimum of 24 hours (48 hours at weekends). It should be stressed that the net does not cover the entire length of the beach, nor does it stretch from the surface to the sea floor.

The success of the operation can be gauged by the number of sharks removed from the nets. Seven hundred and fifty-one were caught in 1940, and by 1948 this had declined to 260. In 1975/76 only 362 sharks were caught off Sydney, Newcastle and Wollongong (two nearby coastal cities) combined. In 1980/81 this figure had dropped to 163.

under some circumstances, but the results have not been consistent.

Many methods have been developed to protect divers from shark attack; some work very well, others are only marginally successful at best. First among these are the various anti-shark weapons. Spear guns alone are not very effective, but if the spear is tipped with a powerhead then this combination (sometimes called a bang stick) can be quite deadly. A powerhead is simply a single-barrelled gun of almost any calibre (.303 is popular in Australia) designed to fire when it comes in contact with the shark. One par-ticularly successful version uses a small explosive charge instead of a cartridge. While effective, these weapons require a good deal of skill on the part of the diver. A shot to the brain is usually necessary for a quick kill.

Gas injection darts were very popular a few years ago, and are still available in some diving supply shops. These weapons work by injecting carbon dioxide gas into the shark's body cavity through a large, hollow needle, causing various problems for the shark. Sharks are about five per cent heavier than the water they are swimming in, so a gas bubble inside their bodies makes them bouyant and forces them to the surface. Larger amounts of gas stiffen their bodies to the point where they cannot swim at all. The main difficulty with these devices is that the gas needle must penetrate the shark's body cavity, and this can only be done from the side or underneath the animal. Head-on shots are not effective. Of course, such weapons are of little value if the shark is not seen first, and in about half of the attacks on divers this was the case.

Several electrical shark repellers for divers have been developed. These are either carried by the diver, or the electrodes are

A diver embraces a large grey nurse he has just killed with the powerhead in his right hand. This type contains a shotgun cartridge which discharges when it is pressed against the shark's body. Other types use a .303 rifle bullet, and are fired at the shark from a rubber-powered spear gun.

incorporated into the diver's wet suit. Electrical repellers work, but have never been widely sold be-cause of the high cost of manu-facture and the limited market.

The June 1974 edition of *Skin Diver* magazine contained an article entitled *Revolutionary Weapon: Anti-Shark Wet Suit*. This turned out to be a black wet suit painted with white stripes. The idea for this unusual suit arose from the observations that pilot fish, which often swim with sharks, have vertical black and white stripes, and that some venomous sea snakes have black and white rings around their bodies. United States Navy scientists tested the suit with blue sharks and grey reef sharks, among others, and found it completely ineffective. Ron and Valerie Taylor, the famous Australian underwater

film makers, have also confirmed that the striped suit does not repel grey reef sharks (see p. 82).

Several attempts have been made to design shark-proof suits. The basic problem with such designs is that they must allow the diver ample mobility, while at the same time providing adequate protection. Since most attack victims suffer cuts that cause shock and bleeding, the main objective is to prevent the shark's razor sharp teeth from penetrating. Severe bruises and broken limbs are not life-threatening, and can be tolerated. This is the sort of compromise that must be made in order to keep the weight and flexibility within acceptable limits.

The United States Navy investigated a material named Kevlar which is widely used in bulletproof vests. Unfortunately, while the material may stop bullets, it did not stop sharks. Kevlar performed well against blue sharks, but failed when tested against the more powerful jaws of large lemon sharks *Negaprion brevirostris*. However, the material is now being used in suits worn by salvage divers to protect them from jagged metal edges and other sharp objects.

A very effective suit has been developed by Ron and Valerie Taylor, together with an American diver, Jeremiah Sullivan. It is simply a light-weight stainless steel mesh suit, similar to those worn by medieval warriors. The material employed has interlocking metal rings, and is widely used in the manufacture of butcher's gloves, aprons and arm protectors. Many tests have now been made in which the Taylors and Sullivan have deliberately allowed themselves to be bitten while wearing the suits. No injury, except for minor bruises and scratches, has been sustained (see p. 142).

The only shortcoming of these shark suits is their cost. A full suit may cost $(US)5200. While this is

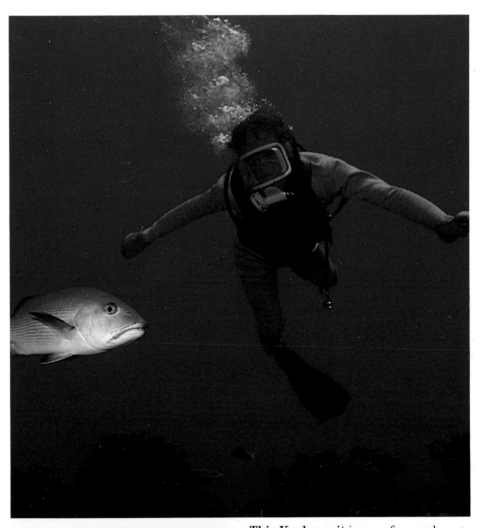

This Kevlar suit is one of several attempts that have been made to find a material that will protect divers against a shark attack. So far no material, other than steel mesh (see p. 142), has successfully repelled the sharp teeth and powerful jaws of a large shark. Even if a suitable material is found, divers will still have to accept the possibility of serious bruising or crushing injuries that a large shark will inflict when it bites.

A blue shark, its body distended, struggles against the effects of carbon dioxide gas injected into it from the dart in its side. Divers attempting to use such a device in self-defence will need to be certain of their aim, because the gas is only effective if it enters the body cavity of the animal.

A **United States Navy** researcher (left), wearing a life jacket, scoops water into a Shark Screen to test its effectiveness. Three inflatable collars which are blown up by the user keep the bag afloat, and these can be brightly coloured to make them obvious from the air. Beneath the water (above) all that can be seen is a dark, shapeless mass which has no attraction whatsoever for sharks. The plastic also prevents blood or urine from escaping into the surrounding water.

out of the reach of most sport divers, professionals and others who must swim with sharks would be well advised to buy one. The high cost stems from the method of manufacture. The mesh must still be made in the same way that it was in medieval times – each of the steel rings has to be linked together individually and welded by hand.

A problem that has received a good deal of attention, especially from the armed services, is that of protecting the survivors of air crashes and sinking ships from shark attack. Unfortunately, the problems of finding and rescuing castaways, and protecting them from attack, can conflict. In order to help make a person visible in the sea it is best if they are wearing highly visible clothing. But sharks are more likely to approach brightly coloured objects than darker ones. For many years the flight crews of various armed services wore, and

still wear, bright international orange – dubbed 'yum yum yellow' – flight suits. During the Vietnam War the United States military changed the colour of flight suits to dark green to make them harder to see on both land and sea. However, life rafts and life jackets continued to be orange or yellow. Bright colours that speed rescue are definitely preferred because the chances of shark attack are extremely small. In the past 20 years there has not been a shark attack reported on a United States serviceman on active duty, and there has only been one since World War II. This is in spite of the fact that there have been many hundreds of occasions when servicemen have had to parachute into the oceans of the world. In cases where the individual did not survive, but the body was recovered, none has shown evidence of shark bite. For this reason little research

on shark deterrents has been done in the United States recently.

During World War II, when large numbers of men and women were being forced into the water from sinking ships and other casualties of war, an urgent pro-gramme to find a chemical shark repellent was initiated. This hastily conducted research resulted in the development of the Shark Chaser, a solid 127-g (4.5-oz) packet of chemicals – copper acetate and a nigrocine dye – which was attached to the life jackets of servicemen. Tests conducted after the war proved Shark Chaser to be completely ineffective as a shark repellent. Its use was discontinued in 1976. Although useless, Shark Chaser probably provided peace of mind for many unfortunate individuals floating in the sea and fearing shark attack.

About 15 years ago the United States Navy developed and tested a

Orange is the most popular colour for flight suits because it is easy to spot from the air during a search. It is an unfortunate coincidence that this is also one of very few colours that have been shown to actually attract sharks.

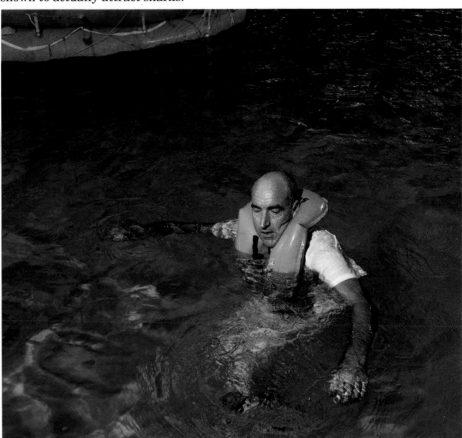

Urgent research into shark repellents during World War II lead to the development of the Shark Chaser – a packet containing copper acetate and nigrosine dye. Its major contribution was to give servicemen peace of mind.

device for protecting people floating in the sea. It is called the Shark Screen, and consists of a large plastic bag which is closed at the bottom and has inflatable collars at the top. When not in use it is folded into a small packet 76 x 114 x 178 mm (3 x 4.5 x 7 in), which weighs about 0.45 kg (1 lb). To use the device, it is unfolded and one or more of the three collars is inflated. The user then climbs into the bag and scoops water into it until the device is completely extended. Once inside, the Shark Screen user is completely hidden from view – all that can be seen from under the water is a large, dark, bulbous shape which sharks are reluctant to approach, even when fresh fish are attached to it. All blood and other potential chemical attractants are kept inside. Even electric fields that may encourage an attack are screened, since the device is made of an insulating material.

Sharks that penetrate the Moses sole's brilliant camouflage get a nasty surprise.

NATURAL PROTECTION

Break Through! 100 per cent Effective Shark Repellent was the title of an article in the September 1975 issue of *Oceans* magazine. Unfortunately, subsequent testing of the repellent has lowered the effectiveness considerably below 100 per cent. The article referred to the discovery by Dr Eugenie Clark that a small, flat fish called the Moses sole *Pardachirus marmoratus* secreted a milky fluid that discouraged sharks and other large fish from eating them. The problem with this substance, and with all the other 200 or so chemicals that have been tested so far, is that a considerable quantity is needed to make a practical repellent. Chemicals

simply disperse too rapidly in the ocean. To use the Moses sole poison as an effective repellent would require that nearly one kilogram (2 lb) of the substance be released continuously per hour. The reason it works for the Moses sole is that the fish releases the toxin directly into the shark's mouth, thereby producing very high concentrations of the chemical, while expending very little of it at any one time.

Despite the fact that initial results were discouraging, work on the Moses sole toxin was still continuing in 1985, when researchers at the Hebrew University in Jerusalem announced that the active constituent resembled household detergent.

THE SUIT OF STEEL

A suit that would give divers protection against shark attack is an attractive possibility. Several attempts have been made to develop one, but the problem is always to keep the garment light and flexible enough for practical use. Only the steel mesh suit has had any real success so far.

The idea for the shark suit came to diver and photographer Ron Taylor in 1967 while he was working with a Belgian scientific expedition on the Great Barrier Reef.

One of the expedition members had with him a pair of gloves made from steel mesh to protect his hands from cuts and scratches. These had originally been made for meat workers to wear while boning carcases – protection from the razor-sharp knives is essential. The first suit was made to Ron Taylor's

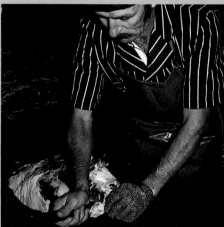

Meat workers wear metal mesh gloves to protect their hands. The material in the gloves closely resembles that used to make the chain mail suits once worn by medieval warriors.

design with the help of Jeremiah Sullivan, a marine biologist studying at Scripps Institution of Oceanography. The finished product weighed some 6 kg (13 lb) – about the same as a diver's weight belt – and was fastened at the wrists and ankles with straps. A hood covered the diver's head, except for the mask.

The dubious honour of being first to try out the new suit fell to Valerie Taylor during a trip to the Coral Sea in December 1978. Nervous at first about the ability of the suit to protect her, Valerie watched as large grey reef sharks circled around, snapping up fish baits as they were released. The sharks clearly knew she was there, but no attempt was made to attack.

The next day, with increasing confidence, Valerie started to handle the sharks – whitetips this time – and even attempted to force her arm into the mouth of one of them. Still they refused to bite, although one did nip her on the leg, but without causing any damage.

Experiments with the suit continued on and off for the next six months until, in June 1980, the prototype received its first real test. On this occasion the Taylors and Sullivan were diving off the

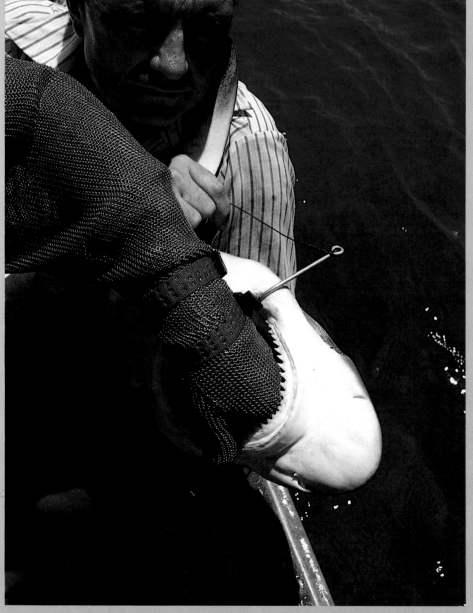

Ron Taylor uses the jaws of a live blue shark to test the suit. While the suit prevents the teeth from penetrating, it offers no protection from the formidable crushing power of a large shark's jaws.

Californian coast with blue sharks *Prionace glauca*, which have no fear in the presence of divers. Experiments showed that the sharks could be tempted to bite by holding a bait in front of the mesh-covered arm, and then withdrawing it at the last moment. Once committed to a charge the sharks seemed unable to change their minds at the last moment. Later Valerie recorded the results of the experiment in her diary: 'I still felt a bit nervous, and like Jeremiah, tended to push the sharks away. Some deep rooted instinct of self-preservation had me defending myself even when I wanted the attack to take place. A big blue shark caught me unawares and latched onto my arm with a sudden thump. I was, to say the least, startled. A natural reaction to seeing a neat set of razor sharp teeth grinding into one's body with mindless fury. The nictitating membrane flicked back for a second as the fish looked at me, an eye black as ebony, and with as much expression gazed into my two blue ones. As the shock wore off, I realized that there was no blood and that it wasn't really hurting. There was just the initial thump and a squeezed feeling. Being pulled back and forth by my elbow was uncomfortable, but while it looked agonising, it wasn't.'

After the initial experiments, the suit was tried on many other occasions, and with several different species of sharks – always with the same success. Plans were made to extend the tests to great whites – the most formidable and powerful of all sharks – but these were postponed. This was not so much because of fears about the power of the shark's bite – which the Taylors believe to be less damaging than is popularly assumed – but because a large great white is quite capable of carrying off both the diver and the suit in one piece.

A two-metre (6.6-ft) blue shark attempts to sink its teeth into Valerie Taylor's arm. Shortly after this photograph was taken another shark bit Valerie's unprotected leg, inflicting a wound that needed hospital treatment.

SHARK FOR SALE

The promise of riches has tempted many enterprising businessmen into investing in shark fisheries, but few have succeeded in making their fortunes from them. Apart from shark flesh, which is widely eaten, only fins and hides are now sold in commercial quantities.

The history of shark fisheries is one of boom and bust. Most species are slow to reproduce, and once stocks are reduced beyond a certain point they take a long time to build up again. In the 1930s and 40s soupfin sharks *Galeorhinus galeus*, then found in huge numbers off the coast of California, were in great demand for the oil their livers contained. In 1939, the fisheries' peak year, over 4 million kg (9 million lb) of sharks were landed. By 1944 the catch had fallen to only 270 000 kg (600 000 lb) as stocks were virtually wiped out. Today, over 30 years later, their numbers have still not recovered.

Sharks are eaten in many parts of the world, although in some countries the flesh has never been popular, except under a pseudonym. Distaste for the idea of eating them probably stems from the fact that sharks consume any unpleasant

rubbish thrown from ships. Sailors have always been reluctant to eat them. In 1771 Peter Orbeck, travelling between Europe and the East Indies, described attitudes aboard his ship: 'If a sailor dies in a place where dog-fishes haunt, and is thrown overboard, he is sure to be buried in the bellies of some of them. Large dog-fishes are never eaten, and small ones but seldom, and in cases of necessity only. They are cut into slices, which are squeezed in water till no oil remains in them; after being thus washed, the flesh is boiled or roasted: the part towards the tail is the best; the fore-part is seldom eaten.'

These days many consider the

TREASURES FROM THE SEA

Hides, oil and fins are the three most valuable products (apart from flesh) obtained from sharks. Today only fins (see p 146) and hides are still exploited on a commercial scale. The shark oil industry declined in the 1950s when vitamin A was first synthesised. Until then shark liver oil had been a major source of the vitamin, especially during World War II when cod liver oil supplies were interrupted.

Shark leather has always been in demand because it is particularly tough, although products made from it are usually expensive because the skins are difficult to obtain and to process. The curing and tanning stages are essentially the same for shark skins as for more conventional hides, but shark skins have the added problem of being covered by hard, abrasive denticles. These must be removed from the surface – in a process known as de-armouring – by soaking the skins in acid or lime.

One of the most successful shark leather manufacturers is the Ocean Leather Corporation of Newark, New Jersey in the United States of America. First established in 1921, the company was originally set up to exploit sharks for oil, hides, flesh and fertiliser. Soon, however, it ran into the same problem that confronts most shark-based enterprises – concentrated fishing rapidly reduces the shark population to a point where it is no longer economic to exploit them. Ocean Leather now concentrates on producing shark leather, and handles about 50 000 skins a year. The majority of the skins come from large sharks, such as tigers, caught in waters off the Pacific coast of Mexico and Costa Rica. Most of Ocean Leather's output is turned into shoes, handbags, wallets and belts.

Shark hides being inspected at Ocean Leather's Newark warehouse.

Shark products on display in a Sydney museum in the 1940s, at a time when sharks seemed to offer considerable scope for exploitation. Now only edible sharks are fished commercially in Australian waters.

Equipment for extracting oil from shark livers at an Australian plant in the 1930s.

Jewellery made from shark teeth can fetch high prices. The white tooth is that of a great white shark, and the brown one a fossil tooth from the extinct shark *Carcharodon megalodon*.

tastiest shark to be the mako *Isurus oxyrhinchus*, and the flesh has been compared to tuna by enthusiasts. In some countries it appears on menus as 'calf fish' or 'sea sturgeon'. The related porbeagle shark *Lamna nasus* and great white shark *Carcharodon carcharias* are also highly regarded.

The most widely eaten species – and probably the most abundant shark in the world – is the piked dogfish *Squalus acanthias*, which masquerades as 'rock salmon' in Britain and 'flake' in Australia. It is heavily fished in American, Canadian, New Zealand, Japanese and Korean waters, and an estimated 34 000 tonnes were caught in 1978.

Another shark that is caught in large numbers for food is tope (also known as the soupfin shark or school shark) *Galeorhinus galeus*. This was the shark that supported huge fisheries off the Californian

AN ANCIENT RECIPE FOR SUCCESS

Shark fins are used in a number of Chinese recipes, although it is shark fin soup which is best known to European gourmets. Various versions of this oriental delicacy are available in restaurants around the world.

All of the four main fins on a shark – pectoral, dorsal, anal and tail – are used for soup making, although it is the lower tail fin that is particularly highly prized. The fins are cut from a shark, trimmed to remove any flesh, and left in the sun to dry for about two weeks. Once dry, the parchment-like fins are ready for shipping, and it is in this form that they are usually sent to China for further processing.

The next stage in the preparation of the fins involves boiling them for several days until the fibres within – which look like uncooked noodles – can be removed. It is these gelatinous fibres that are dried and used in soup making.

There are many recipes for shark fin soup, and all involve soaking and cooking the dried fibres for several hours before adding chicken stock and a variety of other ingredients. Most commentators, however, seem to agree that the shark's fin itself has little or no flavour. Perhaps very few have tasted the 'real' soup, which is reputed to take several days to prepare at the hands of a master cook.

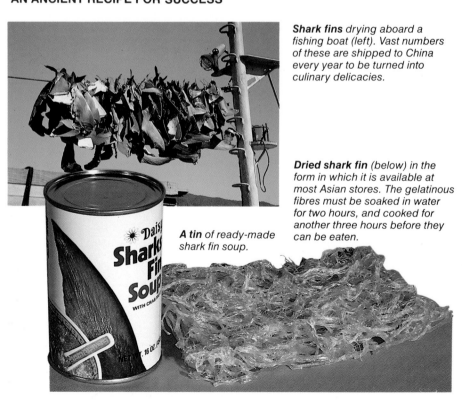

Shark fins drying aboard a fishing boat (left). Vast numbers of these are shipped to China every year to be turned into culinary delicacies.

Dried shark fin (below) in the form in which it is available at most Asian stores. The gelatinous fibres must be soaked in water for two hours, and cooked for another three hours before they can be eaten.

A tin of ready-made shark fin soup.

coast in the 1940s, and also a South African fishery at about the same time. Both industries declined because of over-exploitation. Tope (known locally as Australian school shark) has also been fished off the coast of Australia since the 1920s, although the industry has had a number of problems. When stocks declined in the 1940s a minimum size of 91 cm (36 in) was placed on any sharks caught. Then, in the 1970s, high mercury levels were found in some large specimens, so a maximum size of 104 cm (41 in) was laid down. Despite these restrictions the fishery continues, but catches are declining.

Although most sharks are edible, there are a few that are actually poisonous to eat. These include some tropical species, and the Greenland shark *Somniosus microcephalus*.

The toxin in the flesh of the Greenland shark has not yet been identified, but this has not prevented the Icelandic people from eating it, as they have done for hundreds of years. A shark is prepared for human consumption by burying it in a pit near the water's edge for several months while bacteria modify the flesh. After that it is cut into chunks and hung in a barn for about six months to cure. Thin slices of *Hàkall*, as it is called, are then ready to be eaten with a glass of aquavit to wash them down. The taste of ammonia is apparently so strong that some intrepid experimenters have compared it to eating smelling salts.

Shark fins also have the reputation of being an acquired taste. The subtle flavour they impart to dishes – particularly to the famous soup – often eludes uneducated palates. There is a constant demand for fins in China (see box p 146) which provide a useful source of additional income for the owners of commercial long-line fishing boats.

At one time oil was among the most important by-products of shark fisheries, but that industry has now almost completely disappeared. At various times shark oil has been used as a lubricant, in oil lamps, for curing leather, in soap making, as a tonic, as an ointment, as a base for paints and as an important source of Vitamin A. Oil extracted from the livers of spiny dogfish has been found to contain

PROBLEMS OF A PIONEERING INDUSTRY

There have been many attempts over the years to exploit sharks commercially, and almost all have ended in failure. The story of the rise and fall of Marine Industries Ltd, started in 1927 at Pindimar, 200 km (125 miles) north of Sydney, by Norman Caldwell and three companions, is typical.

The sharks were caught in nets which were left in the water overnight, and early hauls were spectacular. On the first day near

Pindimar – in a bay which locals considered to be free of sharks – 30 were caught, ranging in size from 45 to 225 kg (100 to 500 lbs). Shark products brought good prices (see below) and Caldwell reckoned that the hide, fins and oil from a 225-kg (500-lb) whaler shark brought in £3 7s 9d for a total outlay of only £1 (the average wage at the time was about £3 10s a week).

Soon, however, problems began to surface.

The catch in any area dropped rapidly after only one day's netting, and the company's small boat was forced to go furthur and further afield to find sharks in adequate numbers. A bigger boat was needed, but declining catches meant that there was not enough money to invest in badly needed improvements. It was soon impossible to continue operations and in 1932 the Pindimar factory was closed down, never to re-open.

Shark products fetched good prices – it was the decline in shark numbers that eventually forced the closure of Marine Industries, after six year's hard work.

Dorsal fin Dried fins were sold in China where they are treated and used as the basis for a highly regarded soup. Large fins take about two weeks to cure and lose about 40 per cent of their weight. Dried dorsal fins fetched up to 6s 11d per kg (3s per lb).

Flesh Dried shark flesh was ground into a meal, rich in protein, which made excellent cattle food. A tonne of dried flesh fetched £20.

Skin Tanned hides, with the denticles removed, were turned into shoes, bags and suitcases. Ordinary shark leather fetched £2 16s 6d per sq. m (5s 3d per sq. ft) and carpet shark leather £5 7s 8d per sq. m (10s per sq. ft).

Head Dried and and ground shark heads were used as fertiliser, and fetched £12 per tonne.

Liver Cut into lengths, the liver was rendered down in a steam-heated kettle. A 4-m (13-ft) tiger shark liver could yield as much as 82 litres (18 gallons) of oil rich in vitamins A and D. Shark oil had medicinal qualities, and was used for human consumption as well as for stock feed. What was left of the liver was dried and turned into meal, which was also fed to animals. The oil fetched 7d per litre (2s 9d a gallon).

Caudal fins The lower lobe of the tail fin is the most valued for soup making. They lose little weight while drying and fetched up to 11s 4d per kg (5s per lb).

Pectoral fins All fins are used for soup making. Pectoral fins fetched about the same price as dorsal fins.

Anal fin Anal fins gave the poorest yield of gelatinous fibres for soup making. They fetched only 3s 5d per kg (1s 6d per lb) when dried.

Zane Grey, author of western novels, including the bestselling *Riders of the Purple Sage,* with one of his Australian trophies in the 1930s. Grey fished for sharks all over the world, and wrote several books about his experiences.

ten times the amount of vitamin A present in cod liver oil, which was once the principal source.

Before World War II most of the vitamin A consumed in the United States and elsewhere in the world was imported from Europe. When war broke out and European fisheries were interrupted, there was a great demand for sharks from waters along the Pacific coast of the United States. In the seven years from 1937 to 1943 thousands of tonnes of sharks were caught, and by 1944 they had virtually been fished out. In 1950 chemists discovered a method of making vitamin A artificially, and the demand for shark liver oil disappeared virtually overnight.

However, one chemical present in shark liver oil – squalene – is still the subject of considerable interest. It is an unsaturated hydrocarbon which is found in large quantities in the livers of some sharks and, to a lesser extent, in the livers of most higher animals. Its function is unknown, but at one time it was suggested that it might be effective against malignant tumours, because sharks were thought to be free of them. Unfortunately, studies showed that sharks do have tumours, but the medicinal properties of squalene are still being investigated.

There are extraordinary quantities of oil in the livers of large sharks, particularly basking sharks *Cetorhinus maximus.* In 1945 author Gavin Maxwell set up a basking shark fishery in the Hebrides, the islands off the coast of northern Scotland, which lasted only about three years, but yielded a lot of information about these giant creatures. Maxwell estimated that an 8.8-m (29-ft) shark, weighing around 6.5 tonnes, contained a 940-kg (2072-lb) liver which might yield 2270 litres (500 gallons) of oil!

There has been a small, but steady demand for sharkskin for many hundreds of years. It was originally valued for its abrasive properties and was used for finishing timber – the denticles acting like grains on sandpaper – and for polishing marble. This product was called shagreen, and was simply pieces of dried skin. The Japanese are credited with being the first to use shagreen on sword handles, where it provided a good grip, even when covered with blood. It was also in Japan that the first sharkskin-covered objects were made in the seventeenth century.

The idea was quickly adopted in Europe – particularly in France – where spectacular use was made of shagreen for covering books, instrument cases and scabbards. Often the denticles were ground, polished and dyed, sometimes forming striking patterns. The best known craftsman in sharkskin was Jean-Claude Galluchat who worked in Paris in the 1760s and 70s, during the reign of Louis XV. The techniques used by Galluchat went out of favour in the nineteenth century, and examples of this type of work are now rare, and are often not recognised for what they are.

Although the use of sharkskin for high-quality work rapidly declined, it did lead to experiments with less exotic shark leathers. Some skins were used with their denticles intact, but in most cases the hides were too stiff. Techniques were developed for grinding away the denticles, but this was a delicate process, and not always satisfactory. It was not until about 1920 that the first successful chemical process was developed for removing denticles, while leaving the skin undamaged.

Shark leather is still manufactured today (see box p 144) and products made from it are

Australian entertainer Bob Dyer with a 567-kg (1250-lb) tiger shark, and his wife Dolly with a 178-kg (393-lb) mako at Watsons Bay, Sydney, in the 1950s. Both held world records for sharks during their fishing careers.

THE SHARK'S REVENGE

Considering the thousands of sharks that are caught each year it is surprising that more of their would-be captors are not injured by them. Only a few dozen cases have been recorded in which professional fishermen or amateur anglers have received serious wounds while handling sharks.

One shark, however, did manage to exact revenge on its tormentors in the most unusual circumstances. In July 1970 a fisherman aboard a 13-m (43-ft) powerboat off the Virginia coast hooked a small, 2.3-kg (5-lb) shark and dragged it aboard. Apparently bored or curious, the fisherman stuffed a small bomb (of the type used to train soldiers) down the shark's throat, set the fuse, and then threw the animal overboard again. As those aboard waited, anticipating the results of their little joke, the shark doubled back and, with immaculate timing, blew up exactly underneath the boat. The boat promptly sank — a large hole blown in its bottom planks — and the despondent owner eventually faced a bill of $5000 to pay for salvage and extensive repairs.

Big game fisherman Alf Dean (foreground) with five great white sharks caught off the South Australian coast. Some of Dean's records of the 1950s and 60s still stand today.

reputed to have twice the life of those made from conventional leather. Shark leather shoes are particularly hard-wearing, although the fact that the leather is extremely dense apparently prevents moisture from escaping through it, and this can be uncomfortable for the wearer.

A few other shark by-products are exploited commercially, although none is yet the basis of a major industry. A small trade has grown up around shark curios, such as mounted jaws and shark tooth jewellery – especially any made from the teeth of a large great white shark – which can command high prices. It appears, however, that there may be more potential in the medical use of shark products.

Various parts of sharks have been used in medicine by many cultures, and from the earliest times. Monsieur Pomet, the French

druggist, reported in 1730 that: 'The petrified teeth of this fish [*Canis Carcharias*] are what are called Glossopetrae, they are hung by the good woman about children's necks, in the imagination that they assist them in the time of cutting their teeth. They are also said to be a cordial, alexipharmick [antidote], and sudorifick [agent capable of causing sweating] taken inwardly, but I believe few have tried them.' In 1826 W. Ainslie wrote in his book *Materia Indica* that: 'The flesh of the Shark-Fish is supposed by the Hindoo medical writers to have peculiar virtues in several diseases; and is particularly noticed ... as a diet to be had recourse to in rheumatic affections.' Modern uses for shark products are less speculative. Shark corneas have been successfully transplanted into human eyes, and a synthetic skin for burn victims has been

manufactured using a chemical extracted from cartilage.

Sharks are among several species of gamefish, including marlin and tuna, that are sought all over the world. Their great size and fearsome reputation has made them attractive prizes for anglers.

The International Game Fishing Association recognises nine species of sharks – the blue, hammerhead, mako, porbeagle, school (tope), thresher, tiger, whaler and great white – which can bring anglers points in a competition. Strict rules govern fishing competitions and records are established by anglers for catching the heaviest shark on various standard weights of line.

Although big sharks, such as great whites and tigers, are the most spectacular sights at the weighing station, it is the mako (nicknamed 'blue dynamite') that is

Exciting moments during a game fishing contest off Port Stevens, on the east coast of Australia. A large great white shark, coaxed to the surface by blood and bait in the water, circles ominously before snatching a 2.1-m (7-ft), 80-kg (176-lb) dead whaler shark hanging from the stern of the boat (left). Seconds later it rises to the surface, its mouth gaping, showing the dead whaler inside (right). After 2½ hours the great white was hooked, but the hook pulled out after the shark had been played for 4½ hours on 37-kg (80-lb) line. Those on board estimated its weight at between 1800 and 2300 kg (4000 and 5000 lb).

most prized as a fighting fish. A mako will jump metres out of the water in an effort to dislodge the hook in its mouth, and can take many hours to conquer and capture. The great white has also been known to leap from the water when hooked, but most other species dive deep, and are gradually worn down by skill and persistence.

THE SHARKS WE EAT

Shark flesh is eaten all over the world, although it is not always identified as such because of public resistance to sharks as food. In the United States mako flesh is often sold as swordfish, which is a delicacy, and in Britain many spiny dogfish end up in fish and chip shops.

Apart from a public distaste for the idea of eating sharks, the only problem with marketing the flesh is that it can develop a taste and smell of ammonia if it is not handled properly. Sharks must be bled as soon as they are captured so that urea is removed from the flesh. This is usually done on board the fishing boat, and involves removing the head and belly flaps from the fish. After that has been done it is almost impossible for a layman to identify what remains as part of a shark.

Melbourne is the major outlet for sharks in Australia, although bins of school sharks (most of which are only about 40 cm [16 in] long), wobbegongs, angel sharks, and perhaps a few hammerheads and whalers are offered for sale at the Sydney fish markets most mornings. The majority of these end up in suburban fish shop windows, labelled as 'boneless fillets'.

A bin of small school sharks for sale at the Sydney fish markets.

Tab. VIII

Catulus major 1 großer hund fisch

Catulus 2 Canicula Aristot. Kleiner Meer hund

Canis Marinus 3

Canicula 4 Galeus canis ein art der kleinen Meer hund

Mustelus Spinax 5 Stachd hund

Mustelus Læuis 6 glatt Seelund

Galeus 7 Hund fisch

Galeus Asterias seu stellatus Sternhund

8

Galeus Stellaris
Galeus Glaucus Venetanus Gesn.

9

Part Three

3

Facts About Sharks and Shark Attack

All 344 known
species of sharks
are described in detail
on the following pages. This
section also includes a
comprehensive guide to
shark records, and maps
showing the locations
of all documented
attacks on humans.

SHARKS OF THE WORLD

On the following pages are detailed all 344 known species of sharks, with illustrations of some of the most interesting and remarkable of them. The way in which sharks are classified into orders, families, genera and species – and the features that help in identifying them – are explained below.

The bull shark, Van Rooyen's shark, the Zambezi shark, the river shark, the Nicaragua shark, shovelnose, the cub shark – these are all the same creature that is found and dreaded worldwide. Common names for sharks can vary from region to region. Abundant sharks or man-killers are dubbed with many names; rare kinds may not get any common name at all.

An international system of naming animals had become necessary by the beginning of the eighteenth century, since by then huge numbers of animals were known. The system of binominal nomenclature (two-name naming) devised by the Swedish naturalist Carl Linnaeus (1707-78) is still used today. Each animal has a generic or genus name (a noun, given a capital letter), followed by a specific or species name (an objective). The names usually come from Greek or Latin, are often in compound forms, and are written in italics. For example, *Ginglymostoma brevicaudatum* comes from the Greek for hinge-mouth, and the Latin for short-tailed. Sometimes names commemorate people or places. Scientific books and journals add the name of the person who first described and named the species, with the date, so the Port Jackson shark is given as *Heterodontus portusjacksoni* (Meyer, 1793).

The system goes further. The base units of the system are the species. (Broadly speaking, if two animals can produce fertile offspring, they are of the same species.) Related species are grouped in genera; genera in families; families in orders; orders in classes; classes in phyla; and phyla in the animal kingdom.

The animal kingdom consists of about 30 phyla, each grouping animals with a particular body plan. For instance, spiders and people are in different phyla, but sharks and people are in the same phylum because they both have backbones. The backboned animals (phylum Chordata) are divided into classes that include reptiles, birds, mammals and the three classes of fishes: jawless fishes, those with bony skeletons, and those with a rod of cartilage for a backbone (the class which includes sharks).

The class of cartilaginous fishes – Chondrichthyes – consists of sharks, rays, chimaeras and ratfishes. Sharks and rays have a unique sort of blood, and have upper jaws slung from their skulls, not fixed as with chimaeras and

HOW THE GUIDE TO SHARK SPECIES IS ORGANISED

The charts that start on page 156 list all known sharks by their most recent scientific names – others that may be found in modern books appear in the index (p 202). Space allows only the more widely used common names to be included, and again these are all indexed. Each shark's range is given with a series of numbers that relate to the map (right). It divides the world into regions which are for convenience only – they are not based on water temperatures or currents. Again, lack of space prevents the inclusion (where known) of a full description of the preferred habitat of each shark, such as rocky or sandy bottom. The first size given is the maximum known; the following two are the average for females (♀) and males (♂).

Frequent new finds and current research make any list of sharks obsolete shortly after publication. This list was assembled with considerable help from the two-volume *Sharks of the World* which was compiled by Dr Leonard J.V. Compagno for the United Nations Food and Agriculture Organisation and published in 1984. It gives considerably more information about each shark than it has been possible to include here, but much still remains to be discovered about many of the world's rarer species.

SHARK DISTRIBUTION AREAS

It is obviously difficult to be precise about the global distribution of animals that move freely in the oceans. The data given in the charts is approximate only, and indicates that particular species have been found in the region(s) indicated, but not necessarily that they never occur in those that are not marked. In some cases the known range of a species might be much more localised than is shown here, but it has been impossible to be more precise in the limited space available. The extent to which some species, such as the bull shark, venture into fresh water has not been mapped.

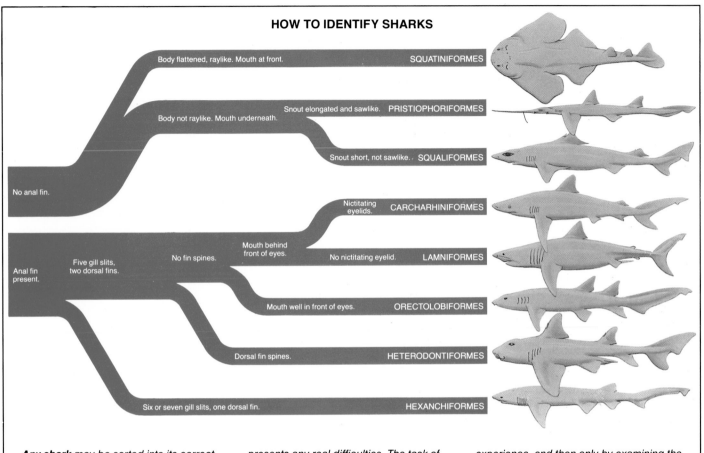

HOW TO IDENTIFY SHARKS

Body flattened, raylike. Mouth at front. — SQUATINIFORMES

Body not raylike. Mouth underneath. — Snout elongated and sawlike. PRISTIOPHORIFORMES

Snout short, not sawlike. SQUALIFORMES

No anal fin.

Anal fin present. — Five gill slits, two dorsal fins. — No fin spines. — Mouth behind front of eyes. — Nictitating eyelids. CARCHARHINIFORMES

No nictitating eyelid. LAMNIFORMES

Mouth well in front of eyes. ORECTOLOBIFORMES

Dorsal fin spines. HETERODONTIFORMES

Six or seven gill slits, one dorsal fin. HEXANCHIFORMES

Any shark may be sorted into its correct order using the simple chart above. Only the task of examining the eye to see if it has a nictitating membrane, in order to distinguish between carcharhinifomes and lamniformes, presents any real difficulties. The task of sorting a member of an order into its family, genus and species is more difficult, however. In many cases this can only be done accurately by an expert after many years of experience, and then only by examining the specimen in minute detail.
Illustrated regional guides to the more common shark species are available for some parts of the world.

---

ratfishes, so they are placed in a sub-class, Plagiostomi (the oblique-mouths). Sharks differ from rays because their pectoral fins are separate from the sides of their heads; they have free upper eyelids, and gill openings on their heads (in rays they are located below the pectoral fins), so sharks are put in a super-order, the Selachimorpha.

Thee Selachimorpha comprises eight orders of sharks. HEXANCHIFORMES (six-gilled shapes), are the frilled and cow sharks. SQUALIFORMES (the Latin word *squalus* originally encompassed all sharks), are the dogfish sharks that include the smallest shark – the spined pygmy shark – and the world's fifth-largest

fish – the Greenland shark. PRISTIOPHORIFORMES (saw-carriers) are the sawsharks, and SQUATINIFORMES (angel-fish shapes) are the angel sharks. HETERODONTIFORMES (different teeth, for their small front teeth and large back teeth) are the bullhead sharks. ORECTOLOBIFORMES (extended [tail]-lobes), the carpet sharks – which includes the whale shark and wobbegongs. LAMNIFORMES (from the Greek lamna, a fish of prey), are the mackerel sharks that include the goblin, megamouth, basking, great white and thresher sharks. CARCHARHINIFORMES (jagged rasp, because of teeth or skin, or both), the ground sharks, include the

requiem sharks and hammerheads.

As the species *Homo sapiens* (Linnaeus, 1758) increases in numbers, and exploits the oceans more and more for food, new species of sharks will be discovered. Other species will be added to the lists just by scientists reappraising the ones already known. Each species has, or once had, a holotype or type specimen, kept in alcohol, or formaldehyde, glycerine and seawater, in a museum or other institution. To reclassify a species, a zoologist may review the published description and draw different conclusions, or re-examine the type specimen. Scientists often disagree on links between species, or on species themselves.

Scientific name	Common names	Distribution*	Size (cm)*	Colour	Notes

HEXANCHIFORMES (Frilled and cow sharks)
Chlamydoselachidae (Frilled sharks)

Scientific name	Common names	Distribution*	Size (cm)*	Colour	Notes
Chlamydoselachus anguineus	Frilled shark, frilled-gilled s, frill s	1,3,4,7,9,10,12,14,15. Bottom, deep	196	Mouse-grey or dusky, paler below	Name means mantled shark + eel; a rare, primitive shark resembling a snake. It has six gill slits, the first nearly encircling the head and looking like a frilled collar.

Hexanchidae (Cow sharks, sixgill sharks, sevengill sharks)

Scientific name	Common names	Distribution*	Size (cm)*	Colour	Notes
Heptranchias perlo	Sharpnose seven-gill shark, perlon s, sevengill s	4,5,6,8,9,10,11,12,13,14,15. Bottom, mainly deep, sometimes shallow inshore	137	Mouse-grey, off-white below	Fierce when caught, but small size prevents it from being considered dangerous.
Hexanchus griseus	Bluntnose sixgill shark, cow s, grey s, mud s, bulldog s	1,2,3,4,5,6,7,8,9,10,12, 13,14,15,16. All levels, mainly deep	482	Mouse-grey, charcoal or russet	Taken for food, but its liver is toxic. Litters range from 20 to 108; size at birth about 65 cm (26 in). Has been found at depth of over 1800 m (5900 ft). IGFA game fish.
Hexanchus vitulus	Bigeye sixgill shark, lesser six-gill s, calf s	5,9,10,12,13. Warm temperate and tropical seas, generally bottom	180	Mouse-grey, off-white below	
Notorynchus cepedianus	Broadnose seven-gill shark, ground s, cow s, broad snout	1,3,4,9,10,12,14,15. Often close to and on surface. Temperate seas	290 ♀240 ♂188	Sandy-grey or russet with dark spots	Aggressive, fights when caught. In captivity has attacked people. Suspected of unprovoked attacks. Possibly prefers rays and other sharks as food.

SQUALIFORMES (Dogfish sharks)
Echinorhinidae (Bramble sharks)

Scientific name	Common names	Distribution*	Size (cm)*	Colour	Notes
Echinorhinus brucus	Bramble shark, spiny s, alligator dogfish, prickle s	4,6,7,8,9,10,11,12,14,15. Bottom, deep, occasionally shallow	310 ♀220 ♂162	Purple-grey or brown, often spotted black	Fat, sluggish, usually covered with evil smelling mucus. In South Africa its liver oil is highly prized for medicine. Is covered in thorny denticles.
Echinorhinus cookei	Prickly shark, Cooke's s, spiny s	1,2,3,12,15,16. Bottom, shallow and deep	400	Grey to brown, white under-side to snout	Has much smaller prickles than the bramble shark.

Squalidae (Dogfish sharks)

Scientific name	Common names	Distribution*	Size (cm)*	Colour	Notes
Aculeola nigra	Hooktooth dogfish	3. Bottom, deep	60 ♀56	Charcoal to black, fin tips white	The 60 rows of teeth in each jaw are slightly hooked.
Centrophorus acus	Needle dogfish	5,12. Deep	81	Light to dark grey	Like all members of the genus Centrophorus, has huge green eyes.
Centrophorus granulosus	Gulper shark, gulper	5,7,8,9,10. Bottom, deep	150	Sandy, paler below	Exploited in Japan for the oil in its large liver.
Centrophorus harrisoni	Dumb gulper shark	14. Deep	80	Colour not known	So far, known positively only from southeast mainland Australia.
Centrophorus lusitanicus	Lowfin gulper shark	7,9,10,12. Deep	160 ♀116 ♂100	Dusky, fin edges white or translucent	Name refers to its occurrence off Portugal, which was part of the Roman province of Lusitania.
Centrophorus moluccensis	Smallfin gulper shark, Endeavour dogfish	10,12,13,14,16. Bottom, deep	98 ♀93 ♂77	Grey, white below	Plentiful off Mozambique and South Africa.
Centrophorus niaukang	Taiwan gulper shark	12. Deep	154	Colour not known	Only known off Taiwan where its liver oil is used.
Centrophorus squamosus	Leafscale gulper shark, Nilson's deepsea dogfish	7,9,10,12,13,14,15. Deep, also pelagic	158 ♀147	Charcoal	Has overlapping denticles on small stalks covering its flanks.

Frilled shark
Chlamydoselachus anguineus
196 cm

Sharpnose sevengill shark
Heptranchias perlo
137 cm

Bramble shark
Echinorhinus brucus
310 cm

*For note on size, and distribution map, see box p154.

Scientific name	Common names	Distribution*	Size (cm)*	Colour	Notes
Centrophorus tessellatus	Mosaic gulper shark, tessellated deepwater s	12,16. Bottom, deep	89	Fawn, pale white bands at fin edges	Centro-phorus means spine-bearing. All in this genus have a strong spine on each dorsal fin.
Centrophorus uyato	Little gulper shark, southern dogfish	5,8,9,10. Bottom, deep	100 ♀82 ♂88	Light mouse-grey, paler below	
Centroscyllium fabricii	Black dogfish	6,7,9. Baffin Island and Greenland. Bottom, deep, sometimes surface	84 ♀64	Chocolate brown, white fin spines	Occurs off the west coast of Africa, also close to Arctic areas where it is commonly taken from near freezing waters.
Centroscyllium granulatum	Granular dogfish	Falkland Islands. Deep	28	Dusky to black	All members of this genus are luminescent.
Centroscyllium kamoharai	Bareskin dogfish	12. Deep	44 ♀43	Charcoal	The denticles are few and far apart.
Centroscyllium nigrum	Combtooth dogfish, Pacific black dogfish, black s	2,3,16. Bottom, deep	50 ♀50 ♂37	Stippled black, white tips to fins	All members of this genus have several rows of comb-like teeth.
Centroscyllium ornatum	Ornate dogfish	11. Bottom, deep	30	Black	Centro-scyllium means spiny small shark. They all have fine dorsal spines, the second much longer than the first.
Centroscyllium ritteri	Whitefin dogfish	12. Deep	43 ♀42	Mouse-grey, black below, white edged fins	
Centroscymnus coelolepis	Portuguese dogfish, Portuguese s	6,7,8,9,12. Bottom, deep	114 ♀92 ♂92	Chocolate brown	Used to be taken in large numbers off Portugal. Netted at 2640 m (8922 ft), deepest for any shark.
Centroscymnus crepidater	Longnose velvet dogfish, golden dogfish	3,7,9,10,11,14,15. Bottom, deep	90	Dusky black, golden or dark brown	
Centroscymnus cryptacanthus	Shortnose velvet dogfish	4,9. Bottom, deep	104 ♀103 ♂78	Dusky or charcoal	Crypt-acanthus means hidden spine. Dorsal fin spines are hidden within the fins.
Centroscymnus macracanthus	Largespine velvet dogfish	Straits of Magellan. Deep	68	Dusky	Only one specimen known, from Straits of Magellan, described 1906.
Centroscymnus owstoni	Roughskin dogfish, Owston's spiny dogfish	5,12,14,15. Bottom, deep	78	Dusky	Named after Alan Owston, an American and a collector of Japanese fish who lived in Yokohama.
Centroscymnus plunketi	Plunket shark, Lord Plunket's s	14,15. Bottom, deep	170 ♀150 ♂115	Chocolate brown	Named after a governor of New Zealand. Litters up to 36. Males and females of same size form separate, large schools.
Cirrhigaleus barbifer	Mandarin dogfish	12,13,14,15. Bottom, deep	122 ♀107 ♂86	Mouse-grey, pale below	Has mandarin-moustache-like barbels or flaps to nose, possibly trailed on sea-floor to detect prey.
Dalatias licha	Kitefin shark, Bonnaterre's deepwater s, seal s, black s	5,6,7,8,9,10,11,12,14,15,16. Tropical and warm temperate seas; deep	159 ♀138 ♂99	Chocolate, often black-spotted	Skin is used for an abrasive leather. Has fringed lips, very strong jaws, and smooth, thorn-like upper teeth, while lower teeth are serrated, wide, triangular. Sluggish but takes swifter prey such as bonito, perhaps by ambush. No one is sure why males more often have fuller stomachs than females.
Deania calcea	Birdbeak dogfish, shovelnosed s, Thompson's s	3,7,9,10,12,14,15. Bottom, deep	111 ♀90 ♂80	Pale mouse-grey	All members of this genus have teeth that develop differently in males and females.
Deania histricosa	Rough longnose dogfish	9,12. Bottom, deep	109 ♀107 ♂84	Dusky	So far known only off Madeira and Japan.
Deania profundorum	Arrowhead dogfish	6,9,100,13. Bottom, deep	76 ♀73 ♂55	Dusky	Little known. Has a long, pointed snout.

Leafscale gulper shark
Centrophorus squamosus
158 cm

Mandarin dogfish
Cirrhigaleus barbifer
122 cm

Arrowhead dogfish
Deania profundorum
76 cm

Scientific name	Common names	Distribution*	Size (cm)*	Colour	Notes
Deania quadrispinosum	Longsnout dogfish	9,10,14. Deep	114	Chocolate	Little known. In Australia, southeastern and southern mainland coast only.
Etmopterus baxteri	New Zealand lanternshark	15. Bottom, deep	75 ♀75 ♂66	Dusky with large black spots below	The skin of all lanternsharks secretes a luminous mucus.
Etmopterus brachyurus	Shorttail lanternshark	13. Bottom, deep	24	Brown, black fin stripes, black below	
Etmopterus bullisi	Lined lanternshark	5,6. Bottom, deep		Charcoal, yellowish spot on head	Little known. No length can be given because the largest measured specimen was immature.
Etmopterus decacuspidatus	Combtoothed lanternshark	13. Bottom, deep	29	Brown, black fin stripes, black below	Known from only one specimen described in 1966. Deca-cuspidatus = ten-pointed. Upper teeth have 8-10 cusplets each side.
Etmopterus gracilispinis	Broadbanded lanternshark	4,6,9. Bottom, deep, and at moderate depths over very deep water	33 ♀33 ♂25	Charcoal, broad black fin stripes	
Etmopterus granulosus	Southern lanternshark	3,4,9. Deep	40	Brown, black below, black fin streaks	Lengths of mature males and females not known; an immature male was 32 cm (13 in.).
Etmopterus hillianus	Caribbean lanternshark, blackbelly dogfish	5,6. Bottom, deep	50 ♀30 ♂26	Chocolate, yellow spot on head	
Etmopterus lucifer	Blackbelly lanternshark, Moller's deepsea dogfish	4,10,12,13,14,15. Bottom, deep	42 ♀34 ♂35	Dusky, paler fins, black fin stripes	Has survived in captivity in Japan.
Etmopterus polli	African lanternshark	9. Bottom, deep	24 ♀24 ♂23	Charcoal, dark bands above fins and tail	
Etmopterus princeps	Great lanternshark	6,7,9. Bottom, deep	75 ♀55	Dusky, black below	Has been found more than 2000 m (6500 ft) down.
Etmopterus pusillus	Smooth lanternshark	4,5,7,9,10,12. Bottom, deep, and surface to deep in oceanic waters	75 ♀42 ♂35	Black, yellow spot on head, pale fin edges	
Etmopterus schultzi	Fringefin lanternshark	5. Bottom, deep	30 ♀29 ♂27	Fawn with dark marks, dark below	All fins have wide fringes of horny 'hair'.
Etmopterus sentosus	Thorny lanternshark	10. Bottom, deep		Charcoal with black marks, darker below	Sentosus means thorny. This shark has two lines of large spiny denticles on flank. An immature specimen was 27 cm (11 in) long.
Etmopterus spinax	Velvet belly	7,8,9. Bottom, medium-deep and deep	60 ♀34 ♂34	Brown, black below with greenish line	Forms large schools; common.
Etmopterus unicolor	Brown lanternshark	12	53	Dusky	
Etmopterus villosus	Hawaiian lanternshark	16. Bottom, deep	46 +	Dusky with black marks, darker below	
Etmopterus virens	Green lanternshark, green dogfish	5. Deep	23 ♀23 ♂21	Chocolate, black-green sheen below	Catching large prey may be done in groups.
Euprotomicroides zantedeschia	Taillight shark	4,9. Oceanic waters off Uruguay and Cape Province, South Africa	42	Brown, black below, light fin edges	Among the smallest of all sharks. A gland below its tail secretes a luminous blue substance. Known only from two specimens (Uruguay, 1966, and South Africa, 1980).

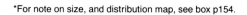

African lanternshark
Etmopterus polli
24 cm

Taillight shark
Euprotomicroides zantedeschia
42 cm

Pygmy shark
Euprotomicrus bispinatus
27 cm

*For note on size, and distribution map, see box p154.

Scientific name	Common names	Distribution*	Size (cm)*	Colour	Notes
Euprotomicrus bispinatus	Pygmy shark, slime shark	Surface to midwaters of Indian, Pacific and South Atlantic Oceans	27 ♀24 ♂19	Fawn to charcoal, clear fin edges	Found near surface at night, making big vertical journeys by day (up to 1500 m, 4900 ft, each way). Luminescent undersides.
Heteroscymnoides marleyi	Longnose pygmy shark	9,10. Probably oceanic	28	Pale brown, translucent edges to fins	Known only from two specimens (Natal, Africa, 1934 and near Ascension Island in the Atlantic, 1980).
Isistius brasiliensis	Cookiecutter shark, cigar s, luminous s, Brazilian s	4,5,9,12,14,16. Oceanic, surface to deep waters	50 ♀44 ♂35	Chocolate, green pupils to large eyes	Isistius from Isis, goddess of light, because it emits a vivid green light from its belly. The glow possibly attracts predators which then fall prey to this shark. It has very strong jaws and long teeth; can clamp itself to prey as big as itself by its lips; it bites, twists and gouges out a plug of flesh. Victims include dolphins and whales. Has been known to attack rubber casings to sonar domes of submarines. Swallows loose lower teeth, perhaps for calcium. Possibly makes vertical journeys of more than 2 or 3 km (well over 1 mile) up and down each day.
Isistius plutodus	Largetooth cookiecutter shark	5,12. Moderate and possibly deep waters	42	Chocolate, paler patch under head	Plutodus = plenty-toothed. Its huge lower jaw teeth are, for its size, the largest of any living shark. Can cut very deep plugs of flesh from victims. A plug of flesh in the stomach of one was the diameter of its mouth but twice as long.
Scymnodalatias sherwoodi	Sherwood dogfish	15. Possibly oceanic	80	Dark brown	Known from only one specimen washed up on a beach in the 1920s in Canterbury, New Zealand.
Scymnodon obscurus	Smallmouth velvet dogfish	4,5,7,9. All levels of oceanic waters	59 ♀59 ♂51	Black	
Scymnodon ringens	Knifetooth dogfish	7. Bottom, deep	110	Colour not known	Has enormous, knife-edged teeth in lower jaw.
Scymnodon squamulosus	Velvet dogfish	12. Deep	69 ♂49	Black	
Somniosus microcephalus	Greenland shark, gurry s, sleeper s	6,7,9, also Greenland, White Sea, Kerguelen I. Surface in cold waters	640 ♀373 ♂293	Greyish-brown	In Arctic and North Atlantic waters, large numbers gather to feed around fishing and sealing operations. When gorging they are apparently oblivious to blows from clubs and other weapons. Their size alone was probably the basis for stories of attacks on people in boats; is now believed harmless. Is taken almost without resistance – simply being lured to surface then lifted with gaffs. Easily fished through holes in ice. Inuit (Eskimos) traditionally used skin for boots, and formed small knives for cutting hair from lower teeth. Usually has one parasitic crustacean attached to each eye which may attract prey towards its host. This shark eats mammals, alive or dead; an entire reindeer minus antlers was found inside one. IGFA game fish.
Somniosus pacificus	Pacific sleeper shark, sleeper s, North Pacific s	1,2,12, also Siberian coast. Shallow in cold waters, elsewhere deep	700 ♀400	Slate	As name implies, sleeper sharks are sluggish yet they can catch swift-moving prey, including seals. Flesh is toxic unless dried or semi-putrid; symptoms of poisoning are like drunkenness.

Cookiecutter shark
Isistius brasiliensis
50 cm

Velvet dogfish
Scymnodon squamulosus
69 cm

Greenland shark
Somniosus microcephalus
640 cm

Scientific name	Common names	Distribution*	Size (cm)*	Colour	Notes
Somniosus rostratus	Little sleeper shark	7,8,12. Bottom, moderate and deep waters	140 ♀108 ♂71		Its comparatively small size shows that it is impossible to generalise about any genus.
Squaliolus laticaudus	Spined pygmy shark	4,7,9,10,12,13. Offshore and oceanic; tropical waters, deep	25 ♀21 ♂18	Mouse-grey, grey or black	Smallest of all sharks. Unique in having a spine on first dorsal fin only. Underside is luminescent. This eliminates any shadow when light comes from above, and predators are less likely to see it.
Squalus acanthias	Piked dogfish, spiny dogfish, skittledog, white-spotted dogfish, codshark, thorndog	Worldwide in temperate and subarctic waters. All levels	160 ♀97 ♂79	Slate, few white spots, paler below	Probably the most common shark. At the beginning of the century 27 million were taken off the coast of Massachusetts every year. Flesh is prized by Italians, eaten in Britain as 'rock salmon' and 'flake' in Australia. Its abundance and non-specialised anatomy mean it is often studied in laboratories, and probably more is known of this than any other species. Gestation period is 18 to 24 months, longer than elephants or whales. May live over 30 years; some scientists estimate nearly 100. Is hated by fishermen who fear teeth and mildly poisonous spines on dorsal fins, and dread the damage it does to nets and catches, but is an important food fish. Is also used for liver oil, pet food, fishmeal, hide, fertiliser. Will enter brackish water. Forms huge schools, sometimes segregated by sex and size. Migrates to stay in water between 7° and 15°C (45° to 59°F); one tagged off west United States coast was found 7 years later off Japan, 6500 km (4000 miles) away. IGFA game fish.
Squalus asper	Roughskin spurdog, roughskin spiny dogfish	5,10,16. Bottom, deep	118 ♀103 ♂87	Chocolate, paler below	Has litters of about 21, each 26 cm (10 in) long.
Squalus blainvillei	Longnose spurdog, Blainville's dogfish	7,8,9,12. Bottom, deep and shallow	95 ♀60 ♂50	Mouse-grey, white marks, white below	Common; often forms large schools.
Squalus cubensis	Cuban dogfish	4,5,6. Bottom, moderate and deep	110 ♀62 ♂62	Mouse-grey, paler below	Common; forms large schools. A large parasitic crustacean lives in its mouth.
Squalus japonicus	Japanese spurdog	12,13. Bottom, deep	91 ♀79	Mouse-grey, white edged dorsal fins	
Squalus megalops	Shortnose spurdog, Spiky Jack, piked dogfish	9,10,12,13,14. Moderate to deep waters	71 ♀62	Dusky to grey, paler below	Megal-ops = large eyes. Like *Squalus acanthias*, this shark has a two-year gestation period (longer than whales).
Squalus melanurus	Blacktailed spurdog	16. Deep	75	Brown, black edges to tail and fins	Specimens found only off New Caledonia. Lashes about when caught and has a dangerous spine on its second dorsal fin.
Squalus mitsukurii	Shortspine spurdog	3,4,5,6,10,11,12,13, 14,15,16. All levels	110 ♀72 ♂77	Dusky, white edges to fins	Common. Sometimes found off New Zealand in water only 4 m (12 ft) deep.
Squalus rancureli	Cyrano spurdog	16. Deep	77 ♀71	Brown	Named for its very long pointed snout. So far, specimens found off Vanuatu only.

Oxynotidae (Roughsharks)

Scientific name	Common names	Distribution*	Size (cm)*	Colour	Notes
Oxynotus bruniensis	Prickly dogfish, humantin	14,15. Bottom, medium and deep waters	72 ♀72 ♂60	Mouse-grey	All members of this single-genus family have large, sail-like, high dorsal fins above a stout body.

Spined pygmy shark
Squaliolus laticaudus
25 cm

Piked dogfish
Squalus acanthias
160 cm

Prickly dogfish
Oxynotus bruniensis
72 cm

*For note on size, and distribution map, see box p154.

Scientific name	Common names	Distribution*	Size (cm)*	Colour	Notes
Oxynotus caribbaeus	Caribbean roughshark	4. Bottom, deep	49	Brown to grey, with dark marks	All roughsharks have upper teeth that are larger towards the back, and lower teeth that point backwards.
Oxynotus centrina	Angular roughshark	7,8,9. Bottom, medium and deep waters	150	Mouse-grey, darker on head	Oxy-notus = sharp back.
Oxynotus paradoxus	Sailfin roughshark, sharp-back shark	7,9. Bottom, deep	118	Dusky, paler below	Roughsharks' large bodies and oily livers probably make them able to hover and coast at the bottom to seek food.

PRISTIOPHORIFORMES (Sawsharks)
Pristiophoridae (Sawsharks)

Scientific name	Common names	Distribution*	Size (cm)*	Colour	Notes
Pliotrema warreni	Sixgill sawshark	10. Bottom, medium to deep waters	136 ♀123 ♂97	Pale grey	Plio-trema = plentiful openings (gills). Sawsharks' 'teeth' on their snouts are enlarged denticles.
Pristiophorus cirratus	Longnose sawshark, common sawshark, little sawshark	14. Inshore, bays and estuaries, and offshore in medium to deep waters	137	Sandy or greyish, brown marks	Sawsharks differ from sawfish in having two barbels near the saw-like snout, and side gills. Much exploited for food.
Pristiophorus japonicus	Japanese sawshark	12. Bottom, offshore	136	Olive-brown	Sawsharks' long barbels probably detect prey disturbed by the snout.
Pristiophorus nudipinnis	Shortnose sawshark, southern sawshark	14. Bottom, medium to deep waters	122	Mouse-grey, paler below	The 'teeth' on the saws of this family are extremely sharp, but, unlike sawfishes, these sharks are inoffensive.
Pristiophorus schroederi	Bahamas sawshark, American sawshark	5,6. Bottom, deep, tropical waters	80	Pale mouse-grey, white below	Sawsharks bear live young. Until birth their saw teeth are folded back so as not to injure the mother.

SQUATINIFORMES (Angelsharks)
Squatinidae (Angelsharks, sand devils, monk sharks)

Scientific name	Common names	Distribution*	Size (cm)*	Colour	Notes
Squatina aculeata	Sawback angelshark, monkfish	8,9. Bottom, medium to deep waters	188	Sandy, with symmetrical white spots	Angelsharks resemble rays but, unlike rays, fins are not attached to the head. This species has large spines on snout.
Squatina africana	African angelshark	10. Bottom, surf zone and deep waters	108 ♀99 ♂78	Mouse-grey, white spots, white below	Like all angelsharks or sand devils, often buries itself in sand or mud, with only eyes and top of body showing.
Squatina argentina	Argentine angelshark	4. Bottom	170	Colour not known	All angelsharks can, if provoked, inflict severe cuts, having strong jaws and sharp teeth.
Squatina australis	Australian angelshark, monkfish	14. Bottom, shallow inshore to deep waters	152	Sandy, many white and grey spots	The large pectoral fins of angelsharks can be cut into steaks.
Squatina californica	Pacific angelshark	1,2,3. Bottom, inshore, shallow and medium to deep waters	152 ♂95	Speckled sandy/russet, white below	Angelsharks' camouflage colouring allows them to lie in ambush waiting for prey. Can bite swiftly with extremely sharp teeth, and people should be very wary of this shark.
Squatina dumeril	Sand devil, Atlantic angelshark	4,5,6. Bottom, shallow inshore to deep waters	152 ♂100	Russet to light grey, white below	Called sand devil because it can inflict severe cuts on fishermen who take it.
Squatina formosa	Taiwan angelshark	12. Bottom, deep		Colour not known	Formosa = pretty, but name refers to Taiwan, not this member of a weird-looking family. Known from only one immature specimen (1972).

Caribbean roughshark
Oxynotus caribbaeus
49 cm

Sixgill sawshark
Pliotrema warreni
136 cm

Australian angelshark
Squatina australis
152 cm

Scientific name	Common names	Distribution*	Size (cm)*	Colour	Notes
Squatina japonica	Japanese angel-shark	12. Bottom	200	Colour not known	In China, much exploited for food and for hide to make shagreen.
Squatina nebulosa	Clouded angel-shark	12. Bottom	163	Colour not known	This, like several angel sharks, has survived in captivity.
Squatina oculata	Smoothback angelshark, monkfish	8,9. Medium to deep waters	160	Sandy/grey, black and white spots	Has large spines on the snout and head but not on the back, hence the name 'smoothback'.
Squatina squatina	Angelshark, monkfish, angel-fish	7,8,9. Bottom, close inshore to moderately deep waters	183 ♀146	Sandy-grey/greenish, white below	Esteemed for food in Mediterranean countries (occasionally, under a sauce, masquerading as lobster). Occurs off Sweden and was named and described by Linnaeus in 1758.
Squatina tergocellata	Ornate angelshark	14. Bottom, medium to deep waters	55	Tawny, prominent rings, blue spots	Has fringed nostrils (present to a lesser degree in all angelsharks). Spines on snout and head, small spines on back.
Squatina tergocellatoides	Ocellated angel-shark	12	63	Prominent rings on fins only	Known from only one specimen taken near Taiwan in the early 1960s.

HETERODONTIFORMES (Bullhead sharks)
Heterodontidae (Bullhead sharks, horn sharks)

Scientific name	Common names	Distribution*	Size (cm)*	Colour	Notes
Heterodontus francisci	Horn shark, horned shark	1,2. Bottom, moderately deep to very shallow waters	122 ♀58 ♂64	Sandy/grey, dark spots, yellow below	Most horn or bullhead sharks lay eggs in spiral flanged egg cases by which they get wedged in crevices. Dorsal fin spines are made into jewellery.
Heterodontus galeatus	Crested bullhead shark, crested Port Jackson s	14. Bottom, inshore and moderately deep waters	152	Tan, dark band below eyes	Egg case has tendrils up to 2 m (6 ft) long that anchor it to seaweeds. Young 17 cm (6.7 in) at birth.
Heterodontus japonicus	Japanese bullhead shark, horned s	12. Bottom, shallow and moderately deep waters	120	Russet-brown, saddle-like areas on back	Several females lay their eggs in one 'nest'. Like other bullheads, uses its broad, paddle-like fins to crawl on bottom.
Heterodontus mexicanus	Mexican hornshark	2,3. Bottom, shallow	70	Bronze-tan, black dots, head stripe	All bullhead sharks grind shellfish between their flat teeth. Some thrive and even breed in captivity.
Heterodontus portusjacksoni	Port Jackson shark, oystercrusher, pigfish, bulldog s	14,15. Bottom, shallow and moderately deep waters	165 ♀112 ♂87	Fawn/greyish, dark bars on flanks	A great deal is known about this shark from tagging and observation. Common, nocturnal. Has 'rest' areas, sometimes used by as many as 16 at a time. Ranges considerable distances from breeding areas, as much as 850 km (530 miles). Females have been seen carrying their egg cases, probably to wedge them in rock crevices. Harmless, although can bite.
Heterodontus quoyi	Galapagos bullhead shark	3. Bottom, inshore and moderately deep waters	59	Fawn/dusky, regular large black spots	Hetero-dontus = different teeth. Both jaws have pointed front teeth for grasping, and flat back teeth for crushing.
Heterodontus ramalheira	Whitespotted bullhead shark, Mozambique bullhead	10,11. Bottom, deep	83	Dark russet, white spots, cream below	Bullhead sharks are the oldest unchanged sharks; fossils have been found in rocks 200 million years old.
Heterodontus zebra	Zebra bullhead shark	12,13,14. Bottom, moderately deep waters	122	Dusky/black, zebra-like stripes	Bullhead sharks have blunt heads with large knobs above each eye.

Angelshark
Squatina squatina
183 cm

Mexican hornshark
Heterodontus mexicanus
70 cm

Port Jackson shark
Heterodontus portusjacksoni
165 cm

Scientific name	Common names	Distribution*	Size (cm)*	Colour	Notes
ORECTOLOBIFORMES (Carpetsharks)					
Parascyllidae (Collared carpetsharks)					
Cirrhoscyllium expolitum	Barbelthroat carpetshark	13. Bottom, offshore, moderately deep tropical waters	33	Fawn, dark blotches across back	Known from only one specimen taken in the China Sea (1913).
Cirrhoscyllium formanosum	Taiwan saddled carpetshark	12. Bottom, moderately deep waters	39 ♀37 ♂37	Pale, six saddle-like patches	Members of this family can change colour slightly to blend into the sea bed shades.
Cirrhoscyllium japonicum	Saddle carpetshark	12	49	Fawn with nine darker saddles	Cirrho-scyllium means orange-coloured dogfish.
Parascyllium collare	Collared carpetshark	14. Bottom, moderately deep waters	87 ♀86 ♂82	Tawny, dark collar and saddles	Occurs only around Tasmania and the southeast of mainland Australia.
Parascyllium ferrugineum	Rusty carpetshark, rusty catshark	14. Bottom, moderately deep waters	75	Mouse-grey, dark bands and spots	From southern Australian waters only.
Parascyllium multimaculatum	Tasmanian carpetshark, T. catshark, T. spotted cat s	14. Bottom, inshore	75 ♂73	Ash, many dark spots, white below	Found near river mouths and rocks in Tasmanian waters only.
Parascyllium variolatum	Necklace carpetshark, varied catshark	14. Bottom, moderate to deep waters	91	Fawn, dark collar, many white spots	Little known. Sometimes caught in rock lobster pots.
Brachaeluridae (Blind sharks)					
Brachaelurus waddi	Blind shark, brown catshark	14. Bottom, inshore very shallow and moderately deep waters	122	Fawn/dusky, white spots, yellow below	Called 'blind shark' because it closes its thick eyelids when taken out of the water.
Heteroscyllium colcloughi	Bluegrey carpetshark, Colclough's shark	14. Bottom, inshore	60	Grey, white below	Known only off Queensland.
Orectolobidae (Wobbegongs)					
Eucrossorhinus dasypogon	Tasselled wobbegong	13,14. Bottom, coral reefs and inshore waters	117	Fawn with dark network	Name means well-fringed nose and shaggy beard. The fringe and beard are formed of flaps of skin. Has reputation as a man-killer in Papua New Guinea, unsubstantiated.
Orectolobus japonicus	Japanese wobbegong	12,13. Bottom, inshore waters	103	Light and dark spots and lines	Wobbegongs have powerful jaws and dagger-like front teeth and can be dangerous if provoked or stepped on.
Orectolobus maculatus	Spotted wobbegong	12,13,14. Bottom, very shallow and moderately deep waters	320 ♀165 ♂165	Brown with lighter bars and blotches	Often seen climbing, half out of water, from one rock pool to another. Its attractive skin is used for bags/ shoes. Wobbegongs possibly catch prey that has merely wandered near or even nibbled on their 'beards'. This shark is disliked by lobster fishers because it gets into pots to eat bait and lobsters.
Orectolobus ornatus	Ornate wobbegong, carpet s, banded wobbegong	12,13,14. Bottom, shallow inshore	288	Brown, light and dark marbling	The tough, patterned skin is used for leather.

Necklace carpetshark
Parascyllium variolatum
91 cm

Blind shark
Brachaelurus waddi
122 cm

Ornate wobbegong
Orectolobus ornatus
288 cm

*For note on size, and distribution map, see box p154.

Scientific name	Common names	Distribution*	Size (cm)*	Colour	Notes
Orectolobus wardi	Northern wobbegong	14. Bottom, inshore, tropical	45 +	Ochre, black fin dots, 3 spots on back	Wobbegongs do well in captivity.
Sutorectus tentaculatus	Cobbler wobbegong, cobbler carpet s	14. Bottom, inshore	200-300	Brown, dark saddles and spots	Suto-rectus = seamed muscle, possibly named for the rows of 'stitching' in form of rows of warty lumps down back.

Hemiscylliidae (Bamboosharks, long-tailed carpetsharks)

Scientific name	Common names	Distribution*	Size (cm)*	Colour	Notes
Chiloscyllium arabicum	Arabian carpet-shark	11. Bottom, inshore and offshore, shallow to moderately deep waters	70	Fawn	Chilo-scyllium = lipped dogfish. Members of this genus have flabby lower lips. So far only found in the Persian Gulf.
Chiloscyllium caerulopunctatum	Bluespotted bambooshark, bluespotted catshark	10	67 +	Dusky, pale blue spots	Rare, little known. Until seen recently in fish hauls in Madagascar, known only from one specimen (1914).
Chiloscyllium griseum	Grey bamboo-shark	11,12,13. Bottom, inshore	74	Fawn, dark/ light bands on juveniles	Sluggish and unafraid; can be caught by hand.
Chiloscyllium indicum	Slender bamboo-shark	11,13,16. Bottom, inshore	65	Fawn, with dark dots and smudges	Spanish and French names include 'elegant' – appropriate for its svelte body and markings.
Chiloscyllium plagiosum	Whitespotted bambooshark	11,12,13. Bottom, inshore	95	Chocolate, dark bands, white spots	Like several of the family, this shark does very well in captivity.
Chiloscyllium punctatum	Brownbanded bambooshark, brown-spotted cat s	11,12,13,14. Bottom, inshore	104	Fawn/russet, dark spots on juveniles	Can live up to half a day out of water. Common on reefs and in ports.
Hemiscyllium freycineti	Indonesian speckled carpetshark, Freycinet's s	13. Bottom, shallow	46	Cream to tan, rusty spots, cream below	The family all have sturdy paired fins that help them to clamber on reefs.
Hemiscyllium hallstromi	Papuan epaulette shark	13. Bottom, inshore	75 +	Tan, large and small dark spots	Little known.
Hemiscyllium ocellatum	Epaulette shark	13,14. Bottom, shallow tropical waters	107	Brown, dark spots, white-edged fins	Abundant on Great Barrier Reef. Harmless (like all this family). Will happily search for food at a reef-walker's feet.
Hemiscyllium strahani	Hooded carpet-shark	13. Bottom, inshore	75	Black 'hood' on head, white spots	Little known.
Hemiscyllium trispeculare	Speckled carpet-shark, speckled catshark	14. Shallow tropical waters	64	Tan, brown spots, bands on tail	Common on coral reefs.

Stegostomatidae (Zebra sharks)

Scientific name	Common names	Distribution*	Size (cm)*	Colour	Notes
Stegostoma fasciatum	Zebra shark, monkey-mouthed s, leopard s	10,11,12,13,14,16. Bottom, shallow, tropical	354 ♀201	Tawny, with dense dark spots	Has prominent ridges on body. Tail is half the total length. Docile. An attractive and popular aquarium species. Lays eggs in horny cases with tufts of 'hair' to anchor them.

Brownbanded bambooshark
Chiloscyllium punctatum
104 cm

Zebra shark
Stegostoma fasciatum
354 cm

Nurse shark
Ginglymostoma cirratum
304 cm

*For note on size, and distribution map, see box p154.

Scientific name	Common names	Distribution*	Size (cm)*	Colour	Notes
Ginglymostomatidae (Nurse sharks)					
Ginglymostoma brevicaudatum	Short-tail nurse shark, nurse s	10. Bottom, inshore	75	Dark brown, paler below	Ginglymo-stoma – hinged mouth. All the family suck prey into their large mouth cavities, and all have remarkably strong skin that makes excellent leather.
Ginglymostoma cirratum	Nurse shark	2,3,4,5,6,9. Bottom, shallow inshore	304 ♀247 ♂241	Mustard/grey, often with dark spots	Large, clumsy, sluggish; generally inoffensive but will bite fast if provoked, and jaws clamped on victims have had to be pried aprart. Is not to be confused with the grey nurse shark of Australia (see sand tiger shark, this page). Nocturnal. Sometimes rests during day in groups of as many as 36, even piled on each other. A popular and hardy aquarium species; some have been kept for 25 years. Is taken for food, and for its skin, and in Brazil fishermen use its earstones (otoliths) as a diuretic.
Nebrius ferrugineus	Tawny nurse shark, Madame X, spitting s, giant sleepy s	10,11,13,14,16. Bottom, inshore, very shallow to moderately deep tropical waters	320 ♀260 ♂250	Tawny	Sucks prey into its mouth, and can reverse this action to spit when caught. Grunts between spittings. Nocturnal; rests in piles in crevices and caves. Thrives in captivity; will bite if provoked.
Rhiniodontidae (Whale sharks)					
Rhiniodon typus	Whale shark	2,3,4,5,6,9,10,11,12,13,14,16. Tropical and warm temperate waters, oceanic and inshore	1265 ♀800 ♂900	Charcoal, yellow spots, white below	The largest shark and the largest fish in the world (larger than small whales). Rhini-odon means file tooth; it has over 300 bands of minute teeth. Is a filter feeder, eating tiny plankton/small fishes, but will also take garbage: the stomach of one revealed a boot, a tin bucket, a wallet and part of an oar. Sometimes groups in hundreds. So inoffensive that people have walked on their backs.

LAMNIFORMES (Mackerel sharks)
Odontaspididae (Sandtiger sharks)

Scientific name	Common names	Distribution*	Size (cm)*	Colour	Notes
Eugomphodus taurus	Sandtiger shark, grey nurse s, sand s, ragged-tooth s, spotted ragged-tooth s	4,5,6,8,9,10,12,13,14. All water levels, surf zone and reefs	318 ♀260 ♂238	Mouse-grey, yellow spots, white below	Has a bad reputation as man-eater in Australia but this may be due to confusion with other sharks as it is inoffensive unless provoked. Popular aquarium species because it looks fierce. Inside the mother, several embryos develop at different stages; the largest, with well developed teeth, eats eggs and smaller embryos; one embryo per uterus survives, to be born about 100 cm (39 in) long. Can swallow air and hold it in stomach for neutral buoyancy. Groups sometimes herd schools of prey. IGFA game fish.
Eugomphodus tricuspidatus	Indian sandtiger	11. Inshore and offshore waters	370 +	Mouse-grey, paler below	This fish is possibly the sandtiger shark described above. The type specimen taken in 1878 was lost.
Odontaspis ferox	Smalltooth sand-tiger, shovel-nose nose shark	1,2,7,8,9,10,12,14,15,16. Bottom, moderate to deep waters	360 ♂275	Charcoal, russet spots, paler below	Despite the name *ferox*, this shark has never been accused of attacking people.
Odontaspis noronhai	Bigeye sandtiger	4,9. Deep	360	Dark brown	Until recently known only from one specimen (1955). Has been taken from between 600 and 1000 m (2000 and 3300 ft) down.
Mitsukurinidae (Goblin sharks)					
Mitsukurina owstoni	Goblin shark, elfins	4,7,9,10,12,14. Bottom, deep offshore, and shallow inshore waters	335 ♂293	Pink-white	Until found off Japan in 1898, believed extinct for 100 million years. Has weird snout overhanging protruding jaws.

Whale shark
Rhiniodon typus
1370 cm

Sandtiger shark
Eugomphodus taurus
318 cm

Goblin shark
Mitsukurina owstoni
335 cm

Scientific name	Common names	Distribution*	Size (cm)*	Colour	Notes
Pseudocarchariidae (Crocodile sharks)					
Pseudocarcharias kamoharai	Crocodile shark	2,9,10,12,13,16. Oceanic, pelagic; sometimes bottom inshore	110 ♀96 ♂92	Grey, paler below, white fin edges	Is a cannibal inside the mother like the sandtiger shark but, mysteriously, two embryos per uterus survive. Can bite very hard when captured. Oily liver gives neutral buoyancy.
Megachasmidae (Megamouth sharks)					
Megachasma pelagios	Megamouth shark	16. Deep, oceanic waters	446	Dusky brown to black	Known only from two specimens. Finding a new giant species that was also a new genus and new family was the most exciting shark discovery this century (off Hawaii, 1976). It has an enormous luminous mouth with 100+ rows of teeth. Lives midwater.
Alopiidae (Thresher sharks)					
Alopias pelagicus	Pelagic thresher, smalltooth thresher	2,10,11,12,13,14,16. Oceanic, sometimes inshore, surface to moderate depths	330 ♀297 ♂276	Grey, white below	All thresher sharks have tails nearly as long as the rest of the body, and they are cannibals within the uterus. All IGFA fishes.
Alopias superciliosus	Bigeye thresher	2,4,5,6,7,8,9,10,11,12,14,15,16. Inshore, and surface to deep offshore waters	461 ♀392 ♂335	Charcoal/purple, large green eyes	Threshers hunt cooperatively, encircling schools of prey and shepherding them with their long tails, used to stun and kill.
Alopias vulpinus	Thresher shark, whiptail s, fox s, thintail thresher	Worldwide in temperate to tropical seas, pelagic, surface to deep waters	549 ♀462 ♂359	Sooty grey, offwhite below	Sometimes leaps out of water. Threshers have been seen to use their tails to 'down' birds skimming the surface.
Cetorhinidae (Basking sharks)					
Cetorhinus maximus	Basking shark, bone s, elephant s, sailfish s	1,2,3,4,6,7,8,9,12,13,14,15. Surface, inshore and offshore	1230 ♀890 ♂650	Deep blue to charcoal, pale below	The second largest shark; can weigh about 4 tonnes. A filter-feeder, it may filter more than 2000 tonnes of water an hour. Often seen basking with dorsal fin above water, even upside down. Pairs or threes swimming nose-to-tail were probably basis for sea monster legends. Gestation may be 3 years 6 months. Is inoffensive unless provoked. One liver can yield 750 litres (165 gallons) of oil, the record being twice as much; the oil once used in tanning and in lamps is now taken for squalene.
Lamnidae (Mackerel sharks, porbeagles, white sharks)					
Carcharodon carcharias	Great white shark, uptail, Tommy, death shark, maneater, blue pointer, white pointer, white death	All tropical, sub-tropical and warm temperate seas, in surf and shallow bays	800 ♂345	Slaty brown or charcoal, white below	The most feared and fearsome of all sharks. Attacks boats, sometimes persisting until boat sinks. Can swim in bursts of high speed. Sometimes leaps out of water, has been known to leap into a boat. Serrated, razor-sharp teeth and powerful jaws allow it to eat almost any animal, including turtles, seals. Will eat carrion like dead baleen whales, garbage. Jaws and teeth fetch high prices as curios. IGFA game fish.
Isurus oxyrinchus	Shortfin mako, bonito s, blue pointer	All tropical and warm temperate seas, surface to moderately deep	394 ♀337 ♂240	Metallic blue, snow white below	The fastest shark and one of the fastest of fishes. Possibly the most prized game fish; puts up furious resistance. Leaps spectacularly, even into boats. Few reliable reports of attacks on humans but when stimulated can be savage and attack swiftly with huge grasping teeth. Considered dangerous. Like other family members, a cannibal within mother. Excellent eating. Jaws and teeth are made into ornaments.

Crocodile shark
Pseudocarcharias kamoharai
110 cm

Megamouth shark
Megachasma pelagios
446 cm

Pelagic thresher shark
Alopias pelagicus
330 cm

*For note on size, and distribution map, see box p154.

Scientific name	Common names	Distribution*	Size (cm)*	Colour	Notes
Isurus paucus	Longfin mako	6,9,10,16. Deep, oceanic, tropical and warm temperate seas	417 ♀331	Blue-black, white below	Mako is a Maori word. Not recorded as having attacked people or boats but its large teeth make it dangerous. Makos can maintain body temperature higher than surrounding water.
Lamna ditropis	Salmon shark, Pacific porbeagle	1,2,12 and Bering Sea, surface to moderate depths, inshore and oceanic	305 ♂210	Dusky, pale below with dark marks	Di-tropis = two-keeled. All mackerel sharks have broad keeled tails but the two Lamna sharks have small extra keel. Salmon are a favoured food of this one.
Lamna nasus	Porbeagle, mackerel shark	3,4,6,7,8,9,10,14,15, also subantarctic waters and Barents Sea, all levels	300 ♀185 ♂240	Slaty blue/ charcoal, white below	Often found in colder water than suits other sharks. A strong swimmer, swift and voracious. Like makos, can keep its body temperature several degrees higher than water around. IGFA game fish.

CARCHARHINIFORMES (Ground sharks)
Scyliorhinidae (Catsharks)

Scientific name	Common names	Distribution*	Size (cm)*	Colour	Notes
Apristurus atlanticus	Atlantic ghost catshark	9. Bottom, deep	25	Brown, dark edges to fins and gills	The catshark genus is one of the largest among sharks.
Apristurus brunneus	Brown catshark	1,2. Bottom, deep	68 ♀46 ♂53	Chocolate brown, pale fin edges	Little is known of any of the catsharks.
Apristurus canutus	Hoary catshark	5. Bottom, deep	45 ♀43 ♂43	Charcoal, darker edges to fins	All catsharks have strikingly flabby bodies and thin skins.
Apristurus herklotsi	Longfin catshark	13. Bottom, deep	31 +	Brown	Known from only one specimen (Philippines, 1934).
Apristurus indicus	Smallbelly catshark	10,11. Bottom, deep	34 +	Mouse-grey	
Apristurus investigatoris	Broadnose catshark	11. Bottom, deep	26 +	Brown	
Apristurus japonicus	Japanese catshark	12. Bottom, deep	71 ♂68	Dusky	Abundant.
Apristurus kampae	Longnose catshark	1,2. Bottom, deep	52	Dusky/black, white fin edges	Like several of the catsharks, found in very deep water (1900 m – 6200 ft down).
Apristurus laurussoni	Iceland catshark	5,6,7,9. Bottom, deep	68 ♀67 ♂68	Dusky to black	None of this family have any colour pattern.
Apristurus longicephalus	Longhead catshark	12. Bottom, deep	37 +	Charcoal	Has a very long snout. Known from only one specimen (1975).
Apristurus macrorhynchus	Flathead catshark	12. Bottom, deep	66	Dun, paler below and pale fins	Most members of this family lay eggs in sturdy egg-cases anchored with tendrils.
Apristurus maderensis	Madeira catshark	9. Bottom, deep	68		Several new members of this genus have been discovered in the last 15 years. It may turn out to be largest shark genus.
Apristurus manis	Ghost catshark	6,7. Bottom, deep	85	Ash	Odd in profile: body very thick in the middle tapering to a narrow snout.
Apristurus microps	Smalleye catshark	9. Bottom, deep	54 +	Dusky or purplish black	Has a fuzzy texture to its skin, like several members of this genus.

Basking shark
Cetorhinus maximus
1500 cm

Great white shark
Carcharodon carcharias
800 cm

Porbeagle shark
Lamna nasus
300 cm

167

Scientific name	Common names	Distribution*	Size (cm)*	Colour	Notes
Apristurus nasutus	Largenose catshark	3. Bottom, deep	59 ♂55	Brown to charcoal	
Apristurus parvipinnis	Smallfin catshark	4,5. Bottom, deep	52	Black	Common in Gulf of Mexico.
Apristurus platyrhynchus	Spatulasnout catshark	12. Deep	80	Dark brown	
Apristurus profundorum	Deepwater catshark	6. Deep	51 +	Dusky or black	Has been found 1600 m (5250 ft) down. Since it was named, others in this genus have been found living in deeper waters.
Apristurus riveri	Broadgill catshark	5. Bottom, deep	46 ♀40 ♂44	Chocolate brown	Males have much larger teeth, jaws and mouths than the females, possibly so the female can be grasped during mating.
Apristurus saldanha	Saldanha catshark	9. Deep	81	Blue-grey	
Apristurus sibogae	Pale catshark	13. Deep	21 +	Reddish white	Known from only one specimen (Makassar Straits, 1913).
Apristurus sinensis	South China catshark	13. Bottom, deep	50 +	Dark brown	Known from only one immature specimen (South China Sea, 1981).
Apristurus spongiceps	Spongehead catshark	13,16. Bottom, deep	50	Dark brown	Unique in having pleats and grooves around gills and throat. Known from only two specimens.
Apristurus stenseni	Panama ghost catshark	2. Deep	23 +	Charcoal	Has an enormous mouth.
Apristurus verweyi	Borneo catshark	13. Deep	30 +	Chocolate	Known from only one specimen (1934).
Asymbolus analis	Australian spotted catshark	14. Bottom, inshore, and at moderate depths offshore	61 ♀57 ♂55	Fawn, russet spots, pale below	Lives in temperate waters off southern Australia.
Asymbolus vincenti	Gulf catshark	14. Bottom, moderate to deep waters	61 ♀49 ♂51	Dusky, dense white spots, white below	Found in southern waters of Australia.
Atelomycterus macleayi	Australian marbled catshark	14. Bottom, shallow	60 ♀51 ♂48	Fawn with grey saddles, black spots	Sometimes found in water merely 0.5 m (20 in) deep.
Atelomycterus marmoratus	Coral catshark	11,12,13. Shallow	70 ♀53 ♂54	Fawn, dark streaks and white spots	Lives in crevices in coral reefs. Does well in captivity.
Aulohalaelurus labiosus	Blackspotted catshark	14. Shallow	67 ♀67 ♂58	Fawn, grey saddles, black dots	Found off Western Australia only.
Cephaloscyllium fasciatum	Reticulated swellshark	13,14. Bottom, deep	42 +	Dun, dark brown saddle, dark spots	When disturbed, swellsharks can inflate their stomachs with water or air to become almost spherical.
Cephaloscyllium isabellum	Draughtsboard shark, Isabel's swellshark	12,15. Bottom, moderate depths	100 + ♀86 ♂69	Fawn, dark saddles with dark blotches	Colouring in the New Zealand form is more distinctly chessboard-like than in Taiwanese and Japanese forms.
Cephaloscyllium laticeps	Australian swell-shark, draught-board s	14. Bottom, shallow inshore to moderately deep waters	97 +	Grey-russet, dark patches, pale below	Called 'Sleepy Joe' because it, like all swellsharks, is sluggish.

Smallfin catshark
Apristurus parvipinnis
52 cm

Spongehead catshark
Apristurus spongiceps
50 cm

Australian spotted catshark
Asymbolus analis
61 cm

*For note on size, and distribution map, see box p154.

Scientific name	Common names	Distribution*	Size (cm)*	Colour	Notes
Cephaloscyllium nascione	Whitefinned swellshark	14. Bottom, moderately deep waters	100 ♂80 +	Fawn, dark saddles, fins white-edged	All swellsharks except the Indian have jaws jointed so teeth are visible when viewed from below.
Cephaloscyllium silasi	Indian swellshark	11. Bottom, deep	36	Fawn with seven dark saddles	A dwarf swellshark.
Cephaloscyllium sufflans	Balloon shark, swellshark	10. Bottom, moderate and deep waters	106 ♀96	Pale with seven darker saddles	
Cephaloscyllium ventriosum	Swellshark	1,2,3. Bottom, shallow and deep waters	100 ♂83	Tan, dark and light spots and patches	Nocturnal. Groups sometimes rest heaped on top of each other. Thrives and has laid eggs in captivity. Young emerging from egg cases have two rows of large denticles used like ratchets to help them out.
Cephalurus cephalus	Lollipop catshark, head shark	2. Bottom, deep	28 ♀21 ♂21	Light/dark brown, green eyes	Scientific name means head-headed; very large gill region is probably an adaptation to life at bottom with low oxygen.
Galeus arae	Roughtail catshark, marbled catshark	4,5,6. Bottom, deep	43 ♀34♂31	Tawny, white outlined saddles	It is possible that the Caribbean subspecies lays eggs while the continental slopes subspecies bears live young.
Galeus boardmani	Australian sawtail catshark	14. Bottom, moderate to deep waters	61 ♂54	Pale grey, white outlined dark bands	Sawtail because of the rows of denticles on the edges of the tail.
Galeus eastmani	Gecko catshark	12,13. Bottom, deep	50 ♀38 ♂33	Dark patches, white tipped fins	'Gecko' because of the slender body. Egg-cases measure about 1.6 × 6 cm (0.6 × 2.4 in).
Galeus melastomus	Blackmouth catshark, blackmouthed dogfish	7,8,9. Bottom, moderate to deep waters	90 ♀66 ♂54	Tawny, dark patches, off-white below	Galeus = dogfish (Greek). The French common name means Spanish dog.
Galeus murinus	Mouse catshark	7. Bottom, deep	63	Brown, paler below	Found off Iceland and the Faroes Islands only.
Galeus nipponensis	Broadfin sawtail catshark	12. Bottom, deep	65 ♀54 ♂54	Light mouse with dark saddles	The males' anal fin is much shorter than the females', a development probably related to the very long claspers.
Galeus piperatus	Peppered catshark	2. Bottom, deep	30 ♀28 ♂28	Tan, black dots, ash below	Found only in the northern Gulf of California.
Galeus polli	African sawtail catshark	9. Bottom, deep	42 ♀41 ♂37	White-edged dark blotches on back	
Galeus sauteri	Blacktip sawtail catshark	12. Bottom, at moderate depths offshore	45 ♀43 ♂37	Brown, black tips to fins and tail	
Galeus schultzi	Dwarf sawtail catshark	13. Bottom, deep	30 ♀28 ♂25	Saddles on dorsal fins, bands on tail	One of the smallest of sharks.
Halaelurus alcocki	Arabian catshark	11. Bottom, deep	30	Charcoal/ash, white tips to fins	Known from only one specimen (1913).

Australian swellshark
Cephaloscyllium laticeps
97 cm

Swellshark
Cephaloscyllium ventriosum
100 cm

Australian sawtail catshark
Galeus boardmani
61 cm

Scientific name	Common names	Distribution*	Size (cm)*	Colour	Notes
Halaelurus boesemani	Speckled catshark	10,11,13,14. Bottom, moderate depths	48 ♀45 ♂45	Brown, black speckles, grey patches	
Halaelurus buergeri	Blackspotted catshark	12,13. Bottom, moderate depths	49 ♀45 ♂39	Fawn, black spots, dark back patches	Like several relatives, the female retains several egg-cases inside uterus until embryos are well developed before laying the eggs.
Halaelurus canescens	Dusky catshark	3. Bottom, deep	70 ♀62 ♂62	Dusky	
Halaelurus dawsoni	New Zealand catshark	15. Bottom, deep	45 ♀40 ♂40	Fawn/grey, pale below, white spots	Found only off Auckland Island and the southern tip of New Zealand.
Halaelurus hispidus	Bristly catshark	11. Bottom, deep	29 ♀25 ♂25	Fawn/off-white, often stripes/spots	A very small catshark.
Halaelurus immaculatus	Spotless catshark	13. Bottom, deep	76 ♀75 ♂71	Ochre	Recently discovered (described in 1982).
Halaelurus lineatus	Lined catshark, banded catshark	10. Inshore, surf zone to deep waters	56 ♀49 ♂52	Fawn, dense flecks, 26 dark saddles	Has an uptilted end to snout. Easily kept in captivity.
Halaelurus lutarius	Mud catshark, brown catshark	10. Bottom, deep	39 ♀35 ♂32	Dun, paler below	Lutarius = muddy; named because of its preference for muddy sea floors.
Halaelurus natalensis	Tiger catshark	10. Bottom, inshore to moderate depths	47 ♀47 ♂43	Tawny, ten dark saddles, cream below	Taken for sport.
Halaelurus quagga	Quagga catshark	10,11. Bottom, moderately deep tropical offshore waters	35 ♂31	Pale, zebra-like stripes, paler below	The quagga, now extinct, was a member of the horse family, striped like a zebra.
Haploblepharus edwardsii	Puffadder shyshark	10. Bottom, surf zone to moderately deep offshore waters	60 ♀50 ♂53	Cream, white speckles, grey saddles	'Shyshark' because when caught they hide their eyes with their tails.
Haploblepharus fuscus	Brown shyshark	10. Shallow, inshore	73 ♀66 ♂66	Reddish brown, vague saddles, white below	Does well in captivity.
Haploblepharus pictus	Dark shyshark	9,10. Bottom, shallow	56 ♀53 ♂56	Mustard brown, dark saddles, paler below	All the shysharks are sport fishes and prey to anglers.
Holohalaelurus punctatus	African spotted catshark	10. Bottom, moderately deep waters	34 ♀25 ♂31	Mustard, brown dots, white fin dot	Unlike most sharks, males of this genus are larger than females.
Holohalaelurus regani	Izak catshark, Izak, shy eye s	9,10. Bottom, moderate to deep waters	61 ♀49 ♂56	Dark brown, dark dots and light lines	Another species that hides its eyes with its tail when caught.
Parmaturus campechiensis	Campeche catshark	5. Bottom, deep		Brown	Known only from one immature specimen (Bay of Campeche, Gulf of Mexico, 1979).
Parmaturus melanobranchius	Blackgill catshark	13. Bottom, deep	85	Pale brown	All members of this genus have flabby bodies.

New Zealand catshark
Halaelurus dawsoni
45 cm

Tiger catshark
Halaelurus natalensis
47 cm

Brown shyshark
Haploblepharus fuscus
73 cm

*For note on size, and distribution map, see box p154.

Scientific name	Common names	Distribution*	Size (cm)*	Colour	Notes
Parmaturus pilosus	Salamander shark	12. Bottom, deep	64 ♀61 ♂56	Brown	Salamanders are tailed amphibians with long bodies. Pilosus – hairy, perhaps for the crest of denticles on tail fin.
Parmaturus xaniurus	Filetail catshark	1,2. Bottom, deep	55 ♀51 ♂41	Dusky brown to black	Very large gill region, probably an adaptation to living deep down where oxygen levels are very low.
Pentanchus profundicolus	Onefin catshark	13. Bottom, deep	50	Colour not known	Has only one dorsal fin, like the frilled and cow sharks. Known from only one specimen (Philippines, 1913).
Poroderma africanum	Striped catshark	9,10. Bottom, surf zone to moderate depths inshore	101 ♀80 ♂84	Ash, dark longitudinal stripes	Often found in caves and among rocks. Does well in aquariums. A game fish.
Poroderma marleyi	Barbeled catshark, black-spotted catshark	10. Moderately deep waters	65 ♂58	Ash, large dark spots on back	Rare.
Poroderma pantherinum	Leopard catshark	9,10. Bottom, from surf zone to moderate depths	84 ♀66 ♂70	Spots/rings in longitudinal rows	Does well in captivity. A game fish.
Shroederichthys bivius	Narrowmouthed catshark	3,4. Moderate depths, inshore and offshore waters	70 ♀40 ♂53	Mouse-grey, dark saddles some spots	Males' teeth are twice as long as females', and their mouths are much longer than females'.
Schroederichthys chilensis	Redspotted catshark	3. Bottom, close inshore	62 ♂59	Pale brown, dark saddles and spots	
Schroederichthys maculatus	Narrowtail catshark	5. Bottom, deep tropical waters	34 ♀34 ♂30	Light brown/ grey, yellow-white spots	Strikingly slender-bodied.
Schroederichthys tenuis	Slender catshark	4. Bottom, deep tropical waters	70	Fawn, darker saddles edged with spots	Occurs off the Amazon River mouth.
Scyliorhinus besnardi	Polkadot catshark	4. Bottom, moderately deep waters	47	Pale, sparse black spots	Scylio-rhinus = dogfish-nose.
Scyliorhinus boa	Boa catshark	5. Bottom, deep	54	Fawn/grey, saddles, rows of black dots	'Boa' because of its colouring.
Scyliorhinus canicula	Small-spotted catshark, sandy dogfish, rough hound	7,8,9. Bottom, shallow to moderately deep waters	100	Sandy, dense dark spots, cream below	Abundant. Eaten as 'huss' and 'flake' in Britain. Thrives in captivity.
Scyliorhinus capensis	Yellowspotted catshark	10. Bottom, inshore and offshore, moderate to deep waters	122 ♀77 ♂83	Grey, dark saddles, yellow spots	Like several shark species, believed to live deeper in warmer waters.
Scyliorhinus cervigoni	West African catshark	9. Bottom, moderate to deep tropical waters	76	Vague dark saddles/spots on flanks	Believed to lay eggs in cases 7 × 3 cm (3 × 2 in).
Scyliorhinus garmani	Brownspotted catshark	13.	24 or 36 +	Large brown spots, vague saddles	Little known – even size of adults is uncertain.

Izak catshark
Holohalaelurus regani
61 cm

Barbeled catshark
Poroderma marleyi
65 cm

Narrowtail catshark
Schroederichthys maculatus
34 cm

Scientific name	Common names	Distribution*	Size (cm)*	Colour	Notes
Scyliorhinus haeckeli	Freckled catshark	4. Bottom, moderate to deep tropical waters	35 +	Tiny black spots on back, dark saddles	Little known.
Scyliorhinus hesperius	Whitesaddled catshark	5. Bottom, deep	47 +	Large white spots and dark saddles	Hesperius = western; named for the region of the Atlantic Ocean in which it is found.
Scyliorhinus meadi	Blotched catshark	5,6. Bottom, deep	49 +	Ash with 7 or 8 dusky saddles	Rare.
Scyliorhinus retifer	Chain catshark, chain dogfish	5,6. Bottom, deep	47 ♀41 ♂39	Yellow-green eyes, cream, brown marks	Stomachs have revealed small pebbles, possibly taken as ballast.
Scyliorhinus stellaris	Nursehound, large-spotted dog-fish, bull huss	7,8,9. Bottom, very shallow inshore to moderately deep offshore	162 ♀125 ♂125	Mouse-brown, dark and white spots	Another shark sold as 'flake' in British fish shops. Skin is sometimes made into leather called rubskin.
Scyliorhinus torazame	Cloudy catshark	12,13. Shallow, inshore to moderately deep waters	48 ♀39 + ♂44	Dusky, dark saddles, some light spots	Females deposit eggs in a nursery area.
Scyliorhinus torrei	Dwarf catshark	5,6. Bottom, deep	32 ♀26 ♂25	Fawn, dark blotches, white spots	Occurs in a limited area, off Florida, the Bahamas and northern Cuba.

Proscyllidae (Finback catsharks)

Ctenacis fehlmanni	Harlequin catshark	10. Bottom, deep tropical waters	46	Russet bars, blotches and spots	Known from only one specimen (Somalia, 1973).
Eridacnis barbouri	Cuban ribbontail catshark	5. Bottom, deep subtropical waters	34 ♀28 ♂27	Dun or ash, off-white below	Very small and slender.
Eridacnis radcliffei	Pygmy ribbontail shark	10,11,13. Bottom, deep tropical waters	24 ♀19 ♂20	Brown, dark marks on fins and tail	The second-smallest shark. Produces one or two young, about 11 cm (4 in) at birth – remarkable as females mature at about 16 cm (6 in).
Eridacnis sinuans	African ribbontail catshark	10. Bottom, deep dark	37 ♂29	Mouse-grey, bands on dorsal fins	
Gollum attenuatus	Slender smooth-hound	15. Bottom, deep	101 ♀101 ♂94	Mouse-grey, paler below	Little known and uncommon.
Proscyllium habereri	Graceful catshark	12,13. Bottom, moderately deep waters	65 ♀51 ♂42	Large and small dark spots	

Pseudotriakidae (False catsharks)

Pseudotriakis microdon	False catshark, dumb shark	6,8,9,10,13,16. Bottom, deep	295 ♀253 ♂234	Dusky	Micr-odon = tiny-toothed, but there are about 200 rows of teeth in each jaw, and the mouth is very large. Sluggish.

Leptochariidae (Barbelled houndsharks)

Leptocharias smithii	Barbeled houndshark	9. Bottom, tropical inshore waters	82 ♀70 ♂67	Ash or mouse-grey	Abundant off river mouths. Males' front teeth much larger than females', perhaps related to mating behaviour. Found in water with temperature between 20° and 27°C (68° and 81° F).

Nursehound
Scyliorhinus stellaris
162 cm

Harlequin catshark
Ctenacis fehlmanni
46 cm

False catshark
Pseudotriakis microdon
295 cm

*For note on size, and distribution map, see box p154.

Scientific name	Common names	Distribution*	Size (cm)*	Colour	Notes
Triakidae (Houndsharks, smooth-hounds, topes, whiskery sharks)					
Furgaleus macki	Whiskery shark	14. Bottom, moderately deep waters	160 ♀121 ♂122	Grey, paler below	'Whiskery' because of moustache-like nasal barbels.
Galeorhinus galeus	Tope shark, school s, soupfin s, vitamin s	1,3,4,7,8,9,10,14,15. Bottom, surf zone to far offshore	195 ♀162 ♂145	Pale bluish grey to purple-black	Galeo-rhinus galeus means shark shark shark. An important food fish. Not dangerous but will bite when caught. A game fish. Tagging shows it can live over 40 years. Can travel 56 km (35 miles) in one day. Formerly so much used for liver oil it was called the oil shark. Can produce 50 pups in one litter.
Gogolia filewoodi	Sailback houndshark	13. Bottom, moderately deep	74	Mouse-grey	Known from only one specimen (Papua New Guinea, 1973).
Hemitriakis japanica	Japanese topeshark	12,13. Close inshore and moderately deep offshore waters	120 ♀106 ♂92	White edges to fins	
Hemitriakis leucoperiptera	Whitefin topeshark	13. Moderately deep inshore waters	96	White edges to fins	Leuco-periptera = white-winged.
Hypogaleus hyugaensis	Blacktip tope, lesser soupfin shark	10,11,12. Bottom, tropical and subtropical moderately deep waters	127 ♀118 ♂119	Ash, off-white below	Like almost every shark occurring near Japan, this fish is an important food source.
Iago garricki	Longnose hound-shark	16. Bottom, deep tropical waters	75 ♀63	Colour not known	So far, found only off Vanuatu. At birth, the young are 23 cm (11 in) long.
Iago omanensis	Bigeye hound-shark	11. Bottom at considerable depths, tropical waters	58 ♀49 ♂33	Mouse-grey, often black fin edges	Large gill region is an adaptation to life in water with little oxygen and a lot of salt. Males are two-thirds the size of females, and weigh one-sixth as much.
Mustelus antarcticus	Gummy shark, Sweet William, flake, smooth dog s	14. Bottom, inshore to moderate depths offshore	157 ♀80 ♂68	Grey, many small white spots	Ant-arcticus = anti-northern, i.e. southern. 'Gummy' refers to its flattened teeth. Has a strong odour.
Mustelus asterias	Starry smooth-hound, stellate smooth- hound	7,8,9. Bottom, shallow inshore to moderate depths offshore	140 ♀85 ♂81	Ash/charcoal, white spots, paler below	Called 'Stinkard' by Irish fishermen.
Mustelus californicus	Grey smooth-hound	1,2. Bottom, shallow inshore and offshore waters	124 ♀97 ♂88	Dark brown/grey, paler below	Will enter muddy bays. Does well in captivity.
Mustelus canis	Dusky smooth-hound, smooth dogfish	4,5,6. Bottom, shallow inshore to deep offshore waters	150 ♀106	Mouse, olive-grey/brown, white below	Can change colour to blend with background. Abundant off the United States, second only to the piked dogfish. Enters lower reaches of rivers but probably cannot live long in fresh water. Often used in research as it thrives in captivity. A game fish.
Mustelus dorsalis	Sharp-tooth smooth-hound	2,3. Bottom, inshore, tropical waters	64 ♀53	Mouse-grey or grey, paler below	Mustelus = weasel, because of its long snout.
Mustelus fasciatus	Striped smooth-hound	4. Bottom, inshore	125	Mouse-grey, paler below	Juveniles have dark stripes.
Mustelus griseus	Spotless smooth-hound	12,13. Bottom, inshore	101 ♀90 ♂77	Mouse-grey or charcoal, paler below	Survives in captivity.

Barbeled houndshark
Leptocharias smithii
82 cm

Tope shark
Galeorhinus galeus
195 cm

Dusky smooth-hound
Mustelus canis
150 cm

Scientific name	Common names	Distribution*	Size (cm)*	Colour	Notes
Mustelus henlei	Brown smooth-hound	1,2,3. Bottom, shallow inshore to moderate depths offshore	95 ♀72 ♂63	Copper, white below	Abundant. Often found in shallow muddy bays and around oyster beds. Does well in captivity. Active and agile.
Mustelus higmani	Smalleye smooth-hound	4. Bottom, close inshore to moderate depths offshore	64 ♀53 ♂46	Mouse-grey or grey, paler below	Tolerates brackish water.
Mustelus lenticulatus	Spotted estuary smooth-hound, white-spotted gummy shark, rig	15. Bottom, inshore to deep offshore waters	137 ♀117 ♂99	Mouse-grey or grey, dense white spots	The only New Zealand smooth-hound. Important to New Zealand fishing industry. A sport fish.
Mustelus lunulatus	Sicklefin smooth-hound	1,2. Bottom, inshore to deep offshore waters	170 ♂103	Olive-brown or grey, paler below	Abundant.
Mustelus manazo	Starspotted smooth-hound	10,12,13. Bottom, close inshore	117 ♀91 ♂81	Mouse-grey, white spots, paler below	Abundant. An important food fish in Japan. Survives in captivity.
Mustelus mento	Speckled smooth-hound	3,4. Shallow inshore to moderate depths offshore	130 ♀88 ♂70	Mouse-grey, white spots, paler below	
Mustelus mosis	Arabian smooth-hound, Moses smooth-hound, hardnose smooth-hound	10,11. Bottom, inshore and offshore waters	150 ♂85	Mouse-grey or grey, paler below	Does well in captivity.
Mustelus mustelus	Smooth-hound	7,8,9. Bottom, shallow inshore to deep offshore waters	164 ♀122 ♂101	Grey, often black spots, white below	Litters of 4 to 15 are about 39 cm (15 in) at birth. Abundant. An important food fish. Also taken by anglers.
Mustelus norrisi	Narrowfin smooth-hound, Florida dogfish	4,5. Bottom, close inshore to moderate depths	100	Grey, paler below	
Mustelus palumbes	Whitespotted smooth-hound	9,10. Bottom, inshore to deep offshore waters	120 ♀90 ♂82	Mouse-grey, white spots, paler below	Sometimes processed into 'biltong,' a dried meat. A sport fish.
Mustelus punctulatus	Blackspotted smooth-hound	8,9. Bottom, inshore black	85	Mouse-grey, spots, paler below	Its dorsal fins are fringed.
Mustelus schmitti	Narrownose smooth-hound	4. Bottom, moderately deep waters	74	Grey, often white spots, paler below	An important food fish in Argentina and Uruguay. Survives in captivity.
Mustelus whitneyi	Humpback smooth-hound	3. Bottom, moderately deep offshore waters	87	Mouse-grey or grey, paler below	
Scylliogaleus quecketti	Flapnose houndshark, flapnosed smooth-hound	10. Surf zone to close offshore	102 ♀91 ♂79	Grey, cream below	Has flaps to its nose that extend to the mouth. A sport fish.
Triakis acutipinna	Sharpfin houndshark	3.	102	Colour not known	Known only from two specimens taken off Ecuador.

Brown smooth-hound
Mustelus henlei
95 cm

Leopard shark
Triakis semifasciata
180 cm

Snaggletooth shark
Hemipristis elongatus
240 cm

*For note on size, and distribution map, see box p154.

Scientific name	Common names	Distribution*	Size (cm)*	Colour	Notes
Triakis maculata	Spotted houndshark	3. Inshore waters	180	Generally has many black spots	Tri-akis = three-pointed (refers to the teeth).
Triakis megalopterus	Sharptooth houndshark, gully s, Sweet William	9,10. Bottom, shallow waters, surf zone and in bays	174 ♀159	Charcoal, often many black spots	Named 'gully' for its liking for crevices. Does well in captivity. A sport fish. Used for biltong (a dried meat).
Triakis scyllium	Banded houndshark	12. Bottom, shallow	150	Indistinct black spots	Often found in bays and at river mouths, occasionally resting in groups. A successful aquarium species.
Triakis semifasciata	Leopard shark	1, 2. Bottom, shallow inshore	180 ♀149 ♂122	Golden brown, dark saddles, black spots	Abundant and harmless. One of the most hardy aquarium species. Often enters muddy bays with tide, leaving as it ebbs. Eats clam necks, possibly removing shells by vigorous shaking once the clam is pulled free.

Hemigaleidae (Weasel sharks)

Scientific name	Common names	Distribution*	Size (cm)*	Colour	Notes
Chaenogaleus macrostoma	Hooktooth shark	11,12,13. Shallow and moderately deep inshore waters	100 ♂82	Golden brown or ash	Hooked teeth and large mouth probably help it snatch and hold fish prey.
Hemigaleus microstoma	Sicklefin weasel shark, weasel s	11,12,13,14. Bottom, moderately deep tropical waters	97 ♀82 ♂77	Ash or copper, black/white fin tips	A specialist feeder on squid, cuttlefish and octopuses. Short mouth probably helps suction feeding.
Hemipristis elongatus	Snaggletooth shark	9,10,11,12,13,14. Shallow inshore to moderately deep offshore, tropical waters	240 ♀194 ♂132	Golden brown or grey	Potentially dangerous because of long teeth (those on lower jaw protrude when mouth is shut), its size and its occurrence in shallow water. Prized as food in India. Similar sharks, twice as large, lived 70 million years ago, worldwide.
Paragaleus pectoralis	Atlantic weasel shark	9. Shallow inshore to moderately deep offshore waters	138 ♀97 ♂97	Golden brown or grey, yellow bands	Also a specialist feeder on squid and octopuses. Small teeth probably suited to holding such soft and squirming prey.
Paragaleus tengi	Straight-tooth weasel shark	12,13. Inshore	88 ♂83	Ash	Little known.

Carcharhinidae (Requiem sharks)

Scientific name	Common names	Distribution*	Size (cm)*	Colour	Notes
Carcharhinus acronotus	Blacknose shark	4,5,6. Moderately deep inshore waters	200 ♀120	Mouse-grey, dark tips to fins/snout	In captivity, faced with intruders, arches its back, raises its head and lowers its tail, perhaps as a threat. Is prey to larger sharks. Harmless. IGFA game fish.
Carcharhinus albimarginatus	Silvertip shark, silvertip whaler	2,3,10,11,12,13,16. Surface to deep, inshore and offshore waters	300	Charcoal, white tips to fins	Plentiful around reefs and islands. Fast, large and bold. Could be dangerous.
Carcharhinus altimus	Bignose shark, Knopp's shark	2,3,4,5,6,8,9,10,11,16. Bottom, deep	300 ♀254 ♂241	Ash, darker fin tips, white below	Unlikely to be a danger since it lives deep down.
Carcharhinus amblyrhynchoides	Graceful shark	11,13,14. Inshore and out to sea, tropical waters	167 +	Charcoal, white streak on flanks	Carcha-rhinus = jagged-shark, or jagged-file, referring to teeth or skin, perhaps both.
Carcharhinus amblyrhynchos	Grey reef shark, long-nosed black-tail shark	10,13,14,16. Bottom, reefs and lagoons, and at moderate depths offshore	255	Grey, tail black edge to tail fin	Curious but generally not dangerous. Has attacked people (at least one fatality); possibly spearfishers were mistaken for their catch. Another shark to adopt postures and swimming patterns to convey threat to intruders.

Straight-tooth weasel shark
Paragaleus tengi
88 cm

Graceful shark
Carcharhinus amblyrhynchoides
167 cm

Grey reef shark
Carcharhinus amblyrhynchos
255 cm

Scientific name	Common names	Distribution*	Size (cm)*	Colour	Notes
Carcharhinus amboinensis	Pigeye shark, Java shark	9,10,11,13,14. Shallow, surf zone, to moderate depths inshore	280 ♀210	Grey, darker fin tips, off-white below	To be respected because of size and large teeth, although no known attacks.
Carcharhinus borneensis	Borneo shark	13. Tropical inshore waters	70	Brown, off-white below	Rare and little known.
Carcharhinus brachyurus	Copper shark, New Zealand whaler, cocktail s	1,2,3,4,8,9,10,12,14,15. Surf zone to moderate depths offshore	292 ♀266 ♂233	Golden brown, cream streak, cream below	Dangerous. Has attacked people in South Africa, Australia and New Zealand. A sport fish.
Carcharhinus brevipinna	Spinner shark, smoothfanged s, longnose grey s	4,5,6,8,9,10,11,12,13,14. Shallow to moderately deep waters	278 ♀224 ♂196	Grey, black fin tips, paler below	Has small teeth but has attacked humans. Often swims fast upwards through schools of prey, snapping all around, emerging still spiralling in a leap out of water. IGFA game fish.
Carcharhinus cautus	Nervous shark	13,14. Shallow waters and reefs	150 ♀135	Mouse-grey, some black fin edges	Timid and probably not dangerous.
Carcharhinus dussumieri	Whitecheek shark, white-cheeked whaler shark	11,12,13. Inshore waters	100 ♀76 ♂73	Mouse-grey, off-white underside	Common, harmless.
Carcharhinus falciformis	Silky shark, sickle shark	2,3,4,5,6,9,10,11,12,13,15,16. Shallow inshore; all levels in open seas	330 ♀259 ♂243	Dusky to sooty, paler below	Called silky for its smooth skin. Is detested by tuna fishers for damage it wreaks on nets and catches; is named the net-eater shark in some parts of Pacific Ocean. Ranks with blue shark and oceanic whitetip shark as most common oceanic species. Not identified in any attacks but abundance and size make it a potential danger. Possibly the cause of deaths after ship sinkings or plane crashes at sea.
Carcharhinus fitzroyensis	Creek whaler	14. Inshore and offshore tropical waters	150	Grey, paler below	The whalers earned their name from their habit of despoiling whale catches in the early days of Australian and New Zealand whaling.
Carcharhinus galapagensis	Galapagos shark, grey reef whaler	2,3,5,9,10,16. Shallow inshore, surface to moderately deep near oceanic islands	370 ♀269 ♂231	Charcoal, white below	Aggressive and dangerous. When excited, will attract others to the area. Known to have killed at least one person.
Carcharhinus hemiodon	Pondicherry shark	11,13,14.	175	Grey, paler below	Little known. Possibly enters river estuaries but such reports are old and may not be reliable.
Carcharhinus isodon	Finetooth shark	4,5,6. Shallow inshore waters	189 ♀157 ♂149	Slate fading to white below	Is-odon means equal-toothed; has same numbers of teeth in upper and lower jaws.
Carcharhinus leucas	Bull shark, cub s, Ganges s, river s, Nicaragua s, Zambezi s, shovelnose, slipway grey s, square-nose s, Van Rooyen's s	2,3,4,5,6,9,10,11,12,13. Shallow inshore, rivers, bays and near wharves	340 ♀242 ♂228	Grey, off-white below	Can live for some time in fresh water; occurs 3700 km (2300 miles) from sea in upper Amazon. Once believed landlocked in Lake Nicaragua but now known to negotiate rapids and return to sea. Jaws and teeth allow it to take large prey, and it will eat almost anything. Eats many other sharks and rays including hammerheads, stingrays and even young of its own kind. Is abundant in many areas where large numbers of people use or enjoy sea or rivers. Is known to have caused several deaths but is not readily recognised so true number of fatalities may be much greater. Possibly the most dangerous tropical shark, even the most dangerous of all. Vastly dreaded in India where it attacks pilgrims in the holy river Ganges, and feeds on corpses consigned to sacred waters. Flesh, fins, hide, liver and carcases are used. IGFA game fish.

Copper shark
Carcharhinus brachyurus
292 cm

Silky shark
Carcharhinus falciformis
330 cm

Bull shark
Carcharhinus leucas
340 cm

*For note on size, and distribution map, see box p154.

Scientific name	Common names	Distribution*	Size (cm)*	Colour	Notes
Carcharhinus limbatus	Blacktip shark, spotfin s, grey s, blackfin	1,2,3,4,5,6,8,9,10,11,12,13,14,16. All tropical and subtropical waters inshore and out to sea	225 ♀184 ♂195	Charcoal, bronze tinged, white below	Often found in mangrove swamps and muddy estuaries. Leaps spinning from water after launching itself upwards through a school of prey. Becomes frenzied when competing for food, and fishermen have seen hundreds churning water to froth. Active, fast, sometimes aggressive. Few recorded attacks on people but is potentially dangerous.
Carcharhinus longimanus	Oceanic whitetip shark, white-tipped s	2,3,4,5,6,7,9,10,11,12,13,14,16. All levels, tropical and subtropical waters	395 ♀225 ♂210	Mouse-grey, copper tinged, white below	Abundant and very dangerous. Hated by tuna fishers and formerly by whalers for harm it does to catches. Perseveres fearlessly when investigating prey. Slow-moving but can move in fast dashes.
Carcharhinus macloti	Hardnose shark, Maclot's shark	10,11,12,13. Inshore waters	100 ♀82 ♂75	Mouse-grey, pale fin edge white below	Was probably cause of many casualties when *Nova Scotia* was torpedoed off South Africa in World War II. Has a gristly beak inside the snout. Like many sharks, lives in sex-segrated populations.
Carcharhinus melanopterus	Blacktip reef shark, blacktip reef whaler, black shark	10,11,12,13,14,16. Shallow close inshore and close offshore	180 ♀113 ♂135	Tan, black fin tips, paler below	Very common on coral reefs in knee-deep water with dorsal fins in air. Occurs in east Mediterranean, probably spreading from Red Sea via Suez Canal. Generally harmless but can be aggressive when bait is around. Has attacked many people, none seriously, but is regarded as a hazard.
Carcharhinus obscurus	Dusky shark, bay s, shovelnose, lazy-grey, black whaler	1,2,4,5,6,9,10,12,13,14,16. From surf zone to far offshore, all levels	400 ♀311 ♂310	Charcoal, copper-tinged, white below	Often follows ships. Has evil reputation but few attacks can definitely be attributed to it. The species most often taken in shark nets off South Africa. IGFA game fish.
Carcharhinus perezi	Caribbean reef shark	4,5,6. Bottom, inshore tropical waters	295 ♀247	Olive-grey, cream below	Abundant on Caribbean coral reefs. Dangerous, having attacked at least two people.
Carcharhinus plumbeus	Sandbar shark, brown s, ground s, northern whaler	4,5,6,8,9,10,11,12,13,14,16. Bottom, shallow inshore, deep offshore	239 ♀100 ♂177	Mouse-grey or copper, pale below	Abundant. Sometimes found in water barely covering it. Common in harbours and estuaries. Skin is esteemed for leather.
Carcharhinus porosus	Smalltail shark	2,3,4,5. Bottom, close inshore to moderately deep tropical waters	150 ♀109 ♂96	Slate, paler below	Common in estuaries. Harmless.
Carcharhinus sealei	Blackspot shark	10,11,13,14. Bottom, shallow, from surf zone to moderate depths	95 ♀81 ♂82	Mouse-grey, off-white below	Common. Too small to be considered dangerous.
Carcharhinus signatus	Night shark	4,5,6,9. Surface to deep, offshore and semi-oceanic waters	280	Slate, large green eyes, paler below	Probably migrates from depths to the surface at night.
Carcharhinus sorrah	Spot-tail shark	10,11,12,13,14,16. Shallow and moderately deep tropical waters	160 ♀130 ♂117	Grey, black fin tips, paler below	Common around coral reefs.
Carcharhinus wheeleri	Blacktail reef shark, short-nosed blacktail shark	10,11. Coral reefs, inshore and offshore waters	172 ♀146 ♂139	Charcoal, black/white fin tips	Aggressive near bait; should be considered potentially dangerous.
Galeocerdo cuvier	Tiger shark	1,2,3,4,5,6,7,9,10,11,12,13,14,15,16. Worldwide in warm seas, surface and at moderate depths, close inshore and far offshore	740 ♀375 ♂298	Grey/black, tiger-like stripes fade with maturity	The shark of the Shark Arm Case. A maneater, second only to great white shark in number of known attacks on people and boats. Fearsome teeth and large mouth allow it to take almost anything: will eat sawsharks, hammerheads, turtles, sealions, jellyfish, lobsters and garbage. One giant weighed over 3 tonnes. Litters are between 10 and 82; at birth measures 51 to 76 cm (20 to 30 in). IGFA game fish.

Blacktip shark
Carcharhinus limbatus
225 cm

Oceanic whitetip shark
Carcharhinus longimanus
395 cm

Tiger shark
Galeocerdo cuvier
740 cm

177

Scientific name	Common names	Distribution*	Size (cm)*	Colour	Notes
Glyphis gangeticus	Ganges shark	11. Fresh water in rivers, estuaries, possibly also inshore waters	204	Brown to grey	Has horrific reputation in India, but the many deaths attributed to this fish were probably caused by the bull shark.
Glyphis glyphis	Speartooth shark	Possibly 13 and 14, probably inshore waters, possibly fresh water	100-300	Grey-brown	Until recently known from only one specimen (1839). More have been caught off Papua New Guinea and Queensland.
Isogomphodon oxyrhynchus	Daggernose shark	4. Tropical inshore waters and estuaries	152	Mustard-grey, paler below	The very long pointed snout and tiny eyes are adaptations to life in murky waters. Harmless.
Lamiopsis temmincki	Broadfin shark	11,13. Inshore waters	168 ♀146	Tan or ash	Little known. A slight potential danger because of large teeth.
Loxodon macrorhinus	Sliteye shark	10,11,12,13,14. Shallow inshore and moderately deep tropical waters	91 ♀85 ♂73	Grey, paler below	Has large eyes. Named 'sliteye' because of the little notches at the hind corners of the eyes.
Nasolamia velox	Whitenose shark, pico bianco	2,3. Moderately deep inshore and offshore tropical waters	150	Mouse-grey white-ringed dot on snout	Little known.
Negaprion acutidens	Sicklefin lemon shark, lemon s, sharp-toothed s	10,11,13,14,16. Surface and bottom, inshore waters, bays and reefs	310	Tawny, off-white below	Generally timid but will defend itself vigorously and obstinately if vexed, and is then dangerous. Thrives in aquariums.
Negaprion brevirostris	Lemon shark	2,3,4,5,6,9. Surface and at moderate depths, bays, near docks and in river mouths	340 ♀262 ♂251	Mustard/slate, fading below	Nega-prion = no saw, i.e. smooth teeth. Dangerous if provoked. Does so well in captivity it is widely used for research.
Prionace glauca	Blue shark, blue-dog, great blue s, blue whaler	Worldwide in tropical and temperate seas, often on surface of deep water	383 ♀276 ♂246	Brilliant blue back, white below	Found in wider range of waters than any other shark. Often seen swimming lazily with first dorsal fin and tip of tail out of water. In courtship males bite females and females develop skin three times as thick as males. Bears litters of up to 135; size when born between 35 and 45 cm (17.7 and 13.7 in). Extremely voracious; will gather round a food source in a frenzy. Packs cause havoc among hauls of fish, launching themselves at nets. Very dangerous; is known to have killed people and is suspected of causing great numbers of deaths after ship sinkings in World War II. IGFA game fish.
Rhizoprionodon acutus	Milk shark	9,10,11,12,13,14. Bottom, from shallow in surf zone to deep offshore waters	178 ♀117 ♂123	Grey above, white below	In India, flesh believed by some to improve the milk production of nursing mothers.
Rhizoprionodon lalandii	Brazilian sharpnose shark	4,5. Bottom, shallow and moderately deep tropical waters	77 ♀65 ♂54	Mouse-grey or charcoal, paler below	Common. Rhizo-prion-odon = teeth with serrated roots.
Rhizoprionodon longurio	Pacific sharpnose shark	1,2,3. Shallow, inshore tropical waters	128 ♀128 ♂75	Brown to grey, paler below	Very common.
Rhizoprionodon ologolinx	Grey sharpnose shark	11,13. Inshore and offshore tropical waters	70 ♀51 ♂45	Mouse-grey or grey, paler below	
Rhizoprionodon porosus	Caribbean sharpnose shark	4,5. Inshore and in deep estuaries, and deep offshore tropical waters	110 ♀94 ♂72	Metallic brown, paler below	Abundant. Taken in large numbers for food.

Daggernose shark
Isogomphodon oxyrhynchus
152 cm

Lemon shark
Negaprion brevirostris
340 cm

Blue shark
Prionace glauca
383 cm

*For note on size, and distribution map, see box p154.

Scientific name	Common names	Distribution*	Size (cm)*	Colour	Notes
Rhizoprionodon taylori	Australian sharpnose shark, Taylor's shark	14. Inshore tropical waters	67	Mouse-grey, abruptly white below	Common but little known.
Rhizoprionodon terraenovae	Atlantic sharpnose shark	5,6. Shallow, near surf zone, in harbours, bays and estuaries	110 ♀97 ♂84	Mouse-grey, white spots, paler below	Enters rivers but does not go far up them. Harmless and abundant.
Scoliodon laticaudus	Spadenose shark	10,11,12,13. Close inshore, lower reaches of rivers, tropical waters	74 ♀51 ♂41	Copper-tinged grey, pale below	Abundant in India and Pakistan. Often found in lower reaches of rivers, but length of survival in fresh water not known.
Triaenodon obesus	Whitetip reef shark, blunthead s	10,11,12,13,14,16. Bottom, shallow, in coral caves in reefs and lagoons	213 ♀131 ♂136	Brown/grey, white-tipped dorsal fin	Able to rest on the bottom. Timid, but can become excited by bait such as speared fish, and will bite humans. IGFA game fish.

Sphyrnidae (Bonnethead sharks, hammerhead sharks, scoophead sharks)

Scientific name	Common names	Distribution*	Size (cm)*	Colour	Notes
Eusphyra blochii	Winghead shark	11,12,13,14. Shallow, tropical waters	152	Mouse-grey, paler below	Has widest head of all the hammerheads, width sometimes half the length of body. Lobes are possibly to increase ability to find and take prey since the smelling and seeing organs are on them. Harmless.
Sphyrna corona	Scalloped bonnet-head	2,3. Probably inshore waters	92	Ashy, white below	The smallest of the hammerheads, its head is rounded and mallet-shaped. Appears scalloped when viewed from above.
Sphyrna couardi	Whitefin hammerhead	9. Bottom, coastal and pelagic, tropical waters	300 ♀232 ♂162	Slate to mouse-grey, pale below	Uncommon. Not known to attack people but its size makes it possibly dangerous.
Sphyrna lewini	Scalloped hammerhead, kidney-headed shark, bronze hammerhead	1,2,3,4,5,6,9,10,11,12,13,14, 16. All levels, tropical and warm waters, inshore and far offshore	420 ♀260 ♂214	Olive-brown, charcoal tips to fins	Most common hammerhead. Probably unaggressive. In some areas, forms huge schools when migrating. Has reputation for attacking people but the large hammerheads are often mistaken for one another. Scientists studying these hammerheads have found them unaggressive.
Sphyrna media	Scoophead	2,3,4,5. Tropical inshore waters	150 ♀116	Grey or mouse-grey, pale below	Sphyrna = hammer. All hammerheads are IGFA game fish.
Sphyrna mokarran	Great hammerhead	2,3,4,5,6,8,9,10,11,12,13, 14,16. Shallow reefs, and at moderate depths offshore	610 ♀365 ♂285	Dark olive, paler below	Sometimes found in water 1 m (3 ft) deep. Diet includes stingrays; these sharks have been found with many stings stuck in their mouths (one had about 50). Feared as a man-eater but is merely a strong suspect. Potentially very dangerous.
Sphyrna tiburo	Bonnethead, shovelhead, bonnet shark	1,2,3,4,5,6. Estuaries, bays and coral reefs, usually shallow waters	150 ♀107 ♂88	Mouse-grey, paler below	Head is quite rounded. Usually found in small groups. Tiburo = Spanish for shark. Closely studied by scientists who have discovered they have a wide range of 'body language' postures.
Sphyrna tudes	Smalleye hammerhead	4. Inshore waters	150 ♀134 ♂127	Mouse-grey, paler below	Known to eat young scalloped hammerheads, and also to enter fresh water. Tudes = hammer (Latin).
Sphyrna zygaena	Smooth hammerhead, balance fish, black hammerhead	Worldwide. Inshore and offshore, sub-tropical and tropical waters	400 ♀257 ♂233	Olive-grey, dusky tips to fins	Often seen at surface with dorsal fins and tail exposed. Considered dangerous. Young 55 cm (21.7 in) long at birth, in litters of 29 to 37.

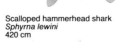

Whitetip reef shark
Triaenodon obesus
213 cm

Winghead shark
Eusphyra blochii
152 cm

Scalloped hammerhead shark
Sphyrna lewini
420 cm

179

FACTS, FALLACIES AND RECORDS

Shark records – especially any claiming great size – are notoriously difficult to verify. The figures quoted here are those considered by most experts to be accurate. They err on the side of caution. It is almost certain that larger and heavier sharks have been seen or caught, but not enough evidence is available to confirm them as records.

The following questions are those most often asked about sharks. Not surprisingly, almost all are concerned with the dozen or so species that are popularly believed to be maneaters – the most 'shark-like' of this diverse and fascinating group of creatures.

Which is the largest shark?

The whale shark *Rhiniodon typus* is not only the world's largest shark, but also the world's largest fish. This plankton-eating giant reaches a length of perhaps 18 m (59 ft). The largest accurately measured specimen, caught off Pakistan in 1949, measured 12.65 m (41.5 ft) long and weighed 21.5 tonnes. There are numerous, almost certainly exaggerated, reports of specimens measuring up to 21 m (70 ft) long.

Next largest, after the whale shark, is the basking shark *Cetorhinus maximus*, also a filter feeder. Data on the sizes of these creatures is more reliable because they have been heavily fished by commercial organisations around the world for many years.

The largest accurately measured specimen reached 12.3 m (40.25 ft) and weighed an estimated 16 tonnes. It was caught off New Brunswick, Canada in August 1851. There are numerous claims made for record specimens which range up to an unlikely 15 m (50 ft), but none have been confirmed.

Which is the smallest shark?

The spined pygmy shark *Squaliolus laticaudus,* which grows to only about 250 mm (9.8 in), is probably the world's smallest shark. Males mature at around 150 mm (5.9 in) and females at 180 mm (7.1 in). A close contender for this title is the pygmy ribbontail catshark *Eridacnis radcliffei* which grows to about the same size. Males of this species mature at 180 mm (7.1 in) and females at 160 mm (6.3 in).

Alf Dean, facing the camera, and a large great white shark. Dean has held the world record for the largest shark ever caught on a fishing line since 1959. His record fish, which weighed 1208.38 kg (2664 lb), was caught on 60-kg (132.27-lb) breaking strain line.

Which is the largest maneater?

Few things in the popular world of sharks and shark stories are as much disputed as the record for the largest dangerous shark to be seen or caught. Considerable fame accompanies any claim to be associated with the largest maneater, so it is hardly surprising that individuals are tempted to exaggerate sightings and encounters. One important point to bear in mind is that the sizes and weights of sharks do not necessarily increase in proportion to one another. Much depends on the sex and condition of the fish.

It is also important to

A thresher shark *Alopias vulpinus* is hauled alongside a fishing boat off the coast of New Zealand. The tails on these extraordinary sharks are about the same length as their bodies. Threshers are thought to be harmless to humans, although there is a story of a fisherman decapitated by the tail of a large thresher in the Atlantic.

Not all shark fishermen use conventional means to secure their catches. This 1470-kg (3234-lb) great white shark was lassoed near Albany by West Australian Fisheries and Wildlife Officer Colin Ostle.

remember that it is often difficult to estimate the lengths of objects in the water, especially when their extremities are submerged or ill defined. In a revealing series of experiments, conducted at the Mote Marine Laboratory in Florida, students were asked to look at two sharks in a pool for 10 seconds, and then to estimate their lengths. Estimates for the length of a 1.8-m (72-in) bull shark ranged from 1.6 m (63 in) to 3.3 m (128 in), with a mean of 2.2 m (85.5 in). For a 1.2-m (46-in) lemon shark the estimates ranged from 74 cm (29 in) to 1.6 m (61 in), with a surprisingly low mean of 1.16 m (45.5 in).

The great white *Carcharodon carcharias* is the largest shark, after the big filter feeders. Its awesome reputation, and the fact that it has been responsible for more human fatalities than any other species, have meant that many myths have grown up around it over the years. It is now difficult to separate fact from fantasy in the stories that are told about it.

The largest great white shark actually weighed appears to be a 3312-kg (7302-lb) specimen caught off the coast of Cuba in 1945. It was 6.4 m (21 ft) long.

The largest great white actually measured was probably a monster caught by fishermen off the Azores in 1978. It was brought ashore and measured by a reliable observer at 9 m (29.5 ft). The giant fish was estimated to weigh around 4540 kg (10 000 lb).

Larger sharks have been claimed, but in every case it is difficult or impossible to verify the facts. There is a second hand report of a 11.3-m (37-ft) great white stranded in a weir at New Brunswick, Canada in the 1930s, but it has not been satisfactorily confirmed. Many claims have been made by sailors and fishermen for record sharks – especially in cases where it has been possible to measure a shark in the water alongside a boat of known length.

One claim often put forward concerns a great white caught off Port Fairy, Victoria in 1852. This specimen, it was claimed, measured 11.13 m (36.5 ft). However, the jaws of this shark are in the British Museum in London where they have been examined by researchers. Comparisons with jaws from sharks of known length seem to indicate that the Port Fairy shark probably only measured about 5.4 m (17.7 ft).

The record for the largest great white (or, indeed, any shark) caught on a rod and line – a claim that is recognised by the International Game Fishing Association – belongs to Alf Dean. His 1208.38-kg (2664.02-lb) monster was landed at Ceduna, South Australia, in 1959. It measured 5.13 m (16.83 ft). A 1566-kg (3452-lb) great white caught by Donald Braddock and Frank Mundus in August 1986 off the US east coast was not recognised by the IGFA, nor was 1537-kg (3388-lb) shark caught by Clive Green off Albany, Western Australia, in 1976. The latter claim was disallowed because whale meat was used as bait, which is forbidden under game fishing rules.

Next largest of the dangerous sharks is the tiger *Galeocerdo cuvier.* The largest accurately measured specimen, which was caught in a shark net off Newcastle, NSW in 1954, measured 5.5 m (18 ft) and weighed 1524 kg (3360 lb). Another shark of the same size was caught off Mackay, Queensland in 1980. Again, there have been exaggerated claims of tigers measuring 9 m (30 ft) or more.

The all-tackle gamefishing

The goblin, perhaps the strangest of all the world's sharks. Specimens of this deep-water species are rarely seen. Most of those captured are taken in deepwater trawls, or on longlines. Freshly caught goblin sharks are a pinkish-white colour.

record for a tiger stands at 807.4 kg (1780 lb), for a shark caught in 1964 off South Carolina, USA, by Walter Maxwell. This giant specimen was 4.229 m (13.88 ft) long.

Two other large shark species are the Greenland shark *Somniosus microcephalus* and the related Pacific sleeper shark *Somniosus pacificus.* In 1895 a 6.4-m (21-ft) Greenland shark was caught in the Firth of Forth, Scotland. It weighed 1021 kg (2250 lb). In 1966 two scientists in a research submarine at a depth of 1219 m (4000 ft) off the coast of California came upon a giant Pacific sleeper shark that they estimated to be 9.1 m (30 ft) long. Both of these sightings were of exceptionally large examples of their species.

Not all sharks are large
It is an interesting fact that of the 344 known species of sharks, only 39 are known to grow to over 3 m

(9.8 ft). Over half – 176 species – are under one metre (39 in) long at their maximum.

Which is the most common shark?
Piked dogfish *Squalus acanthias,* which are found in waters around the world from the coasts of Scandinavia to southern Chile, are probably the most common sharks. At various times they have supported important fisheries in several countries. It has been estimated that in 1904-05 some 27 million were taken off the coast of Massachusetts, USA, alone. On occasions longline fishermen have reported catching a piked dogfish on nearly every hook on a 1500-hook line. These sharks grow to a maximum size of only about 1.6 m (63 in).

Which is the rarest shark?
Fourteen sharks are known from one specimen only, but in most cases

these are fish that have a limited range, and perhaps live at great depths in the ocean.

It is a remarkable fact that a species of shark that can grow up to 4.5 m (14.8 ft) escaped detection until 1976. Only two specimens of the large, filter-feeding megamouth shark *Megachasma pelagios* have so far been caught. The first was discovered in strange circumstances when an oceanographic research vessel hauled in two parachute sea-anchors from a depth of about 165 m (541 ft) in waters off Hawaii, to find a megamouth entangled in one of them. It was suggested that the shark had been swimming along with its mouth open to catch small crustaceans when it encountered the parachute, which became entangled in its tiny teeth.

Which is the strangest shark?
This title must belong to any one of the hammerhead sharks (*Eusphyra blochii* or *Sphyrna sp.*) or to the bizarre, deep-water goblin shark *Mitsukurina owstoni*.

No really satisfactory explanation has been put forward for the strange shape of the hammerhead's head. It has been suggested that the wide separation of the fish's nostrils, and its habit of swinging its head from side to side while swimming, may enable it to

detect smells over a much wider area than would otherwise be possible. Other theories suggest that the shape of the head may make it a more efficient swimmer, with better manoeuverability.

The first specimen of a goblin shark was captured in waters off Japan in 1898. Fossil teeth from this strange shark had been known since the middle of the nineteenth century, but researchers had assumed it was extinct. Goblin sharks live in the deep oceans and are therefore rarely seen. The strange projections on the tops of their heads are probably an adaptation for feeding, although almost nothing is known about the lives of these curious creatures.

Which shark is most dangerous to humans?
Of the 344 known species of sharks, only about 27 are known to have attacked people or boats. Another 12 species are suspected of attacking people, and a further 28 have the potential to be dangerous. The most dangerous sharks

(excluding the plankton eaters) are all over two metres (6.6 ft) long.

Of the sharks positively identified in attacks on people, three stand out as being most dangerous – the great white *Carcharodon carcharias*, the tiger *Galeocerdo cuvier* and the bull *Carcharhinus leucas*. Between them these three sharks have been responsible for at least 80 deaths. The most blamed was the great white with 32 attacks, next was the tiger with 27 attacks and last the bull with 21 attacks.

How long do sharks live?
The life span of sharks has been something of a mystery for many years. Only recently, as the results of tagging studies start to become available (see p 47), has it been possible to make realistic estimates. Generally, it appears that the slow-growing sharks live longest. Both the Port Jackson shark *Heterodontus portusjacksoni* and the whitetip reef shark *Triaenodon obesus* probably live to about 25 years, while the tope shark

---

REAPING THE BENEFITS OF FRIENDSHIP

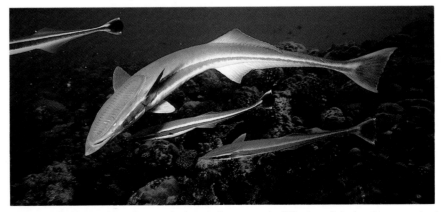

The remarkable sucking disc on the head of a remora is difficult to dislodge once attached.

Sharks are often seen with two companions – pilot fish and remoras. The relationship between pilot fish and sharks is little understood. They do not appear to depend on sharks for food, nor do they lead sharks, as was once suggested.

Remoras have a disc on the tops of their heads with which they can attach themselves to the skin of a shark, or any other large fish or floating object, by vacuum action. Remoras, like pilot fish, do not generally share a shark's food – the only benefit they receive from the association seems to be free travel.

Galeorhinus galeus and the piked dogfish *Squalus acanthias* may have a life span of around 40 years. Scientists have claimed that some piked dogfish may live as long as 100 years, and a similar figure is sometimes suggested for large great white sharks *Carcharodon carcharias*.

How fast do sharks swim?

Most sharks are slow swimmers, only reaching maximum speed while chasing food. Few actual measurements have been made, but the work that has been done suggests that the warm blooded species, such as the mako *Isurus oxyrhinchus*, porbeagle *Lamna nasus* and great white *Carcharodon carcharias* can all sustain higher swimming speeds than other sharks. On occasions makos will leap from the water, and in order to do that they must reach at least 35 km/h (22 mph) in short bursts. Other researchers claim to have measured steady speeds of 39 km/h (24.5 mph) from blue sharks *Prionace glauca,* with short bursts of 69 km/h (43 mph), although this seems unlikely.

An idea of normal cruising speeds can be gained from tagging studies of sharks during migrations. The fastest sustained trip so far recorded was by a mako which covered 2413 km (1500 miles) in 86 days at a rate of 28 km (17.6 miles) a day. Shorter journeys of 400 km (248 miles), or more, in seven days are common. This means the journeys must have been accomplished at speeds of at least 2.4 km/h (1.5 mph). However, because sharks do not normally swim in straight lines all the time, they would have covered considerably more than 400 km during such a journey. During normal day-to-day activities sharks are thought to swim around at a much more sedate pace of about 1 km/h (0.7 mph).

How deep do sharks go?

So little is known about the great ocean depths that it is impossible to give an accurate answer to this question. A number of deep water sharks have been caught below 3500 m (11 500 ft), but they may easily descend to the deep ocean floor on occasions (the deepest ocean trench plunges to 11 038 m [36 204 ft] below sea level).

Some deep water species, such as the cookiecutter shark *Isistius brasiliensis,* rise to the surface to feed at night, making a remarkable journey which involves a vertical swim of around 7 km (4.4 miles) there and back.

Which shark is the greatest traveller?

This distinction undoubtedly belongs to the blue shark *Prionace glauca*. Migrations of from 2000 to 3000 km (1200 to 1700 miles) are common, and the record so far is for a journey of 5980 km (3740 miles) from New York State to Brazil.

Other sharks are also great travellers, and records exist of movements of over 2500 km (1550 miles) by makos *Isurus oxyrhinchus,* tigers *Galeocerdo cuvier* and sandbar sharks *Carcharhinus plumbeus*. Bull sharks *Carcharhinus leucas* have been found over 3700 km (2300 miles) from the sea in the upper reaches of the Amazon, so they are presumably capable of swimming that distance.

Do sharks live in fresh water?

Only two species of sharks are conclusively proved to venture into fresh water – the bull shark *Carcharhinus leucas* and the Ganges shark *Glyphis gangeticus,* although half a dozen others are suspected of entering streams, and several can tolerate brackish water for short periods of time.

At one time bull sharks caused considerable confusion. They are found in one major lake, Lake Nicaragua, and many rivers, including the Ganges, the Zambezi, the Mississippi, the Tigris and the Amazon. Researchers thought that several of these populations were in fact different species, and named them accordingly. Only in recent years has it become obvious that they are all bull sharks.

Bull sharks have also been confused with the only other proven freshwater species, the Ganges shark. This is an extremely rare fish which is known only from a few specimens taken from the Ganges and Hooghly Rivers in India. It has acquired a fearsome reputation as a maneater, but this may be undeserved; the real culprit may be the bull shark.

Is it true that sharks must turn on their backs to attack?

It is often asserted that sharks cannot bite while swimming the right way up, which is completely incorrect. This idea was first put forward by Aristotle in 330 BC in his *Historia Animalium,* and is still believed by many people today. Sharks can, and do, attack their prey in whichever way is most convenient.

Are sharks attracted by human blood?

This is another 'truth' that is frequently quoted. In fact experiments have shown that sharks do not appear to be particularly interested in the blood of any mammal, although they are very sensitive to extremely small concentrations of fish blood in water. Further confirmation of this fact is provided by the number of cases in which sharks have bitten humans once and then lost interest. Despite this, some experts still suggest that anyone with an open wound would do well to avoid swimming in water where sharks may be found – just in case.

WORLD GAME FISHING RECORDS FOR SHARKS

John Robinson, *an Australian angler, once held the world record with this 620-kg (1422-lb) tiger shark. The title is now held by an angler in the USA.*

Broadly, the aim of game fishing is to catch the largest possible fish on the lightest possible line. Ten weights of line may be used, ranging from 1 kg (2.2 lb) breaking strain to 60 kg (132.27 lb) breaking strain. Records are established for the heaviest fish of each species caught on the various line weights. Local records are verified by the various national associations, and world records by the International Game Fish Association in the United States of America.

Strict rules govern the sport, the expressed aim being to give the fish a fighting chance. Lines, hooks, rods and other equipment must comply with a rigid set of definitions. Only the angler who hooks the fish is allowed to play it – no other person is allowed to help, or to touch the rod or line.

The following records are for 'all tackle' – any weight of line up to the maximum of 60 kg – and were those recognised by the International Game Fishing Association in January 1989.

Bob Dyer *and a great white shark weighing over 900 kg (2000 lb). Dyer died in 1984, but many of his fishing records, for various line weights, still stand today.*

Species	Weight	Length	Place caught	Date	Angler
Blacktip shark	122.75 kg 270.56 lb	245.00 cm 96.46 in	Malindi Bay, Kenya	21 Sept. 1984	Jurgen Oeder
Blue shark	198.22 kg 437.00 lb	363.22 cm 143.00 in	Catherine Bay, NSW, Australia	2 Oct. 1976	Peter Hyde
Bull shark	222.26 kg 290.00 lb	228.60 cm 90.00 in	Dauphin Island, Alabama, USA	30 Aug. 1986	Phillip Wilson
Copper shark	145.30 kg 320.31 lb	245.00 cm 96.46 in	Portimao Lagos, Portugal	5 Sept. 1987	Rudolf Streur
Dusky shark	346.54 kg 764.00 lb	297.18 cm 117.00 in	Longboat Key, Florida, USA	28 May 1982	Warren Girle
Greenland shark	775.00 kg 1708.56 lb	408.00 cm 160.63 in	Trondheimsfiord, Norway	18 Oct. 1987	Terje Nordtvedt
Hammerhead shark	449.50 kg 991.00 lb	447.04 cm 176.00 in	Sarasota, Florida, USA	30 May 1982	Allen Ogle
Lemon shark	180.07 kg 397.00 lb	304.80 cm 120.00 in	Dunedin, Florida, USA	29 Apr. 1977	R. M. Guccione
Mako shark	489.88 kg 1080.00 lb	345.80 cm 136.00 in	Montauk, New York, USA	26 Aug. 1979	J. L. Melanson
Porbeagle shark	210.92 kg 465.00 lb	281.94 cm 111.00 in	Padstow, Cornwall, England	23 Jul. 1976	Jorge Potier
Sandtiger shark	144.24 kg 318.00 lb	251.46 cm 99.00 in	Nags Head, North Carolina, USA	25 May 1986	Dave Wolfe
Sixgill shark	466.00 kg 1027.00 lb	329.00 cm 129.53 in	Faial, Azores Islands	13 Nov. 1987	W. P. Reece
Spinner shark	86.18 kg 190.00 lb	203.20 cm 80.00 in	Flagler Beach, Florida, USA	3 Apr. 1986	Gladys Prior
Spiny dogfish	6.37 kg 14.06 lb	98.00 cm 35.58 in	Kenmare Bay, Co. Kerry, Ireland	29 May 1988	Horst Muller
Thresher shark	363.80 kg 802.00 lb	487.98 cm 192.12 in	Tutukaka, New Zealand	8 Feb. 1981	Dianne North
Tiger shark	807.40 kg 1780.00 lb	422.91 cm 166.50 in	Cherry Grove, South Carolina, USA	14 Jun. 1964	Walter Maxwell
Tope shark	33.00 kg 72.75 lb	146.05 cm 57.50 in	Parengarenga Harbour, New Zealand	19 Dec. 1986	Melanie Feldman
White shark	1208.38 kg 2664.00 lb	513.08 cm 202.00 in	Ceduna, South Australia	21 Apr. 1959	Alfred Dean

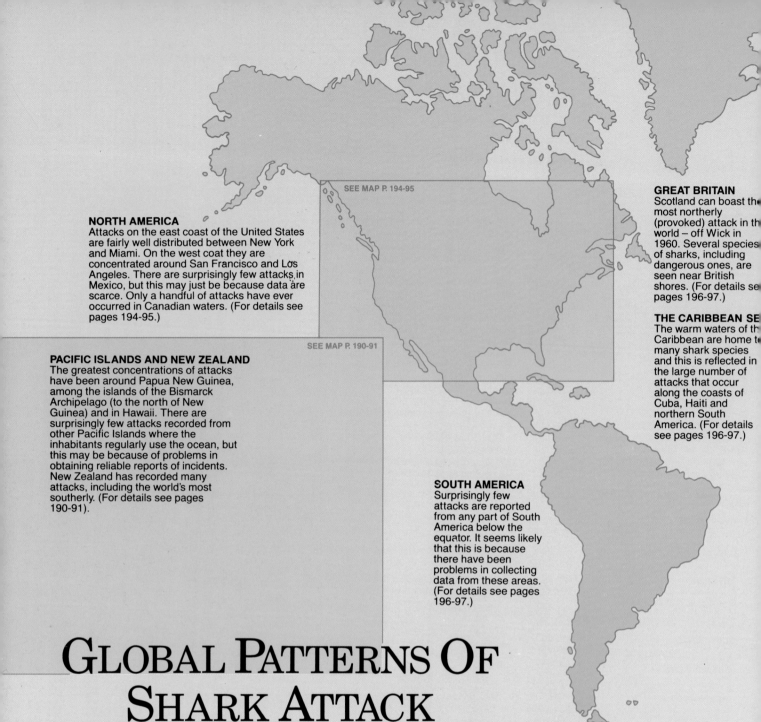

SEE MAP P. 194-95

NORTH AMERICA
Attacks on the east coast of the United States are fairly well distributed between New York and Miami. On the west coat they are concentrated around San Francisco and Los Angeles. There are surprisingly few attacks in Mexico, but this may just be because data are scarce. Only a handful of attacks have ever occurred in Canadian waters. (For details see pages 194-95.)

SEE MAP P. 190-91

GREAT BRITAIN
Scotland can boast the most northerly (provoked) attack in the world – off Wick in 1960. Several species of sharks, including dangerous ones, are seen near British shores. (For details see pages 196-97.)

THE CARIBBEAN SE
The warm waters of the Caribbean are home to many shark species and this is reflected in the large number of attacks that occur along the coasts of Cuba, Haiti and northern South America. (For details see pages 196-97.)

PACIFIC ISLANDS AND NEW ZEALAND
The greatest concentrations of attacks have been around Papua New Guinea, among the islands of the Bismarck Archipelago (to the north of New Guinea) and in Hawaii. There are surprisingly few attacks recorded from other Pacific Islands where the inhabitants regularly use the ocean, but this may be because of problems in obtaining reliable reports of incidents. New Zealand has recorded many attacks, including the world's most southerly. (For details see pages 190-91).

SOUTH AMERICA
Surprisingly few attacks are reported from any part of South America below the equator. It seems likely that this is because there have been problems in collecting data from these areas. (For details see pages 196-97.)

GLOBAL PATTERNS OF SHARK ATTACK

The following pages examine, with maps and graphs, shark attacks around the world. Sites of almost all known recorded attacks are pinpointed, and attack figures are broken down month by month, to see if any seasonal patterns emerge.

In 1958 the United States Navy provided funds for a Shark Attack File to be established at the Smithsonian Institution in Washington, DC. Using old records, reports from scientists, divers and news clipping services, the project compiled a file of 1652 attacks from around the world before funding ceased in 1967. It remains the most detailed list of attacks available.

The information was analysed by Dr H. David Baldridge at the Mote Marine Laboratory in Florida. In assessing the reliability of the information on the File, he noted that in 90 per cent of cases accounts were based largely on information provided by people who were not at the scene of the attack. He also pointed to a geographic or cultural bias in the File – cases came predominantly from English-speaking countries. This presumably reflected a language barrier, rather than any scarcity of attacks in other regions.

Despite these problems, David Baldridge's analysis provides the most reliable picture of shark attack patterns that exists. It also overturns some long and widely held beliefs about shark attacks and shark behaviour.

Over two-thirds of all the documented attacks have occurred since 1940. This is an average of about 28 cases a year, world wide, (less than the 100 cases often cited as a likely average).

All but four of the attacks in the File occurred between 47°S and 46°N. Generally there were very few attacks near the equator, rising to a peak in the middle latitudes and falling off again in colder waters. The correlation between

THE MEDITERRANEAN SEA
Many species of sharks, including some dangerous to humans, are found in the Mediterranean. Several attacks have been recorded in the Adriatic Sea, off the coasts of Italy and Yugoslavia, including the most northerly recorded unprovoked attack in 1934. (For details see pages 196-97.)

EAST ASIA
There is a small concentration of attacks around Singapore, and a few have been recorded off the coasts of China and Japan, but less than might be expected. (For details see pages 196-97).

SOUTH ASIA
The Ganges delta and the Persian Gulf are both areas notorious for shark attacks. However, reports of many attacks on these coasts probably do not reach researchers. (For details see pages 196-97.)

AUSTRALIA
Australia has recorded more attacks than any other country on earth. The majority are concentrated around the major cities, and the others are distributed in a way that reflects the large number of people who live on the coastal fringe. (For details see pages 188-89.)

AFRICA
The most remarkable feature of African shark attacks – apart from those that take place in South Africa – is that there appear to be so few of them. This is almost certainly due to the fact that most occur in remote areas and are not reported. (For details see pages 192-93.)

P. 192

SEE MAP P. 193

SOUTH AFRICA
Most attacks in South Africa occur around Durban, on the Natal coast. A few take place around Cape Town, but none have been recorded on the Atlantic coast north of that city. (For details see pages 192-93.)

SEE MAP P. 188-89

SEE MAP P. 190-91

water temperature and shark attack, however, has more to do with the likelihood of people being in the water when it is warm, than with sharks preferring that temperature. The 'shark attack season' in any locality would be the time when the water was warm enough for humans (above 20°C; 68°F) and not too hot for sharks (less than 30°C; 86°F).

Only a third of recorded attacks were fatal, and the number of fatal attacks is declining. This decline could be due to the greater likelihood today of a victim receiving prompt medical attention.

Baldridge's most significant conclusions concern shark motivation. Only one-quarter of all attack victims received the types of wounds that suggested that the shark's main interest was in feeding. Only 20 per cent of all attacks involved more than one strike, and in only four per cent of cases did the shark behave in a frenzied manner. None of these findings indicate that sharks, which are extremely efficient marine predators, are particularly interested in eating humans.

Baldridge also found no evidence for the popular theory that wounded or bleeding people were more likely to be attacked, or that sharks were attracted to any mammalian blood.

The attacks plotted on the following maps and graphs are taken from a list of approximately 1200 attacks that were in the Shark Attack File in 1967. They show unprovoked and provoked attacks – the latter being where a shark was caught, trapped, speared or somehow aggravated before it eventually attacked.

Attacks on boats, on victims of sea and air disasters (where there is no way of knowing whether the victims were alive or not before the attack) and other doubtful attacks have been excluded from the maps and graphs. The numbers beside some of the markers indicate the number of attacks at that location, and not the number of victims.

187

AUSTRALIAN SHARK ATTACKS

The earliest known attack in Australian waters was in 1803 at Hamelin Bay in Western Australia, when a Mr Lefevre was attacked by a shark and died from his wounds. The unfortunate man was the first of 319 recorded Australian shark attack victims – over one-quarter of all the unprovoked and provoked attacks from around the world recorded in the Shark Attack File.

The distribution of attacks around the coastline largely reflects population densities and the popularity of water activities. With about 220 attacks listed in the file, the east coast of Australia might, on the face of it, appear to be one of the most shark infested areas on earth, but this high number really only reflects the fact that there are a large number of beaches on this coast, with many people using them.

Sydney beaches were notorious for attacks until meshing was introduced in the 1930s. Since then there has not been a shark fatality at a Sydney ocean beach (up to the end of 1988), although attacks still occur within the harbour.

The seas off southern Australia are one of the main haunts of the great white shark, *Carcharodon carcharias*, one of the most dangerous of all sharks. Many of the shark sequences for the film *Jaws* were shot there, and nearly all the record-breaking great white sharks have been caught in these waters. After California, the southern coast of Australia has the second highest incidence of great white shark attacks.

For many years Bass Strait was thought to be the southern limit of shark attacks in Australia. But in January 1959 a naval rating was attacked and killed several hundred metres off Port Arthur in the south-east of Tasmania. Five days later another attack occurred off Port Davey in the south-west. They remain the most southerly attacks in Australian waters.

Unprovoked non-fatal attacks ○
Unprovoked fatal attacks ●
Provoked non-fatal attacks ○
Provoked fatal attacks ●

TIMOR SEA

Wyndhar

Broome

INDIAN OCEAN

Port Hedland

Tropic of Capricorn

WESTERN AUSTRALIA

Geraldton

Perth
Fremantle

2

Esperance

Two-thirds of Australian attacks occurred south of the Tropic of Capricorn, and 80 per cent took place in the five warmest months of the year between November and March.

Attacks north of the tropic were concentrated around the Great Barrier Reef and Torres Strait Islands – both areas where there are a lot of divers. Only 51 per cent occurred between November and March, the southern summer, because more people are likely to go into the water all year round.

Per cent of total
40
30
20
10
0
J F M A M J J A S O N D
Month of year

Per cent of total
40
30
20
10
0
J F M A M J J A S O N D
Month of year

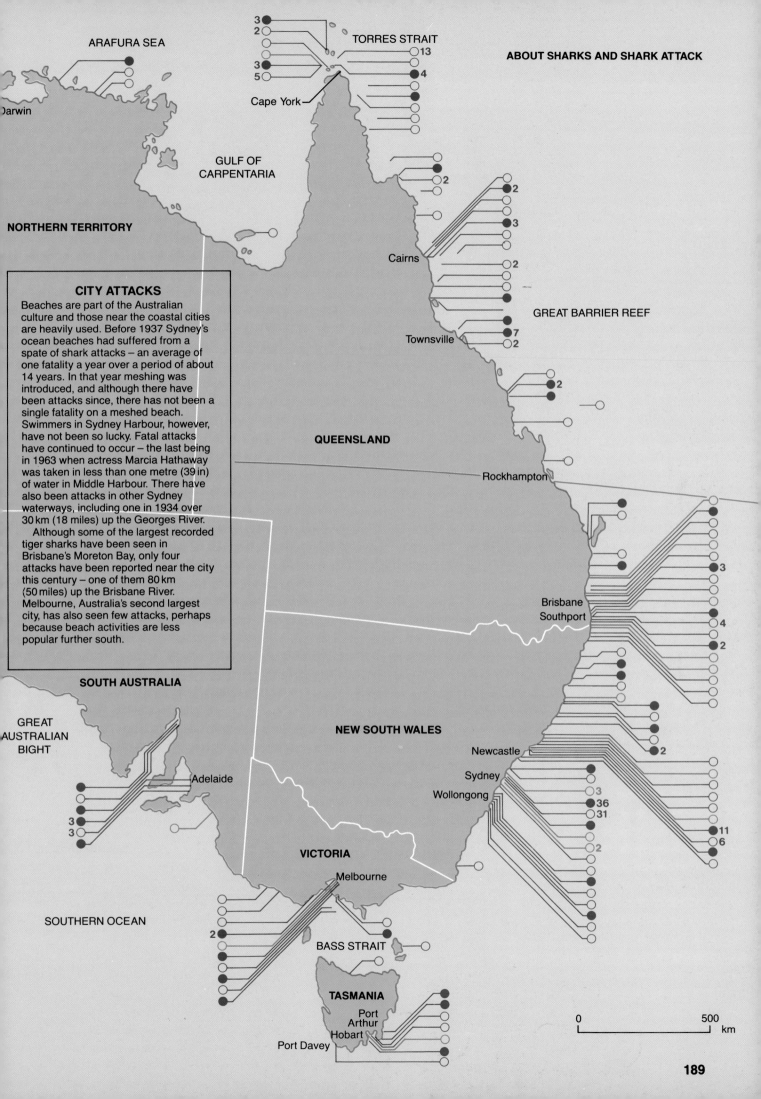

ARAFURA SEA

TORRES STRAIT

ABOUT SHARKS AND SHARK ATTACK

3
2
13
3
5
4

Cape York

Darwin

GULF OF
CARPENTARIA

NORTHERN TERRITORY

2

2

3

Cairns

2

GREAT BARRIER REEF

7
2

Townsville

2

CITY ATTACKS

Beaches are part of the Australian culture and those near the coastal cities are heavily used. Before 1937 Sydney's ocean beaches had suffered from a spate of shark attacks – an average of one fatality a year over a period of about 14 years. In that year meshing was introduced, and although there have been attacks since, there has not been a single fatality on a meshed beach. Swimmers in Sydney Harbour, however, have not been so lucky. Fatal attacks have continued to occur – the last being in 1963 when actress Marcia Hathaway was taken in less than one metre (39 in) of water in Middle Harbour. There have also been attacks in other Sydney waterways, including one in 1934 over 30 km (18 miles) up the Georges River.

Although some of the largest recorded tiger sharks have been seen in Brisbane's Moreton Bay, only four attacks have been reported near the city this century – one of them 80 km (50 miles) up the Brisbane River. Melbourne, Australia's second largest city, has also seen few attacks, perhaps because beach activities are less popular further south.

QUEENSLAND

Rockhampton

SOUTH AUSTRALIA

GREAT
AUSTRALIAN
BIGHT

Adelaide

NEW SOUTH WALES

3

4

2

3

Brisbane
Southport

Newcastle

2

Sydney

3

Wollongong

36
31

2

11
6

3
3

VICTORIA

Melbourne

SOUTHERN OCEAN

2

BASS STRAIT

TASMANIA

Port
Arthur
Hobart

Port Davey

0   500
km

TAIWAN

SOUTH
CHINA
SEA

PHILIPPINE SEA

WAKE
ISLAND

PHILIPPINES

MALAYSIA

MARSHALL
ISLANDS

GILBERT
ISLANDS

INDONESIA

PAPUA
NEW GUINEA

3
2
2
2
5

2
3

2

2
2

SOLOMON
ISLANDS

3

NEW
HEBRIDES

NEW
CALEDONIA

3

1
4
3

AUSTRALIA

NORFOLK
ISLAND

4

NEW ZEALAND

TASMAN SEA

North Island

Auckland

Wellington

Christchurch

South Island

Unprovoked non-fatal attacks
Unprovoked fatal attacks
Provoked non-fatal attacks
Provoked fatal attacks

TASMANIA

SOUTHERN OCEAN

Dunedin

Invercargill

Stewart Island

0   1000
km

Tropic of Cancer

MIDWAY ISLANDS

HAWAIIAN ISLANDS

Pacific Ocean attacks show no obvious shark attack 'season', since nearly all the island groups are in the tropics where diving, swimming and fishing are year-round activities.

PACIFIC OCEAN

CHRISTMAS ISLAND

Equator

New Zealand attacks show a marked seasonal pattern. None were recorded at all in the months between April and November, reflecting the small number of people who are prepared to venture into cold southern waters at that time of the year.

PHOENIX ISLANDS

UVALU

TOKELAU ISLANDS

WESTERN SAMOA

AMERICAN SAMOA

TONGA

COOK ISLANDS

FRENCH POLYNESIA

FIJI

Tropic of Capricorn

NEW ZEALAND AND PACIFIC OCEAN ATTACKS

PITCAIRN GROUP

The map shows the locations of 189 attacks that have been recorded for the Pacific area – 37 per cent of which were fatal – a proportion that is in line with the Shark Attack File as a whole.

Among the cultures of the Pacific islands the importance of sharks is reflected in folklore and myth, in shark gods and shark legends. It would have seemed likely that a large number of attacks should have been recorded from these islands, at least since regular records of dates and facts were kept

after western contact. However, isolation and distance have meant that probably only a fraction of the incidents have reached the Shark Attack File.

The area with the greatest concentration of recorded attacks is Hawaii. Most have been on fishermen – mainly of Japanese extraction – and ordinary swimmers seem to have been relatively immune.

One of the worst mass shark attacks of modern times took place with the sinking of the steamer

Negros off Bondoc Peninsula in the Philippines in 1927. Fifty-five people died, many of them having been taken by sharks as they floundered helpless in the water.

The world's most southerly recorded attack was on 27 January 1962 at 46°S, off the southern end of the South Island of New Zealand. Norman McEwan received deep gashes to his wrist from a 1.5 m (4.9 ft) shark while swimming in waist-deep water. More attacks, some fatal, have been recorded from other parts of the South Island.

AFRICAN AND SOUTH AFRICAN ATTACKS

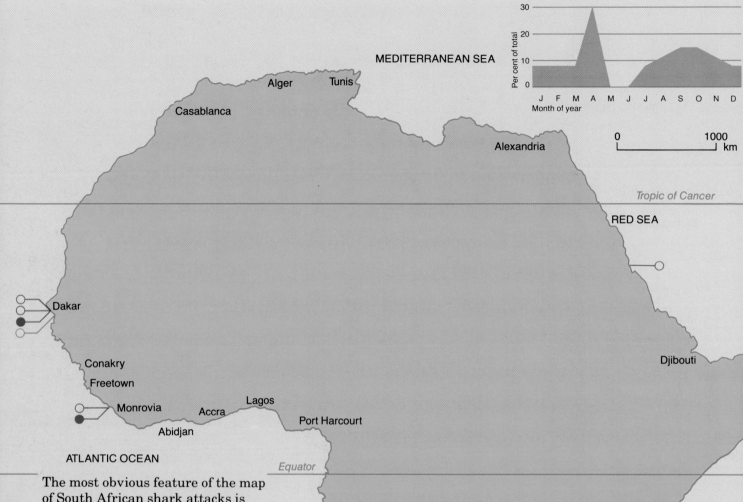

There is no obvious seasonal pattern to attacks over the greater part of Africa. However, these figures are far from complete, so no significant conclusions can be drawn from them.

MEDITERRANEAN SEA

Alger   Tunis

Casablanca

Alexandria

Tropic of Cancer

RED SEA

Dakar

Conakry

Freetown

Lagos

Monrovia   Accra   Port Harcourt

Abidjan

ATLANTIC OCEAN   *Equator*

Djibouti

Mombasa

Dar-es-Salaam

Luanda

Moçambique

Tropic of Capricorn   Walvisbaai

Maputo

Madagascar

Cape Town

INDIAN OCEAN

SOUTHERN OCEAN

The most obvious feature of the map of South African shark attacks is the number concentrated along the eastern coastline of that country. Few people swim along the Atlantic coast due to a cold current that sweeps in from the polar regions, and there have been no recorded attacks along this coast between Cape Town at 34°S and Monrovia, in Liberia, at 6°N. The currents along the eastern coast are warmer, however, and more suitable for water activities.

There is an over-representation of South African attacks which is almost certainly due to the fact that reports of attacks from there were more easily available to researchers compiling the Shark Attack File. It is also noticeable that the majority of recorded South African victims were white, although this group

CITY ATTACKS

Three-quarters of all South African shark attacks have occurred along the beaches of Natal. Durban, the capital of Natal, is the country's major holiday resort and has the greatest concentration of swimmers. Records of early attacks were scantily kept and the earliest known were three, all fatal, that took place in 1906. There are no records of any more attacks at Durban until 1943. Over the next eight years the city suffered a spate of shark attacks – 19 in all. The attacks threatened the popularity of the city as a tourist resort and in 1952 the city council acted, erecting mesh nets along the main beaches. Only three attacks have occurred since, none of them fatal.

South Africa's other major coastal city, Cape Town, has no record of any attacks. The sea there is considerably colder than it is along the Natal coastline, and attracts fewer swimmers.

SOUTH AFRICA

Walvisbaai

Lüderitz

ATLANTIC OCEAN

0 — 400 km

Cape Town
3
2
2

Port Elizabeth

East London

INDIAN OCEAN

NATAL

Durban

Tropic of Capricorn

2
2
8
15
2
2
5
4
3
2
2
3
2

SOUTHERN OCEAN

Unprovoked non-fatal attacks	○
Unprovoked fatal attacks	●
Provoked non-fatal attacks	○
Provoked fatal attacks	●

makes up less than 20 per cent of the population. It seems likely that this was because more whites take part in water sports, rather than a preference on the part of sharks for people with white skins.

Attacks on the beaches of Natal account for three-quarters of all South African cases. In 1940 a remarkable sequence of five fatal attacks took place just south of Durban, the capital of Natal.

Natal was also the location of one of the worst mass shark attacks on record. In 1942, off the northern coast, the *Nova Scotia*, carrying 1000 Italian prisoners of war, was torpedoed. Most people on board died, with a large, although unknown, number taken by sharks.

Another notorious incident, also involving a shipwreck, took place about 100 km (62 miles) to the east of Cape Town at Danger Point when a British troopship, the *Birkenhead*, went aground in 1852. Many of the 455 lives that were lost were due to attacks by packs of sharks.

South African attacks, as in other temperate regions of the world, show a strong seasonal pattern. Seventy-five per cent took place in the five warmer months from November to March, when many people go swimming.

Per cent of total

40
30
20
10
0

J F M A M J J A S O N D
Month of year

UNITED STATES AND CANADIAN ATTACKS

North America, after Australia, has the highest incidence of shark attack in the world: 253 have been recorded in the Shark Attack File – 225 of them along both coasts of the United States, and the remainder in Mexico. Thirty-two per cent of all attacks were fatal. The most northerly (confirmed) attack was off Swampsott, Massachusetts (42° 28'N).

Of the United States attacks, three-quarters took place along the east coast. This coastline is longer than the west coast and the proportion is in line with the relative numbers of people living along the two coasts. The west coast, however, probably has the greatest concentration of great white sharks in the world. Almost 40 per cent of all great white shark attacks have occurred along a 200-km (124-mile) stretch of California.

One of the most notorious of all shark attack sagas occurred off the New Jersey coast in 1916. Over a period of 12 days, along a densely populated section of the coast, five people were attacked. The response was hysterical. Guns and explosives were used against anything that moved in nearby waters for a period of several weeks in an attempt to find the shark responsible. It was assumed that the attacks were the work of one rogue shark (although that theory is now in doubt).

Although sharks, including species dangerous to humans, are common in Canadian waters, there appear to have been been attacks. Author R. M. Ballantyne reported an incident that took place in 1848 in which an Indian family were attacked while canoeing in the Gulf of St. Lawrence. They only escaped by throwing a baby overboard to distract the shark. On another occasion a warden was menaced by a shark while he was crossing ice floes near Basque Island in 1940.

UNITED STATES OF AMERICA

San Francisco

3
2
2
2

3
3
3

Los Angeles

San Diego

2
2
3

PACIFIC OCEAN

Unprovoked non-fatal attacks	○
Unprovoked fatal attacks	●
Provoked non-fatal attacks	○
Provoked fatal attacks	●

0   500
└──────────┘ km

CITY ATTACKS

Few shark attacks have occurred in the New York area. Apart from the notorious events at Matawan in 1916, slightly to the south, in which five people were attacked in 12 days, there have only been five or six attacks in the New York conurbation. Further south, Charlestown, South Carolina, and Miami, Florida, have each suffered a similar number of attacks.

Along the Pacific coast of the United States – one of the main areas in which great white sharks are found – there have been six attacks in the Los Angeles area and in San Francisco, near the northern limit of west coast attacks, there have been two. One of the latter was at Bakers Beach, within sight of the Golden Gate bridge, in which Alfred Kogler, an 18-year-old student was fatally mauled by a great white shark. Further south, around San Diego, there have been five attacks, all in the 1950s, but only one of them was fatal.

Both the east and west coasts of North America cover roughly the same range of latitudes, so it is not surprising that they show essentially the same seasonable patterns of attack. Eighty per cent of east coast attacks (right) took place during the five warmest months, as did 67 per cent of west coast attacks.

GULF OF SAINT LAWRENCE

Saint Lawrence

Swampsott
Boston

New York

ATLANTIC OCEAN

Savannah

New Orleans

Tampa

Miami

GULF OF MEXICO

Tropic of Cancer

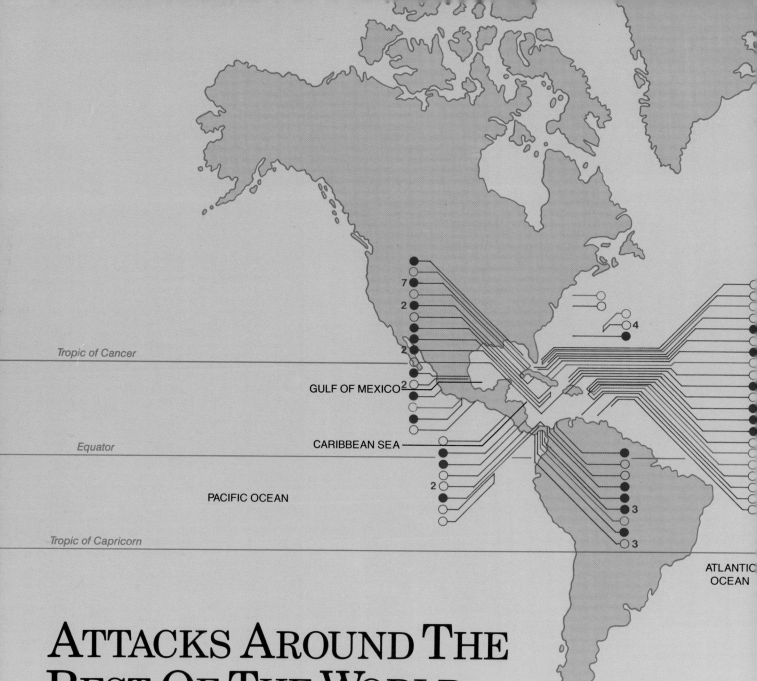

Tropic of Cancer

GULF OF MEXICO

Equator

CARIBBEAN SEA

PACIFIC OCEAN

Tropic of Capricorn

ATLANTIC
OCEAN

ATTACKS AROUND THE REST OF THE WORLD

This map shows the locations of shark attacks in areas that are not included in the preceding maps.

Europe has been relatively free of attacks, although a number have been recorded in the eastern Mediterranean, especially in the Adriatic Sea. The most northerly Mediterranean attack was in the Adriatic in 1934 when 18-year-old Agnes Novak was fatally injured near Susak, Jugoslavia.

The only other European cases outside the Mediterranean both involved sharks caught by fishermen. The most northerly of all attacks took place in the North Sea off Wick, Scotland (58° 26′N), in 1960, when Hans Schapper was bitten on the arm by a small shark

that had been dragged on board a trawler in a net full of fish.

Two-thirds of European attacks have been fatal – twice the world-wide average.

An area with a particularly bad shark attack record is the Persian Gulf. A number of fatal attacks have taken place in the pearl beds and fishing grounds at Ra's At-tannūrah, Saudi Arabia. The river complex at the head of the Gulf is also dangerous. Fatal attacks have occurred 150 km (93 miles) up the Karun River near Ahvāz in Iran.

Another area notorious for sharks is the Ganges Delta, which straddles the border between India and Bangladesh, especially the Hooghly River that flows through

Calcutta. In 1880 alone 20 people were attacked in this area. Further to the east, in Singapore, Hong Kong and China, there have been numerous attacks on divers, swimmers and fishermen.

It seems strange that a small number of attacks (four only) seem to have taken place in Japanese waters. This could be a result of language difficulties that have prevented attacks from being recorded by American researchers.

The same problem may occur in South America which has not apparently been the site of many shark attacks at all. The only recorded South American attack below the equator was at Buenos Aires in 1954. It was not fatal.

MEDITERRANEAN SEA

Iran
ARABIAN GULF

Saudi
Arabia

Japan

China

Bangladesh

India

RED SEA

ARABIAN
SEA

PHILIPPINE
SEA

5

4

Singapore

2

3
3

7
5

INDIAN OCEAN

SOUTHERN OCEAN

Unprovoked non-fatal attacks	○
Unprovoked fatal attacks	●
Provoked non-fatal attacks	○
Provoked fatal attacks	●

Attacks in the Caribbean Sea show
little seasonal weighting – not
surprising for a tropical region of the
world. However, almost half the
Caribbean attacks were fatal – a higher
proportion than the world average.

Per cent of total

40

30

20

10

0

J F M A M J J A S O N D
Month of year

The monthly breakdown of attacks in
the Mediterranean Sea shows an
expected bias towards the warmer
months of the year – 90 per cent took
place in July, August and September,
when many people are swimming.

Per cent of total

40

30

20

10

0

J F M A M J J A S O N D
Month of year

GENERAL INDEX

*Page numbers in bold type indicate main entries, while those
in italic refer to illustrations. See separate species index on
pages 202 to 207 for names that appear in the species charts
(pages 156 to 179).*

SPECIES INDEX

The following index lists both the common and scientific names of all the shark species that appear in the charts on pages 156 to 179. Alternative common names, and some outdated scientific names are also included.

AB

Aculeola nigra 156
African angelshark 161
African lanternshark 158
African ribbontail catshark 172
African sawtail catshark 169
African spotted catshark 170
alligator dogfish 156
Alopias pelagicus 166
Alopias superciliosus 166
Alopias vulpinus 166
alopiidae 166
American sawshark 161
angel fish 162
angel shark 162
angel sharks 161-2
angular roughshark 161
Aprionodon brevipinna see
    Carcharhinus brevipinna 176
Aprionodon isodon see *Carcharhinus isodon* 176
Apristurus atlanticus 167
Apristurus brunneus 167
Apristurus canutus 167
Apristurus herklotsi 167
Apristurus indicus 167
Apristurus investigatoris 167
Apristurus japonicus 167
Apristurus kampae 167
Apristurus laurussoni 167
Apristurus longicephalus 167
Apristurus macrorhynchus 167
Apristurus maderensis 167
Apristurus manis 167
Apristurus microps 167
Apristurus nasutus 168
Apristurus parvipinnis 168
Apristurus platyrhynchus 168
Apristurus profundorum 168
Apristurus riveri 168
Apristurus saldanha 168
Apristurus sibogae 168
Apristurus sinensis 168
Apristurus spongiceps 168
Apristurus stenseni 168
Apristurus verweyi 168
Arabian carpetshark 164
Arabian catshark 169
Arabian smooth-hound 174
Argentine angel shark 161
arrowhead dogfish 157
Asymbolus analis 168
Asymbolus vincenti 168
Atelomycterus macleayi 168
Atelomycterus marmoratus 168
Atlantic angel shark 161
Atlantic ghost catshark 167
Atlantic sharpnose shark 179
Atlantic weasel shark 175
Aulohalaelurus labiosus 168
Australian angel shark 161
Australian marbled catshark 168
Australian sawtail catshark 169
Australian sharpnose shark 179
Australian spotted catshark 168
Australian swellshark 168
Bahamas sawshark 161
balloon shark 169
bamboo sharks 164
banded catshark 170

banded houndshark 175
banded wobbegong 163
barbeled catshark 171
barbeled houndshark 172
barbeled houndsharks 172
barbelthroat carpetshark 163
bareskin dogfish 157
basking shark 166
basking sharks 166
bigeye houndshark 173
bigeye sand tiger 165
bigeye thresher 166
bigeyed sixgill shark 156
bignose shark 175
birdbeak dogfish 157
black dogfish 157
black shark (for combtooth dogfish, also kitefin shark) 157
black whaler 177
blackbelly dogfish 158
blackbelly lanternshark 158
blackgill catshark 170
blackmouth catshark 169
blackmouthed dogfish 169
blacknose shark 175
blackspotted catshark 168, 170, 171
blackspotted smooth-hound 174
blacktail reef shark 177
blacktailed spurdog 160
blacktip reef shark 177
blacktip sawtail catshark 169
blacktip shark 177
blacktip tope 173
Blainville's dogfish 160
blind shark 163
blind sharks 163
blotched catshark 172
blue pointers 166
blue shark 178
blue whaler 178
blue-dog 178
bluegrey carpetshark 163
bluespotted bambooshark 164
bluespotted catshark 164
bluntnose sixgill shark 156
boa catshark 171
bone shark 166
bonito shark 166
Bonnaterre's deepwater shark 157
bonnethead 179
bonnethead sharks 179
Borneo catshark 168
Borneo shark 176
brachaeluridae 163
Brachaelurus waddi 163
bramble shark 156
bramble sharks 156
Brazilian shark 159
Brazilian sharpnose shark 178
bristly catshark 170
broadbanded lanternshark 158
broadfin sawtail catshark 169
broadfin shark 178
broadgill catshark 168
broadnose catshark 167
broadnose sevengill shark 156
broadsnout 156
brown catshark 163, 167, 170

C

brown lanternshark 158
brown shyshark 170
brown smooth-hound 174
brownbanded bambooshark 164
brownspotted catshark 164, 171
bull huss 172
bull shark 176
bulldog shark 156, 162
bullhead sharks 162
calf shark 156
Campeche catshark 170
carcharhinidae 175-9
Carcharhiniformes 167-79
Carcharhinus acronotus 175
Carcharhinus ahenea see *C. brachyurus* 176
Carcharhinus albimarginatus 175
Carcharhinus altimus 175
Carcharhinus amblyrhynchoides 175
Carcharhinus amblyrhynchos 175
Carcharhinus amblyrhynchus see *C. wheeleri* 177
Carcharhinus amboinensis 176
Carcharhinus azureus see *C. leucas* 176
Carcharhinus bleekeri see *C. plumbeus* 177
Carcharhinus borneensis 176
Carcharhinus brachyurus 176
Carcharhinus brevipinna 176
Carcharhinus cautus 176
Carcharhinus dussumieri 176
Carcharhinus falciformis 176
Carcharhinus fitzroyensis 176
Carcharhinus floridanus see *C. falciformis* 176
Carcharhinus galapagensis 176
Carcharhinus gangeticus see *Glyphis gangeticus* 178
Carcharhinus glyphis see *Glyphis glyphis* 178
Carcharhinus hemiodon 176
Carcharhinus isodon 176
Carcharhinus japonicus see *C. plumbeus* 177
Carcharhinus lamiella see *C. obscurus* 177
Carcharhinus leucas 176
Carcharhinus limbatus 177
Carcharhinus longimanus 177
Carcharhinus macloti 177
Carcharhinus macrurus see *C. obscurus* 177
Carcharhinus maculipinnus see *C. brevipinna* 176
Carcharhinus maou see *C. longimanus* 177
Carcharhinus melanopterus 177
Carcharhinus menisorrah see *C. amblyrhynchos* 175 or *C. dussumieri* 176
Carcharhinus milberti see *C. plumbeus* 177
Carcharhinus nicaraguensis see *C. leucas* 176
Carcharhinus obscurus 177
Carcharhinus oxyrhynchus see *Isogomphodon oxyrhynchus* 178
Carcharhinus perezi 177
Carcharhinus platyodon see *C.*

G

frilled-gilled shark 156
fringefin lanternshark 158
Furgaleus macki 173
Furgaleus ventralis see *F. macki* 173
Galapagos bullhead shark 162
Galapagos shark 176
Galeocerdo arcticus see *G. cuvier* 177
Galeocerdo cuvier 177
Galeolamna macrurus see *Carcharhinus obscurus* 177
Galeolamna stevensi see *Carcharhinus plumbeus* 177
Galeorhinus australis see *G. galeus* 173
Galeorhinus chilensis see *G. galeus* 173
Galeorhinus galeus 173
Galeorhinus omanensis see *Iago omanensis* 173
Galeorhinus zyopterus see *G. galeus* 173
Galeus arae 169
Galeus boardmani 169
Galeus eastmani 169
Galeus melastomus 169
Galeus melastomus murinus see *G. murinus* 169
Galeus murinus 169
Galeus nipponensis 169
Galeus piperatus 169
Galeus polli 169
Galeus sauteri 169
Galeus schultzi 169
Ganges shark 176, 178
gecko catshark 169
ghost catshark 167
giant sleepy shark 165
Ginglymostoma brevicaudatum 165
Ginglymostoma cirratum 165
Ginglymostoma ferrugineum see *Nebrius ferrugineus* 165
ginglymostomatidae 165
Glyphis gangeticus 178
Glyphis glyphis 178
goblin shark 165
Gogolia filewoodi 173
golden dogfish 157
Gollum attenuatus 172
graceful catshark 172
graceful shark 175
granular dogfish 157
great blue shark 178
great hammerhead 179
great lanternshark 158
great white shark 166
green dogfish 158
green lanternshark 158
Greenland shark 159
grey bambooshark 164
grey nurse shark 165
grey reef shark 175
grey reef whaler 176
grey shark 156
grey sharpnose shark 178
grey smooth-hound 173
ground sharks 167-79
Gulf catshark 168
gully shark 175
gulper shark 156
gulper sharks 156
gummy shark 173
gurry shark 159

H

Halaelurus alcocki 169
Halaelurus analis see *Asymbolus analis* 168
Halaelurus bivius see *Schroederichthys bivius* 171
Halaelurus boesemani 170
Halaelurus buergeri 170
Halaelurus canescens 170
Halaelurus chilensis see *Schroederichthys chilensis* 171
Halaelurus dawsoni 170
Halaelurus hispidus 170
Halaelurus immaculatus 170
Halaelurus lineatus 170
Halaelurus lutarius 170
Halaelurus natalensis 170
Halaelurus quagga 170
Halaelurus vincenti see *Asymbolus vincenti* 168
Halaelurus labiosus see *Aulohalaelurus labiosus* 168
Halsydrus maccoyi see *Cetorhinus maximus* 166
Halsydrus maximus see *Cetorhinus maximus* 166
hammerhead sharks 179
Haploblepharus edwardsii 170
Haploblepharus fuscus 170
Haploblepharus pictus 170
hardnose shark 177
hardnose smooth-hound 174
harlequin catshark 172
Hawaiian lanternshark 158
head shark 169
hemigaleidae 175
Hemigaleus microstoma 175
Hemipristis elongatus 175
hemiscylliidae 164
Hemiscyllium freycineti 164
Hemiscyllium hallstromi 164
Hemiscyllium ocellatum 164
Hemiscyllium strahani 164
Hemiscyllium tricuspidare see *H. trispeculare* 164
Hemiscyllium trispeculare 164
Hemitriakis japanica 173
Hemitriakis leucoperiptera 173
Heptranchias perlo 156
heterodontidae 162
Heterodontiformes 162
Heterodontus francisci 162
Heterodontus galeatus 162
Heterodontus japonicus 162
Heterodontus mexicanus 162
Heterodontus portusjacksoni 162
Heterodontus quoyi 162
Heterodontus ramalheira 162
Heterodontus zebra 162
Heteroscyllium colcloughi 163
Heteroscymnoides marleyi 159
Heteroscymnus longus see *Somniosus rostratus* 160
hexanchidae 156
Hexanchiformes 156
Hexanchus griseus 156
Hexanchus vitulus 156
hoary catshark 167
Holohalaelurus punctatus 170
Holohalaelurus regani 170

IJKL

hooded carpetshark 164
hooktooth dogfish 156
hooktooth shark 175
horn shark 162
horn sharks 162
horned sharks 162
houndsharks 173-5
humantin 160
humpback smooth-hound 174
huss, bull 172
Hypogaleus hyugaensis 173
Hypoprion macloti see *Carcharhinus macloti* 177
Hypoprion playfairi see *Carcharhinus melanopterus* 177
Hypoprion signatus see *Carcharhinus signatus* 177
Iago garricki 173
Iago omanensis 173
Iceland catshark 167
Indian sand tiger 165
Indian swellshark 169
Indonesian speckled carpetshark 164
Isabel's swellshark 168
Isistius brasiliensis 159
Isistius plutodus 159
Isogomphodon oxyrhynchus 178
Isurus glaucus see *I. oxyrinchus* 166
Isurus oxyrinchus 166
Isurus paucus 167
Izak 170
Izak catshark 170
Japanese angel shark 162
Japanese bullhead shark 162
Japanese catshark 167
Japanese sawshark 161
Japanese spurdog 160
Japanese topeshark 173
Japanese wobbegong 163
Java shark 176
Juncrus vincenti see *Asymbolus vincenti* 168
kitefin shark 157
knifetooth dogfish 159
Knopp's shark 176
Lamiopsis temmincki 178
Lamna ditropis 167
Lamna nasus 167
Lamna philippi see *L. nasus* 167
Lamna whitleyi see *L. nasus* 167
lamnidae 166-7
Lamniformes 165-7
lanternsharks 158
largenose catshark 168
largespine velvet dogfish 157
large-spotted dogfish 172
largetooth cookiecutter shark 159
leafscale gulper shark 156
lemon shark 178
lemon sharks 178
leopard catshark 171
leopard shark 164, 175
Leptocharias smithii 172
leptochariidae 172
lesser sixgill shark 156
lesser soupfin shark 173
lined catshark 170
lined lanternshark 158
little gulper shark 157

M

NOP

QRS

ACKNOWLEDGEMENTS

Many people and organisations assisted in the preparation of this book. The publishers would like to thank them all, particularly:

Australian Museum, Sydney; Mr Foster Bam; Bank of England; Guy Bevan; Henri Bource; John Casey, National Marine Fisheries Service, Narragansett; Coledale Surf Club; Dr Leonard J. V. Compagno; Robert Curry; Stephanie Davenport; Wade Doak; Sara Dodds; Rod Grainger of *Bounty Hunter*; Howard Hall; Peter Huck; Robyn Hudson; Stuart Inder; Eric Love; Mitchell Library, Sydney; Museum of Applied Arts and Sciences, Sydney; National Library of Jamaica; Newcastle and Port Stephens GFC; Ocean Leather Corporation; Qantas Airways Ltd; Sean Semler; Linda Spain; State Library of New South Wales; Dr J. D. Stevens; Dr Leighton R. Taylor, Waikiki Aquarium; Dr Tony Underwood; Robert J. Woodward.

The following organisations and individuals provided photographs and gave permission for them to be reproduced.

6-7: Ron & Valerie Taylor. 8-9: Ron & Valerie Taylor. 12: Photri. 14: tl, Kathie Atkinson; others, Ron & Valerie Taylor. 16 and 17: tr, tl, Dianne R. Hughes. 20: David Doubilet. 21: United States Navy. 24: t, Bill Wood; b, Ron & Valerie Taylor. 26: Ron & Valerie Taylor. 27: United States Navy. 28: tl, Nick Otway; bl, br, Ron & Valerie Taylor. 29: Foster Bam. 30, 31: David Doubilet. 33: Ron & Valerie Taylor. 35: Ron & Valerie Taylor. 39: t, Susan Turner; b, Noel Kemp. 41: Noel Kemp. 42: tl, Noel Kemp; tr, Susan Turner. 43: t, Neg. No. 32603. Courtesy American Museum of Natural History; b, Noel Kemp. 44: S. Church. 46: t, United States Navy; b, H. Wes Pratt. 47: Stephanie Davenport. 48: National Marine Fisheries Service – Narragansett Laboratory. 49: T. Halavik. 50-51: Ron & Valerie Taylor. 52-53: Ron & Valerie Taylor. 55: t, Ron & Valerie Taylor; b, Neg. No. 29665, courtesy Dept. Library Services, American Museum of Natural History. 56: United States Navy. 57: Howard Hall. 60-61: Mansell Collection. 62: National Museum, Naples/Agenzia Fotografica Luisa Ricciarni, Milan. 63: Kunsthistorischen Museum, Vienna. 64: t, b, Nick Otway. 65: t, Mary Evans Picture Library. 67: box, all Peter Goadby. 68: Peter Goadby. 69: t, Mary Evans Picture Library; b,

BBC Hulton Picture Library. 71: tl, Stuart Inder. 72, 73: Ron & Valerie Taylor. 74-75: The Photo Library. 76, 77: Ron & Valerie Taylor. 78: t, c, Ron & Valerie Taylor; b, Bill Wood. 79: Ron & Valerie Taylor. 80: Ron & Valerie Taylor. 82, 83: Ron & Valerie Taylor. 84: Ron & Valerie Taylor. 85: tl, Ron & Valerie Taylor; tr, West Australian Newspapers Ltd.; b, Mansell Collection. 86: Ron & Valerie Taylor. 88: K. J. Waddingham. 90: Henri Bource. 91: Ron & Valerie Taylor. 92: Mary Evans Picture Library. 93: Ron & Valerie Taylor. 94: Mitchell Library, Sydney. 95: Ron & Valerie Taylor. 96: Photo Index. 96-97: Bob Mossel. 98: John Fairfax & Sons Ltd. 99: Mary Evans Picture Library. 100: Metropolitan Museum of Art, Wolfe Fund, 1906. Catharine Lorillard Wolfe Collection. (06.1234). 101: t, b, Mary Evans Picture Library. 102: t, Mary Evans Picture Library; b, Ron & Valerie Taylor. 103: Mary Evans Picture Library. 104-105: Mitchell Library, Sydney. 106, 107: Ron & Valerie Taylor. 108-109: Australian Museum/Camera Lucida. 110, 111: Wade Doak. 113: National Library of Jamaica. 115: John Fairfax & Sons Ltd. 116: John Fairfax & Sons Ltd. 117: tr, Ron & Valerie Taylor. 118: John Fairfax & Sons Ltd. 119: tr, John Fairfax & Sons Ltd. 121: Brown

Brothers. 122, 123: Brown Brothers. 124, 125: Brown Brothers. 126: Ron & Valerie Taylor. 128, 129: Ron & Valerie Taylor. 130, 131: Ron & Valerie Taylor. 132: b, Ron & Valerie Taylor. 132-133: Museum of Fine Arts, Boston. 134: Museum and Historical Research Section, Bank of England. 136: Ron & Valerie Taylor. 137: tr, National Marine Fisheries Service – Narragansett Laboratory. 138: Ron & Valerie Taylor. 139: t, Foster Bam; b, United States Navy. 140: United States Navy. 141: tl, United States Navy; tr, Qantas; b, Ron & Valerie Taylor. 142, 143: Ron & Valerie Taylor. 144: t, Ocean Leather Corporation; bl, br, Museum of Applied Arts and Sciences, Sydney. 145: BBC Hulton Picture Library. 146: t, c, Ron & Valerie Taylor. 148: Eric Love. 149: t, Peter Goadby; b, Ron & Valerie Taylor. 150: t, Mark Deeney. 151: t, Mark Deeney; b, David Burford, Fish Marketing Authority of NSW. 180: t, Ron & Valerie Taylor; b, New Zealand National Publicity. 181: Australian Information Service. 182: David Rodgers, NSW Department of Agriculture, Fisheries Research Institute. 183: t, United States Navy; b, Ron & Valerie Taylor. 185: Peter Goadby. Position of photographs on the page: t – top, c – centre, b – bottom, l – left, r – right.

The publishers acknowledge their indebtedness to the following books and papers that were used for reference, and in the preparation of text and illustrations.

General reference *About Sharks and Shark Attack* David H. Davies (Routledge, London, 1965); *Animal Facts and Feats* Gerald L. Wood (Guinness Superlatives, Enfield, 1982); *Blue Meridian* Peter Matthiessen (Random House, New York, 1971); *The Book of Sharks* Richard Ellis (Grosset & Dunlap, New York, 1976); *Danger Shark* Jean Campbell Butler (Robert Hale, London); *Discover* magazine, various editions (New York, 1985/86); *Fangs of the Sea* Norman Caldwell and Norman Ellison (Angus and Robertson, Sydney, 1937); *Fishes of New Guinea* Ian S. R. Monro (Dept of Agriculture, Port Moresby, 1967); *Fishes of Tasmania* P. R. Last (Tasmanian Fisheries Development Authority, Hobart, 1983); *The Fresh and Salt Water Fishes of the World* Edward C. Migdalski and George S. Fichter (Knopf, New York, 1976); *Great Shark Stories* Ron and Valerie Taylor with Peter Goadby (Collins, London, 1978); *Shark Attack* H. David Baldridge (Berkley, New York, 1974); *Shark Attack* V. M. Coppleson (Angus and Robertson, Sydney, 1958); *Shark Attack: A Program of Data Reduction and Analysis* H. David Baldridge (Mote Marine Laboratory, Sarasota, 1974); *The Great Shark Suit Experiment* Ron and Valerie Taylor (Ron Taylor Film Productions, Sydney, 1981); *Harpoon at a Venture* Gavin Maxwell (Penguin, 1984); *The Histories* Herodotus (Penguin, 1968); *Life of Sharks, The* Paul Budker (Weidenfeld, London, 1971); *Man is the Prey* (Panther, London, 1971); *Maneater Man* Colin Thiele (Rigby, Adelaide, 1979); *Megamouth – A New Species...* Leighton R. Taylor, L. J. V. Compagno and Paul J. Struhsaker (California Academy of Sciences, 1983); *Myth and Maneater* David Webster (Angus and Robertson, Sydney, 1972); *National Geographic* magazine, various editions; *Reader's Digest Book of the Great Barrier Reef* (Reader's Digest, Sydney, 1984); *Shadows in the Sea* Harold W. McCormick, Tom Allen and Captain William Young (Weathervane, New York, 1963); *The Shark Arm Case* Vince Kelly (Nelson, Sydney); *Shark Attack in Southern African Waters* Tim Wallett (Struik, Cape Town, 1983); *Shark – Killer of the Sea* Thomas Helm (Robert Hale, London, 1962); *Shark-O* P. F. O'Connor (Secker and Warburg, London, 1953); *Shark, The: Splendid Savage of the Sea* J-Y. and P. Cousteau (Cassell, London, 1970); *Shark – The Killer of the Deep* Zane Grey (ed. L. Grey) (Belmont, New York); *Sharks* (Wildlife Education, San Diego, 1983); *Sharks: An Introduction for the Amateur Naturalist* Sanford A. Moss (Prentice-Hall, New Jersey, 1984); *Sharks and Shark Deterrents* P. W. and C. Gilbert (Underwater Journal, 1973); *Sharks and Shipwrecks* Hugh Edwards (Lansdowne, Melbourne, 1975); *Sharks and Survival* Perry W. Gilbert; *Sharks – Attacks, Habits, Species* Peter Goadby (Ure Smith, Sydney, 1959); *Sharks – Killers of the Deep* Michael Bright (Omega, London, 1984); *Sharks of Australia* G. P. Whitley (Pollard, Sydney, 1981); *Sharks of the World, vols 1 and 2* Leonard J. V. Compagno (FAO, Rome, 1984); *Sharks of the World* Rodney Steel (Blandford, Poole, 1985);

Sharks – The Search for a Repellent Theo W. Brown (Angus and Robertson, Sydney, 1973); *Trawled Fishes of Southern Indonesia and Northwestern Australia* Thomas Gloerfelt-Tarp and Patricia J. Kailola (ADAB); *The Water World* J. W. Van Dervoort (Union, New York, 1884). **The Mysterious Lives and Habits of Sharks** Brain to body-weight diagram, p 21, adapted from Moss, Sanford A., 1984. Sharks – an introduction for the amateur naturalist, Prentice-Hall, New Jersey, p 126. **The Shark's Remarkable Senses** The original work presented here was carried out at Cornell University, Ithaca, New York; the Mount Desert Island Biological Laboratory, Salsbury Cove, Maine; the Marine Biological Laboratory, Woods Hole, Massachusetts; the Lerner Marine Laboratory, Bimini, Bahamas; the Mote Marine Laboratory, Sarasota, Florida. Dr Perry W. Gilbert, the author, deeply appreciates the use of the facilities at each of these institutions. Portions of this study were supported by the US Office of Naval Research, the Mote Scientific Foundation, and the Elizabeth Mote Rose Research Fund. Critical editorial assistance of the author's wife, Claire K. Gilbert, and typing of the manuscript by Linda M. Franklin are gratefully acknowledged. References cited in the text and used in preparing illustrations: Budker, P., 1959. Les organes sensoriels cutanes des selaciens. In: Traite de zoologie, Tome XIII, Fasc. 2, p 1047. Corwin, J. T., 1978. The relation of inner ear structure to the feeding behaviour in sharks and rays. In: Scanning electron microscopy. Johari, O. (ed.), pp 1105-1112, Chicago: SEM, Inc. Daniel, J. F., 1934. The elasmobranch fishes. p 259. Univ. Cal. Press, Berkeley, California. Dijkgraff, S. and Kalmijn, A. J., 1963. Untersuchungen uber de Funktion der Lorenzinischen Ampullen an Haifishchen. Z. Vergl. Physiol., vol. 47, pp 438-456. Gilbert, P. W., 1962. The behaviour of sharks. Scient. Amer., vol. 207, pp 60-68. Gilbert, P. W. Biology and behaviour of sharks. Endeavour, New Series, vol. 8, no.4, pp 179-187. Gilbert, P. W., Hodgson, E. S., and Mathewson, R. F., 1964. Electroencephalograms of sharks. Science, vol. 145, pp 949-951. Hodgson, E. S. and Mathewson, R. F. (eds.), 1978. Sensory biology of sharks, skates and rays. pp i – ix, 1-666, US Dept of the Navy, Office of Naval Research. Kalmijn, A. J., 1971. The electric sense of sharks and rays. Journ. Exper. Biol., vol. 55, pp 371-383. Kalmijn, A. J., 1974. The detection of electric fields from inanimate and animate sources other than electric organs. In: Handbook of sensory physiology. Fossard, A. (ed.), vol. III, pp 147-200, Berlin, Heidelberg, New York: Springer-Verlag. Murray, R. W., 1960. Electrical sensitivity of the ampullae of Lorenzini. Nature, vol. 187, p 957. Murray, R. W., 1962. The response of the ampullae of Lorenzini of elasmobranchs to electrical stimulation. Journ. Exper. Biol., vol. 39, pp 119-128. Popper, A. N. and Fay, R. R., 1977. Structure and function of the elasmobranch auditory system. Amer. Zool., vol. 17, pp 443-452. Tester, A. L., Kendall, J. I., and Milisen, W. B.,

1972. Morphology of the ear of the shark genus *Carcharhinus* with particular reference to the macula neglecta. Pacific Science, vol. 26, pp 264-274. **Inhabitants of Ancient Seas** Bauchot, R., Platel, R. & Ridet, J-M., 1976. Brain-body weight relationships in Selachii. Copeia, 1976, no. 2, pp 305-310. Duffin, C. J. & Ward, D. J., 1983. Neoselachian sharks' teeth from the lower Carboniferous of Britain and the lower Permian of the USA. Palaeontology, 26, pp 93-110. Karatajute-Talimaa, V. N., 1973. *Elegestolepis grossi* gen. et sp. nov., ein neuer Typ Placoidschuppe aus dem oberen Silur der Tuwa. Palaeontographica, A, 143, 35-50. Maisey, J. G., 1982. The anatomy and interrelationships of Mesozoic Hybodont sharks. American Museum Novitates 2724, 1-48. Maisey, J. G., 1984. Higher elasmobranch phylogeny and biostratigraphy. Zoological Journal of the Linnean Society 82, pp 33-54. Maisey, J. G. & Wolfram, K. E., 1984. 'Notidanus'. In N. Eldridge & S. Stanley (eds), 'Living Fossils', Springer-Verlag, pp 170-180. Mader, H., 1986. Schuppen und Zahne von Acanthodiern und Elasmobranchiern aus dem Unter-Devon Spaniens (Pisces). Gottingen Arbeiten zur Geologie und Palaontologie 28, pp 1-58. Thies, D. & Reif, W-E., 1985. Phylogeny and evolutionary ecology of Mesozoic Neoselachii. Neues Jahrbuch fur Geologie und Palaontologie, Abhandlungen pp 169, 333-361. Turner, S., 1982b. Middle Palaeozoic elasmobranch remains from Australia. Journal of Vertebrate Paleontology 2 (2), pp 117-131. Young G. C., 1982. Devonian sharks from south-eastern Australia and Antarctica. Palaeontology, 25, pp 817-843. Zangerl, R., 1981. Chondrichthyes I, Paleozoic Elasmobranchii. Vol. 3A Handbook of Palaeoichthyology (ed. H-P. Schultze), Gustav Fischer-Verlag, Stuttgart/New York, pp 115. **Sharks in the wild** Information on shark movements in the Atlantic Ocean from Casey, J. et al. The shark tagger, 1977-1985. National Marine Fisheries Service, Narragansett, R. I. Stevens, J. D. 1976. First results of shark tagging in the north-east Atlantic, 1972-1975. J. Mar. Biol. Ass. UK 56, pp 929-937. Information on Australian tagging results from Pepperell, J. Gamefish tagging 1981-82 – 1984-85. New South Wales Dept. Agric., Fish. Div. Tracking of white shark using sonic tag from: Compagno, L. J. V., 1984. FAO species catalogue. Vol. 4 Sharks of the World. FIR/S125 Vol. 4. Part 1. Segregation of sexes from: Bass, A. J., D'Aubrey, J. D. and Kistnasamy, N. 1976. Sharks of the east coast of southern Africa. SA Ass. Mar. Biol. Res. ORI Invest. Rep. No. 45. Growth and ageing of sharks: Prince, E. D. and Pulos, L. M. (eds), 1983. Proceedings of the international workshop on age determination of oceanic pelagic fishes. NOAA Tech. Rep. NMFS 8. Growth rate of sandbar sharks – Casey et al. (above). Growth rate of Galapagos whalers: Bass, A. J. and Smith, J. L. B. 1977. Long-term recoveries of tagged sharks. Copeia, No. 3. **Sharks of the World** Diagram on p 155 adapted from Compagno, Leonard J. V., 1984 Sharks of the World. p 3, FAO, Rome.

Typesetting by Smithys, NSW, Australia
Colour reproduction by Colourscan Co. Pte Ltd., Singapore

Printed and bound by
Dai Nippon Printing Co. (HK) Ltd, Hong Kong for
Reader's Digest (Australia) Pty Limited
26-32 Waterloo Street, Surry Hills
NSW 2010, Australia